Dear Dr. Pullias

A Healing Epistolary Friendship Between
Generations: Earl V. Pullias, Ph.D. and
Debbie Bumstead - 1968-1978

Other books by Debbie Bumstead
The Dream Time An Account
of a Ninth Grade Girl of the 60s
The Destruction of Alice: A Novel
Apricot

Dear Dr. Pullias

A Healing Epistolary Friendship Between Generations: Earl V. Pullias, Ph.D. and Debbie Bumstead - 1968-1978
Debbie Bumstead

Dear Dr. Pullias is a work of non-fiction. Some names have been changed.

ISBN-13:978-1500426316
ISBN-10:1500426318
Printed in the United States of America

To the Memory of Dear Dr. Pullias
from Dear Debbie

Debbie - Self portrait - 1973

Dear Debbie:

It was a special joy to me to see you yesterday. Almost a year had gone by I guess since I saw you, so I wanted to see what time and experience had done—so far as one can tell from what is to be seen—which I suppose is not very much. In fact, we know each other more chiefly through writing than in any other way. Perhaps it always will be so. That is all right. I suppose it is very hard to be sincere in other contacts.

I liked your home there: that is what I saw. I don't know how the inside would be, but the yard, the grass, the trees, the barn, the cows lowing across the way spoke to

Sample of Dr. Pullias's penmanship

Table of Contents

Since you were a very small child I have been deeply interested in you, and I believe in the most beautiful sense ... have loved you very much. But probably I have not communicated that feeling very well. I did not really know how, except perhaps some in these letters, to surmount that thick and high wall of shyness and perhaps other feelings and fears that separate people. I hope the deep, deep kindness I have felt has in some measure come across.
Earl V. Pullias

Dear Dr. Pullias, there is so much importance in love, don't you think? Everything thrives best with the care of love, I feel love for just that simple fact – I love the way anything, person, place, or thing, ANYTHING looks, feels, is the best with care and love.... Bad things change, disappear, reappear with the minute; Good things are ever under, through and forever. You are a friend forever, Debbie

Introduction

Dr. Earl V. Pullias and my grandpa, Trowbridge H. Bumstead, had been best friends when they both worked at Pepperdine University in Los Angeles in the 1940s. When my grandparents left the work to live on their country property outside Hemet, California, they continued the friendship with the Pulliases, who came on weekends and vacations to their adjoining acreage in the rocky hills. My father, Max Bumstead, built the adobe home called *Sleepy Hollow* on *Random Acres* where Grandbee and Grandpa lived, and, on *Luiseno Land* - named for the ancient people who had lived there - the two buildings for Dr. and Mrs. Pullias. Of their cabins, one was brick, large with fireplace and a kitchenette, and the other, up a winding path and cuddled between huge boulders, a tiny wooden writing study called The Four Winds. Through the years there was a lot of visiting between *Sleepy Hollow* at the base of the hills and *Luiseno Land*, a mile or so up a winding road. I was born in 1954, and counted the Pulliases as part of my extended family.

When I was seven Dr. Pullias and I both fell in love with the book **Rabbit Hill** by Robert Lawson and its Franciscan motto, "There is enough for all." When I was eleven, on a visit to see him at *Rabbit Meadow*, as he now called the clearing where his cabins stood, Dr. Pullias asked me why I liked my fifth grade teacher so much. I said, "Because he's fun!" and Dr. Pullias used this anecdote in one of his chapters in **A Teacher is Many Things** which he was writing at the time with co-author, James D. Young. Dr. Pullias and I continued to share good books with each other. Then in a store one day, I bought some postcards with Rabbit Hill-like pictures of little animals at play and sent them to his home in L.A. Dr. Pullias wrote back, encouraged me to write letters to him, and so it went on. I was 14 and Dr. Pullias 61 when we began our twenty plus years of pen pal correspondence.

Dr. Pullias saved all of my letters to him. But in those early years, not thinking ahead, I hadn't taken care to save every letter from him - I'm just glad I saved as many as I did! Dr. Pullias told me later when he gave me the first batch of my letters that he himself had thought he might use them in a writing project, but now he didn't think he had time, and maybe I could do so myself. So, here they are, our gathered letters from 1968 through 1978, with a few added from 1979, all together for the first volume of **Dear Dr. Pullias**. Maybe Dr. Pullias would have added words of interpretation and explanation if this had been his project. But I've just plopped the letters down in the best order I could figure (some letters don't have dates) and let them reveal their story as is. In my letters I've also left the original bad spelling and questionable grammar, which both improve slightly, as the years pass.

Young, shy, troubled Debbie Bumstead and old, wise, kind Earl V. Pullias tell an unusual yet universal story of friendship and love between generations in **Dear Dr. Pullias**. I hope the younger readers of this volume will recognize themselves in both Debbie and Dr. Pullias, and seek out help or give help needed. For older readers, I hope Dr. Pullias will inspire you to search for and continue the good work of mentoring young people.

***

In 1965 Dr. Pullias gave my father a copy of his just published book, **A Search for Understanding**. I have it now, on my desk, and many times between then and today, I've opened it to study the three photographs of Dr. Pullias and read the "Glance Backward" he'd included in the first pages of this book of essays on education and psychology.

Here is Dr. Pullias as a little boy! How I loved this picture.

And here he is in 1945, a professor and Dean at Pepperdine University in its first years. I used to look at this photo to see the man who was already being called great, yet who called my Grandpa great as well. Also at this time Dr. Pullias knew my father and mother as students: my parents met and fell in love at Pepperdine.

Then, here is a picture taken in 1964 when Dr. Pullias was in his late 50s. This is the man with whom I became friends.

I grew up knowing a little of Dr. Pullias's life history. He had been a farm boy in Tennessee, born in 1907 to parents who encouraged their children to learn and go far. I knew he had gone to college, that he had a Ph.D. and that he was a psychologist who helped people, as well as a college professor teaching teachers and a famous writer in his field. As a teen, I observed and felt he had a loving marriage with Mrs. Pullias, which I contrasted with my mom and dad's dissolving one. I liked Calvin, the Pulliases' son, who was a young man when I met him. Later, I learned there had been another son, John, who drowned in the ocean; this news made my heart hurt, since the existence of death had already touched me with mystery and dread. I knew that during the years when Grandpa Bumstead and Dr. Pullias were close, they loved to listen to classical music together and then have long philosophical discussions. Later these types of thoughtful conversations were a constant background to my childhood years, as Grandpa, my father, my aunt, and other family members continued to get together to talk.

But when Dr. Pullias and I began writing to each other, my knowledge of him shifted. Now, he wasn't my grandpa's best friend, my dad's advisor, my mother's confidant; instead he became mine in a new personal way that no one else owned. Soon, the whole family knew of our correspondence; so much so, that whenever Dr. Pullias wrote to another in the family, I was called over to decipher his penmanship. I became the expert on Dr. Pullias.

***

In one of his earliest letters to me (Letter #8), Dr. Pullias mentioned two parts of his childhood which affected him deeply. One was the witnessing of animals suffering on the farm, and the other was that during his schooldays, he hated some of his teachers, the ones who were mean and uninspiring. Now, later, I have found at least three different writings of his in either book or essay mentioning these two subjects, so they must indeed have been important in his development as a person.

Another reminiscence of his youth that charmed me (Letter #285) concerned his learning to train fine horses with a mentor of his own, a Civil War veteran who took him to help at horse shows. He also told me in Letter #314 that his own grandfather, a Greek immigrant, had been a Cossack Cavalryman who had had a wonderful horse with which he fought in the Crimean War.

Recently I found one page of a 1929 letter from Earl (Dr. Pullias) to Pauline (Mrs. Pullias), that was posted on the Pepperdine University Archives site, where Pullias's personal and professional papers are listed. In the letter, again the horse makes an appearance as Dr. Pullias tells how he rode in the rain out to the mailbox to find a thick letter from Pauline. When the rain let up, he stopped and read her loving words. The page of the letter he wrote back to her describing this experience is sweet and full of love – he was kind in his writing even as a young man.

Dr. Pullias sometimes mentioned to me how Mrs. Pullias had responded to something I'd written, and whenever I visited at *Rabbit Meadow*, there she was - dear Mrs. Pullias, as bright and cheerful as a songbird hopping around her tall slow-talking stork of a husband. Once my mother said that Mrs. Pullias told her that when Dr. Pullias seemed a little too idealistic, she would bring him back to earth and show him that he was a human after all. I did notice, myself, that when we were all together, that while my parents and grandparents and I looked to Dr. Pullias reverently, listening to hear his wisdom, Mrs. Pullias treated him more as an equal, a person she loved and knew deeply as a human man.

Because the collection of **Dear Dr. Pullias** letters shows mainly the intellectual and emotional relationship Dr. Pullias and I had, I would like to just mention some of my physical encounters with him. In my early childhood and my teen years, as I've mentioned, we often met out at the hills of Hemet and walked together along the dirt roads there. I remember the day I accompanied the family, my grandparents, and the Pulliases on a hike. Grandpa held a witching stick and paced a little valley, waiting for the stick to point to water. When the dowser turned down in Grandpa's hands, there my father made a mark and later he dug a hole and built a little wishing well of wood.

And when I was a teen, Dr. Pullias and I hiked down from his cabin to this well one day, and he told me the story of the fellow who searched for wisdom, went far and wide, and then was told to go to the tallest mountain where there stood a well, and when he looked down into the well, he would see the secret of life. Of course, he saw himself reflected in the water of the well. This was my first introduction to the search for truth, and I guess it may sound obvious, but the story was new to me, and as Dr. Pullias and I sat beside the well on the bench under the arbor, I felt like I'd been given some special knowledge that not everybody knew.

On another occasion, one dark stormy night our telephone rang at home. Dr. Pullias was calling from *Sleepy Hollow* to see if my father could come out and help him get the big car unstuck from the mud. I got to come, too, and we drove halfway up the dirt road in the rain toward *Rabbit Meadow* to find the Pulliases' big black car resting in a flash flood rut. There in the night wilderness I felt fresh and alive, proud of my dad for his fix-it ways, and full of love for Dr. and Mrs. Pullias. After the car was able to drive on, we all met up at their main cabin and had warm drinks before the fireplace. Dr. Pullias's favorite words from the Greeks: Truth, Beauty, Goodness, and Love could be applied to that wonderful night - TBGL as we knew it by code. See how many times this code is mentioned in **Dear Dr. Pullias**!

Dr. and Mrs. Pullias sometimes came to our house in the town of Hemet, too. Once, while still a teen in high school, I was kissed by my friend; after their visit, as he left, Dr. Pullias paused by the front door, took my face in his large hands, and planted a kiss on my forehead. Oh, I felt loved! But as the very first epigram (see above) in **Dear Dr. Pullias** indicates, there was a physical shyness between us, insurmountable most of the time. How I wish now I'd been able to hug him more, talk to him more easily in person, maybe even tease him like I usually do with people I love. I daydreamed of living with him and his wife, of being his child, of being rescued from the problems of life I had at the time. Maybe he had a similar daydream once in awhile, too, but mostly we relied on written words sent by post to deepen our connection and to create our amazing friendship.

Still, I loved being with him in person – he was a tall lanky man with a remarkable voice, oh, his voice! Full of Tennessee it was, without any twang, with only soft gentle warmth that reflected his heart, I'm sure. I can hear him now, asking me as I dismounted my horse at Rabbit Meadow one fine day, "Debbie, do you think Prieta would mind if I took a ride on her?" It was a pleasure giving him a boost up, and seeing his long leg swing over Prieta's bare back. In memory I see now, with deep love for his friendship and sorrow for his loss, Dr. Pullias riding the black long-tailed mare along the sandy path away from me, his back tall, his shoulders strong, my friend, my friend.

1968

I sure am happy today! It's good to be alive today! Debbie

There are few things so wonderful as learning and developing more and more the great things that lie undeveloped in you. In most people they are never developed and this is one of the saddest facts of life. There will be hard, unpleasant, discouraging days. We must learn how to deal with these and not be turned aside by them. Dr. Pullias

Debbie Bumstead

Dear Dr. Pullias

Postmarked February 23, 1968

Dear Uncle P. -- (Daddy told me to write this)

We went to Idlewild and I got 3 cards something like this one especially for you. I read Joanna and Ulysess. It was very good. Next I'm going to read A Killing Frost. Did you ever read Lord of the Flies or Dibs In Search of Self? I would like you to write me if you're not busy. Thanks for being a great friend Love, Debbie

2.
Dear Dr. Pullias

I'll send the cards some other time because I want to write you a letter instead.

I guess I just don't know enough good words, because I had to write something someone else wrote in Joanna & Ulysess. Do you know how it is when you have something great in your head but you can't write it down? That's how it is with some books I read.

I really do recommend that you read <u>Lord of the Flies</u>. Its one of my favorites for this year and last along with <u>Brothers of the Sea</u>, <u>Dibs</u>, and <u>My Friend Flicka</u>.

Tonight Tim & me will go to the library and I will try a get <u>A</u>

<u>Killing Frost</u>. It sounds good.

The way that lady worked with Dibs is fasinating. I think I might be a child pscaligist. When you worked with people that way were you a child or adult pscaligist?

<u>A Killing Frost</u> is still out.

I really don't know what to write about. You will have to ask more questions.

Please write soon

Your friend Debbie

P.S. I'm calling you Dr. Pullias because that name just fits you.

3.
Postmarked April 10, 1968

Dear Dr. Pullias, I'm on Uncle and Aunt Rae's boat. We're sailing in the Long Beach Harbor. Its very exiciting. The ocean reminds me of almost jelled jello when you jiggle it. The color is either dark or light, deep or shallow. Bye, Debbie

4.
Postmarked April 26, 1968

Dear Dr. Pullias

Dear Dr. Pullias

Thank you for the think full letter. Sorry I didn't write sooner but I have been pretty busy.

Last Sunday I went to a jimcana and watched some friends ride there horses. Do you have any suggestions of good books? I can't find any, lately.

I can't talk well with people so I like writing like you said.

Your friend, Debbie

5.

Dear Dr. Pullias

Your letter to me wasn't to me. I'm returning it to you.

I finally got <u>A Killing Frost</u>. It was very very good. I think the author remembered what she used to think when she was Ramie's age because she showed a girl's thoughts very good. I have often thought of some of the things Ramie did. Please tell me what you thought of the book.

Yesterday morning I watched the birth of a kitten. Our cat had three kittens. All of them are striped. Do you want one?

I'm reading a good book. Its called <u>The Lion</u>. It's about a young girl who has a special understanding and power of animals in Africa. You might like to read it. The author is Joseph Kessel.

Grandpa is reading Sylvia Wilkinson's first book, <u>Moss Grows on the North Side</u>. As soon as he's finished I'm reading it. Have you?

Tina our poodle adores those kittens. She will lay in front of the box and watch them all day. Every once in a while she gets up and licks them, but Mamma cat doesn't mind at all.

I guess that's all I can think of to write.

Well, bye, Your Friend, Debbie

6.

Dear Dr. Pullias

Thanks very much for sending the three books. I have already read The Kinship of Animals before. I found it very good. I was in 6th grade then and my teacher who was a good teacher was very interested. I have started The Wind in the Willow a few times before but I never finished it. Yesterday I read The Little Prince. I found it very good and thoughtful.

I'm in history right now. Last period was English with Mrs. Loper. In my mind she should not be a teacher Everything about her bothers me. Watch her talk look at her mouth working to hard for the words. Listen to all the ekums and ummms. Look at the way her dress fits her tightly look at her tummy sticking out. Look the way she waves her hands and walks. Listen to the way she chops poor Richard who may need chopping but certainly not from a teacher. Look at how she thinks she's the best. Listen to how her voice is boreing and irratating. Ughh! I wish she would find this letter and take some advice. I have often thought the day before schools out to put a note on her desk saying:

"Don't think you're such a high and mighty adult because it makes you like a spoiled immature child."

But I won't. Richard is a loud-mouth and should be talked to reasonably because he is intelligent. But Mrs. Loper calls him names and makes him talk back to her which I don't blame him.

It seems I can't stand to write much more on her so I won't. And you might not like my criticizing her. I don't think women should be teachers but men who are easier to talk to and funner, and they seem to be able to get closer to their students than women. I not going to be a teacher because of this and also I don't want the worry. Does John like me? Oh, do I look ok? O my O my.

That's all I guess. Thanks again Your friend, Debbie

7.

Dear Dr. Pullias,

The mama cat is looking listening. Where are they she's asking. But I don't know so she leaves my room. I don't know if she knows they are dead, that a black tom came in the night and bit their throats. She doesn't know that I heard them and went down and saw them with blood running out, that I kicked that tom not with hate but with anger.

I blame my parents for taking them down in the basement when I told them not to. I blame me for not making my wish to have them upstairs stronger. I blame the mama cat for not being there to fight. I blame the tom for killing tho' this was his way. I blame that hole in the basement where cats go in and out.

Dad said that he thought the mama cat would protect the kittens but I said she was out. I thought that he should have thought. My mother doesn't stay with me to protect me every minute.

Well, now that I've said that I don't feel any better like people do in books who "get it out of their system." but I don't feel worse either.

Frosty, our altered cat, really fought that tom afterwards he was really mad. He loved those kittens but he never showed it because of his dignity.

Thank you for the letter. That's a good agreement about the letters.

Well, that's all for now I guess.

Sincerely, Debbie

8.

Los Angeles

May 24, 1968

Dear Debbie

As a friend I am sure you will understand when I tell you that these weeks have been very demanding and so I seemed to have no energy left to respond to your letters both of which I appreciated and found very interesting. I could tell you some of the things I have been doing, but I believe they would not be very interesting.

Your feeling about the kittens who met a seemingly cruel and untimely fate brought up deep memories and many feelings from my own experience. Adults often times do not seem sensitive to a younger person's concerns and feelings. I recall when I was a boy I with great patience and care raised a chicken from a tiny chick to a large rooster. He was a good friend and followed me about -- one day when I was away my parents decided he was in the way so they killed him and cooked him. I think they thought it was all somewhat funny, but I was deeply hurt and saddened. Other similar things happened that left scars in my mind.

Also I was interested in your feeling about the teacher. In the main, my school experience was bad - teachers were often, for many reasons I suppose, much they shouldn't be as teachers or as persons. And I too came to almost hate teachers and even learning. And then somewhere along the way I came to feel that one of the great needs of the world is good teachers. So I have tried to be one and later through writing and in other ways help others to be. So life goes.

I am glad you liked *The Little Prince*. If things I suggest or send do not speak to you - do not catch your interest - do not try to read them. I will have more time later this summer and hope to suggest some good things. I hope my delay in writing will not discourage your writing.
Sincerely, Earl V. Pullias

9.
Dear Dr. Pullias
    I am glad to receive your letter to me. Thank you. I was wondering why it was a long time before you wrote but the other night Grambe told me you were correcting lots and lots of papers. Were those papers final exams or something?
    Summer always seems the death season. Everything important to me has died in the summer, my great grandma, my little cousin, my devoted chicken Charlie, and now first the kittens not in the summer really, but the mama cat is dead I think. We have a orange stubb tailed tom cat, Toby. He has a cancer or something in his neck and its getting bigger & bigger. Mom says the vet may have to put him to sleep.
    Summer is also a fun time because no school! and swimming! And watermelon!
    I got a new kitten. Pixie is her name & she's very cute white &

8

Dear Dr. Pullias

fluffy. We have 5 animals. That's not too many.

I'm sorry I haven't gotten those books to your place on the hill.

Toby's lump drained out and he's better. Just like a cat.

Well I guess that's all. Nothing interesting has been happening around here or in my head so that's why this letter isn't so interesting.

Please tell me what your work is like. All I know is that you teach teachers True?

Goodbye Your Friend Debbie

P.S. Woody isn't feeling well he won't eat and his legs are weak. Today we may take him to the vet. We took him he has a fungus. We have to bathe him every day in this stuff and even that might not help but it <u>must.</u>

10.

Dear Dr. Pullias,

Thanks for the letter & list. Thank your friend for her trouble for me, please. I think I will enjoy those books more when I'm older but you see I don't care for some biographies very much now. That doesn't mean I'm ungrateful. I am very much grateful. I'll look for them at the library.

It sure was nice seeing you but I never really studied your face Usually I study people's faces and draw them in my mind. All I notice is your eyes & mustache. I don't think I've had time to look at you much. Always when I picture you you look like Albert Einstein.

At supper we were talking about that religious dome or whatever that Mrs. Pullias wants. Its all sounds very interesting but how can you sit in a dome and see the truth. Religion or God is not something to see but to believe in if you choose. Oh I don't know what I mean. Maybe I misunderstood that dome thing.

Today when we went to your house I sure had fun. We haven't been doing much this summer and that was a nice change for us. Woody, too.

I'd like to know when you are coming back to your little place here because Woody & me sure had lot of fun. I don't like to go out by my self because I'm afraid of those rattlesnakes

I was gald to meet Calvin a second time. He's a pleasant sort of fellow

Well Good-bye Your Friend
 Debbie

Debbie Bumstead

P.S. Those designs on your envelope are made by a spirograph. Joe when he was in Germany bought it for me. Its really something. So many nice designs you can make or copy. Debbie

11.
Dear Dr. Pullias,

I sometimes think entirely too much. Maybe not Maybe others think a lot Maybe everybody. I can't tell. Sometimes like just a while ago I think whats that ant right there thinking? Then I think of what its thinking. How can you think what an ants thinking I think. Oh boy isn't this confusing I just can't seem to convey what I'm feeling or rather what I'm thinking.

Sometimes I think I'm crazy. Would you believe it? Maybe its easy to believe because maybe you felt you were crazy once too. Maybe everyone feels that. But if you think you're crazy then you aren't maybe because some crazy people some don't think they're crazy but they are maybe they know they are crazy. Oh gosh this is a mess.

Last night I sitting on the truck watching our 3 cats and I began thinking how they are so different. Toby is so forthright (?) if he wants to be petted he'll come to be petted but Frost will run toward you stop all of a sudden lick his tail quite thoroughly then walk to you. It's enough to make you laugh but if you laugh he will make an even longer delay by maybe washing his feet. Well I watched them till dark thinking what they were thinking but not doing a very good job. I always think that animals think in pictures not words. After that I began thinking why I was thinking that. Then I got off petted them both said goodnight & went in. (humph)

Enough of that (too much in fact) Thanks for the letter I enjoyed it. I keep meaning to get those books up there but never do.

I can hardly wait till I go swimming I love to swim. Water is so so -----. I'm going up to Reno sometime soon but you can mail a letter to me here then when I'm up there I'll write you or something.

Your friend, Debbie

P.S. Sorry for writing your address upside down. Good bye.

12.
Dear Dr. Pullias

Dear Dr. Pullias

Thank you very much for the letter I would like very much to hike to the top of Hemet Bute. I imagine the veiw is pretty good.

I haven't gotten that book yet I guess I'll get it tomorrow. Thank you for it.

Next Monday Mom & I are going to Reno for about 3 weeks. Then I'll have 2 weeks before school starts. I don't know how in the world I will find my rooms in that high school but I guess I won't be the only one.

In your letter you said maybe I should keep a notebook of thoughts. Well last year sometime a friend showed me her diary and I decided I wanted one too but not like hers. Hers was just this happened & this, so unpersonal. She didn't write down her thoughts. I got a diary for my thoughts but I would write in and forget for so long and just once and a while I write in it. I only write in it when I am MAD or depressed. So when I read it later it seems silly so I tear it out & throw it away. Well not really silly but not the way I really feel except then. Well theres one messy mixup paragraph. Even I hardly understand it.

I am very interested in Math. I'm only a B student in it but I enjoy it very much. For this next school year I am taking Algebra I. I also very interested in Art. I like to draw and paint but I like to when I have someone else to draw with. My main interest though is thinking not what I'm thinking but other people are. I might look at Tim whos looking at one of the cats and I make up things he could be thinking. Maybe I see a girl or boy at school looking at the teacher but is he listening? I might say to myself what are you thinking right now as I'm writing this or what will you think when you read this. I don't know what you will be thinking but I ask myself anyway. Crazy? Right.

Well good-bye Your Friend

A\ Bitter (Mary) Bee (Deborah) of Noble Birth (Alice)

P.S. Yesterday I looked up all sorts of names too see what they meant. It's quite interesting.

13.

Dear Dr. Pullias,

I sure am happy today! It's good to be alive today! We are home in Hemet again and I'm very happy about it.

I had lots of fun in Reno. We were very busy most of the time.

11

Terry & Marie stayed over 5 nights. We went swimming a lot and out to eat. We played with the dogs and went to see their uncle's four calves. It was all very nice (what a silly word: nice).

My father has fixed the house different. Now I have a bright, sunny room that used to be a kitchen. One wall is made of stuff you can pin pictures to. He said we could paint the room. I am going to have it light blue on the wood work & pretty light blue flowered wall paper on it. I hope.

We'll get Woody today I guess. He'll probably be all well from his fungus and he'll be smooth and silky. I'll take him to the high school track and run with him. I'm going to teach him Come, Sit and for an easy trick Shake hands. One time Tim and I were sitting in the front yard and Woody was sleeping on the porch near his house. Tim and me tryed this experiment Tim started beating up on me and I screamed and yelled. Woody to the rescue! Lightning on his feet, Thunder in his voice! Up he jumped onto Tim's chest: he wanted to play, too. He wanted to play but I bet that would really scare someone beating up on a person. Our family sure feels safe with him. Our widowed neighbor says she doesn't feel safe when Woody is out at Jan's. Everybody loves him He loves everybody.

I sure liked your book. I read most of the first chapters and the very last one. That was the best. About a teacher being a person.

I am very happy today and I hope you are too. This supposed to have been a very happy letter and it is.

Your happy friend, Debbie

14.
Dear Dr. Pullias,

School has just started here and I know it started there a week ago. I expect that's why you haven't written yet.

Well, school today was fun. At first finding my classes was hard. I have 3 men teachers & 3 women. I always think that usually men teachers are funner and just better.

In art the teacher said to sketch an interesting person so I drew you but it didn't turn out very good. I think I'll have fun in there except for those big 11th grade boys who laugh at people's last names. Ekumm. I may go thru' another year of Bummy, Dagwood, Blondie ect. ect. I don't mind and I guess that helps because they give up after a while.

Dear Dr. Pullias

I didn't worry much in August about school and my teachers. And that's the trouble, thru elementary school I use to spend nights in the summer worring about whether my teachers would like me and whether I would get good grades and so on. Then when I went to school I always made good friends with my teachers, got good grades, really had fun. Then in 7ᵗʰ grade all rush rush rush got to get this and that done within the hour. This and that within the year. No time to talk about things that make you friends. I made about 3 teacher friends in both 7ᵗʰ and 8ᵗʰ grade (about 13 teachers) and also they forget so easily (because of 200 students a day) that they weren't much of friends either. You are a teacher and my friend but you don't forget what I say much. I perhaps am wrong. You're a teacher tell you side of the story, please.

I have read Manxmouse and it was good, cute, too. But I only read ½ of The Strange One. It bothered me for some reason so I didn't like it. One thing tho' I liked was the way the author showed all threes thoughts and feelings.

Well Goodbye and please write only when you have time.

Your friend, Debbie

15.
Dear Dr. Pullias,

I'm glad you asked me why we feel so good and sometimes so down. I never even thought of that before. Maybe its physical because when I'm tired or sick I am depressed and when I feel good my bones tingle and I want to run. (This is so messy because this is the first time I've thought about it and my thoughts aren't organized) Sometimes though I feel good and I think or see something depressing like war pictures or such. I begin to think that leads to something else and soon I thoroughly depressed.

This morning Joe & me took Woody out to Random Acres. He sure had lots of fun running. We hiked the hard way to your place and saw your new signs and that string with the bells. Is that to call down someone up there? We bought some pop (Joe says you should have a pop machine up there). I showed Joe the place where the bees are and they were so slow, sick, I guess. I bet you have lots of fun there making things and enjoying the place.

School is very fun this year, so far. English class has three teachers one teaches literature (I'm with it) one language and one reading. We are in class for 5 weeks then we rotate then we go back to one huge classroom with two teachers. Every single day we have to get out paper and write in our journals on some subject. I don't know whether it's a good idea or not.

In Life Science one day they showed a real human brain in a film. It was all pink and wrinkly with blue veins running acrosst it. Just like its supposed to look like. But isn't weird to think that that stuff in my head is operating my hand to write and its thinking. Whats inside I wonder? Just the same stuff.?

Theres a book about a lazy African rabbit and his lazy African friends called Zomo the Rabbit by Hugh Sturton. It is written in a funny way. In some parts you just have to laugh out loud. I read Lawrence of Arabia and it was pretty good. I am very interested in Arabia, Lawrence, Mohammed the prophet and all that.

Well, goodbye Your friend, Debbie

16.
Los Angeles
Oct 12, 1968
Sunday morning

Dear Debbie

I am glad that you and Joe were able to come with Woody out to our place and be a part of its freedom, quiet and beauty. I hope you will come often either when we are there or when we are not there. We would like for it to be a great good place where people (and animals) can be free and unafraid to think and feel deeply. I would like for you to help me think about how this could be done. Mrs. P & I plan to come up there this coming Friday night and will be there Sat. and Sun. We would be glad if you and whoever would like to come would drop by while we are there. Don't feel any need to but just come and be one of the land and rocks and us.

I was interested in your ideas about moods. You are probably right that one's physical condition or bodily health has much to do with a person's psychological feelings. Also the reverse is true: that is, our psychological mood seems to affect our bodies greatly. For example, I suspect a dream will influence the way we

feel the following day. Or often a single pleasant or unpleasant incident will greatly influence the way we feel physically and psychologically for a day or longer.

Perhaps as we mature and learn we understand ourselves better and know something of what to expect of ourselves and others. Or even, we might get to the place where small things do not hurt us so badly. At least, when we understand we can manage more wisely. But all of this is the deep and interesting problem of mental health which we will be studying all through life.

I was much interested in hearing about your school work. I believe you will move steadily now into a stage where you will greatly enjoy the process of learning - even as we often do it in school! There are few things so wonderful as learning and developing more and more the great things that lie undeveloped in you. In most people they are never developed and this is one of the saddest facts of life. There will be hard, unpleasant, discouraging days. We must learn how to deal with these and not be turned aside by them. That is, we must learn to work even when it is not interesting. I make progress on the new book.

All good wishes, your friend, Earl V. Pullias

17.
Dear Dr. Pullias,

How did life begin? That's what we were talking about in science last week. it's a very interesting subject and I'm glad it has at last come into Science classes. The teacher thinks it happend by accident and most of the kids think of the Bible. Well, how did life begin and How should or will I or anybody know and Why does anybody want to know? I want to know but why do I want to know and what if I did know then I wouldn't have it to want to know which wouldn't be any good on account I want to know.

Oh, did I tell you Joe might be a teacher? One day I told him he'd be a good teacher and he said yeah sure teaching kids Colombus discovered America I told him what about the Norsemen he said remeber the Indians then we dicussed all that stuff and he said he might be a teacher He's going to San Diego College.

Tim is going to Woodbury in L.A. for an art major He wrote us a letter and boy he must be having a ball!! He told us he actually liked history which is something and all that. All what? Everything.

I haven't had any bad nightmares lately which is surprizing because usually when school starts I don't have much time to daydream. I sort of like those nightmares because there interesting but I don't really understand dreams. I mean how can your head work without you knowing it? But really your head would be the one knowing it and your head is the one that dreams. Like now my hand was writing that down but my head didn't understand it any more than I did. Just now my head felt overpowering confusion but my stomach felt it too. Maybe the nerves by accident sent confusion to my stomach.

I don't feel much like writing more now Goodbye

Your friend, Debbie

P.S. Thank you very much for your letter and I'm sorry this one is confused and mixedup. D.B.

18.

Dear Dr. Pullias,

Why has my head been so full of beutiful descriptions, stories and thought. If I should try to write them only something would come out that sounds too much of what it is, so that if someone were too read them they would not think of beuaty but of how too much this is of what it is. As someone would read this they would only smile and not think of my sadness and confusion. When I read this over it to makes me feel so, oh, I don't [know] a word that has a meaning of something like confusion but not so quite, I am not confused, it is only that I feel I can do more but it does not come out into my hands and through my pencil.

Why do I feel this way when all my heart and head cheers for life and I sing in my whole body. Why, right now, do I cry at the beauty of life when I should shout and laugh.

This didn't start as a letter for you, Mr. Pullias, it started as something to write, but now it is a letter just for you. Will I be glad to know you will read it? Yes, someone must know how I feel and you cannot tell parents. They live to near and are not what they should be.

Your friend, Debbie

Dear Dr. Pullias

19.

Dear Dr. Pullias,

I was very happy to see you last Saturday. Anne, Woody, & I had lots of fun, yelling & singing to the hills and hiking.

That last letter I wrote to you was only of that moment, I do not feel that way always, of course.

I am having so much fun in school! Every class is so much fun and interesting except geography, but that's only one boring hour in six. The work is pretty hard and takes time in all my classes. I wonder why it is that I am having fun in my classes and doing only average work when in geography I am getting better grades on tests?

I asked Miss Kerr my liturature teacher where she took her training and she said Santa Barbara University I was surprized because that is where I thought I might go because my father said the city was pretty and the pychology was a main thing there but I don't know yet.

Monday I go to language for 5 weeks. It is a new method, now. We have the English that is like Math and not nouns, verbs, graph sentences and that stuff. It sounds interesting.

I don't think about what other people think about me any more. Is that good or bad? I think it is good because I am not so self-conscious and that means I am a happyer person. And to me I am a very important person so I ought to be happy sometimes. But then your friends are important too. No, if your friends are friends then they like you just the way you are.

Goodbye

Your Friend, Debbie

20.

Dear Dr. Pullias

I have nothing much too write. Everything goes on in much the same way everyday. My thoughts are occupied with school mostly. I wonder why that is that way. Why don't I everysingle day do something different I mean completely different. Why do I spend my time sitting in a desk for 6 hours learning? Why do I listen? Why do I draw, write, think? Why do I live? Why will I die? When I am dead how I'll just be dead I'll be dead and know no more. OH what a stupid topic.

I have to give up Woody because he disturbs the peace. What am I going to do without him. **Sit around this house and get fat.** Darn.

Debbie Bumstead

Woody is mine.

Music is getting to be very interesting to me. I don't really understand how its made I mean why does it make you listen. Why is it so beutiful. I wonder why I like some songs and not others. Maybe its poetry for you to listen to instead of reading it. Everybody ought to have someway to make theirselves music. Instraments, singing, or whislting Or even hearing.

Looking at this cat somebody ought to make music to discribe a cat Its eyes. Maybe people too. Maybe dandilions! Maybe hands. Names?

We get our grades next week I think I will gett a good grade in Algebra I. I'm very interested in Math. I think will take 4 years of it tho' I only [need] 1 to graduate.

Thanks alot for your letter to me

Your Friend Debbie

21.

Dear Dr. Pullias,

I really got a surprize the other day when I found out I got an A in Science! That teacher is very good. He trys to keep the interest of us people in the adience. But sometimes he doesn't. All the kids (not all) in there are more or less the way out or in crowd. That is, they don't try much. All they need to do is listen.

Friday in Science Mr. Greene called me up to the desk to talk. He showed me a very hard test we all took. Out of all 130 tests about, I was the only one too get a 100% He talked about my grades and subjects and he said he thinks I am a underachiever. Someone who does not [measure] up to the capabilites because there is no challenge. I would like to have someone explain this more to me as I donot understand to well. I don't think I could ask Mr. Greene and I would not like to go to the counselor. But I believe it should be someone who knows this school And maybe I will ask my science teacher. Something will turn up.

I bought myself a book called The Family of Man it is a collection of photographs. I like it a lot.

You are probably busy so I'll stop now.

Your Friend

Debbie

P.S. My other grades are B for Algebra B for Art C for Geography, B

Dear Dr. Pullias

22.

Dear Dr. Pullias,

I don't know how to start writing about this subject. It is please to be kept in confidence in fact I don't want to ever talk about it: Well Tim came home Thankgiving and he was in my room and we were talking about college and Tim told me about an experience concerning marjana Oh darn I wish to God he hadn't tried that or even told me his "beautiful" experience. I don't know much about majana but in Sience we discussed it. It's a very interesting subject.

Can I get into college without 2 foreign language years in high school? I like to learn Spanish and have had about 4 years of it (same thing over and over). But I don't like the way they teach it. It's not a right way but then, how are you supposed to learn it.

Up at your place on the hill my father and I went. I played archery (at a sack on a bush) and if you should find 2 arrows don't think someone was shooting at your animals or house.

I like to play archery. I just learned a few weeks ago. Its fun reminds me of the Middle Ages. I am so interested in the Middle Ages or Dark Ages. I wonder why? Why the Middle Ages and not the Renesiance? Why am I interested in World War II and not W.W. I? Is it the way I grew up or what. I am interested in Communism but not in Democracy but I know I wouldn't like to live in a Communism government.

Joe showed us a "zilch." It is weird. Wow. This is what you do take plastic bread wrappers and braid them. Hang them from a coat hanger with a pan of water underneath then put it on fire. Its slowly unbraids and three little dribbles of it fall on fire and give off the most weird sound and then go pssss on the water it keeps going on & on. It has to be dark and quiet. The whole family was really surprised by it its unbelievable.

Thanks for your letters and your friendship.

Your friend Debbie

P.S. An enjoyable book is The Hobbit by J.R.R. Tolkein

23.

Debbie Bumstead

Los Angeles
Dec. 24, 1968
Dear Debbie:

Your good letter came and as always I appreciated it very much. I am glad you can speak to me about things in confidence. I shall always, of course, keep anything you may wish to say to me in confidence. Thus I hope you will feel completely free. Only then does a friendship and letters have the greatest meaning.

I am glad you went out to our place with your father and to do your archery. It is a very fine activity: I used to enjoy it very much, but have not done much in recent years. I saw only one of your arrows that you lost. It was near the green pepper tree next to the road that leads to our cabin. I stuck it in the ground near the tree so you can get it when you go back out. I hope you go often. It is a good place for the heart and soul.

Thanks for mentioning The Hobbit. I enjoyed this book and some others by the same author very much. I wish I had thought to mention it to you as something you might like. This author is a very good writer, I think. I would like to know why you think his writing is so interesting. Of course, the story is good, but there is a special quality about the writing that is hard to describe.

I was very glad for the Christmas vacation to come. The break in school routine and demands is pleasant. Christmas is in many ways a beautiful time, but in some ways and sometimes it makes me feel sad. Wonder why that would be?

The writing has come along pretty well this fall. I have finished all the main chapters now - 17 in all, in addition to an Introduction. I am not sure if it needs a closing chapter or not. Will have to decide on that. I hope the book will be readable. I am glad that many teachers seem to be reading A Teacher is Many Things. Maybe it will do some good.

This afternoon I drove out to the cemetery where our son John and his friend, Gordon are buried. Perhaps I didn't tell you about this boy. He and his friend about the same age were drowned when they were 18 years old. They were swimming in the ocean near one of the beach cities. It helps me to think to go out there now and then. Life is strange.

Dear Dr. Pullias

I hope you are having a fine Christmas. Earl V. Pullias

24.

Dear Dr. Pullias,

I would not know why you sometimes feel sad at Christmas. To me it is fun because I like to go shopping and spend lots of money and to help others pick out something to get. Then everybody wakes up early and everybody's eyes are shining and smiling with secrets. Maybe you are sad because you remember the thrill when you were small or maybe you think of Christ and the sins of man or something happened that was sad near Christmas. I don't know.

The Hobbit was a really weird book. What about it I don't know but I think of black and white slick pages when I think of the book. I guess it seemed so true. It was very interesting book.

I am very interested in poetry. I was writing down the ones I liked. I have read 2 books by Peter S. Beagle and I going to see if I can find some poetry by him. The books were; The Last Unicorn which is really really good A Fine and Private Place is strange. I have never read a book like his.

I went up to my Grandmas the other day. I climbed up the hill behind their house. I was sitting on a rock and Tina was bustling around and I felt like I was the only one in the world alive even when I saw people or cars but I know that if I saw they have a worried face or if they cried then I should no I am not much importance to anyone I'm only very important to me and I feel my feelings but what am I to the person in the house in the back of ours and what is she to me just a person to illustrate my point which isn't getting on to well.

There was 102 words in that sentence very bad English. Tch Tch.

Oh well life may be strange but its sure fun.

Your friend, Debbie

Debbie Bumstead

Dear Dr. Pullias

1969

I was very glad .. we were able to talk a little while there before "The Four Winds." Wouldn't it be interesting if we could meet and talk there again two days before your 20th birthday? And even your 30th? We would see what we have been able to do with life, and what it has done with us. The rocks, the sky, the hills, the clouds, the birds will be quite the same. They have not changed much since the Indians sat where we were sitting and perhaps talked of what they thought was fundamental. **Dr. Pullias**

I wonder why I write you all these personal things. Every teenager ought to have someone to write to…. Just to write things that you can't say. Thank you. Debbie

Debbie Bumstead

Dear Dr. Pullias

25.
Dear Dr. Pullias,
What do you teach? What is your new book about? I sure like to write. I wonder if it is programed or whatever in my genes or that I grew up liking words and liking to put them together. I remember writing and drawing picture stories for my grandma when I was in second grade. Now they look so funny. I write to pretty many people and I like to get letters back. In English we have this journal that we write about 5 min. each day. Our thoughts. I always look forward to these and the teachers write that they enjoy mine.

Now in English the whole 2 classes are together again. We haven't gotten really into the quarter so I donot know what we will be doing. But I think they said we will be put into small groups according to your ability. The teachers are very young and the way they hand out so many ditto papers and laugh. It just makes me think they are playing a game and us students are members of the game. In a comments part of one of our assignments I wrote that and she said I was right! That they had to do something to make themselves enjoy their job.

This quarter I think I got better grades. Tho' in Algebra I I slipped down from a B to a B-. In Art I received an A. A B in P.E. and an A in Life Science. I have not gotton my Geography or Enlgish grades yet.

I was very happy to see you and Mrs. Pullias that rainy night. It was very good to see you eat and drink. Ha you could laugh but it is that I like to be able to picture people as people. I remember when I was in elementary 6th grade my teacher got mad or maybe I was getting old enough to realize he was human. Anyway, I think teachers who teach youngsters are not really human to the child. After and in 6th grade I kept trying to see and understand that teachers had feelings.

I remember my 5th and 6th grade teachers were very pleased with me. I wonder why once they get to know me adults very much enjoy me and it is the same with small kids. But I donot have to many friends my own age. Those I do have tho are good. But I can only think for me so I can not see why.

My father is at your cabin. He took my microscope and is going to see if he can take some pictures through it.

Hoping you may have time to write, I will close.

Your Friend, Debbie

26.

Los Angeles

Feb. 29, 1969

Dear Debbie:

I had intended to write you a few words on your birthday. To be fifteen is an interesting experience, but I suppose really no more interesting or meaningful than to be twenty or forty or sixty or eighty. Human life is an interesting drama. It unfolds in a special way and each part has its special characteristics.

The special thing about the stage of life you are now in is that you are now making the transition between childhood and adulthood. In the next four or five years your full self as a woman will begin to take final shape. It is not that you will not change after that, but a great portion of what we are emerges by the time we are twenty-five. I hope there will be great years of growth and learning for you. Life is really a wonderful adventure. But we ourselves have much to do with how it unfolds.

I was very glad you walked back up the road and we were able to talk a little while there before "The Four Winds." Wouldn't it be interesting if we could meet and talk there again two days before your 20th birthday? And even your 30th? We would see what we have been able to do with life, and what it has done with us. The rocks, the sky, the hills, the clouds, the birds will be quite the same. They have not changed much since the Indians sat where we were sitting and perhaps talked of what they thought was fundamental.

Thanks for listening to the chapter. It was one of the harder, more concentrated chapters. Some I believe would be more interesting. The rain today is beautiful. I wish I was there to see it fall on those rocks. I hope the second semester goes well.

Sincerely, Earl V. Pullias

Dear Dr. Pullias

27.

Dr. Pullias,

Thank you very much for the letter. Yes, it would be very interesting to talk again in 5 or 15 years, just to see what has come. I wish I could talk more freely with you and my teachers, but instead I just listen. There are so many questions which I want to know the answers to but since I cannot get the answers from others I try to work and think them out myself.

But there are some things that cannot think out because I donot know enough about them. One that has been puzzling and frightening me recently is nightmares. Do they mean anything and if they do what? And what causes them?

I read somewhere that you are unconscious in sleeping and when you are waking you come out of the unconscious to the id and to slow down waking you dream. So your dreams are all in the id?

For my birthday I received a canary, Pooka, who sings so beautifully. He's a flity and active light yellow. He makes you think of imaginary lands and flowers.

My father and I are both interested in the mystery initials TBGL.

I'm reading an interesting book called The Annotated Alice. It is the two Alice books plus notes on the puns and strangenesses. Alice's adventures have always fascinated me. I, when I get through reading them, usually continue with more weird adventures with me as heroine.

There's one long note about dreams and being awake, and madness. I am still trying to understand it. To do that you must read each important word carefully all the while thinking and concentrating on what is trying to be gotton across. It is very interesting.

Perhaps it is the same with your book. As I listened and concentrated I understood I did not think up an opinion of it. I only knew as you said you were writing something new. As you looked at me and asked me what I was thinking of it, it was not that, Dr. Pullias, I was looking at you and understanding it.

Your Friend,

Debbie

Dr. Pullias,

Thanks a lot for the letter.

This letter in with this note was written a couple few days ago, but was't sent becauce I have no stamp.

When I read over it I don't know about it. Oh, well.

Monday we are going to do our choral reading to the class.

Maybe because spring and summer bring with them more freedom I don't [think] to much of my work but I am so much more free with myself. I making friends with teachers and students who I wanted to make friends with at the beginning of school.

In fact one teacher is trying to make friends with me. She is my P.E. teacher. I realized at the beginning of school she wanted to be friends but she is shy and I am shy. Today we started to talk about our art work. She likes to draw.

I like friends. DEB.

28.

Dear Dr. Pullias,

Thanks very much for your letters.

I had been reading one of my Grandma's books about astrlogy. It went into great detail about how you can recognize what certain people were born under what sun sign. It is strange how some of those really fit the people who were born just then. All those planets in a precise position when you are born. But how does that have anything to do with it? I thought it is recorded in your DNA and what your envirment is and all this goes to make yourself up. And that's what I'll go on thinking. But it is still interesting and many times correct. What do you think about it?

My brother Tim brought home a friend from college to stay the weekend. He was from Hong Kong and had studied five years in England. He was very polite and really respected my father. I guess he was brought up to respect oldersters.

The sun sign for me says these people often live thru' the day storing the happenings in their brain for later reference. I find this is very true with me for at night I spend a lot of time just going over the happenings and thinking why. Why did he say that? Why did she act that way? What was she thinking then? All sorts of things. I also go over what I say and think these questions about myself. Sometimes I do think of someone I do not even know the name of even animals. I don't know maybe all other people think that, too. Do you know?

Dear Dr. Pullias

I was hiking in the hills a few days ago and I really love to do that! Oh, I just like to walk alone or with the dog and just be. Doing that if you want you can pretend you are living in the past or the future. You can sneak and go as quietly as you want or be happy and run down hills and be noisy. Then if you have a friend with you you can show them weird rocks and yell and sing. But where is it going.

I wonder why I write you all these personal things. Every teenager ought to have someone to write to. Be they adults or not. Just to write things that you can't say.

Thank you.
Your Friend
Debbie

29.

Dear Dr. Pullias (in Greek letters), or, Delta rho Pi upsilon lambda lambda alpha sigma,

Thanks for the letter. I'm glad it finally came. Tomorrow we start swimming: I CAN HARDLY WAIT! What nonsense. So what? I feel
N o n s e n s e i c a l.

A few long weeks ago I was writing a poem in Art And the teacher came to see what I was doing. I covered it with my aRM (IT WAS MINE) but he lifted my hand and read and left silently. I was terribley hurt and Angry and could not like him at all for a week or so but as ALL THINGS COME AND ALL THINGS GO I greatly enjoy that class now. There is a fun friend in there and she is
N o n s e n s e i c a l.

The teacher, too is sort-of
N o n s e n s e i c a l.

In English today us as a group read our dumb poem to the teacher: "I think Debbie's own teeth can't hear her." I wish I could talk LOUDER! I could. I can write LOUD.

Shes fun and sort-of
N o n s e n s e i c a l.

TODAY WAS SO FUN! I FEEL LIKE DANCING. I smiled at everyone and even if I didn't know them. They smiled back. TRA-LA! My chest hurts from
!HAPPINESS!

Debbie Bumstead

When I write all this it reminds me of a poem in A TEACHER IS MANY THINGS. Its all about the Exhortation of the Dawn.

I sure like it.

Have you ever been told a joke so funny you can not stop laughing? That's what happened to me in science. Oh.

Well I think I will saunter off to the land of Nod and all my happiness will melt into dreams. Dreams of Yesterday.

I wish I had a wishbone.

Nonsenseical

Me

Deborah,

or,

Delta epsilon beta omicron rho alpha

30.

Dear Dr. Pullias,

I'm so angry with myself I would like to talk or write to someone. My father is not usually here, my mother would not respond, my brother, Tim, bugs me with his laziness. In English today we had panel disscussions on novels we were assigned to read (ours was All Quiet on the Western Front). Our group was disorganized (we had kidded around all the time we were to be preparing), unprepared, and so this made us all "unspeakers." Oh, darn.

In a way I should be pleased. In Geography awhile back I'm ashamed to say I had a D average. I brought that up to a C+ average with a report and today (Oh frabjous day!) with only 2 test grades (84 B and 158 A+++++...) I broght it up to a A- average. Fantastic.

In science I also think I did good on the final.

I am learning to play tennis. I practice at the high school and on weekends my father and I play. I think its fun to bap that ball around.

I hope you are coming out to your cabin over Eastern vacation. Once when I went out there, there was a stream I followed aways. In some places it is really beautiful.

Your Friend,

Debbie

31.

Dear Dr. Pullias,

I was thinking about school and a friend came to my mind. He is mentally disturbed I think and belongs to the special class at the high school. Somehow he just became a sort-of friend. He calls me pudding face (?), Linda (?), and Deb, and hits me gently on the arm or says stickum up. (He is not mentally retarded) But I have never once said anything to him! I feel no real need to, but it puzzles me. Maybe I have a perfectly winning smile.

I wonder why people become friends and why friends need friends. I wonder why people must love others and be loved. I was talking with my father and he said you must love yourself before you can give love. I wonder if loving yourself is the same as understanding yourself. Perhaps you must love yourself but not think of yourself.

Oh, I so like hiking up in those hills. It seems like magic sometimes. You know it could be magic because books with magic are fictional which is not true so what is true magic? Maybe I experience true magic when I am walking out there. See?

When I was up there in those magic hills talking (for some reason I don't like that word. It makes me think of harshness, just the sound of it) with you you said that you thought that I was different which I think also, but I wonder if you were a friend (and you probably are) of another girl or young man wouldn't you think that person different, too? Everyone is different and special.

I am looking forward to starting school Monday. This week we will have "rube day" which probably will be lots of fun. Oh, wonderful school! I might say about it: "Absence makes the heart grow fonder."

Your Friend, Debbie

P.S. I have been doing some oil painting and finished a dark blue, yellow, and green jungle scene which if I use my imagination turned out like I wanted it.

P.S. #2 I got a B in Algebra. I was sort of disappointed because I had worked so hard at being neat and handing in assignments on time, studing for tests and taking notes

32.

Debbie Bumstead

Dear Dr. Pullias,

My father said that you had been up on the hill making a speech. What's your speech about? I'd still like to know what you teach. Are you an administrator?

This semester has turned out very good in the way of grades. Mostly I have gotten As and B+s. They really surprized me. In a way it was sort of sad to leave for some of the teachers will not come back. It's strange to think you will never see again a person who helps you learn something very important. And you want to continue to know them espially the ones who have tooken a great interest in you personally. But they will be gone. And next year you will have the same teachers but with different people inside them.

I am earning four dollars a week from my mother so if I should continue to, then I would have $208 in a year! Also next month I will take care of this ladies two dogs for $5 aweek.

I have been doing a lot of art work. My teacher, the last day, gave me 4 jars of florescent paint and some cardboard to work on. The other art teacher who is also a friend gave me a picture for Tim and a ceramic jug I gave to my father. For a large still-life I drew I received a ribbon from the county. That is probably the only one you would like because the rest are sort-of modern art. (That's probably why it got a ribbon.)

I don't think I ought to write more because you're probably still busy.

Your Friend,
Debbie

P.S. Look at this paper closely. It has little ridges in it. I wonder why?

33.

Dear Dr. Pullias,

Today my father and me went up and got your letter which he'd been keeping for me and my report card which pleased me very much. I walked down alone and stopped by the Lost Spring (WOW: It's really lost now) and read the letter. It was so beautiful! The rocks were pink with the sunset, the weeds near them all mauve and still. And the plants near me were large and green and pungent. There was a bird playing by himself in the sky. I looked up at the old man in the moon.

Dear Dr. Pullias

I think he was sad.

My mother and me went to Reno for a month. Sometimes it is fun there because I have a couple of good friends but it is kind of boring otherwise.

Onetime a friend and I went to see the royal Lipazzan stallions perform. They're sure wonderful!

To me I think that we should talk to as we write. I think that talking is about as important as writing in a different way. I can talk to and question strangers politely and with family members I can discuss, talk, sing, whiltse easily but then there are those people like you who are strangers yet people who I know well and they know me well. These are the people I think of mostly. This is where most of my teachers are too.

Summer is so fun. You have nothing to hurry up with. You can stay up till midnight (like right now) and you can wake up at 4:30 to eat warm bisquits. You can go out in to a silent morning world and sit with just thoughts. No hurry.

We Bumsteads are endowed (right word?) with this quality all the year. My father calls it the Bumstead Curse, but I think it is good. You may only live once but if you hurry through that life, being busy and hurried, then it is not worth living, is it? What do you think?

I have been doing a lot of photography which is fun and interesting. My father says I'm too good at too many things. (?)

I want to write you about my games that I play with people sometime. My mind sure is weird. How about yours?

Your Friend,
    Debbie

34.
Los Angeles
Aug 14, 1969
Thursday night

Dear Debbie:
    Probably I should have asked you before I spoke to your Dad
about fixing up your room for this fall. If you think it is a good
and workable idea, I would like to speak to him again about it
and perhaps send a little money to help with whatever cash outlay
might be involved. I suspect a nice room with some privacy
might be good for you now. You let me know what you think.
    I believe I understand what you said in your last letter about
the "Bumstead Curse." Those feelings and tendency are not all
bad: they are often the symptom of fine thought and talent. The
trick is to use this moodiness and feeling of just wanting to <u>be</u>
rather than wanting to <u>do</u> in creative ways. You and I working
together will learn to do that over the years. Then we will have
the best of the Bumstead trait and the best of other traits that
will enable you to learn how to work so you can use, and enjoy the
use of your abilities and talents as they unfold.
    Frankly, I am very proud of the progress you have made both
in the attitude toward and your skill in doing well your school
work. That is just a beginning of your growth. Before school
starts I want you to reread three chapters of <u>A Teacher Is Many
Things</u>. "The Teacher as an Inspirer of a Vision of Greatness",
"The Teacher as a Bridge between Generations" and "The T. as a
Person." Hope all goes well there and that many good ideas
come.
    Your friend, Earl V. Pullias

35.
Dr. Pullias,
    It was real nice seeing you Monday morning. I wish I had gotten
up earlier.

Dear Dr. Pullias

We are having a yard sell hear but nobody buys anything.

I appreciate very much your concern about my room. It's very nice.

I'm looking forward to school but I don't espially want the summer to hurry up.

There is nothing to write about. My [eyes] have [been] so much better that it makes them ache to have on my glasses. I owe it all to sunflower seeds.

Well, I hope I will see you guys again soon

Yours, Debbie

P.S. My mother has said she'd like to talk or write to you but I don't know if she will.

36.

Dear Dr. Pullias,

There is an open house tonight in which the parents go to all your classes in schedule and see your teachers. Last year my father and I went but this year my mother is going, too. I will stay home. She is not really intrested in my school work the way my father is. I mean she is concerned but not interested. It is just that she wants to have Daddy to think she is trully interested.

It is hard to live with this fakery. I know 3 sides to it. When my mom complains when he's gone, constantly making excuses for him, like 'Oh he's so independent...' And then when my fathers home she's always doing something, trying to please him with something she's not. Then there's Daddy's side where he wants to be alone and do things.

It all just rattles me up. It shows up in school. 2 teachers have asked me what's the matter. Even that breaks me up. I just can't seem to let people help.

My geometry teacher is concerned. He says by the way I talk to him I'm a very good student. But still I'm getting a C- average so far.

I got a progress report for a D+ average in History. What cruddy start for 10th grade.

Now you know my troubles. And there's not time to tell you everything that should offset this problem but still it dominates me.

2 classes out of 6 is not horrible but it is 2 very important courses.

And I should be happier. Maybe this year is jinxed.

I've entered a equestrian club and plan to enter an Art club. Clubs are important I guess but I'm not very clubby.

I hope you are well, happy, and thriving up there in L.A.

Your Friend, Debbie

37.

Los Angeles

Oct 14, 1969

Dear Debbie:

Your letter came today. I was very sorry to hear that things do not go so well. Last year was a happy and good year for you and I was thankful and glad for you. Perhaps they cannot all be good, but I am hoping this one will straighten out before too long.

I believe I understand what you say about the home situation. As time goes on I am hoping this type of thing will not bother you so much. I have found that it is almost impossible to understand other people, especially our parents. People often marry, I don't know quite why, who are not very well suited to each other. Even when they want to do otherwise, they hurt each other. Especially, when we want so very much to be loved and accepted we do things that may have the opposite effect. Strange, but true.

You cannot do much to solve all of this. Perhaps you can learn to understand it better, and as much as you can, accept and love them both. It will help a great deal if you can become keenly interested in your work and in doing it well. The clubs will be good if they interest you: horses are wonderful. Write me about how things go. Just writing will help.

Los Angeles is a huge and noisy city. There is much that is beautiful and good here and much that is ugly and bad. It seems that crowdedness always brings out the worst in people. I will always like the quiet country best: open sky, sand, trees, leaves, grass, happy growing, living things. But of course, everywhere there are friendship and love: they are very good. Keep your heart and head up.

Sincerely, Earl V. Pullias

38.
Los Angeles
Nov. 2, 1969
Dear Debbie:
I just finished a book I think you might enjoy or like: <u>A Crack in the Sidewalk</u> by Ruth Wolff. It is a good story, is about a teen age girl, and has some good psychology in it. Hope you can find it there.

Your letter came and as always I was glad to receive it. I was glad to learn that things were better than when you wrote before. The school work will straighten out: I want you to do a very good job, if just for the sake of doing it, and also to get ready for college which will be a great experience when it comes.

You asked or rather wondered about my attitude toward the war and toward all war. War is a horrible, dreadful, wasteful, foolish thing. Perhaps some time human beings will cease to try to settle their problems in such a destructively foolish way. I suspect though it will not be in our life time. Someway we have to have better people and it is my hope that better teachers and wiser parents can eventually produce enough better people to make a better world. In the meantime, I don't know what is best to do. I would guess if we did not have police it would not be safe for you there in your house or for you to take a walk alone or for me to sit here writing to you. Often in life, Debbie, I have found we have to choose between the lesser of two bad things, rather than what we would really like.

We are eager to come to the hills. Enjoy this beautiful fall as much as the problems of life will allow.

Your friend, Earl V. Pullias

39.
Dear Dr. Pullias,
I guess we both thought of writing each other at the same time. Your letter I very much liked getting today because I am staying home from school with the second cold in a row. I don't understand getting another cold because I am usually so healthy. It worries me.

That book you wrote of makes me want to read it right now.

Maybe my mother will take me to the library.

It is nice to think that you thought of me on your trip and got that little wooden animal. My antelope is rather lonely.

Our children's library is soon to get a bunch of new books. That will be neat!

Bye, Debbie

40.

Dear Dr. Pullias,

Tonight it is still Thanksgiving night. I think this Thanksgiving was my most ever Thanksgivingest Thanksgiving. It was because my father was so sick and his eyes were all old and watery. And I went for a walk in the morning with the wind blowing. Everything looked so clean and quiet. The little children were dressed in pink dresses or green sweaters. I felt sad and all I thought of was the sounds of raking leaves and just walking. Do you know what I mean?

When my uncle and aunt and cousin came to eat I looked at my uncle Hersey to often. I could see his wondering why but some days I get to looking to long. I think it is just my eyes resting but I don't know. Tonight my dad said I had been watching him all day like I thought he was going to die.

I was sitting in the car waiting for my mother some days ago, this lady was sitting in a restaurant looking at me, I turned my head toward her and she got all flustered and turned away. When Ma was backing out she turned again and looked at me and even as we drove off she turned full round on her stool to watch me. I wonder what I look like from the outside of inside me. What was she thinking I wonder. If she had been oldish I wouldn't really wonder but she looked only 35 or so. Mmm.

Do you think I have any special way of writing? I mean when I read of over it, it doesn't seem different. It's different from others but, well I don't know.

I hope you had a nice Thanksgiving. Your Friend, Debbie

I decided to write some more this morning.

What makes the wind blow? I never could find a reason. When trees are blown all about it reminds me of an amoeba with all its leaves as protoplasm. Palm trees make me think of mad people waving their arms around. I wonder why I find comparisons? Why can't I just accept trees as being trees and not looking like anything but just trees? I do that with people I know, too. I wonder why I do. Is it a bad habit? Anne and me are making the movie-film cartoon for Tim on Christmas. Its lots of fun but I don't know if we'll finish. I'll have to do most myself. Anne is always busy. Why is it that I am not busy anytime. I have time to visit friends and walk and think while my friends have just got to do this or that. I think I must be awful lazy.

There are too many Is in this letter. I wonder why?

> Till time stands still
> And knows what it's all about,
>> Debbie

41.
Dear Dr. Pullias,

Thanks for the paper of yours. I read it. Isn't it really weird that I should write you that last letter asking about the book and the poem in it?

I think perhaps, I don't agree with the writing of that book. It seems like a textbook on philosophy or the search for truth. Isn't that something a person thinks out for himself? Can you say "the pursuit of truth calls for skill, persistence, application"? Can you teach somebody how to find truth? Not to me.

The other day when it was raining so very hard and nice I was stringing some beads and the string broke and the beads fell. That made me think of a poem to write:

> Rain
> God has broken
> The string to a fine necklace
> Of the tears he has cried.

Maybe it is not a poem but just a sentence. Anyway.

I wish I'd come out there when you were there but I'm the only one in the family who likes to hike so no one takes me out. I'm old enough to have a license but no one will take me driving to practice. That was the Complaint Column.

Pretty soon I'll be able to play some songs on the guitar.

> Oh well, bye
>> Your Friend,

Debbie Bumstead

Debbie

P.S. I am desperate for a good, well-written book. Do you know any?

42.

Dear Dr. Pullias,

I am sorry of your illness and that you could not be here over Thanksgiving vacation. It rained. I had a nice vacation in a sort-of sleepy thoughtful type way.

Immortal

This morning when I was walking to school I thought so many thoughts that when I got to my class the last thing I remembered doing was putting the dog out. And when I was in my class and thought of the time it had taken me it seemed like an eternity or no time at all. If I was immortal probably my life would be in that feeling. I would be there and never grow old and never grow young and walk in the hills for more than a year and never know. I could sit in the grove of pepper trees and crunch pepper tree leaves for several days or several years depending on how I felt. I could pick up a brittle stick and take an hour to do so and a walk with my friends would not last even a second in my life. I could not get married and have children for they would be old and wrinkled and dead before I would take time to blink my eye. Perhaps I would see wars and the end of mankind and then perhaps I would walk alone over rubble and skelitons. I would be lonely and my loneliness would last for an eternity but be no time at all.

That was a paper I had written for English last quarter.
Well, I guess I will quit. Hmmm.
Your Friend, Debbie.

43.

December - 1969

Dear Dr. Pullias,

I really liked seeing you yesterday. It was the first time I have felt completely free to come up and talk with you or maybe not free but at ease. It is a surprizing change and I am pleased.

Today I read A Teacher is a Person again. It is my favorite chapter

40

Dear Dr. Pullias

in your book. What you write about the classroom being a place for teachers to watch the ways of people is very good I think. Even as a student it is an interesting place. I really like to just watch, listen, and talk to all these people. Everybody is so wonderfull!

But isn't it good to go away alone and think about what you've said, heard, and seen?

I know only one girl who thinks this way, too, that everyday at the end of a school day she is looking forward to tommorrow. But I think perhaps she looks more toward why people act and look the way they do and I am more interested in the thoughts and feelings people (including me) have and why. I don't know.

It's night, the wind is blowing and it smells like rain. I wish I was on a rock out there, alone, with no fear for just awhile. What are you thinking about it? I hope the wind does not blow to hard our walnut tree.

Queer looking bugs jump all about my new room.

It is very private though buggy. I like it very much but I do not know really if it will get finished. I can fix it like I want tho'.

On this record called 'Hair' there is a song called What a piece of work is Man with the words in your book. You have probally heard of the musical 'Hair'? What do you think of it?

So far I have squished two hard little bugs in here. It is easy because I can think of them biting me at night but when I'm walking outside and should look down and see I'm stepping on a insect I feel so cruddy. I can never bring myself to smash a spider when it just stands there. They seem so important when you see them alone. Even a rattlesnake is beutiful when you can not feel its poisen.

Anne told me she's giving me a pscheldeldlic unicorn picture for Christmas. This is my most favorite animal. They are perfect. I'm making her a paper-mache marrinette because she likes them so much.

I'm so very glad I feel now that I want to talk with you. I mean this feeling of compression (right word?) is gone and I am very glad. It's good.

School starts Monday. Hope it goes well with you.

Your Friend, Debbie

Debbie Bumstead

1970

Your last letter made me very sad. All of life often makes me sad. Yet of course there is much joy and beauty in life: the two are forever intermingled and intertwined. I find it is very good to be sad, especially if that sadness results from the truth. The truth is a precious thing and often you who are younger perceive and express the truth-some aspects of it- better than those of us who are older. **Dr. Pullias**

Those dreams still come, those ones about dead children.
Debbie

Debbie Bumstead

Dear Dr. Pullias

44.
Dear Dr. Pullias,

I am sorry I haven't written. I'm sorry you haven't written. Hmmm

Last time I was up at your place to see you guys, afterwards I got to thinking that the problem with my relationship with you is that you're too concerned with me. Everytime I go up there you say "Let's go for a walk" or "Let's go up to the Four Winds" and then when we're up there you ask questions about me and I sit there in a straight chair, my feet tracing the bricks and my hands breaking a twig. I feel like a dumb little kid.

I have some friends in Reno that I write to, whenever we write we write about what has happened to us and things we feel. But when I see them in the summer we do things and talk opinions and funny happenings. See?

My friends all have horses and I so immensly enjoy riding that I decided to get a donkey. Go ahead and laugh. This horsy friend has worked it all out, where to keep it, feeding it, so on. Now, my only problem is MONEY. I'm going to earn some from Ma. It is so earthy and beatiful to ride on a horse. I don't know about a donkey, but I can try it!

This weekend my friend Carrie, and my English teacher may go on a trail ride. I hope we do. The teacher will have to borrow me a horse, if she can.

I'm taking guitar lessens. They're intresting.

We had class finals this week. I am doing pretty good in all my classes except Geometry

I hope all of you people are great OK.

Your Friend, Debbie.

45.

45

Debbie Bumstead

Los Angeles
Feb. 1, 1970
Dear Debbie:

Your last letter made me very sad. All of life often makes me sad. Yet of course there is much joy and beauty in life: the two are forever intermingled and intertwined. I find it is very good to be sad, especially if that sadness results from the truth. The truth is a precious thing and often you who are younger perceive and express the truth-some aspects of it-better than those of us who are older.

I am very glad you told me just how you felt: I understand what you said quite fully and deeply. I should have seen it myself. You do not seem so foolish and stupid as you say you feel when I asked you questions. But as one writer says "questions are pressure." Although also questions can be a sincere desire of a friend to know more and to understand more. Yet one knows that understanding and knowing cannot be pushed but must grow. I will remember that.

Perhaps it would help a little to say another word: the next four or five years will be crucial in your life. If you get a vision of the best that is in you and learn to grow toward it, your life will grow toward the good and beautiful thing it can be. There are hundreds of false roads you can take and they all lead to nowhere, and often worse than nowhere. A single friend can sometimes make the difference.

Horses are wonderful. I hope so much you were able to take the ride. And I too have long wanted a donkey. If you get one, maybe we could have his company some when we are there.
Sincerely, Earl V. Pullias

46.
Dear Dr. Pullias,

Thank you very munch for the letter. Your letters always smell nice and strange. I liked that one especially because it showed more you in it.

I think, maybe, I don't think that questions are a friend's way of communicating. Maybe a different kind of friend. Nothing can be said either way because one is as the other; itself. Oh, no! There comes my philosophy of all things and if ever I try to say it, I can't. I think my father knows what I mean by all of it but perhaps I can say it better than write. Are you now thoroughly confused?

In English last quarter we had a few writing assignments and I did very well on all of them. In fact (brag, brag) my English teacher began to look with new respect at a quiet girl who says hardly a thing. So I got an A in there for the semester.

I did quite well in German and P.E., too. I feel good and have fun in these classes. All this year I have been uninspired in art work. I do good but I don't feel good.

This semester our teachers were changed around. I have the same Geometry teacher. In there I got a C+. Mr. Axminister does not like me and unfortunately I have the same feelings toward him. Tuesday we are going to have team-teaching, in <u>Geometry</u>! Aaaggghhh!!!

Hhmmmm. What would I do without school?

You should see my room! It's getting pretty neat. Its got all contrasts there are bright jungly curtains, a floresent unicorn poster, a crazy quilt, an Indian rug, and a bunch of stuffed jungle animals.

I like my German teacher very munch. He is so kind. It would be hard to know anyone kinder. I think I will like my new history teacher, too.

Well, good-bye   Your Friend, Debbie.

47.
Los Angeles
Feb 10, 1970
Dear Debbie,
I wonder if the rain falls tonight on the hills and rocks of Hemet? It is hard sometime to realize that existence goes on all over the world. We are sometimes inclined to feel that things and people exist only when we know about them. Rain has been falling almost all day today. I like the steady fall of a gentle rain.

Once when I was about your age I liked to ride a large, beautiful horse we had on the farm. Some time I would need to ride to the back of the farm in a downpour of rain. I can see now the slick, reddish coat of that horse and smell the wonderful odor of a healthy horse.

You are doubtless right about questions. I shall try to learn not to ask them, but just to wait and to listen and that which I need and want to know will come better.

The school results sound very good to me. I am especially glad that you are coming more and more to enjoy the process: that is the real hope of making life good. I guess it would be difficult to explain your philosophy to which you alluded - I would like to hear more about it - perhaps later maybe?

I am glad you liked my more frank letter.
Good wishes, Earl V. Pullias

48.
(Feb. 1970)
Dear Dr. Pullias

We are signing up for classes next year. In science I am going to take chemistry which will be completly new to me. In English I'll get a semester of Creative writing.

My brother Joe (alias Gomez, Quasimodo...) along with a few friends bought some land in Oregon. They are going to go live up there come summer and we may go up, too. That sounds really neat.

I just turned 16 a few days ago. My mother says I look 13. Maybe I am socially immature. Maybe it is just part of my thinking machine. People seem to treat me like I'm a curious, serious, little kid! Last Friday I was reading in Geometry and my teacher comes by and says "Debbie" just like I was a baby. But I like it because that is just me! So what?

Last year 2 days before I was fifteen on a Sunday I sat on a hard rock and listened to a poem from your book. It seems like it was about space? How is your book faring? I'm interested in it. I sure haven't seen you guys in a long time.

When you are listening to nice music or listening to poetry, or just barely listening to soft voices around you, you get different, sort-of ultra-thoughts. They make you think dark forest green thoughts that sort-of roll around in your head or push to get out.

Tomorrow is Pete the dogs birthday #1. It's raining.

What do you think about things like the earth?

Dear Dr. Pullias

Your friend, Debbie

P.S. I have kept a diary pretty well so far this year. I can't seem to write thoughts in it but I write what I liked about the days and I write my dreams. I like to read over it later.

49.

(May 1970)

Dear Dr. Pullias,

Thank you for the letter. It gave me a lot to think about.

I still don't want to be a teacher at all but more and more I find myself wondering about what I would do as a teacher or what I would think. As a student I may write a paper on a teacher of mine, if I were a teacher would I might write a paper on a student? You never seem to write about an espially good student you have or one you have a personal interest in. It seems to me that students would affect a teacher much the same way as a teacher affects students. I don't know.

My mind may grow more effective and beuatiful but I don't know about my body.

When I am around some girls I feel fat and horribly pimply. I feel like I have a double chin. When I am around boys I feel dainty and like a girl. I feel so much better in a man teacher's class because I feel so nice.

Children, I think, get the idea that grown-ups are not really human with different interests just like kids who have different interests. I mean I sort-of have the hard to get rid of feeling that when you grow up you're always flooded with finaicial problems and how to send Junior through college... Where did I get that idea? Maybe it's true?

My mother's birthday is Sunday. I think I will make a couple of bead necklaces for her.

I think people are going about this earth pollution thing wrong. I don't litter, for instance, not because I want to save the earth but because it seems to me that the earth feels good when I put trash in a trash can. My room looks pretty messy but in actuality it feels good with everything cluttered.

The day after I got your letter you should have seen how hard I concentrated in History. Would you believe in Geometry I have done my assignments three nights in a row?!

I hope you come out soon.

In Geometry my tests scores for this quarter so far are 103% (!), 80%, 94%. Wow!

Your Friend, Debbie

P.P.S. A small peice of creative writing of mine appeared in our Literary Issue newspaper. It was a special newspaper for the end of the year. Most of the subjects were about earth.

50.
Los Angeles
June 3, 1970
Wednesday Night

Dear Debbie:

Thanks for your letter: it was a good letter for me. I was sorry I did not let you know that we were coming to Hemet last week end. I had to work a good deal, but it would have been good to see you.

Teaching may not be for you. But one never knows what the future will bring. I remember when I was your age and younger of feeling that I would never be a teacher. In fact, I felt this would be the last thing I would ever be. I am not sure what brought the change in my mind.

I have many thoughtful and interesting students. Now and then I have written about them, but more often I guess I have written and thought about my teachers. That is not quite true, for I have often <u>thought</u> of my students - in fact, that is much of what a teacher does. Had you thought that in addition to being a friend, you are also a student of mine?

It will be wonderful if your mind can learn to concentrate: then learning will be easy, often quick, and will have a depth and clarity that will surprise you. Your body will grow beautiful too: a good mind and spirit needs a good body in which and through which to function. Give that growth a half a chance and it will come: like other beautiful living things grow.

May 31 is also Mrs. P.'s birthday. Wish we had dropped by your house as we left for home. I hope you made the necklace for

Dear Dr. Pullias

her.

Your friend, Earl V. Pullias

51.

(June 1970)

Dear Dr. Pullias,

Today was the last day of school. It doesn't seem like it. It seems like tomorrow I will go to school as usuall. It's hard to think that I'll never be a 10ᵗʰ grader again and I'll never see the teachers who are leaving again. In just three more months I'll be a Junior then a Senior and then what will I do? It is all very scary.

I always get my best grades the last quarter. I got As in History, P.E., and German. In Geometry I got a B instead of a C+. Next year I can hardly wait to see what Chemistry's like. I don't even know what its about. I also took Creative Writing.

My crayon pictures on my bulliton board look like they were done by a crazy person. I wonder if I'm crazy. I have always puzzled over why people look at me and treat me like I'm strange. Even you do.

That was a dumb paragraph.

Well, the other day Daddy left or something and my mother said "I just don't know what to do" so I said "Divorce him." I don't know what divorcing does espially but I think my father needs a big kick in the pants like he's always complaining that Tim needs.

We haven't heard from Tim in about 2 months. His girlfriend asked me about him a couple of times. I'll have to write that to him, it might make him feel nice.

Well, bye, Your Friend, Debbie.

52.

Dear Dr. Pullias,

Well, do you have a yard where you live in L.A.? Does Mrs. Pullias grow things? I like Mrs. Pullias because she makes me think of a little girl who is pleased about everything around her.

Sometimes I wish I wasn't so shy. It's so maddening.

Can you sometimes feel like the earth is so bursting with things that grow up. The grass and trees and flowers seem so fierce, sproting up where they can be so strong. But I think of New York and it seems like a blight on earth and like it hurts. Like a bunch of pimples. But when I am in a big city I like so munch because of all the people to look at and think of. Well, and I wonder if the street on which so many cars and trucks and people crossing and getting killed thinks like in Simon's song; "I'd rather be a forest than a street/Yes I would/If I only could/I surely would."

I am writing this at about midnight tonight and I am listening to records. Who is Frank Lyod Wright? When I go to bed at a regular time all I do is toss and turn till midnight or so, so why not do something then? Hmmmm, my writing as acted kind-of funny in this letter. It hardly makes sense.

The next letter you write to me I think should go up to Reno. We are leaving for there Monday. My mother wants to stay at least 6 weeks because she wants to get a divorce. Well, if we stay that long I shall surely die of boredom. Perhaps your letters will revive me.

Your Friend, Debbie.

53.

In Reno, summer 1970

Dear Dr. Pullias,

I told my mother that you wished she would not get the divorce and she said she had wanted to talk to you badly. She gave me a letter my father wrote to her on the day you wrote mine. He wrote that he wished that there was no divorce also but that it would be better and that my mother would be able to grow. I, too, think it a good idea. I am not grown-up and I don't know all about love and things but I know what I feel when I live with two people who love each other but constantly make each other unhappy and everyone else around them.

In this 16th year I begin to feel that all I have experienced and felt and all I have read and learned is starting to grow inside me and fit together like a puzzle and come out in my thinking more to my satisfaction. Sometimes I get a feeling that I want to read about anything and everthing and look and stare at all I can see and all that I could see and to feel whatever I feel and not just let it slip by. Is that what you mean being a drifter you let all that slip by?

My room is on a secound floor and when I look at the window I see the neighbor's place. I know these people through Marie, a friend who's father lives there. She lives with her mother but she wants to live with her father. Her problem is not anything like mine but still I think I know how she feels. Anyway these neighbors are so interesting to me. They are two girls there visiting and a pregnat lady about to have a baby and Marie's big brother and her father who I like very munch and his new wife. There are also 5 or 6 horses, 11 or so dogs, cats, and ducks and a skunk and a goat. Brinna, the wife reminds me of my 9th grade English teacher I so admired. I get so extremely shy with people I want to know and I want to talk to them but I wish I were not so shy.

There was a deer up at your cabin? What did it do? I have never seen one in the wild. Except once when we were little kids we were all riding in the car and a whole herd ran out in front of us and one jumped over the car. We were so thrilled.

Tim is supposed to get a special discharge very soon.

I have so munch to write but perhaps it will all save for another time. I would like to write a dream I had last night. I was in India and on the ground were long lines of dead children and there was a manure pile and tethered to the top of it was two kids. I came back later and they were dead. I went into a house that was full of junk to buy a kitten and the whole litter of kittys were malformed. Some had mange and one had three eyes and it looked at me so evil.

That's sickening.

Please write soon.

Your Friend, Debbie.

P.S. I like the name Deborah, too, but if you call me by that name please pronounce it Deborah and not Debra which I dislike.

54.
Los Angeles
July 17, 1970

Dear Debbie:

How good to receive your interesting and free letter! Your writing skill is developing beautifully: that is because you are developing, for writing is in essence a reflection of one's **being** - oneself. Your feeling about things coming together and making meaning in this year of your life is an aspect of the growth and life adventure I envision for you: it should go on from stage to stage through all of your life.

Yes, <u>not</u> seeing and feeling and searching for knowledge and understanding is part of what I mean by <u>drifting</u>. Beyond that, I mean the failure to develop goals or ideals for oneself: ideals about all aspects of oneself toward which you can be growing all your life. Thus with God's help, one becomes what he is capable of becoming as a person. We'll talk more about this later.

The divorce problem is very complicated. Usually it does not settle anything. Your parents have many years to live long after you will have gone out on your own. Really they need each other on that long road. But I guess some time there is no other way but to separate and divorce, but I wish it were not so in their case.

The deer was interesting and beautiful. I came out of the back (north) door of The Four Winds and he was feeding not far from the cabin on the flat toward Hemet Butte. The noise of the door frightened him and he began bounding toward the hills to the north and was soon out of sight. I wish I could have seen him close.

Your friend, Earl V. Pullias

55.

In Reno, summer 1970

Dear Dr. Pullias,

I am thinking of how to begin this letter. I was thinking of writing the feelings I had when I began thinking about school and being at home and the pleasant routine of waking up every morning to go to school, to have friends over after school to eat cookies till the bus comes and all that sort-of stuff. Sometime I will write about it in depth, maybe for my Creative Writing class I took for first semester.

Darn. I think I would give anything for a pen that doesn't skip! Aaaggghhh!!! It bugs me to death!

Anyway I was writing about routine. Or anyway I am now. Anyway I like routine. When ever I go to Thrifty's for a ice cream cone I always get a 10 cent cone with a scoop of Black Walnut on the bottom and Orange Sherbut on top. When I go to Baskin-Robbins I always get Fresh Strawberry. What has that got to do with anything? Boy what a crazy letter.

Dear Dr. Pullias

I hope I get Miss Kerr for Creative Writing.

Have you ever been to Europe. Have you been in Germany in the forests and visited castles? I would like to some day.

Tim is supposed to get a Special Discharge and may be up here next week. That will be super neat! Wizzo! Groovy! Tough! Tomorrow a cousin of my mother's is coming to visit. She has two kids to make friends with. Besides the two friends I already had here I've made friends with a 13 year old girl who goes to my Grandmother's church. She has a 2 year old sister who made friends with me, too. I have an aquantence with a boy who also goes to that church. That's strange for me to make some many friends so quickly. I was reading in a women's magazine under my horoscope, Aquarius, it said "you will be meeting new friends late in July and early in Aug…" Isn't that amazing! Really weird! Really Strange!

Hmmmm.

Please write Supersoon! OK?

Your Friend, Debbie.

P.S. I read a really good book today. It was <u>A Walk to the Hills of the Dreamtime</u> by James Vance Marshall.

It was in Australia and these two half-caste kids who have grown-up Christian meet up with a Aborigenie tribe. The different ways of life are -- well anyway it is a good interesting book that makes you think about things and also tells about the Aborigenies ways of survival.

56.

In Reno, summer 1970

Dear Dr. Pullias,

Well, it is about 10:30 or 11:00 this Friday night and I am so glad inside. I wanted to share it. Tim is supposed to be here tommorrow afternoon! He is out of the army and I am glad of that but I am glad, too, that he went through all that. I think that he is also glad of going through it. I think that it has been a fight for himself and that he feels he has won it.

These days have been so full. The first of this week Louise, a cousin of my mom's came and with her, her new husband, his two children, and a 23 year old Mexican boy she is helping put through college. The boy was so smiley and sincere and the husband was kind and funny to me. What was so nice about them was that they seemed

to like me and accept me for what I am. I mean that many people I am
with continually say "Why are you so quiet!?" or "You look so sad." It
makes me dislike being with them. Anyway in the 3 days they were
here, I fell to liking them eversomunch. I had a lump in the throat all
the day after they left and today has not been munch better but Tim is
coming tomorrow and Sunday is usually nice, too.

Even though extra nice things are happaning here and I am
enjoying myself on the outside and beautifull feelings are with me,
inside I can feel my nerves tightening to a knot and I have frightful
dreams. I want so much to go home and calm myself down and listen
to my music (I get none at all up here) and write and just calm down
inside. I can tell busy cities are not for me.

Thank you for the wonderful letter. You wrote more about your
own self and I liked that. I always write about myself to you, don't I?
Boy, will I be glad to get home. I really beleive that "Abesense makes
the heart grow fonder" but absense is good. I always look forward to
coming up here in the summer.

Perhaps you have really liked being alone for 2 weeks but perhaps
then you will be so glad to see your family again. Perhaps we learn
something from absense.

I have not see Calvin and Frances for along time. I hope I see
them someday.

Bye, Your Friend, Debbie

P.S. A good book is <u>Tistou of the Green Thumbs</u> by Maurice Druon

57.

Dear Dr. Pullias,

I wish I could not start every sentence with I. Would, I mean.
Trees do something to me. The wind blows the leaves but the tree
seems to me to be doing it himself and thinking and bending and
singing to me. There is a tree with bunched leaves out a window here
and when a breeze comes up the bunches nod up and down and make
me laugh. They look like a baby waving bye-bye. Part of our walnut
tree fell down today. At night before I fall asleep in that time you're
just able to control what you think I sometimes walk through deep
green forests with a friend. Everything is there and there are deer. It is
real.

When I have a very bad dream after a few days it is usually sort of
silly but there is one that I had in 7th or 8th grade that scares me still. I

Dear Dr. Pullias

was at the Elem. School and I noticed some green puddles on the ground. I looked down into one and there as if standing in a hole full of green water tilting his head up at me was a dead child. There was such a horrible look of terror in his face but it was dead. It was as if the child had been sent to hell but shouldn't have been and was being tortured. And was looking and reaching for me to save. That was what it looked like but I didn't even think of saving it.

Ugh. It makes my stomach tense up even now.

I will be glad school starts soon. I got the teacher I most hoped and prayed I wouldn't get for creative writing.

Write soon please, Debbie Bumstead. Your Friend.

58.

September 1970

Dear Dr. Pullias,

That trip sounded pretty neat! Michigan is a state I always wanted to learn about or visit. I think probably because the name is nice to say. It is so wierd for me, and I think about this alot, to realize someone, enyone, is living and doing and thinking about something all the while I am. I like books, espially children's books, that go into this.

I am sort-of watching a program about a homosexual. It seems like that a life thinking that way would be so one-sided. I mean, a person who thinks this way might eliminate in his mind the whole of an oppisite sex. I don't know how important sex is to life. My father once told me that it was like life was a cake and sex is icing on top.

Those dreams still come, those ones about dead children. Besides that I just have such weird dreams. Night before last I had a dream that Grandbee died in a storm on the hill because she was hiking up the hill to your place to see if my father was OK. The feelings we all had after she died were very real. I have had a series of dreams about Granbee this year. In only one other did she die.

Maybe this is that I have an obsession about death, I don't know. The first death that really affected me was when a little 2 year old cousin died. I kept thinking about his mother looking in his crib and finding him there dead. That was in 7th or 8th grade.

I hope you write soon. What subjects are you teaching? I went to the Elem. School yesterday with a friend and seeing all those kids, I thought it would be nice to just know them all. For friends.

Debbie Bumstead

Your Friend, Debbie.

59.
Los Angeles
Sept. 28, 1970

Dear Debbie:
I am glad you liked the sound of my trip. It would have been nice if you could have gone along with me to help me observe and get ideas. I also have often thought how strange it is to think of all the people of the world carrying on their lives: in a sense, it seems that action takes place only where we are.

In regard to the dreams about death and especially about the death of a child, I suspect the cause roots back into that early bad experience with the death of your 2 year old cousin. An early experience of this kind can leave some scar, especially if you can't talk it over with someone. I would suggest that you get a notebook and keep an account of your dreams in it. Note also what thinking about the dreams brings to your mind. Often a dream is trying to say something to you indirectly, so that the things the dreams suggest to you may be more important than the dream itself. Also, write freely to me about your dreams - that will help.

We will talk much about sex in the years that lie ahead. Your mind is touching now on two of the most complex and sometimes difficult problems in life: death and sex. We must learn to handle both of them with great wisdom. If we take reasonable care we can learn about both of them gradually. Let me help as a friend in any way I can.

Sincerely your friend, Earl V. Pullias

60.
Dear Dr. Pullias,
I am sorry that I have not written very soon.

Tim bought a new truck. It is dark green and when you are in it, it is like a fish. One night we went out to test his four wheel drive in the

58

mountains. Mama and him were talking and I was left to my own thoughts. I liked it and in the hills it was exciting thinking of murderers hiding out or hiking at night over the rocks and exploring. He is pretty pleased with it.

This school year I sort-of feel a difference in myself. I didn't mind being alone. Is this bad? I feel like being gentle with people and myself. I don't know, I just <u>feel</u> different.

Creative Writing is creepy. The teacher is a regular old bag and she's not even weird in a interesting way. Her mind is closed and when I'm around people with closed minds my own mind closes like a clam against them. But still through all this I want to be nice to her. She believes that one should write for someone while I write for myself. If I wrote for her, yig, what a bore my writing would be. No, I am writing all this here without even thinking about it.

My chemistry teacher is pretty nice because he is quiet and smiles at you.

Well, you will be surprized to hear that I have been imagining myself as a teacher and what I would do. It all started when one night I was telling Tim about the Minoan Age and White Corpuscles to my mother. Tim said I would make a great teacher.

I had a nightmare Sunday morning with a dead kid with bloated stomach and purple bruised face. Monday evening I got sick from thinking of it and eating a hamburger. What do dreams of dead children mean. I have so many of them, I hate them.

I hope you are feeling better? Your Friend, Debbie

61.

Dr. Pullias,

It is the next day now and my father told me that Mrs. Biddle, my Crea/Writ Teacher called them (my parents) to ask them (my parents) how she should ask me if she could publish some of my stuff. She's weird. I do not know why she could not just ask me to my face! When I get through writing something like that I feel like just letting it go away from me into the trash or anywhere. I feel like it did me good while I wrote it and it made me feel good right afterwards but when it is done it is done.

Well, I guess I ought to study my chemistry. I do not understand a single bit of it.

Now it is the next day after the next day! Today I banged up my finger in basketball and I was going to type a letter to San Diego for information. These is what I would like to know from you:

I was wondering if you have to get a degree if you want to work. I don't even know if I want to go to college that way. To get some sort-of degree you have to take Enlish courses and maybe something you don't want to take. When I look through this course pamphlet Joe gets for U.S.R. I see very many that I like and I would like to take them but can I take anything I want? I don't understand. I guess I ought to find out soon because you have to have thngs decided before next year.

Sunday the 13th our little riding club is going out to a friend of mine's house where she has Arabians and then to another place, too. Hmmm

Write soon, OK?
Debbie

62.
Dear Dr. Pullias,

In German today Mr. Forte wrote a note to me on one of my papers. He asked me if I would like to help teach German to elementary kids next year or be his teacher's aide for high school. There was this girl in my Art class who helped a Elem. Teacher and I thought I would like to do that. I would not like to be a hi-school aide, though, and I wouldn't want to teach kids German if I had to take German III, too. Mr. Forte said I have a rare talent for languages. I do not really think so but that would be fun, to teach kids.

My Crea/Writ teacher is pleased with my writing and I am doing well in History. I like my Chemistry teacher very munch though he's not a very good teacher. Art OK and in P.E. I am in Tennis II. Its fun.

I find this year I feel good when I learn or do homework. It is just a good feeling to have done something. I don't know what I mean.

At a store I bought a hand-carved in Africa, antelope. It is very beautful. I have, since I was very young, always wanted carved wooden animals. This is my first. Maybe I will start another collection. So far I have a collection of china animals and one of stuffed animals.

Things are really beginning to look up for me, how about you? I would still like to know about your teaching and also I would like to know where and how you lived when you were a little boy. Your mother sounds interesting. I like old people, too.

I am going to ride to the library now and I will mail this. A friend and I went window-shopping for fun for Christmas (already). I like to buy things.

Your Friend, Debbie

63.
Dear Dr. Pullias,

Well, I know I have not written.

You know, if I could send a little envelope full of all the thoughts I just thought to write you then I wouldn't have so much problem. When you open the envelope all the little thoughts drift into your head and you understand what I have thought to you without me sweating it out trying to write what I really feel and mean.

Joe was telling us about a philosophy he read about and it was that everything is a part of you and you are part of it and when you look at something you are looking at yourself. I do not understand that. I see all the people and in my mind they come toward me and ask something of me. And in my mind they are asking me to give them something of myself and I do. I am writing for you and it is something inside me just for you because in my mind you are asking me. Not pressureing me but asking me sadly. I write for everyone who asks me in their mind. And I draw for my art teacher and I smile for people and all of it and everything is for myself and I ask people in their minds to reach out and touch me, also.

I thought sure I would get a C in Chemistry and I was so worryed I would get a D because I got Ds on the tests but when I asked Mr. Reed he said I was getting a B+. Wow! It was because I handed in all my assignments. Wow! I am so happy about that!

We have rented our front apartment to a oldish Mexican couple. Well, I was hoping for children but they're nice. They will move in Dec 14. I asked my Mother and she said maybe we would rent the back one too and rent ourselves an apartment. I would like to live where I could have a pony and enjoy my childhood before I graduate. Anne and me entered that riding club the English teacher I like put on again.

61

Debbie Bumstead

I don't know. I can never get used to her at all but I would like to be her friend. She is sort-of like my father in that she can really hurt you by saying something that's true but not the kind of truth you say to someone. You know? The only time you enjoy her is in a conversation but I am to shy to start one with anybody. I am the shyest person I ever knew! It is not self-consciousness but I guess it just part of my personality.

My Crea/Writ teacher gave me an A for my writing but I didn't do so good on her tests so for the quarter I got a B+. In my other classes I got about B+'s too. That is pretty good for me for the 1st quater.

How are you guys? I sure haven't see Calvin in along time.

Mr. Liefman at the Harford Funeral Home is hooked on my mother. It is sort-of funny. He called her one night that she might come down to the Funeral Home and talk. He left a scented pen in her car when it was parked at the school. Every once in a while he drives by our house very slowly.

Your friend, Debbie

P.S. Our library has that book by E. Goudge and the others too but they are always out. I have been reading <u>Winnie the Pooh</u> and <u>Brer Rabbit</u> for fun.

64.
(Dec 1970)

Dear Dr. Pullias,

I hope you and your family have a nice Christmas. Aren't you glad to have 2 weeks of no school? I am!

That weekend I saw you up at the cabin was the best weekend I ever had in a long time! I don't know. Something about living like a family diffent from my own and you were there and you are wonderful and Mrs. Pullias and that other guy who is something like Tim, my brother. And then the country is me. Then and Pete with me. Everything. The next day, Sunday, our little club of four girls and Miss Kerr went on our field trip and it was so fun talking and laughing in the car. I don't know why I was the center and everyone was talking to me and I got embarrased. We had fun.

Sometimes I play a game, but I don't do it on purpose. It is playing like I am not interested in whats going on around me. Like at school I'll look out a window when a teacher is talking and pretend not to have the slightest interest in what he or she is saying but really I am listening intently. Or if we have company I may sit in a chair and flip through a magazine like I'm reading but I'm listening. I wonder why I do that? I remind myself of Frosty, one of our cats who acts the same way. I guess I am a great eavesdropper.

I thought about any deaths I'd known and between 6th grade summer and 8th grade there were sure alot. The first was my baby cousin. Then various gory deaths of puppys and kittens, one smothered, one pulled out by pliers and flushed down the toilet, three premature sickly kittens. Then my great-grandmother died and I saw her and then the kittens who were eaten by the tom. That is the one I remember most. I keep thinking I am forgetting one very horrible one. Maybe I'm thinking of a nightmare though.

Have you ever read I Never Promised You a Rose Garden? Everyone tells me it is very good. It is about a 16 year old girl in an insane ayslum. I'm reading it now. It's by Hannah Green.

Your Friend, Debbie.

65.
Christmas Day - 1970
The Four Winds
Dear Debbie:
    This note paper I use only on very special occasions to write to very special people. So I write you a note on Christmas day of this first year of the 1970 decade, and immediately my mind in imagination begins to look backward and forward. Ten years ago you were six soon to be seven, and if we go back to 1950 you were not yet born. But that is all a matter of time - now back to Christmas 1900 and very few people we know would have started

their lives.

But to look forward is equally interesting or more so. Ten years from this morning you will be a good almost 27, with lots of fine experience and education (which is the same thing) behind you and with excellent abilities and skills to be used in the living of life: writing, teaching, observation, adventure. I will be older, and as people count time, beginning to be old, but that too will be interesting. And it will be very good to have a friend 27 to think about life with.

Our task is to do the best we can the things at hand. The rest will take care of itself as life unfolds.

Your letter came. Thanks. We are very glad you liked it here and want you to come whenever you wish.

Sincerely, Earl V. Pullias

66.
Dec. 30, 1970
Dear Dr. Pullias,

Tonight I am alone in our little apartment. I am glad. This place is rather small for four people. I wonder if I will enjoy living alone when I leave.

Lately I have very munch thought of what my life shall be like when I am older. I am really getting up there near, I am almost 17. Your note came when I was thinking of these things. I have decided for sure I'm going to college. There are many things that I want to try. I want something to say that I can teach. I want something to say I can help mentally disturbed people. I do not want to get married, untill I am very much older. I do not very much want babies. Children but not babies.

When I have learned what I need to, to do what I want, I think I shall still take school courses. I want to live in a little house and have a dog and a pony for my spare time in the outskrits of a town.

There! That's an idea of my goals. Here are some things that worry me: in college I am scary of dormitories. I have a bad idea of them. I do not want to belong to a sorority. I am afraid I will be lonely after college. Maybe by that time single people may adopt children. I do not want a husband because I am scared I would get tired of him.

Dear Dr. Pullias

I hope you will not get sick. I hope you are feeling well. I have been feeling rather blah. Maybe its because there's not much to do.
Your Friend, Debbie.
Oh, I still feel like writing. I hope you will not be bored. Tomorrow I am going to sew. It is so hard. But I want to learn. I would like to have nice clothes. Well, now I do not feel like writing on.
Debbie.
P.S. I am reading <u>The Trumpet of the Swan</u>. It is very fun to read. When I was little I read one of this author's books called <u>Stuart Little</u>. It affected me like <u>Rabbit Hill</u>.
Dec. 31,1970
This is the last day of the year. That's weird.

Debbie Bumstead

1971

*The ideas related to Earth Day are wonderful.
Perhaps eventually we can build a world in which
all days of the year will have the spirit of Earth
Day and people will hurt the earth and its
creatures, including other people, <u>less</u> and will
teach and heal and help them to grow into what
they can and should be <u>more</u>.* **Dr. Pullias**

*It's very maddening to be a genious one day and a complete flop
the next.* Ha Ha. Debbie

Debbie Bumstead

Dear Dr. Pullias

67.

Dear Dr. Pullias,

I feel so depressed. I feel like crying right here in chemistry. It is the lull or depresion that comes after something wonderful has happaned. I wonder if it that is what all people go through.

The semester has started today and almost all my classes are the same. For Intermediate Composition I got a teacher I do not care for. I so wanted Miss Kerr and then I did not get her. I know that I can not have everything. Rats.

There is something that I would like to tell you and it is that I get these headaches. It started after we moved to the back apartment. There was Joe and Tim and Mamma and me in those three rooms. Every so often I would get feeling maybe like claustrophobia. I pressed my head so hard with my hands against my temples. Maybe now that Joe and Tim are gone to Oregon I will not have that. It made me feel so helpless and hopeless.

Well, now I know. I did just have Int/Comp and I feel like it is busy work. It will change maybe. But then I will find out if Crea/Writ was a Comp. class and perhaps I'll change to a literature class. Today I can not think to think it out because my head aches like my brain is expanding and trying to explode.

Maybe when I get home I will have a dish of ice cream to cool my eyes. It is 6th period with 30 minutes to go. The question is… will I make it? 30 min is a long time. For 2 minutes I look at the reflection in my glasses that shows an elargement of my eye and lashes. Wierd. 28 minutes to go. For 10 minutes I look at a magazine with another girl and explain to her a picture showing a lady feeling for breast cancer. 18 minutes. Whew. 18 more min and now I do not know what to do. Maybe I will try and think, something I do not do often at school even tho' this is the place for it. I think I feel better. Your Friend, Debbie

68.

Debbie Bumstead

Dr. Pullias,

Today is the day after yesterday when I wrote that first part. I stayed home from school today. I sewed a little and read a lot and once when I laid down for a nap I had a very clear dream. When I awoke from it, my heart was thumping and my head felt so <u>clear</u>. I was glad. Because another thing that started when we squished back into this part of the house is that all my dreams I could not remember well and they didn't leave feelings in me. I guess I would rather have nightmares than those vague, gray, linty-type dreams. Maybe yesterday was a climax to feelings and clausterphobias that were mounting up in me.

Remember the time I wrote about wanting so much privacy? And then about my parents troubles that affected me so much? They went away just like this one has. At least, I hope it is gone. Now, I feel pretty good. I certainly don't feel like crying. That was the worst one I can remember having. I mean the climax with that head ache.

I sure thank you for listening to my dumb troubles. Too bad every girl or boy, man or woman even couldn't help each other like this. Now that's a thought to finish on. Bye, Debbie

69.

Dear Dr. Pullias,

Sometimes I wonder what kids who get straight As think about in class. Do they listen attentively and work when they're supposed to and so on I wonder. One time, for instance, in History our teacher was lecturing and he was adding to an answer I had just given. He was addressing me in front of the class, and I was supposed to be listening but I wasn't. Even though I nodded my head as though I <u>was</u> listening I was truthfully thinking about his skull and what it would look like if his face skin peeled back showing all the muscles and then that pulling back showing his skull. (Gorey!) I also thought I would certainly like to pop that yellowhead sprouting from his nose (I hate yellowheads!).

I have had some strange new thoughts come to me lately. Things I never thought of before. I like it and sometimes in my head I write things and explain things out very clearly instead of letting things fly around loose up there. I have had strange dreams. I sure think it's great to have them. They set the pace for the next day and they give me something to think out when I should be listening "attentively." Once about a week ago I had a very bad dream about black widows.

Dear Dr. Pullias

Ugh. Don't you ever have dreams? My mother and father never talk about theirs. Maybe when you're grown-up, dreams are not so important. I think I tend to dwell deeply on things that are no use at all out in the world. I don't even know what is important to older people.

As I read over this letter it pleases me because I knew what I was writing and everything came out in a nice way.

I hope you write soon,

Your Friend, Debbie.

70.

Dear Dr. Pullias,

I wish that it would not take so very long to make the friends I want to make. It takes so much time and I do not know if its deeper for that. The real first remembrance of you was when I was in 5th grade. Then I really wanted be your friend but it took all the way till last year before I could really feel you were my friend. I mean I know you were a great friend but I have to come to the point were I don't regerd you as some kind of god which I'm inclined to do with my favorite people.

I'm reading a book titled Person to Person: The Problem of Being Human. You are soposed to substitute yourself in for person. The first part is about values and how as you grow up parents, teachers and others tend to put their own values into you so you are not really you in your thinking of the way to do things, what is most important, what is good and bad. There are two athors, one the pschologist, says the infant has a system of values his own then this process of "introjection" happens, and then if the person at an older age sees what has happened to him goes to a therapist then he can come to know himself better. I wonder what would happen if a person grew up fully independent of being put these values on? Would he be a better person? Carl R. Rogers and Barry Stevens are the authors.

I will look for that book you mentioned. It sounds interesting. (Today I found it and started it).

These are the grades I'm getting I think. In P.E. I'm getting an A which is a real suprize to me. In Geometry its on the line between C+/B-. I have a feeling he's going to give me the C+ to snap me out of lazyness. In English, German, and Art I get disappointing Bs. In History again on the border between C+/B-. I think if I talk with him he'll make it a B-.

Debbie Bumstead

I think if I just get to know my history teacher I'll get better grades but there comes that "long time making friends" bit again.

Saturday my parents, Anne, and me are going to an open house at Redlands University. It looks like it will be interesting. Anne (a friend) is going there if she gets good enough grades. It seems like a nice place because there are so little many students. I've always wanted to take a sensitivity training course. Do you know about them? What is your opinion?

I wish you could come out sometime when it is raining because I think that is the best time to walk in the hills.

Your Friend, Debbie

P.S. Sorry this paper is so hard to read on account of this pen on account I used it on account I wanted to, on account I sometimes do what I want, on account I want to.

71.
February 21, 1971
Dear Dr. Pullias,

It is Sunday night and I am listening to records. This evening I have been working on a collage. It is a picture of two little girls talking. When you don't have a good book to read and no one to talk to, do you sometimes draw? Sometimes I can imagine you sitting at your desk with heaps of papers to grade piled around but there you are doodling! Maybe a picture of a grasshopper or some thing.

And now comes a song that I like to listen to. It is so soft. There is a line that I like: "I've got nothin' to do today but smile…" Oh, well.

Maybe you would be interested in knowing what I am taking for classes next year. They are: Govt./ Cultural Anthropology; Social Poetry/ Lit of the West. World; P.E.; Senior Studio (Art); Work Educ.; Ind. Study. The work education class is the elementary teacher experience and the independent study I hope to get for Crea/Writ.

Do you have a big house there?

My brothers came home from Oregon. I guess they just didn't like it.

For my birthday my father gave me three small moss covered rocks and a large bowl. So I started my little garden yesterday. I am using the bowl for a pond. It sure is fun to plan it out.

So now I am 17 years old. I don't feel any great difference.

Dear Dr. Pullias

Actually there is nothing munch I can think of to write about. How did you guys feel the earthquake?

Your Friend, Debbie.

72.
Feb. 24, 1971
Dear Dr. Pullias,

Thank you for the letter. When the earthquake came here it was just real long and rocking. Sort of a nice feeling, I guess. It didn't scare me like some earthquakes do.

My writing was coming along just great, you know, I was enjoying writing and my thoughts went onto the paper very easily. But then my new Crea/Writ teacher, Mr. Hill said I ought to try to write either poetry or short storys because these things I do are inbetween and are neither one nor the other. He said there was nothing wrong with them, that I just might try something different. So I did. But I wasn't at all satisfied with the free verse I did and the story I tryed was so dumb I threw it away. And now I can't even do my regular things anymore! It's sort-of like, I guess, a mental block in my mind. I sure hope I get over it! It's very maddening to be a genious one day and a complete flop the next. Ha Ha.

I still don't know what college I want to go to. Do you know where I can find the names and addresses of colleges so I can write for information?

When I went hiking last time up in your place I also felt like there were less birds. It was so quiet. The rocks seem even deader than they already are without the little animals.

Write soon,
Your Friend, Debbie

73

Debbie Bumstead

73.

April 22, 1971

Dear Dr. Pullias,

Well, today is Earth Day, did you know that? It seems like everyone in Hemet forgot and nothing happaned like last year when the kids at school went crazy and cleaned up the campus and made promises to do their best and all that. In my very little way I celebrated this day. I watched the trees blowing in the breeze from my history class window 2 stories up and I felt very friendly toward them. I picked up a eucalyptus tree seed pod and carried it around untill 4th period when I left it on my desk in Crea/Writ for Mr. Hill. I hoped that he would notice it and think about Earth Day, too. On a test paper in German, I wrote "Happy Earth Day." to Mr. Forte and when he picked it up he saw it and said, "Happy day to you, too, Debbie." And now I am writing to you on this green paper on Earth Day and maybe when you read this you will think of the hills out here that you like so much, OK? Sometimes I just wish there was someone to share these thoughts I have and they could understand without laughing and there is these people like you and Mr. Hill and Mr. Forte and Miss Kerr and there are so many. I wish that I could be with these people more often. I like them very much.

I am very excited about going to college and learning about psychology and children and helping them when I get out of school. It is something to look forward to and I think it is very good to have something always to look forward to because then you don't feel like killing yourself or anything. I hope that I will always have something to look forward to even when I am very old. If I don't have anything then, I would surely feel like dying. I might even look forward to death.

This summer I want to learn a lot about colleges and I want to have answers to my questions. I wish that I will be able to visit some to see what they're like. I guess they are just about like high school.

One of my friends is going to Redlands University. I went there once to visit and I liked it because it seemed small and there were trees and it was nice. I like the city of Redlands, too, what I have seen of it. But I do not know anything about the college or anything. Mostly I remember the art class because we went in there and looked at all the pictures. I remember in one of the dormotories there was a bunch of kids sitting around and it was dark and spooky looking. I didn't like

74

that. It started raining and we ran from shelter to shelter and laughed and then we left. It was a nice visit, really.

Write soon, Your Friend, Debbie.

74.
Los Angeles
May 2, 1971
Dear Debbie:
Your letter was a great joy to me. The warm greeting on Earth Day gave me strength and encouragement coming from a dear young friend, especially. The ideas related to Earth Day are wonderful. Perhaps eventually we can build a world in which all days of the year will have the spirit of Earth Day and people will hurt the earth and its creatures, including other people, <u>less</u> and will teach and heal and help them to grow into what they can and should be <u>more</u>.

I was as glad or even more glad to hear of your feelings about college and your plans to go. You have some good time to get information and to make your plans. Redlands is a beautiful small place and a fine college. That type of college would be best for you to spend the four years for your B.A. or B.S. degree which is called the undergraduate years. Then if you should find that study interesting and wanted to go on for more advanced studies you would probably go to a large University -- perhaps USC where I work. But in life although it is very good to plan, it is also good not to think too far ahead but take one interesting step at a time. They would have books about colleges out at the J.C. there, or perhaps at the library. I know a lady at the J.C. that took her doctor's degree here who is very nice and would be interested in talking with you: Dr. (Mrs.) Mildred Hight - very nice lady.

Your friend, Earl V. Pullias

75.
Sunday, May 30, 1971
Dear Dr. Pullias,

Debbie Bumstead

I don't know why my home life is so miserable. I think that I will be glad to move away to college and after that to a place of my own. Perhaps at first I will be scared a little and lonely but I want to go as soon as I can; I won't be going to the Junior College and staying at home, I want to go away. I hope that I could be happier or I mean more at ease, I don't know, when I am left here.

Do you know of Johnston College? It is a part of Redlands University. I think that that is where I want to go. The reasons being, it is a small college with a few people to the teachers and you figure out where you are going, what you want to be and they say that their emphasis is more on "learning" than "teaching." That is what I would like. Also you can register in some of the classes in the University, too, so I will be able to learn and be taught what I want, so that I can go to be and do what I might really want.

Are you glad that school is almost out? I guess I am but I don't know. Summers are all the same, it seems, and maybe that is the good of them. I remember the summer I went to my great-grandmother's funeral, no, I only remember the incident and not the whole summer. There was the summer after sixth grade that I learned about sex. My brother, Tim and cousin, Donna told me dirty jokes and I learned that way. Last summer I don't remember so good. Do you have a special summer you remember?

There is a boy who's name is James in my Art class and I think that he thinks interestingly. We write to each other a little, he is a good writer. I like him because he's different, you know? But he's not all that different, I guess.

Write soon please.

Your Friend, Debbie.

76.

Dear Dr. Pullias,

A couple of days ago we went to the beach. That was the funnest day of this summer. Do you like the beach. I liked it even though it was kind of crowded but I wish I could have seen some of the ocean life like limpets, urchins, jelly fish and things like that. Where are they?

What can you do with so many people in the world? It seems like there are too many but I can not think that it should be any other way.

Dear Dr. Pullias

I don't feel we ought to try and change things. But we ought to start doing things in a perhaps righter way and in time things would be changed without us even touching them and hurting them that way. I can't explain it. I ought to think of an example.

I really want to get into that Johnston College in Redlands. It is exactly what I want. I mean I like the idea of it and I would enjoy being part of that experiment. But I also want a deep type learning thing and I can have that by taking some of my classes in the University part. I want both and there it is.

La Verne College is something like Johnston and that might be a second choice but it doesn't have a University type thing with it so I don't like it as much.

Do you know of any colleges that I might like?

I checked a book out of the library all about "The Forest"! Wow, is it interesting! I would like to learn awhole lot about the forests.

When I look through a college catologe at the courses I would like to take some subjects you hardly even get into or talk about in high school. Here are the ones that sound interesting to me that I don't know anything about:

1. Philosophy
2. Theology
3. Religion
4. Biology
5. Psychology

Philosophy sounds espially interesting.

When are you going to be out in the hills?

My mother said I could have a couple of kittens when they're ready to leave their mothers. That's something to look forward to.

We are pretty sure I am suffering from an ulcer. I can understand that.

Write soon.

Your Friend, Debbie.

77.
Los Angeles
June 17, 1971
Dear Debbie:
I have been so neglectful about writing! Can you find it in

your heart to forgive me? Perhaps you can if I tell you a little about my work these weeks. In addition to all the work connected with the closing of school - papers, grades, etc. - I agreed this year to make five graduation talks for colleges. The last one is tomorrow night. In a way, I enjoy the opportunity to try to teach what I believe, but also it is a strain. I will be better now.

I can understand your being miserable at home. In part it is your time in life, but also, it is the situation there. I think you will be better when you are away, but you are growing and learning. Often in life, Debbie, we have to take what we have and use it for learning and growth. Try to think of what you have: a good mind, a developing body, a sensitive spirit. And around you all the wonders of nature and life to observe, to think about, and to write about. These are all materials you can use to learn and grow. Almost above everything, I want you to learn to rise above any condition and find your own good life. It is of utmost importance that you learn to work well for really nothing is done of worth without work.

Yes, I know about Johnston College. It sounds interesting and is worth looking into. You will be making your decision about college before too long.

I would like to hear more of James. Maybe the two of you can be friends and learn together. Write when you wish to even if I don't.

Your friend, Earl V. Pullias

78.
July 8, 1971
Dear Dr. Pullias,

Thank you for your helpful letter. It was here when we got back from Reno. We stayed up there just a week.

Do you think you know me pretty well? I don't know if a person can really know a person really good just from writing but maybe you can know a person better from his writing, I don't know. Anyway if you feel you know me pretty good I would like you to fill out one of these recomendation papers. If you want to. I guess I will send it to you after school starts. I thought I would also ask Mr. Hill my

Dear Dr. Pullias

Crea/Writ teacher and Miss Kerr or maybe one of my P.E. teachers.

I got these application forms and things from Redlands today and it is pretty exciting! The only problem I think I would have in college is having to share a bedroom. Did I tell you that already?

There is money for me from my Grandmother in Reno but she said it would be better to get a student loan because they don't charge interest or something like that.

Do you remember me writing to you about those bad dreams about dead and bloated and mutilated babies? Well, I have noticed lately that I have these same dreams but something inside my brain doesn't let them get horrible and quite so gory. For instance there was one where Mr. Hill was walking on a muddy beach and there was a beat-up child on the beach and I, the dreamer wasn't in the dream till later but I could see it and I could have seen the kid, I could have gotten a close-up veiw, I think I even thought of why I wasn't seeing it close-up, but my dream sort of eased over that part and then Mr. Hill called some people and they came down to get the child and it was still alive and then I was the kid and Mr. Hill was going to take care of me.

It just seemed so strange. Like the little film-maker who makes my dreams deliberately skipped a little over that part so as not to frighton me. It still scared me. And it happaned in several other dreams, too.

Well, I have been taking tennis lessons and we had a tournament at the end and I won women's singles championship and also my partner and I won women's doubles championship. Wow! It was even in the paper! Hemet News (haha) It is exciting but not terribly great or anything. Now I am going to take some more lessons. They're free.

Write soon.

Your Friend, Debbie

79.
Friday, 13, 1971, August
Dear Dr. Pullias,

Sometimes I feel like I am feeling so many things. I feel like my perceptions are the highest they have ever been and I feel that they will stay that way; that everything that I come across in every day will be there with something special in it. Do you see? It just happaned today that I thought of that; everything I see or hear or feel is what it is and I like it that way. everything is just so much there.

I have thought of that before and felt it but today it seems different. Do you know what I am feeling? Have you felt it?

What is your backyard like? Is there a big tree and you sit under it at a card table writing a little letter to me? And when you are writing do you sometimes think of my ways like I think of yours now?

James is a musician, did I tell you that? I guess he might even be called a slight fanatic about classical music like Beethoven. He wants to go to some music school in Boston.

It is nice with him. I can still be my individual self with my own thoughts and actions, he's on the other side of the sidewalk walking his own way and there are two of us. I always imagined with a boy you're supposed to hold hands and be as one. I don't think I could get along that way. With James I am never hoping and praying that he'll come visit, I like him to but I wouldn't miss him if he left my life completely. Except I'd miss the way he's the only guy who is that way that I've met.

My mother has a boyfriend who wants her to marry him. He calls her up every night and talks for an hour on the wonderful things she is and how he could really "dig" her. My mom sounds cross when she talks to him and he repeats things so she repeats her cross answers. Its kind of funny but also it sort of bothers me. She likes him though, I guess. I hope she does because I wouldn't want her talking that long if she didn't like it.

I didn't think ulcers were so serious. James said he had two and he had to eat baby food. I wonder what troubled him. I really do...

Write soon, ok?

Your friend, Debbie

P.S. I'll write to that college in San Diego.

80.
Los Angeles
Aug. 17, 1971
Dear Debbie:

I did not wish to imply that ulcers are so bad -- many people doubtless have them -- but they are not good, and I would like for you to be well. Our bodies are the instruments with which we live life: if they are in good shape then the chances are better that our lives will be better. I would like for you to take good care of your body and take a wise pride in it as you grow older.

It would be hard to describe what our backyard is like. I am sorry we do not have a big tree -- I would like to sit under a big tree as I often did when I was about your age and in the country. Our youngest son, John, liked machines and electricity very much, so when he was a small boy -- eight or ten maybe -- we built a sort of work shop for him here in the backyard about ten feet by seven I guess. Two or three years ago I fixed it up a little and now use it for a study. There are banana trees by the front door and lots of rose bushes by the north window. I think you would like it as a place to work and think.

No, you didn't tell me much about James. I am very glad you have a friend with whom you feel so free -- few things are better. I hope you will listen to classical music with him: the more you listen, the more you will like it. When will he go to Boston -- perhaps not for another year?

Mrs. Pullias and I plan to come to our hills tomorrow (Wed.) and stay over until Sunday. If it is convenient for you we would be glad for you to come out and visit us - Sat. perhaps or another day?

Sincerely Earl V. Pullias

81.
Tuesday, Sept. 21 1971
Dear Dr. Pullias,

Thank you for your letter. I had very much fun on my visit with my aunt and uncle and small cousins.

I don't know if there is something physically wrong with me or if it is mentall worry and fatigue but lately (maybe since November of last year) I sometimes have a terrible time and even though its usually after a slight unhappy happening and should only warrant a bad mood I go into horrible crying. And I writhe around on the bed and press my hands as hard as I can against my temples and sort-of gasp and cry. When I try and calm down and breathe deeply and evenly my head hurts so much. Afterwards my head feels so heavy and sleepy I can't move it very good. I thought I better tell someone about it because it doesn't seem quite normal. It doesn't happan that often, only about 4 times I've had it and this afternoon was one. I don't know, maybe worries build up. Also afterwards my skin feels very sensitive and I'm cold and I can't think well.

Yours, Debbie

I do not feel like writing but I will soon write again to you. I better mail this or it will get out of date and I won't feel the same.

82.
Los Angeles
Sept 24, 1971
Dear Debbie:

Your letter came yesterday. I am very pleased that you felt free to tell me about your special problem. I have a few suggestions that may be helpful.

1. The kind of symptoms you describe are frequently related to a girl's monthly periods, particularly as she is coming into full maturity. There is no very good explanation of this fact, but I think it helps some that many young women have a similar problem.

2. You didn't ever tell me if you saw the doctor about your "ulcer" problem. I hope that problem too is connected with emotional strain and will soon be better. But my point is that you should see a doctor for a good general examination. Sometimes there is a little something wrong that pulls a person down and makes ordinary problems more difficult. So it would be wise to have a general examination and see if everything seems to be all right physically.

3. It would be good if you could develop pretty good routine habits. Get to bed regularly; especially eat a little more regularly than many of us do; take your exercise; (tennis is very good and swimming if you have a place); and do your school work regularly so it won't bother you too much. In short, build yourself up physically.

4. Write to me freely if there are things that worry you -- don't let them fester in your mind.

5. Take care when you are in "bad" spells such as you told me about not to let anyone tempt you to try to overcome them by wrong means: drugs or sex are the most often suggested.

Your friend, Earl V. Pullias

83.
Los Angeles
Oct. 15, 1971
Dear Debbie:

I have been a little worried about my friend in Hemet. I have not heard since you told me about not feeling well, but I hope all goes well and you have your school underway. I have wondered if you got your teaching assistant assignment. But I remember that we agreed that friends write only when they feel they wish to: that agreement we must keep.

I have had a little bit of a rough time the past ten days or so -- last week I took something like the flu and have had a hard time getting over it. I believe I am a little better today, and hope to be back at teaching soon. Just as soon as I am back on the job I must send you the names of some other colleges.

Let me know what you have been thinking about college. Is there anyone there that you might like to go to college with? Of course, it is not necessary that you go with someone -- you will find friends when you get to college, but if there was a friend to be with the first year it might help a little.

My regular work requires so much time now that I haven't been able to write much lately. I would like to change that if I can. I hope you continue to write down your thoughts. It seems to be true that the more we write the easier it is for us to express our thoughts.

A few weeks ago our old cat that is a descendant of cats we have had since long before you were born came walking in with a youngish and somewhat wild female who ten days later produced a group of kittens. I didn't have the heart to take the old cat's bride away and now my conflict is worse than ever! Life is too complex.

Your friend, Earl V. Pullias

84.

Debbie Bumstead

October 23, 1971
Saturday evening
Dear Dr. Pullias,

I am very sorry I haven't sent you a letter in a long time. I started writing about five and each time I ran out of things to say and when I waited awhile then it got out of date. I was sorry you were sick and thank you for your helpful hints in the first letter.

Hey! You ought to keep all your new kittens and name them T.B.G. and L. Haha. What do they look like?

The teacher assitent class I have I enjoy extremely much. I have one boy whom I tutor out in the hall. There was a boy I had before who was really emotionally disturbed in some way. I don't know how and I liked being with him very much but finally he had to go to a special class. The boy I have now is sort-of nervous but he's really a healthy regular boy. I like him. This is third grade. I really don't know why I like being with children so much. My friends can not really enjoy being around them at all, Anne and Becky and Carrie.

As for colleges I have changed my mind again. Mr. Hill told me of the University of California at Santa Cruz which is small, caters to the individual and also is not as expensive as private colleges. Is there any more small state colleges or universities? I think I would much rather pay less and still get educated if the place is small. But I have to have applications in in November, don't I? Is it possible to start college in the winter quarter and still get a room? Answer please!

Well, I have alot to do today. This morning I have to wash dishes, work on my government report, and work in my garden and in the afternoon we are going to look at a horse. My mother has a lady friend who will keep it free for me if I let her little boys ride it sometimes. That's a deal to me! And when I have to sell it she said she might buy it. It will cost $150 to me if I get it.

Your Friend, Debbie.

85.
Thanksgiving 1971
Dear Dr. Pullias,

Yesterday at school I had an appointment with Mrs. Hight. I thought she was a very nice woman and she seemed fairly interested in me, wanting to help. You know, it is sometimes a wonder to me how some grown-ups know exactly what to say and don't stumble with their lips and never run out of things to speak of. Not really all that perfect but anyway that is the impression I got of Mrs. Hight. I guess she just knew her business very well.

I think but am not sure that I would rather go to Santa Cruz than the state colleges. It is just a feeling against the state colleges, maybe because I don't know much about them. Mrs. Hight mentioned junior colleges with dormitories and that sounded really good because they would be small, wouldn't they? I don't know how much they cost. Is it just room and board? You can get two years college credit in junior colleges, can't you?

You know, at times I think I am a little young and nervous for coping with the wilds of university or college life. I don't know what I mean but I worry about things that are happening around me; I get headaches and cry and get sick in my stomach. But I think I have strength, too. I trudge through and get over these bad times and there is not a trace of them left afterwards. Even though I'm having a hard time I can keep myself going pretty well. So either way -- if I go to a Junior college and get used to things gradually or go to a University and really jump into it -- I think I'll make it. Do you?

I really hope you will tell me when you are next going to visit your cabin. I think it would be very fun for my little friend and me to make the long excursion to your cabin and we could explore the roads and trails around there on our horse and pony. I guess it looks pretty funny: a tall girl on a tall black horse and a little girl on a little black pony riding together. Misty is a very good rider and I am getting better. I like it!

I am all alone this evening. I do not get scared or lonely but evening is the very best time for me to have someone around to talk and do things with. I guess that is the same with my mom and brother but they have someone to go to and I don't.

Tonight I would like to have a discussion of some kind, philosophy or something. Do you like to talk that way? I wish someone could be here suddenly just for a little while. How about you or Mr. Hill or Miss Kerr or Aunt Raechal or Daddy or how about James. Yes, I really feel like talking with James. Maybe we could get in our coats and go for a walk, maybe we could go to the bookstore but it wouldn't be open on Thanksgiving, would it? We could get milk and grahem crackers, take our ease around the heater and talk about ways of life and thinking. Sigh... James moved away a long while ago. Too bad, he was the only person my age that I have every really liked and enjoyed in all ways including intellectual. All good things come to an end, don't they? Not really.

Your friend, Debbie.

86.
Los Angeles
Dec. 11, 1971
Dear Debbie:

Friday I came down with a dreadful head cold so it did not seem wise to try to come out this weekend. I am a little better today and hope to be back on the job next week if possible. We tried to call you several times today, but no answer. Hope we didn't disappoint or inconvenience you too much. Next time we will do better!

Someone brought this writing paper to me from England. She is a former student of mine who knew how much I like Shakespeare. Have you had much contact with Shakespeare -- sometimes called <u>the bard </u>-- yet? Later you will come to know him.

Hope all goes well there. I am a little disgusted at being sick again -- but that does little good!

Your friend, Earl V. Pullias

Dear Dr. Pullias

1972

You were wondering if you are different. Yes, I believe you are different from most girls in many deep and important ways.... it is important that you continue almost above everything to be yourself. Some one has said that we grow more and more to be our true selves as we grow older: as we are enriched by learning and by experience. You will find that this being yourself will mean that you will be alone often and feel alone. This I suspect is one of the prices of being special in a significant way and finding more and more meaning in life as you develop. Dr. Pullias

I feel like singing because of all my love for the beautiful people, the children, the green plants surrounding the world, the humming sparkled weather. My whole life it seems is in me; everything I see or do moves within me the bursting that is me.

Debbie

Debbie Bumstead

Debbie Bumstead

Dear Dr. Pullias

87.

Monday Jan. 1972

Dear Dr. Pullias,

I'm sitting in this government class which is two stories up and I can look out the window at the tops of trees. That's about all I can say for this class except that I can write in here without any bother. Hmmm.

Sorry I missed you yesterday. I spent the whole day with Misty who is ten and emotionally disturbed. At least her mother says she is but I can't tell when a kid isn't normal. All I know is she is kind of "high" some of the time and yesterday she really was. I guess because she was going out with me and that was new. First we went to a restaurant and had hamburgers, then we went out to see Prieta (the horse) and then we went shopping. She came to my house and she stayed over night. She was really excited at that.

Somehow this is what I would like to do for a career. I don't want to just sit with a kid in a room but I want to take him places, go to the beach, out to eat. Do you know if that would help a kid? I sort of think it would and I wonder if there are any clinics or whatever that do that? I know that there are times you must sit and be quiet and then with them I would like to draw or talk. Somehow I will have to develope this idea.

Why do you think I should not go to Santa Cruz? I received a card from Stanislaus saying they reserved a space for me. Well.

I really don't know what to write, really, I really don't know. Last night Misty asked me what problems I have and the only one I could actually think of was 1. My Govt. class is boring. I was amazed because I thought I might be a person with problems but I'm not. Isn't that great?

Right now I am in my English class and I've been observing this girl who came in sort of late and she was self-conscious. She had on a very short dress and her notebook fell. She was terribly embarrassed and then she put her hands in the places where pockets in her dress might have been but there weren't any pockets there. Poor kid.

If you are going to be out next weekend I'll come out. I feel like hiking and letting my brain get some restful air.

I guess my mother told you about us having Prieta bred. The stallion is an appaloosa and this colt will be my mother's. She is the one who wanted the appaloosa. I wanted to breed her to our friend's Arabian. Maybe I'll do that next year.

Your friend, Debbie.

88.
Dear Dr. Pullias,
Hello again.

Today I am staying home from school. My body feels like its made out of a stack of different colored building blocks so that each part of me has a certain hurt or ache. Its wierd. And when I move around my arms and legs feel all trembly and shaky.

My brothers, both are living here now and yesterday Tim had his girl-friend and another friend over from 3:00pm till 11:00. I don't know but when people are around for such a long time I get all nervy. Even when I go in my bedroom. Then they were gone and I was in bed and my mind just went in a circle around the apt. First the living room, Joe was sleeping in there, next my mom's room, shes there sleeping, then the bathroom, down the steps in the basement, there was Tim, last was my room and me in there. My brain just went around and around. My temples hurt feroisly (sp). I can't understand why that affects me so wierdly. Do you know why I feel that way when people are all living close? I would sure like to know.

What will it be like when I have to have a roommate in college? Will it be different? DB

89.
Los Angeles
Jan. 26, 1972
Dear Debbie:

Dear Dr. Pullias

Your letter - really two letters I guess - written before I saw you and Misty up at our place last Saturday came. As I have said often before, I am glad that you can speak to me reasonably frankly, in writing especially. I know your situation there all crowded together, and many other factors, is extremely difficult. I hope you can hold out and stay reasonably well until you go away to college. The having a roommate in college will be altogether different, I think.

You never told me what your doctor said. Reasonably regular habits of sleep, eating, exercise (play and riding your horse) are very important. I don't want to "preach" or seem to but one's health is important: the condition of one's body effects everything about a person - especially the way he sees things. Frankly, I don't think there is anything really wrong with you psychologically more than there is with any person of your nature who is growing up: a painful process for anyone.

You were probably peeved at me about Santa Cruz, and I can understand how you would be. It is very difficult to make clear why it seems to me that it might not be wise for you to go first there, but I may be wrong, and so let's wait and see if you are admitted and then I'll be glad to talk with your mother about your going.

There are many new things that could be done in teaching. The doing of very interesting things with children, such as you mention in your letter, is one of them. A teacher with imagination has a great deal of freedom. Then there is also the work of dealing with individual children, or with children in small groups, who have special development problems: you might be especially good at this kind of thing. I doubt if there is much wrong with Misty that would not be overcome quickly under your care. We must talk more about this.

Your friend, Earl V. Pullias

90.
Los Angeles
Jan 29, 1972
Saturday night
Dear Debbie:

Debbie Bumstead

Yesterday Mrs. P. and I needed to come to Hemet for a little business and so we drove on out to our place in the hills. We had a picnic lunch there among the rocks. Things seemed strange and especially quiet and in a way distant -- they stood out almost like in a picture, a painting of reality. We thought of you and wondered what would be best for you. And if we could help.

We were both quite impressed with the way you dealt with Misty the day you people came by. I had an idea that may be worth considering: if Misty's people felt they could afford it do you think they might be willing to give you room and board and let you tutor and guide and help M? I believe you would be excellent with her, and for her. Not only would you help her, but it would give you fine experience in what may become your life profession. The additional value of course would be to get you away from the crowded condition there at home, and give you some more experience away from home before you go to college.

Of course, I have said nothing of this to your mother. I was sorry I had spoken to her about Santa C. without talking to you about it first. It is not my way, and I didn't intend to. The idea of being Misty's tutor and companion may not be good or possible but I thought it interesting and worth mentioning. Tell me what you think.

I hope your writing goes well and that you got some good teachers this semester. Please feel free to tell me of any things that worry you -- I would like so much to be your friend if in some way we can bridge the gap of generations. My teaching work starts again the second week in Feb. I am hoping to write a little this coming week.

Sincerely, Earl V. Pullias

91.
Jan. 31, 1972
Dear Dr. Pullias,

That is a very interesting and exciting idea about being a live-in tutor for Misty. The problem is their house is nearly as crowded as this one. The mother and father are pretty old (Misty is adopted) and they sleep in the living room. Misty has a pretty big room but it is not private. Then there is one other bedroom that is occupied by a big brother. There is a small empty room next to the kitchen but I don't know if they want to make it into a bedroom. There are also a couple of little cabins on the property.

Anyway I will mention the idea to the mother, Mrs. Graves. She is extremely interested in tutoring and helping kids who are smart but are pushed behind the real smart kids. We have talked together about this. She is very interested in teaching. And sometimes I feel she wants someone to talk to her about this thinking of hers because every time I go in we start talking about that.

I can't think how I am with Misty that would impress you. I know that I have two ways with her - one - intellectual, with us talking and discussing things and two - fun, doing enjoyable things. I also know that I do not treat her as adult to child. When she acts "cute" I don't really think oh how cute and I don't think she likes that. I'm not sure if she likes me but I guess it is like that with children. I don't know. How could I help her?

It is the next day and I talked to Misty's parents. I read that part of your letter to Mrs. Graves and when I finished she said, "I think the Lord has answered our prayer." She was excited and she showed me the bedroom where I thought the brother lived but he doesn't. It is a small dingy room and cool and it is rather like a hole but to me it looked very delightfully private. It is almost as crowded as here but the places to escape are more private and there are more of them. The lot the house is on is huge.

The father was a little more dubious.

Tonight I find myself comparing what I am doing and feeling here with what I might be doing there. I think things might be quieter there even if Misty likes to talk. I feel my being would only have one person, Misty, to cope with instead of three here.

This semester has started out with two new classes that I feel will be very interesting: Sociology and Literature of the Western World. These are my grades for last sem. Govt. B+ ,Social Poetry B+ or A, Work Experience A, German II A, Art A, P.E. A.

What are you teaching this semester?

Write soon, Your friendly Debbie
I like you alot.

92.
Los Angeles
Feb. 5, 1972
Dear Debbie:

As you probably know, I had not received your letter when I saw you Thursday: it was here when I got home. Thanks very much for it. I appreciated all your letters but especially the line "I like you a lot" which you know I can return.

I hope the arrangement to be a companion and tutor for Misty went well. I cannot say just why I thought you were especially skillful with her. The important thing is you are <u>sincere</u>, <u>authentic</u>, <u>yourself</u> with her, and you like and respect her, but do not let her dominate or take advantage of you with either cute or ugly ways. She as a growing girl will show many sides. I am confident she has good potential and I believe you will help her to grow as she can and should. Doing things that are fun together and teaching her directly will both help. In the meantime you will learn and grow: all will take time. It might be helpful if you let Mrs. Graves borrow your copy of <u>A Teacher is Many Things</u>. The house and the large lot sound interesting. Let me hear more about them as things develop. Take care you preserve time for you own study, writing, and just being alone.

Congratulations on the fine grades on your courses. As I said before, the grades in themselves are not so important, but they represent your ability to do a job well: they will be a means to other things. I hear better things about Santa Cruz, and if you should be admitted, I'll talk to your mother. Now, let's do the things at hand.

I'll tell you about my classes a little later. One is on teaching, especially college teaching; the other about the history of colleges and universities.

Your friend, Earl V. Pullias

93.
February 16,1972
Dear Dr. Pullias,

Thank you very much for the book. I think it has many good ideas with that organic learning. I put Misty in those kids place learning that way and it would have good for her if she had started out learning that way. But she has already half learned the standard-type way so how could she start over?

This is what we are doing. First she does her homework and I try to explain things, I make her read the directions which otherwise she would not do and we illustrate problems on her blackboard. Second we work maybe a page in these workbooks her mother bought and wants her to do. Third she reads to me books we checked out of the library. Fourth, and this is the funnest for me, she writes in a journal we started about what happaned to her that day and I write down the words she has to have help on to spell. Then after she's through I give her a little spelling test on those words. All through these lessons we sometimes laugh or after one she runs around. But when she is consentrating she does well. Her spelling is terrible.

Her mother I know loves Misty very much but she nags so much at her that I almost go crazy. Nag, nag, nag! She is a very old woman with no teeth and her voice doesn't turn you on to do something. Maybe that is why she has to nag. She thinks Misty has a disease called dyslexia. Do you know anything about that?

They eat healthy foods here so I may become very healthy.

I am so involved with school, riding Prieta, being with Misty, and doing my own homework I have very little time to be just me and alone. But when I do get a little time for that I enjoy it very wonderfully. I haven't done any creative writing in a long time. For a couple of weeks I have remembered my dreams and have written them down in a notebook. They're interesting.

Do you like to be alone? I guess some people don't. Do you remember your dreams?

Another thing about living here is everyone goes to bed so early. 9:00 or 9:30 and I usually stay up till 10:30.

Well, good-night.

Your friend, Debbie.

P.S. You can write to the same address.

P.P.S. I will be 18 on the 18th. That's magic! It only happens once in a lifetime. 18 on the 18th.

94.

Debbie Bumstead

Los Angeles
At home
March 12, 1972
Dear Debbie:

This is my 65th birthday and I wanted to write you on this day. I suspect 65 seems very old to you -- in a way it is, but however one may seem or look, he does not feel too different as he grows older. In a deep sense, the experience is very interesting especially if one can continue to learn and thus really stay alive. I am sure that is what makes the difference in people - not <u>years</u>, but whether they have continued <u>to learn</u>.

I have just returned from a week's trip out of the city: to Chicago for a conference, then to Tenn. to visit relatives and particularly my mother, and to visit the college I attended many years ago. It was especially interesting to talk with my mother who is now 92 years of age but still very alive and interested in many things. She wanted very much to go on to school and college, but was not able to do so.

I hope things go well at the Graves' and with Misty. It will take time to help her; do it in your way. Take care not to let her dominate you or take undue advantage of you. That would not be good for either of you. Observe carefully and learn all you can, but do not work so hard at her problems that you do not enjoy her and the work. We hope to be up this weekend. Would be good to see you and the horses.

Sincerely, Earl V. Pullias

95.
Los Angeles
Backyard Study
March 21, 1972
Dear Debbie:

It was very good to have you and Misty visit us. I was sorry there were some complications that may have made your visit somewhat less pleasant, but there are nearly always complications in human life. I have always tried as best I could - not always with success surely - to use even the complications as a means of learning and sometimes interest and even fun. Those of us interested in the human mind and personality never lack for material to study - there are always ourselves and others.

You are doing a significant job with Misty. I will not try to say why I think so, but I sense important change which is natural to healthy growth and learning. I do not wish to over emphasize the point, but in that situation, in fact, in almost any situation you will have to take care to protect the aloneness you need not only for your own work but also just for being.

Be sure you let me help if anything at all worries or concerns you. It is quite valuable to feel completely free to speak with a friend in whom you have confidence. My work is a little hard, and I, like you, am not writing much, but I guess that comes and goes.

Your friend, Earl V. Pullias

96.
March 30, 1972
Dear Dr. Pullias,

I am sad, too, right now, and I don't know what to do. This afternoon I went to my mother's house to be alone because I knew she was with friends. I thought she would be gone untill tomorrow but she came home and I did so want to be all alone. Then she fixed a drink and I felt helpless and mad so I left.

But I still didn't want to go back to the Graves' but it was night; where could I go? I drove to the Plaza and wandered around in the stores. I drove to where I keep Prieta and I thought it would be nice to be by her but then I didn't think I ought to go in there to their yard at night so I came back here to the Graves's. Right now I wish I was somewhere else where I could cry. I can't cry here…

For me too, that juniper tree place is very wonderful to think about. I think because it is a hidden and isolated place and that makes it seem very much more natural. Perhaps tomorrow I will go out there to be alone and I will hike down there. Maybe I will bring Pete, my dog. I like to be with him and I think he misses me living at home because he has started digging holes again. Hmm.

I have just had a thought; I will go take a bath. Taking a warm alone bath would comfort and warm me. I will write more after it.

Debbie Bumstead

Ah, now I do feel better. I can see my ribs through my skin. It looks pathetic. Ha ha.

I have three large notebooks filled with creative writings. I am planning on gradually typeing them all out neatly and placeing them in order by their dates. The thing I like most about my writings is the comments my teachers wrote on them. These comments, I think I will type in red type right along with my writing. I hope it will turn out nice. It may take a long time.

You, I would like to read them, if you want when I have typed some.

I feel like I have not written in this letter what I wanted. I want to thank you and Mrs. Pullias for letting us spend the night. It's something I always wished to do. I had fun.

Stanislaus sent me a housing list thing and it looks as if the rooms are mostly private rooms in family households with kitchen priviledges. The average price about $70.00. There are some listings of girls who want roomates to share apts. The cost is the same. I'm not sure which I would do best in.

Since I have begun helping Misty with her homework I think I do my own homework much more thoroughly. I guess the studying feeling is in the air. All my classes are interesting.

I think now I will go in the living room, sit on the warm couch and read my book; *Dracula*.

Your Friend, Debbie

P.S. I have started Misty reading poetry. They are short yet interesting and challenging, I think. Will write more later date.

The next morning:

I opened your letter to add this terrible dream I had last night. This is it:

I was at a beach and there were thosands of people laying around but they did not make any noise. The sun did not seem to be out. There was two little boys with me and we were suposed to go find Misty. We feared that she might be drownd.

One of the boys found her body and called me. I went into the water toward him and suddenly he said, "Oh! Don't step on it." And I looked down and saw that my foot was almost about to step on this blue bloated fleshy little body. Oh. I was scared to pick it up and I asked the little boy if he wanted to do it but then I realized I was an adult and this is something I must do. So I picked the limp body up and carried it to shore. People gathered around. Mrs. Graves was there.

Then I was at school in a classroom and it was there that the thought came to me that Misty would not be around anymore. She was dead. Not just away for a day but dead. I was afraid I was going to cry in class.

Then somehow I found out that in the class before this one, in my German class I had fallen sound alsleep and it was all a dream about M. being dead.

What a terrible dream. It seems almost as if when someone mentions dead baby dreams, soon after I have one. You asked me about them and I had this one. About a month ago I told Mr. Hill about them and after that talk I had one.

Strange.

Tim asks if you would like to buy a cord of assorted wood for $50.

It is evening now and I will mail this tomorrow. I am staying the night here at home and I may stay another day because I am very weak. I guess I hadn't eaten much the last week and today my stomach gave out and I got terrible shakes and pains. I was so hungry I couldn't even eat. Do you think that made me dream that dream? It is all very interesting to me how things connect.

I would like to sleep like a log tonight. No dreams.

Write soon. Debbie.

97.
April 6, 1972
Dear Dr. Pullias,

Troubles, troubles, everywhere. Did you have or do you have troublesome times like mine? All of the time there is something, it seems. Something. Not really always. It just seems like I write only bad things to you. I hope you realize that isn't all my life. My stomach trouble has come again but I don't think it is from nervousness. A new sympton is added to the others and this is the shakes. I start shaking. My mother thinks it is vitamin deficiency.

Well, I won a state scholarship for $450. A question I have is why can't you use it on room & board: It says that you can use it only on necessary fees not books or supplies or R. & B. I only need $165 for a year in fees. That's strange.

Another bad dream last night. About this really terribly fat kid falling in a fire and burning. I saw his legs burning with crackles and bubbles in the flesh and then the black bones just sort of crumpled up.

You should see Prieta now. Her hair is all shed out and she's very black and slick and shiny. She now has a scattering of white spots on her withers. I think she looks very pretty, indeed. She runs and trots when I want her to and we can turn quick at a run. The only thing I don't like is the way she shys so much. It scares me. One time something really scared her and she took off. I was holding on for dear life! But I guess you have to expect that with horses who are so afraid of silly things.

I've decided to try and live here at least untill school's over and then maybe 2 weeks into the summer. But I don't want --

April 9, 1972

Yesterday, Saturday, I was here at Mama's place and Mrs. Graves called on the telephone. She told my mom that it would be best for me to leave, move out. She did not give me any explanation at all which I thought was rather unfair. Anyway I moved out double quick. And that's that. It was an experience even if I didn't accomplish anything.

I rode with Misty today and she said nobody even told her I was leaving and when she came home and saw my room empty she was shocked. It would be a surprise, I guess. It'd be like you had a dream and when you woke up everything was gone.

98.
April 16, 1972
Dear Pullias,

It would be nice to go to Cal Western if I got the money. I like the campus, I like San Diego. Its just that I am so very tired of trying to figure it all out. I have to figure out where to go, how to fill out forms, classes, worst of all I have to work out the money bit and where I'm going to stay. Its hard for me because I'm all alone with no one to really help me the instant I have questions. My counselor can't take time, you are too far away, Mr. Hill doesn't know that much about it. I want to just get it done.

Dear Dr. Pullias

I wish I did not have to worry about money but I do. If I can get over guilt feelings this is what I could do: get all the schlrships I can then get a loan for the rest of the money I need. This loan you don't have to pay back untill you're through with college than its 3% interest. If I can't pay it back my grandmother could pay. Its just that I don't want to get anything from my grandparents. It bothers me.

Another thing that bothers me is that you say Cal Western would be much better than Stanilaus though why you don't say. But Mr. Hill says a state college is better because in Cal Western you tend to get kids who have money but no brains and the same with teachers. Personally Cal Western is nicer probably because I know what it looks like. The money bothers me so much.

April 18, 1972

I feel much better today. A new outlook on life every day. Do you think if I send in this change of college card to the Calif. Schlrship place saying I was going to Cal Western they would change the amount? I figured out the money I could get in the margin. Is that about right?

For one year
Ca. Scho.....1000
Loan....1000
Mother... 720
Work... 800 (?)
Little sca....300
3820

I really don't have time to find out if Cal Western would take me before I have to send in everything to Stanilaus. What if I decided to go to C. W. and they didn't take me but it was too late to go back to Stan.? Wow, I just want to have it finished. Tired. What did the person say on the telephone?

I wish that you will answer all my questions. Write soon.

Just think if I go to Cal Western; James lives in San Diego! Oh, brother..

Your friendly friend, Debbie.

99.
Los Angeles

Debbie Bumstead

April 20, 1972

Dear Debbie:

I am at USC giving an Exam in one of my courses -- a dreadful thing to do I guess, but seems to be a part of life. Your letter came today and I just had time to read it before I came down here. But I am eager to reply. To be brief and clear let's list the answers:

1. There is not much difference between colleges - the difference will be between teachers, and there will be some good and some not so good anywhere - as has been the case in high school.

2. I am not sure that Cal Western will be so much better than Stanislaus, but if you could make it there it might be more pleasant and interesting.

3. I am sure Cal W will admit you - I talked to the man about that.

4. The finances (or money) are a difficult problem. Let us see if we can work it out. I know it will not be easy.

5. Fill in the Admission blanks for Cal Western (you should have received them by now). Just fill them in the best you can and don't worry too much.

6. Fill in the scholarship applications blank. Give your situation just as clearly as you can and don't hesitate to indicate how bad it is. They have some scholarship money and I believe will help us.

Note: In case you run into trouble with either of the blanks get in touch with Dr. Hight. She will be glad to help. Put my name in as a reference if they ask for a reference on either or both blanks.

7. Do what you mentioned in your letter about your State Scholarship and lets see it they will raise it if you are accepted at a private college. Tell them you are going there (Cal W) and mention how much the tuition is.

8. Maybe I can help you to see that borrowing from your Grandparents, if you need to, would not be bad.

9. Keep your place at Stanislaus. Don't worry about the place to stay (board) - I'm sure that can be worked out later.

10. Don't let all the blanks and directions bother you - they are not nearly as bad as they sound. I felt the same way when I

was going to college, and when I got there it all worked out.

11. If for some reason neither of the places works out - which I don't think will happen - Dr. Hight told me she would help you to find a nice home to stay in near the community college there in Hemet and you can spend a year there and go off to college the next year.

And don't forget to laugh or smile.

Your friend, Earl V. Pullias

100.
April 26, 1972
Dear Dr. Pullias,

I'm sorry I haven't written for so long. I appreciated your letter that explained things so clearly.

I have a picture for you. In fact I have two pictures for you.

My mother and I are sewing a lot this weekend. My mom wants to make me a nice outfit for graduation.

Also today we went to San Diego. Did you know that Cal Western is moving to the Elliot campus? Well, we visited that place and it is in a eucalyptus forest place. It is very nice, I guess. My mother loved it, she wants me to go there very much because I will be protected. She doesn't mind about the money.

We went and visited San Diego State and that place was huge and we didn't like it.

I went to visit Mrs. Hight at the J.C. She was afraid that I would get up there and would suddenly run out of money. She wants me to go to the J.C.

Next Friday a friend is taking me to Disneyland. I haven't been there in a very long time.

Well, I don't have much to write. What are you doing? When will you be up? Down, I mean.

School is going very well. I find my Socology class very interesting, the teacher is a good sensitive person. His name is Mr. Phil Simon. Mrs. Hight knows him, I wondered if you did.

Oh! Did you know that Misty fell off a horse and broke her leg terribly? She's been in the hospital a long time.

Your Friend, Debbie.

Debbie Bumstead

P.S. My night's have been very full of dreams. Dream after dream and in the morning sometimes I remember three dreams clearly. Wierd.

101.
Los Angeles
May 7, 1972
Dear Debbie:
Our letters crossed in the mail as often happens with friends. Your letter and the admission recommendation came today. I am sending the recommendation off tomorrow. I am confident there will be no problem about your being admitted. It is important that you receive a scholarship from there to supplement the other scholarships you will have. Be sure to put your Cal Western scholarship application in and I will write in support. I have hopes that we can get a good scholarship for you.

I am glad you and your mother could visit Cal W. There is a good chance they will not move the college but that is confidential so do not speak of it except to your mother if you wish. Of course, it really wouldn't matter too much if it were moved, but I doubt if it will be.

I am glad you saw Dr. Hight. She is a fine person and very interested in you. I can understand her concern, but I would suggest that we see if we can get arrangements worked out to go to Cal Western this coming year. If we can't, then we will work something else out. I believe it can be done. It is good that your mother likes the idea.

I'm real sorry about Misty - poor youngster. We'll have to talk about your experience there sometime.

It is wonderful to know school goes so well. Sociology is a good study, and it is encouraging to have a fine teacher. Really, you are just now learning how to learn - from now on it should be better and better. If it works out that way, it would not be bad to spend a year or even two in the J.C. Let's see. Hope to see you on the weekend.

Your friend, Earl V. Pullias

Dear Dr. Pullias

102.
May 8, 1972
Dear Dr. Pullias,

Fall is a nice enough season and it does seem rather sad but I like winter and summer. My mind likes winter and my body likes summer. To me it is very monotenus the way spring must always follow winter, summer always comes after spring, fall never fails to be right after summer and so on year after year. It even sort of bothers me, wow! There's no variety! Some people feel this is something wonderful to rely one; the fact that the seasons always come in order. Well, that's all right with me. I'm not saying I don't love the seasons, its just the way they come. What do you think?

Last night and the night before I had two very scary dreams that were very similar. One was a dream about the man who takes care of Prieta and he was chasing me off his property, threatening me with a rifle. The dream last night was of Mr. Farmer my art teacher who went crazy and threatened the art class with a knife. I like these two men well enough; they are very nice to me. They are both similar in body structure; not fat but big, with terribly big arms and hands. I have a feeling these dreams sort of reflect the feeling of smallness I get when I'm around them. Maybe the threatening with weapons has something to do with sexual organs, who knows. I like men who are thin.

On Saturday I will, I hope, ride Prieta up to see you and maybe a friend, Carrie or Anne will come, too. Carrie has always wanted to meet you ever since I mentioned you to her in 7th or 8th grade. She has never had the chance. She has problems with her parents because they never let her do anything. She has two horses, one is very young and silly and it is a sort of blue gray color. Anne's horse is brown and stocky and rather silly, too. Prieta is not really very silly, she's too mature.

Dr. Pullias, don't worry too much about my health. It is improving all the time. I eat well here at home because I can fix my own meals. I have learned to avoid some things, for instance oranges which really make me feel sick. I wonder how I will do in college.

How are you? Do you eat well?

My grandma Bumstead had a heart attack. Its terrible.

Debbie Bumstead

My uncle Frank is dying of cancer. He's 52.
Strange how things happen.
    Your friend, Debbie.

103.
May 27, 1972
Dear Dr. Pullias,

Hi. Today is Saturday and in an hour I am going on a ride with Carrie on Prieta. Did you enjoy your little ride on her?

I was just talking to my grandma and she mentioned that Misty is still in the hospital. I had thought she went home a long time ago and that is why I didn't go to visit her. I wish I had known. I told her mom I would exercise Misty's ponies but I have an absolute dread about going out there. And the longer I wait the more dreadful it seems. It is mainly Mrs. Graves, I guess, I know she is harmless to me but she really scares my insides. She's wierd.

I want to keep in touch with Misty, but I don't like Mrs. Graves hanging over us like fuzzy old spider. She makes me think of nightmares.

Yesterday I got a letter saying I was accepted into Cal Western so now I am waiting to see if I get any financial help. I hope I do. I went through the catologe and picked out all the courses I would take in four years. I have it all figured out! Of course I can change it if I want.

If you died before I died would people read my letters? I don't want them to. I just wanted to know because I saw a TV movie where a lady read the personal letters her husband got when he died.

I am reading a very interesting book called I'm OK - You're OK. Have you read it?

I never knew you had worked with colts before. I wish you would write to me some of your memories. I like to know how people have grown up.

Carrie is going to a "dude ranch" part of the summer as a teacher teaching kids to ride. She is very excited and she wants to see if this is the kind of work she might want to do. I hope she enjoys it because I just do. I think I would enjoy it but I'm not too good at riding. Although I did do a pretty good job teaching Reggie and Randy (the kids where I keep Prieta) the fundamentals.

Dear Dr. Pullias

Something that has always absolutely fascinated me is the way people are different from each other. I like to think about my friends who are interested in different things and they will all live their different lives. I like children because of that. Tomorrow I am taking Reggie and Randy out hiking. We may go up to your cabin.

Your friend, Debbie.

May 28, 1972

Sometimes I get a feeling, a very happy feeling that makes me think of something that happened a long time ago. For instance when I listen to the birds around here I get a tremendous sudden happy feeling and I think of the book <u>Rabbit Hill</u>. It used to be I just got the feeling and didn't think of the book but I felt I should be remembering something and I found out what it was a couple of years ago.

Another thing is when I wake up very very early in the morning to do something different from going to school I have terrific pressing excitement feelings in my chest. I don't know why. It might be that whenever our family was going on a trip somewhere we would get up to go very early.

Listening to the crows caw early in the morning makes me feel the feelings I had when we as a family went down to the boat in San Diego.

Do you suppose that when I read <u>Rabbit Hill</u> I also listened to some birds?

It's interesting. I wish I could know what someone else thinks like that. I wish I had someone who wrote to me like I write to you. Its interesting to me a lot. Is it to you?

Reggie, Randy and I saw Mrs. P, Cal, and Frances when we went hiking. We had fun except for our two unfortunate incidents. The first was when Duchess, the German Shepard dog of the boys got stuck under Dr. Cain's car. I went to get him to help us only he was in his underwear. It was funny. He came out after dressing and mumbled and grumbled. We spent a long time trying to figure out what to do; poor Duchess was half under half out and she couldn't budge. And it was so hot! Finally Dr. Cain used a shovel as a lever to lift the car up and I pulled her out.

The second incident was when we were coming down from Hemet Butte and the boys were running down. Randy, the little skinny one took a flip, landed on his back and started screaming. He scraped himself up pretty bad because he didn't have a shirt on. He was really hurting. We walked to your cabin and Mrs. Pullias comforted and cleaned him up. He felt much better then and we went into town and bought some ice cream.

Well bye, Your friend, Debbie.

104.
Thursday morning
June 1, 1972
Debbie:

There were so many things I didn't respond to in your letters that I want to write a little more this morning. I liked Prieta very much - she is interesting and <u>pensive</u>. It had been so long since I rode any that I felt a little awkward riding, but that soon would be over, I'm sure: experience is a fascinating thing. In almost everything it reduces awkwardness, and even fear, although in the case of fear it has to be the right kind of experience. We hope later to have a horse or maybe a donkey.

I have not read <u>I'm OK-You're OK</u> but I would like to this summer, and then we'll talk about it. I would like for you to try your hand at some of Willa Cather's books that I mentioned a little earlier: <u>My Antonia</u>; <u>Death Come for the Archbishop</u>; and <u>The Lost Lady</u> (maybe this summer) , which I have read recently and found good writing.

Yes, the feelings you describe in your letters are very interesting to me. I will tell you more of my feelings a little later, I hope. I know quite well what you mean.

My work is very demanding just now - end of school: papers, grades, speeches, but that is life! Write when you feel like it. Your letters are good to receive.

Sincerely, Earl V. Pullias

105.
Los Angeles
June 4, 1972
Sunday afternoon

Dear Debbie:

Thanks for the very personal invitation to your high school graduation. I liked that type much better than the formal printed ones. We would like very much to come to the graduation exercises, but I am speaking for a Junior College graduation that same afternoon so we cannot come. We will be thinking of you - and hope to see you soon.

I am real proud of the record you have made in high school. You have done well under what were sometimes difficult circumstances, but more important, you have developed a great deal in many ways. The next four years will be even more important and interesting. From 18 to 22 a person grows into the adult he is likely to be in life. I don't want that to sound too final, because of course, we go on learning all through life - or at least we should and can - but the college years are the bridge between youth and adulthood.

Perhaps your most important achievement in high school is that you have learned how to do your school work well - how to study and work: these are extremely important in life whatever one does.

You are on your way: I am thankful and glad because you are my friend. I am eager to see the pictures you have for me.

Sincerely, Earl V. Pullias

106.
June 14, 1972
Dear Dr. Pullias,

I am typing this letter because my hand is very tired of writing but at the same time I feel like writing you a letter. This is my solution. Notice as you read the great skill and style with which I type. Ha ha.

Several things have happened during the time in which I have not written you. Firstly I was accepted in to Cal Western. Secondly I received $1500 of support 750 of which is a loan. I also received $150 from a Hemet Scholarship. At this time I can not remember the thirdly and forthly (maybe even the fifthly) things that have happened. They will come later.

Your pictures patiently wait to meet you.

Oh! Thirdly has just come to me. I chanced across a book in the library titled The Art of Child Placement. I thought this might be a good job for me because it involves children and getting to be friends with them and helping them and going places with them. On the other side it also seems like it would be a good steady job to keep me from becoming too much like other Bumsteads in the family. What do you think and know of this occupation?

Have you ever read The Diary of A.N.? It is an extremely good book. Anyway I can relate with the girl in it very well. She had many of the very same problems and thoughts and experiences that I have had. I really would have liked to have been friends with her and it was hard to think that in actuality she was just a fictional character.

I can hardly believe tomorrow is the last day of school. It certainly doesn't seem like it. I want to get a summer job but I kind of don't know how to go about it. I was riding my bike around the other day and came upon a preschool. I thought I might inquire into that. If they have preschool in the summer.

Typing is sort of impersonal, is it not? But sometimes its fun.

Write soon when you are not busy.

Your friend, Debbie.

P.S. Keep my letters as you like study them as you like but why don't you write on the cover of the folder to send them back to me. If I die before you though you may do what you want with them.

107.

June 1972

Dear Dr. & Mrs. Pullias,

This is to thank you for the exquisitly (sp) nice pen. I am writing with it here. Thank you also for all of your thoughfullness and the nice times I have at your cabin.

I picked this card for you because a long time ago for Christmas we received a card from you with a bird on it and my father said, "Once Dr. Pullias said to me that if there were such a thing as reincarnation he would like to be a bird."

Thank you again.

Your friend, Debbie.

108.
Los Angeles
June 24, 1972
Dear Debbie:

What a nice thank you card! And the note on it was you, and that is good. We are so pleased you liked the pen, and hope that it will remind you of our friendship through the years that you have it. It was very good to have you at the cabin and about. To have you move in and out freely as one of the family is very good. I had hoped we might all go over in the juniper tree area, but we'll have to do that next trip, maybe.

I am deeply thankful and pleased that the plans are shaping up for you to attend a small college in a town where you want to be and near the ocean: do you suppose it is too many good things?! I am writing your mother saying I talked to you about the educational fund to be set up in a bank there and used as needed only for that purpose, and that you felt all right about it. Let me know if there is anything else I can help with.

I am pleased you remembered the card with the bird on it we sent for Christmas and what your father said about my liking birds especially. It might be very interesting to come back as a beautiful bird! I believe it is their great freedom of movement and their apparent joy in life that appeal so much. Debbie, if you should find out your father's address, send it to me. I want very much to stay in touch with him.

Your friend, Earl V. Pullias

109.
July 6, 1972
Dear Dr. Pullias,

Last week I went to that camp thing for girls in Idylwild and I met 10 very interesting girls and we all stayed in a very rustic large lodge house. I enjoyed the setting and the people immensly but there were several things I did not like. Like having a real patriotic whoope flag ceremony twice a day and dressing for dinner and three horrible classes in Parlimentary Procedure.

The last week in July I am going again: this time as a counselor to

Debbie Bumstead

four 13-14 year old disadvantaged girls. One of my roomates who I liked very much, Jan is also coming to counselor four other girls that same week. It will be interesting, I think.

When I was there we had a counselor lady come talk to us individually. She gave us a mental health test and I scored very high on maturity, extremely extremely high on having someone to tell my problems to (guess who?) and my future plans and goals. I was low in what I thought of myself (?). It was quite fascinating and the lady and I had quite a rapor with each other. I liked her.

Starting tomorrow I will be working at the child care center in San Jacinto. It is going to be volunteer, no money, shucks. I will probably enjoy it and I want to find out about nursery schools. I have been reading "The Montessori handbook" and I have been thinking about it.

Another thing we did at the lodge was a lady analized our handwriting. She said so many true things. She said my writing showed I had extremely well thought out plans for the future (wow) but that people had to draw me out because I didn't talk much. She said I was poised but that my writing showed that I was irratated at myself.

My mother is going to be gone for 2 weeks so I will be here alone. I invited my 3 little cousins to come spend a couple of days here next week. I hope they can come.

Since I won't be able to drive to San Diego I will have to register for classes by mail.

These are my first choices

1st quarter	2nd quarter	3rd quat.
Matrix Art	English	Natural Science
Psychology	Math	Drawing
Literature	Philosophy	Afro Asian Heritage

Here are my alternitives
 Statistics, Design, Philosophy of Life, Politics, N.S. II Soicology

I could not find any history course with Civilization in it so I don't know what Mr. Box teaches.

I won't send in the form untill you write back.

Write soon.

Love, Debbie

P.S. You should see Prieta. She is FAT! I mean real fat. Her belly, that is.

110.
Los Angeles
July 10, 1972
Dear Debbie:

I wish you could see my small study here in the backyard. I believe you would like it. This morning, and often, I have a candle burning on my desk, and above the desk a little to the right I have put your picture - the one with the leaves and toadstools - which I like very much. That should help to keep the spirit of a friend near.

Your letter was a joy to receive. First to the business about the courses for the fall quarter. I was able to talk with two of the men I know at Cal Western and so received some suggestions about the courses. One of the men whom I respect and who knows the teachers and the courses well, suggested that you might be wise to make one shift your sequence of courses: he thought you might take the philosophy the first quarter and the literature the second. This would enable you to get Dr. Box in the philosophy in the fall quarter which I believe would be a good relation. They suggested a Mr. Fortbrook for your Matrix Art and a Dr. Pitts for psychology both of whom they recommended highly. This arrangement would take care of the fall and then you could figure on the details of the next courses a little later when you are there. (If you can't get Dr. Pitts in psychology, then a Dr. Jacobs will be good.) It is wonderful to have your plans for college taking shape.

The Idyllwild experience sounded very good - the next one will be even better. I hope the two weeks alone go off well. I am delighted you will be working at the child care center - tell me more about it later. I must see our dear Prieta! Am a little pushed today. Will write more later.

Sincerely, Earl V. Pullias

111.
July 21, 1972
Dear Dr. Pullias,

Debbie Bumstead

Hi.

This summer certainly seems to be eventful. I always seem to be doing something or going to be doing something. I don't know if I like that. Tomorrow I will be going to that camp and I'm afraid I'm not leader enough to dominate the actions of four girls who are my age almost. Anyway I'll try to be at least compainable and at the end of the week I bet I'll be pooped.

Did I write to you that Prieta stepped on a nail? She has been out of comission for a long time and had to even have surgery to get rid of the absces. Twice a day my mother and I must try (though sometimes its hard to succeed) to soak her foot in a basin for ½ hour. Its boring for all three of us.

After we soak Prieta I ride the young donkey-pony they have there because I am trying to train him to be a riding pony. He is very sweet. Probably just the donkey you would like to get if you ever got one. His name is Sam or Sambo and he's very furry and dark. His mama is a plain old gray donkey who lays down when you get on to ride. Ha ha. She's funny.

School for me does not start untill Sept. 23. I tryed to get the courses you said but there was no way of getting the teachers I wanted.

I have been reading some books on teaching by Montessori and Caroline Pratt. Very interesting! Fascinating, in fact. I like Sylvia Ashton Warner's way best so far I think. But it would be easy to have a combination. What a day dreamer I am! I've worked out a whole new school up to the 6th grade. It would be interesting to have a better way of teaching for high school. Do you know any good books on teaching or rather education in new ways? I'll have to read yours all the way through.

Terrible dream last night. Crunch someone eating a bite out of a man's face. That was strange. See you later.

Your friend, Debbie.

112.

Dear Dr. Pullias,

We will be going on an airplane to Reno Saturday morning. I hope I don't get sick. We'll be up there (in Reno not the airplane) about 2 weeks, maybe more. You can write if you want. Address: 2100 N.

Dear Dr. Pullias

Virginia, Reno, 89503.

I liked my second week at Idyllwild much better than the first. There were 8 14-15 year old girls and us two counselors. We each had four to look after. They were all girls with some kind of troubles. All of them except one were rather lazy (like me) and had to be prodded to get things done. All of them talked very very much about their familys. A pychologist came one evening and we had a group session in which everyone told about themselves and their lives.

The main thing they had to do was make a dress or blouse, plan a fashion show and show it to the old ladies of Idyllwild. They did a real fine great job with some help from us counselors: Jan doing the proding and me doing the structural planing and writing.

Two girls I became interested in especially were Elizabeth from Riverside and Tracy from Palm Springs. Elizabeth was from a family of 13 kids and she was loud and tuff but still she was younger than me and was respectful. We struck up a very nice friendlyness. Man, does she have a tuff life!

Tracy was very quiet and had a speech problem. You could see she was used to being teased terribly. One thing that was very nice to happan to her was I asked her if she wanted to introduce the entertainment at the fashion show. She agreed hesitantly and asked me to write what she would say. Anyway she did it and did it quite well, she thought and after the show you could just see her glowing. She plans to write to me.

Well, here is my father's address:
463 Klute St Apt 1
Santa Rosa, Calif. 95401

Your friend, Debbie.

113.
Reno, NV
Dear Dr. Pullias,

Thank you for the letter. It is nice to get one somewhere different from home. I am looking forward to going home because I feel like riding Prieta and because I am going to invite my little second cousins to come again. I've made up some things to do this time to take up the long hours we spend in the house out of the heat. Games of observing and drawing and making up stories and dictating things that have happened to them to me. I don't know how to tell of my feeling for the middle boy, Steve. He is about 8, I guess and I have a very special interest in him and love for him. He is so full of wonder.

There is a great library up here and I have checked out quite a few books on primary schools. A very good one is from Britain and is called The Teaching of Young Children. When I think of teaching in a school I do not want to give up my want to have the fun of kids but when I think of just fun I want to teach them, too. I would like to keep about 7 children all the time and teach them, too. You know? I could do that but I don't think I would get paid. Do you know an instance in which I would? Its important.

Dr. Pullias! Sorry! You'll have to find another 18 year old slave. I'm probably not much better at housework than you! Of course maybe two crummy house workers are better than one, or would they be twice as bad?

Last night I had a dream about Dr. Cain. Wow, what a character to suddenly pop up in a dream. He was my science teacher and was showing me an experiment. The night before I had a bad dream, the first in many months. Dead kittens, thousands of dead white kittens on lush green grass. It was wartime and I was escaping with my mother and a guy in a jeep. We drove by these kittens. This dream was brought on by the third session of the movie War and Peace. Did you see that movie? I thought it was very good. But I did not like the dream. I have very often dreams about stores. I can't figure out what stores have to do with anything. Its strange. The stores are department stores or small ones and they are usually closed but I am in them, often with my mother or grandmother.

All summer I have been working and working on thinking about what I would do after college. I have been thinking and writing and figureing so much I can't stop. I'm getting tired of it.

Well, I hope you know the real me because that's who I've been all along. Surprize! Now you know: I'm me. Isn't that something. My grandmother doesn't seem to know the real me because she seems to be so sure I don't really love her. When I am around her I feel like a very ugly kind of person. I feel like she thinks I'm grabby and very cruel. I'm afraid to discuss things with her because if my opinion is different she thinks I'm being mean to her. She is a woman who would need some kind of help if she wasn't so far gone. I really don't know how to do anything for her except write letters.

Enough of that. Sometime I would like to write you about my friend, Marie who lives across the way here in Reno. She's a good kid.

We will leave here on Monday. See you sometime. Write soon.

Your friend indeed, Debbie.

114.

Dear Dr. Pullias,

We got back here in Hemet Monday afternoon and then I suddenly got very sick like I have never been before. It was miserable. Now it is Wednesday and I feel pretty good except my stomach muscles are so sore from throwing up I can't move around. Last night I had a dream that I was staying out at my Grandparents old house in Random Acres. I saw you driving a huge kind-of old-fashioned van up the road and I waved but you didn't see me.

I got my class schedule and for fall I have Art, English, P.E. & Pyschology. It didn't work out like we wanted.

Write soon, OK?

Debbie.

P.S. Have you read a book called The Primal Scream? I have not yet but my brother Joe read it and now he is really turned on about it. He wants to go through Primal Therapy. When he came up to Reno he talked for an hour or more to me about how it is so true and then he bought me a copy. I'm on the second chapter and all I can say is that it is just interesting.

I can hardly wait for college. But I was wondering what happans if you get sick like I did and you don't have a lovely mamma to help you along? Ha ha.

115.

Los Angeles

Sept. 2, 1972

Dear Debbie:

After I left yesterday I felt that there may have been something you wanted to say to me or ask me, and I did not give you proper time. If that were so, you will write to me. For most thought and feeling writing is easier for some of us than talking.

Wonder why that is so?

Your letters - the one written at Reno and the one after you came home were very good: they were you. I was real sorry you were sick: a person surely needs a mother or some one who can take her place when he is sick. I know you were partly joking about getting sick at college, but if you should there will be someone.

Perhaps I should mention a thing or two from my experience. You are likely to be a little frightened between now and the time you go to San Diego. Sometimes you may wish you had never decided to go. That will pass and when you get to college there will be some disappointments, especially until you get use to things. Then it will be a great adventure.

I am so pleased you are interested in various approaches to education. It is a fascinating subject offering much opening for the imagination.

We will talk more of your Grandmother. I wish she could know the real you or at least a part of it. I suspect she is much more deeply interested in you as a person than it seems. But the gap is very wide, I know.

Hope you and Prieta can visit us Saturday. Did you try any of the Cather books?

Your friend, Earl V. Pullias

116.
At Cal Western, San Diego
Sept. 22, 1972
Dear Dr. Pullias,

Its nice here. I like it. Its comfy and warm and I can go up to the lounge to watch TV if I want. I have plenty of time alone in my bedroom and my roommate is very compatible. Her name is Debbie Sjoberg and she's quiet and studious but quite a bit more out-going than me. She spends a lot of the day out with four of the girls down our hall.

The first couple of days I was also going around with these four girls but I did not like it. I tried to think why and then I had it; they are just terribly boring to me, or maybe not boring but superficial. And they do not listen, they only talk. They're nice enough but no fun for me. Do you know what I mean? One example of the way we don't fit is my sense of humor. My roommate to me is hilarious, her movements and facial expressions show how she is thinking. She is absent-minded and sometimes without her saying a single thing I fall into peals of laughter, laughing untill I cry but no one else observes and they act as if I'm crazy or something.

I feel sleepy and good tonight because pretty soon I can go to bed and sleep warm. I feel good because tomorrow's Saturday and I'm going to take a walk off campus. I feel good because its looks like I'm going to have a nice psychology teacher. He looks like Dr. Cain only younger; he even smokes a pipe. His name is Dr. Jacobs. He is running his class this way; every Monday is a lecture, Tuesdays are experiments, Weds. are small groups discussing things, Fridays are tests. Sounds interesting. He's pleasent.

My English teacher I'm not sure about but I will probably get to know him pretty good as that's the way it is with English teachers and me. His name is Mr. De Seager.

My art teacher, too, seems kind and friendly. His name is Calvin Fortbrook. I'm not sure, though, about his assignments. I have a Mr. Richardson for Creative Writing but I have not met him yet.

Sept. 23. I went for a long walk today down to Shelter Island. I went about 10:30 and I ate lunch there and then came back. I enjoyed my outing very much. I felt quite grown-up because I was so far away from my family members

I'm afraid I may have some trouble with my English and Art classes because for the past two years I've had Creative Writing and Senior Studio, both of which are completely free. You did what you wanted. I liked that.

I feel good! Do you?

The library here is great.

Please write very soon! I liked your letter.

Your loving friend, Debbie.

P.S. What's your middle name? Vincent?

Debbie Bumstead

117.
September 27, 1972
Weds.
Dear Dr. Pullias,

It is 9:00 in the morning and I have an hour before I leave for English. I'm chewing gum. I'm listening to the radio, I'm writing. I am aware of a stiffness in my back. I hear squeaking out in the hall and cans banging. I'm wondering what you'll think when you read this. I'm wondering what my English teacher will think of my assignment. I am extremely aware of the brillant squares of fabric on my quilt where I am sitting. I hear a nice song on the radio and my foot moves in rythmn.

I enjoyed your letter with the upmost of pleasure. Last year I started and read part of a book called <u>Fig Tree John</u>. It was about a place in Utah, I think or near there about an Indian. It told of the Indian's belief that the Salt Lake was how the gods punished the white people for taking the desert and making it productive. Anyway this one

Indian wanted to see this Lake so he took his wife and they went there and settled down. That's as far as I got.

Flying was not my favorite experience. It was interesting to see out the window; it looked as if it were a map. But I still didn't like it much. I really didn't like it when the plane shook. But we got where we were going in a hurry and that was nice.

Last night was rather hectic for my roommate. Earlier she had received a letter from a girlfriend. Later the girl called her and told Deb that she loved Deb's boyfriend. The girl was all upset and said she was sorry and everything. Deb was not really upset just insulted. After the call every one in the hall gathered in our bedroom to discuss it. Everyone analized the letter about three times over. Deb said that the girl and her boyfriend were coming up to San Diego next weekend to see a football game. Instantly all the girls exept me told her to invite them both over here so they could meet them.

It made me think of my dad bringing Geets home. So later I told Deb that experience and how Geets went wacky and threw a shoe at me. Deb told me about her father who married another lady. She also has two older brothers. And lived with her mother alone. Her birthday is February 8 and mine is Feb. 18.

That was dumb last night. I must be really different than most girls. I mean, really really different!

Tomorrow is Thursday and I have only one class in the A.M. so afterward I am going to take a walk to the elem. school near here and see what kind of volunteer stuff I could do on Thursdays.

Hope everything goes well with you.

Your friend, Debbie.

118.
Los Angeles
At home
Sept. 27,1972
Dear Debbie:

It was very good to get your letters. I was eager to hear how things were going. To get a reasonably congenial room mate is a great help, and to have a pleasant room "down a hall" I know was a dream of yours. It is interesting that both of you are "Debbie."

What a delight the walk alone must have been! That is a beautiful area.

The classes are likely to be all right: some good, some so-so, some perhaps bad: that is life at college. I have found if one keeps his eyes open, he can learn almost as much from one as another. Really that is not quite true: a really good teacher is a wonderful thing.

You may have concluded or <u>found out</u> that I am a little crazy. I mentioned enclosing a check for a little special fund for you this fall, and then didn't enclose it? Mrs. P. asked me to mention that we wanted to give you something more for graduation, and didn't quite know what would be good so this can make that up a little. Do what you please with it.

The "V" in my name stands for Vivon. I have heard my mother say how she happened to choose the name but now it has slipped my mind. I will ask her when I write again. I am so glad you are feeling well. College can be a great learning and living adventure for you: I believe it will be.

My speeches in Utah went well, although that trip and all the work around the beginning of school were a little tiring. I am feeling better now. The drawings in your letter were wonderful.

Your friend, Earl V. Pullias

119.
Los Angeles
Oct. 7, 1972
Sat. night.
Dear Debbie:

It is good to have a friend to whom one can write when he wants to. There does not need to be a reason - just the need or wish to write. Just the desire to reach across the miles and the years and think and feel with someone of common interests and concerns. That is one of the goods in life.

Your last letter crossed my last one to you in the mail. I was interested in the incident about your roommate, Deb, and the girls who came in to respond to it. You were wondering if you are different. Yes, I believe you are different from most girls in many deep and important ways. I cannot now say what those ways are - perhaps I will never be able to say very precisely or clearly. But I can say that it is important that you continue almost above everything to be yourself. Some one has said that we grow more and more to be our true selves as we grow older: as we are enriched by learning and by experience. You will find that this being yourself will mean that you will be alone often and feel alone. This I suspect is one of the prices of being special in a significant way and finding more and more meaning in life as you develop.

I hope things go well there. Your walks sound very interesting. I hope you can find some school where you can help and learn: that will come. College is a great experience in many ways. I would like for it to be a fine time of physical development for you. I believe you will come to feel well and find a wholesome joy in the good use of your body: health is a fine thing.

My work has been a little hard this fall, but should be better now. I need time to be alone, to think, and to write. I must tell you more of my activity and thought.

Sincerely your friend, Earl V. Pullias

120.
Los Angeles
Backyard
Oct. 15, 1972
Dear Debbie:

It is a lovely mid-October morning: the sky is that remarkable blue that comes only in Oct., the air is crisp and fresh, the red roses are blooming (not seeming to know or care it is fall and winter is on the way) here in the yard. So it is a good time to talk a little with a friend before I go to church.

You seem to be very fortunate in your room mate. Most people are not so wise and sensitive to another person's feelings and unspoken wishes. Perhaps a deep and long time friendship can develop between you - that is rare, but when it comes is one of life's finest things. Give her my regards if it seems wise.

There is much about your childhood and growing up that you will need to consciously understand and eventually integrate into your personality. It is natural and good that you loved and love your father so, and that the memories arise and bring tears. Of course, you loved and love your mother also, but in different ways - the two producing conflicts often, but that is the nature of life. These things will all take their proper place in your life and thought as you grow toward full maturity.

The C's are not bad in the beginning of college work. You will catch on and move into B's and A's as you get more experience with college. Take care to develop a good, consistent, regular work schedule: learning to work effectively, as I have often said, is one of life's most important achievements, whatever one wishes to do. I'm sorry about the creative writing teacher, but that seems to be pretty typical - you were lucky in the Hemet teachers.

Your friend, Earl V. Pullias
P.S. I am sending you the book <u>I'm OK</u> - thinking you might need it. We are very pleased at the use of the gift we sent. Your room sounds so comfortable and cozy!

121.
Oct. 20, 1972
Dear Dr. Pullias,

That letter was very nice; I liked it.

It is about 15 after 3 in the afternoon and I am waiting for my mother. I'm going home for the three day weekend. It'll be good to get out for awhile and remember what its like in old Hemet. Maybe I'll go to the show with a friend or play tennis at the new high school. I'll ride my snazzy horse, call on Misty, and I'll eat good yummy delicious home-cooked Debbie Bumstead dinners. I'll hug my splendid Mamma and say hi to her every time she looks at me. I'll help her move, too.

Did you know she's moving? The house was a friend of hers' but they're moving, too. it's a very large house with three bedrooms and a huge living room. Also it is out in the country.

I wonder what made her move? I hope it wasn't me wishing for a big house and only that. But its nice and only $100 a month. She wants to have the apartment finished up and rented out. Then in awhile she wants to get a mobile home. That sounds right for her. I can easily imagine her in a trailor court.

Dear Dr. Pullias

During the thanksgiving vacation a girl wants to come home with me because she can't very well go to her home in Conneticutt. She's a rather high strung girl who laughs excessively but she's nice. She's a little young. I wonder how she will feel in all-white Hemet, not bad, I hope.

There is another girl here and I just don't understand her problem. She is constantly borrowing things! She borrowed my paints (used them all up, too) some drawing sheets, pen and ink, pen. She never gave them back and I didn't want to ask for them back. She also borrowed my roommates spoon, poetry book, & piggy bank money. This weekend she's borrowing a girl's sterio, another girl's TV and she was going to borrow a girl's Teapot but the girl refused. I'm glad, I think. Maybe she'll begin to realize what she's doing. Do you know what's with her? She's nice enough, otherwise; she's teaching me to play my recorder. Maybe she believes we are indebted to her.

English is going better. In Psych. next Tuesday we're going to Casa Blanca, a mental hospital.

Love, Debbie.

122.
Oct. 26, 1972
Dear Dr. Pullias,

I recieved the book today. Thanks.

Over the three day weekend I went home. It was very beautiful. All the days felt like Christmas. One Sunday Carrie and I went riding in the lovely Hemet weeds. We went to Miss Kerr's house, found her roofing, and talked a long time. Miss Kerr and I have been writing each other.

On Saturday night I had a bad dream. It went this way:

First I dreamed that we were living in a dark adobe house in the country. Joe seemed to be there and Mamma. A hallway with Persian figured rugs led me to a bedroom. In this dark room I dimly saw a girl making a bed. It might have been me. On one side of the bed I saw the small carcass of a baby. I was very frightened; my heart started to pound, but I said to myself, "I must not let this dream get bad." So I went on down the hallway to another bedroom. I woke up very afraid.

Last night, though, was far worse. I went to bed before my roomate and I must have gone directly to sleep. It seemed more like half-sleep to me. Anyway something, I don't know what, scared me terribly. I couldn't breathe and my body was tight or tense. My mind felt like it was being pressed together. Suddenly I woke up (but I felt like I was awake all the time). Deb had just turned out her light and she asked me if I was awake. I said, "Yes." She asked if I had had a bad dream (today she said I had been gasping). But I couldn't answer. I tried to say but I just couldn't. I was so scared. Then I began to think about dead children dreams. I was so frightened I was going to have one that I tossed and worried and perspired. Its hard to write you how afraid I was. I can't say.

I started to sort of cry. I said, "Debbie?" She was awake still so I asked her, "If I get scared will you come over?" She said, "sure! What scared you?" I answered "I don't know." Then she asked me if I had dreamed something but I couldn't answer. I couldn't say it.

Then I continued to worry about dreaming. I couldn't sleep. It was a nightmare just being awake. I finally turned on my night light and read Bible stories till I fell asleep. I didn't have any bad dream.

Today I could tell about the dream I had of not breathing but when I thought and wanted to say about the dead children dreams I couldn't. My heart beat harder and I got nervous. It was really freaky.

So no one here knows what is frightening to me. If I told someone I think they would not believe I was serious. But you know, don't you? Do you know why I am afraid? I don't know.

My English teacher wrote on my last paper that he'd like to talk with me. That will be interesting. Its strange that I really enjoy talking but it doesn't show, I guess.

What is your basic philosophy of life?

Do you know what I'd like to do? Well, I think I'd like to join the Vista volunteers for a year, next year or the next year. Do you know anything about this service?

I am very sleepy. My eyes are burning. Will I go to sleep if I get in bed? My roommate is out with a friend. I felt sort-of dumb about having asked her to come over if I got scared. I mean, she's only as old as me and besides that what could she do? But I felt better when I did ask her because half of the horror of a bad dream is when you wake up and you're scared. It might be good if someone real and alive were sitting on your bed. (I don't' know if it would be good because nobodie's been around when I had a bad dream, but it sounds good.)

It's late now but I've not yet gotten ready for bed. Instead I've been sketching out my final painting for the art class. Did I tell you about this project? I really have become involved in it. The teacher asked us to paint to music and I decided to do it to classical music. Wow! I'd like to be a conductor conducting music in color. Well, that's what I did. I did about five preliminary paintings spending about 20 minutes on each. I really got into the music. One of the paintings I did to a very vibrant piece by Tchaikovski (spelling?) I like it best.

Well, I think I will now depart to sleep. So good night,
sleep tight,
Don't let the bed bugs bite
Wake up to the morning's glad light
Happy and brite.
Yes indeedy.
Love, Debbie

123.
Nov. 3, 1972
Friday
Dear Dr. Pullias,

Thank you for the letter. I was getting awfully lonely for some letters. I haven't gotten any for 1 ½ weeks and that's a long time for me!

Well, I don't know what to do about these dreams! I can't believe how scared they make me and how numerous they are coming at me now. I write them down but writing them makes me remember the next nights dreams better. I want to remember them because they're interesting but I don't want to feel frightened.

Debbie Bumstead

There are two types of bad dreams for me. The most prevalent is the dark murky repulsive dream of death or bloatedness. The other type seems to be full of a sort-of buzzing brightness and when I wake up I'm frozen. Always in the latter type of dream I wake up lying on my back with a pecular pressure on the base of my head. Do you suppose the pressure on a special part of my brain produces the dream?

Please tell me all you can about Vista. I don't know anything about it.

Very tired of so many years of school. I ought to take off one year. I feel I'm so dumb about living in the world and I want to learn before I'm too old.

You know the one thing I really miss here? Boys! I never am able to come in contact with men here; it is a totally girl place. I miss my brothers, I miss you, I miss Mr. Farmer and Mr. Hill, I miss my little boyfriends out where Prieta is. I never knew how much I liked to be around boys. Perhaps something will develop. At least I talk to my art teacher every once in awhile and at least my psychology teacher sometimes winks at me, at least I've had a few conversations with male students.

Tell me, why am I so shy?

Hey! I was so naughty! Tee hee! We had to write in my expository writing class a theme using persuasion. Well, I wrote in my favoritest fun way all about persuading Mother Nature to send me a windy day. I didn't do it expository and it was so fun! I wonder what he'll think of it.

Our research paper is due before Thanksgiving. I'm going to write on some aspect of open education.

Please write soon

Love, Debbie.

124.

Note clipped to Debbie's returned letter:
Debbie: I thought you might wish to have this letter at hand when reading mine. Write. If I can help in any way let me know. Please return the letter to me later; I want to keep it with your others. What beautiful days these are! Don't fail to see them.

Dear Dr. Pullias

Dear Dr. Pullias,

I feel like stating the facts simply:

1. College classes are, in the main, irrelevant to my personal individual interests.

2. It is more profitable for me to work on my own on all subjects, save science.

3. It is proven that I do indeed study and think and write in depth on anything that so inspires me.

4. It is proven that I am indeed highly motivated toward search for knowledge and will be so even in the absense of school.

5. College classes, though challenging, stunt my growth toward important aspects in my life.

Therefore it can be deducted that:

1. If I continue to dedicate four more years wholey to college I will at the end of that time know much about nothing and nothing about everything (to me).

2. If I stop college to learn on my own I will work on all subjects that I am fascinated by but are never offered in college and after four years I will know much about everything that is important and still better I will still be searching.

Therefore the ideal solution can be gathered from this data. Either that I:

1. Find Somebody to Support me while I do my learning Thing, or

2. Find a Living which incorporates my interests so that I may Learn while earning Money, or

3. Find a Job which may be awful but gives me Time to Learn.

Well, that sums it up simply, doesn't it? Now I only have to find a way to get my solution.

What do you think?

Your friend, Debbie.

125.
Los Angeles
Nov. 19,1972
Sunday Morning
Dear Debbie:

The rest of the family and I made a one day trip to Hemet

yesterday. The trip is a little long for one day, but we had about four hours there and it was beautiful indeed. When I returned last night your letter was here waiting for me. It is a sincere and thoughtful letter, as your letters nearly always are. You asked me to say what I think of your ideas and conclusions. So now I respond to the request as frankly as I can - as friends speak to each other.

First, let me say that I believe I understand the ideas you express, chiefly because I have felt them myself and often came near to acting upon them. Had I done so, I would have been cut off from the opportunities that have given some meaning to my life. I would have been caught in a web that would have destroyed the freedom which I had to have - in short, I would have drifted into poverty, dependence, "failure" that really enslave a person and eventually cause a person to develop very undesirable ways of defending himself. I have seen thousands take that road, and I know it leads to worse than nowhere. Of course, I would hate to see you take it, although I know how appealing it is, and that it may be the only road many can take. Now let me answer your ideas one by one as sincerely and briefly as I can:

1. Often college classes are, or seem to be, irrelevant to our personal interests. As a rule, with effort and persistence and a little sense of humor they can be made to relate to our interests and our long-time goals - not completely, but some. A good teacher helps very much, and they are very scarce: I have a dream for you to be a great teacher.

2. As a rule, it is not possible for a person to work on subjects on his own. He moves from one thing to another and bogs down. I find this to be true of excellent advanced students. It sounds good, but will not work.

3. You are right that you write well on things that inspire you. But you, like other people, need a great deal of learning as a background and as a means in order that you can really do well in the areas of your interests.

4. I am sure that you are highly motivated toward a search for knowledge, but this would not likely last long in the absence of school - not at this stage of your development.

5. Really the college classes need not stunt your growth

toward the important aspects of your life. Used wisely they will be an important means to that growth just as high school was.

Now to your conclusions:

1. You need not know "much about nothing" and "nothing about everything" if you continue in college. True, much of the study may be uninteresting and even harmful, but as an experience it is the best means toward your goals - almost, in our world, the only means.

2. If you stop college you will likely find yourself blocked in practically everything you want to do. Soon you will likely cease the search or the search will become defeating and frustrating.

3. If you found someone to support you, the demands on you for the support would keep you from doing what you want to do - there would be little or no freedom there.

4. At this stage of your development no job will give you the money you need for freedom and still enable you to learn and grow. Look around you at the people who have taken that way, and you'll see that they have neither the money nor the freedom.

5. A job that will be "awful" as a rule will not give you time to learn.

So there is what I think, as you requested. Let me try to summarize: education, formal education, as unpleasant and meaningless as it often is - I always hated it up through the years - is a means toward the freedom and the opportunity one must have. Without it the chances are great that you or anyone else will be defeated and eventually crushed. This does not mean that the college there is the best one for you, or that you might not wisely drop out for a while. It does mean that you are at a very crucial stage when you might make a very bad decision.

Practically, I would urge that if possible you finish your present quarter in as good shape as possible, and if you can, complete the year to give the experience a real chance. That would enable you to continue your education sometime later when you decided to do so. Your scholarships are very important - try not to lose them.

Debbie, this is a long letter and it may sound "preachy." Try your best not to take what I have said in the wrong way. I am pretty confident I am right, but at the same time I know how strong your feeling is and as I said I understand it. You are

needed in the world, but you can do what is needed only if you
are prepared. Have a fine Th.S. holiday.
  Your friend, Earl V. Pullias

126.
Nov. 28, 1972
Dear Dr. Pullias,

My thoughts seem to have produced a quite positively negative
reaction from you! I wrote that letter with a certain amount of humor
which you seemed not to catch. Please do not take it too seriously. It
is what I think, but it's a little radical and unpractical for me to act fully
on. Perhaps you are not aware of my commen sense which takes care
of me and doesn't let me wander.

Despite this I do disagree with many of your ideas concerning
higher education but then, I'll not change you as you cannot change my
views. And I don't even want to persuade you to change.

My roommate with whom I shared some of your thoughts asks
you very seriously what you mean by saying that formal education
provides the background to do things well in your interests.

My roommate is having problems again with her personal life.
There's this guy who's married and he keeps pestering her. Debbie is
friends with him, likes him and everything but feels he's beginning to be
too demanding, wanting to be with her all the time. She doesn't know
how to tell him to bug off.

I most certainly will be continuing all through this year here. I
never thought I wouldn't. My classes for next quarter are Math
(beginning), Drawing, and Developmental Psych. I wanted to take a
natural science class but it was full.

It seems as if I could do more of what I want if I didn't go to
college full-time. I'd like to do something with children during the day
and take maybe 2 classes at night. What's the hurry, anyway, to
graduate? I've got all my life and after that I'll just die. On this basis, I
can realize that I might as well live the happiest and the most
compatible way I can with myself. I do not have to force anything on
myself unless I think I want to because I will be dieing anyway. You
may think its selfish to think that way but its not. Its not, because in
order to be happy, I personally, enjoy loving people-children and so to

be happy I will try to make them happy. But if I don't make someone happy that's all right because we're both dieing some day anyway. And since everyone dies I can very easily accept the idea of death as a part of life.

Now, what do you think?

Your friend, Debbie.

P.S. I got a letter from James. May be seeing him.

P.P.S. My gosh! I weighed myself today, found I had gained <u>12</u> pounds since beginning of school. I weigh 112 pounds

127.

Hemet

Saturday Dec. 16, 1972

Dear Dr. Pullias,

I have been home for a week spending most of my time in this house alone reading or writing or thinking. I have my music playing; I have the windows to look out at the shifting green plants; I have my mind clear and open for thoughts to come as they wish. And I have been thinking and changing my mind about some things.

About two days ago I found a book by Hugh Pratner called <u>Notes to Myself</u>. I didn't read it all, just the first subject he speaks of: living for the present. I have been so silly, making out plans for all of my future, trying to find a way to get to the future the quickest way, and saving things for future use. Since last summer all I have done is think about the future. Perhaps this is why I have not been happy with every day like I always used to be. Now I think I will change myself back to my happier self - where I am glad <u>one</u> day is here for my benefit.

I don't know if I wrote you that James and I are corresponding once more. We write medium to long letters discribing things we like such as snow, wild places, San Diego, Victorian houses, forests, etc. I did not know that a boy could be so sensitive. Or rather I didn't know a boy could be so sensitive and not be scared to show it. I like him.

What a lot of thinking I have thought this week! I thought about my shyness and I thought perhaps it is not all shyness but a slowness to open up due to mistrust, lack of interest to make friends, and the feeling that no one will be interested in what I say. I think with grown-ups and children I have a bit of true shyness but at least I'm open with them. With my peers, though, it's slowness and not shyness at all, I don't trust their concerns. I wonder why. I probably have an iferiority complex. Sometimes I think it is that, sometimes I think it is only that I feel no wish to make a lot of friends my age.

The writing address here is P.O. Box 653, Hemet, 92343. The house number is 26528 Soboba Street. When are you going to be at the cabin?

Merry Christmas, Your friend, Debbie.

P.S. Prieta in nearly bursting! 12 more days!

128.
Dec. 21, 1972
Thursday
Dear Dr. Pullias,

I feel like writing a lot to you tonight. I've just finished eating a bowl of ice cream so I'm shivery. This house is large and has many show places for my mother's antiques of which she is exceedingly proud. She says she is throroughly delighted with the house. I'm glad.

My vacation is being very pleasant and restful to me. I feel like singing because of all my love for the beautiful people, the children, the green plants surrounding the world, the humming sparkled weather. My whole life it seems is in me; everything I see or do moves within me the bursting that is me.

I suppose life is ever changing. Because I have had three very wonderful days I think it will continue so well. Life continues, its true, and that gives me comfort to remember that happy days come as often or more often than sad ones. Anyway! Let me tell you about my three consecutively gorgeous days. Someday maybe you can speak of one of your happy days. It's good to share, isn't it?

Looking back, I suppose it was four days because James came to visit on Monday. He stayed the afternoon and ate dinner with us. We went for a long walk down Soboba. Mostly he talked and he talks exceptionally well, mostly I laughed and I like to laugh. When we came back to the house it was dark and we drove to the store to get food. We took occasional detours to see the Christmas lights on houses and to look at the cottage he lived in when age four. After we ate back here he left. He said he would come again (he lives in Anza now) and of course he'd write.

I don't remember what I did Tuesday but Tuesday night I had a extremely comforting slightly sad dream. In it Mr. Hill, my old creative writing teacher came up to me and because I would be leaving high school forever he put his arm around me and pressed me against his side. I hugged him hard with my head against his chest. There was a tremendous feeling passing between us. He said, "Come see me each Christmas."

I have these dreams very rarely in which the feeling of comfort, security, something, some feeling which can not be reproduced in any part of real life, comes to me. And the day after such dreams is always wonderful in a sort of lonely hurting happy way. So Wednesday I felt the dream, thought of Mr. Hill and James and my roommate, and sat outside in the sun.

Then today at about noon I went over to check on Prieta (her foal comes soon!) and began to play with Reggie and Randy the kids there, making a dirt castle and digging a big hole. Company came and the company had a boy about two who was sent to play with us. I watched him and thought I would not mind having a two year old. He became excited about the donkeys and horse and wanted to ride. I said, "Go ask your mom." He danced away, very little, calling, "Mom! Mom! Mom!" I thought, "how could such a little fellow understand me." Anyway in the course of the afternoon I felt very responsible, holding him on the donkey, holding him in my arms while the others rode so that he would not get trompled. I thought, "yes, indeed, I'd not mind having a two-year-old." Of course, I'd not mind having Reggie and Randy, Stevey and Scotty, Misty, and Vincent either! Sigh.

My hand is very tired, whew. My dreams seem to have turned to informational for awhile. They have informed me of Christmas presents, names I'd forgotten, and answers to questions. One dream I had a few weeks ago after a letter you had written on getting involved in sex gave me my belief and aspirations (?) in this subject. I dreamed I was walking with a guy but we were simply friends making ourselves better friends by only continuing to be friends. I thought "it's a very slow pleasant, very very slow building up of friendship." And that's the way I feel it might should be. I think I might even be a bit wierd in the way of sexual relations. I thoroughly enjoy the feeling I get when around boys and men but the thought of kissing and intercourse kind of ruins my fun. I don't think I'm scared, its just that I want to be <u>friends</u>. Do you know what I mean? Do you think that's wierd?

I like James very much because, you know, tho' I have not

discussed it with him, I think he feels the same way! I believe its rarer for a boy to feel that way than a girl. What do you think?

Well, one more thing to write about then I'll be off to bed! I have been reading my text books for Developmental Psychology next quarter. Its quite fascinating, I'm half way through (halfway through a text book? Wow!) and I think I'll enjoy learning about children growing up. If you know of a book, I am especially interested in Behavior Modification and would like to learn more about it. I tried it once on Misty (without knowing what it was). You see, when I was living there one thing that irratated me most was her whining before going to bed. Whine, squeal, complain! One evening we went outside to see the ponies. I said, "Misty, I will give you 25 cents a week if you try very hard not to whine at bedtime. Just hop in those Pjs, brush your teeth, and wow, off to bed." I told her her whining wasn't bad it just hurt my ears. Anyway it worked. I don't think it hurt her, do you? Of course I only stayed there two weeks [months] after which Mrs. Graves decided I must leave. Maybe she found out and didn't like the idea, quien sabe?

Also, another idea, in Dr. Jacob's class I learned much about reinforcement, positive and negative. I read that the positive was much more effective in establishing behavior, true? I thought what if the world began rewarding good behavior instead of punishing bad behavior? What if on the news they told all good positive things? I think things would be better, don't you?

I must stop writing or I may become hysterical because of everything I am thinking! Too much to write on 500000000000000000 pieces of paper on both sides!

Your friend!

Debbie!

Friday - Another great day. I took Reggie and Randy out hiking. I sat on a hilltop and watched them climb a bigger hill and remembered that when I was their age I began exploring the hills with my friend Jeff.

Also I received my report card (I can hardly believe I still get them - I'm almost 19) and got a B in Art, a B- in Expository Writing, and an A in Intro. to Psychology. I was quite pleased.

Dear Dr. Pullias

1973

Living away from home [at college] with no one to depend on except myself most definitely appeals to me. I am so fond of this independent feeling that I even enjoy it on deepest darkest nights when I am really alone, and I enjoy it when I wander alone by Saturday along city streets in such a vast city. This great feeling has pervaded the whole year as a pleasing under-theme. Debbie

It was a special joy to me to see you yesterday. Almost a year had gone by I guess since I saw you, so I wanted to see what time and experience had done .... You looked good to me. Your legs were brown and firm, you arms likewise. I would guess you are in better health than you have been in a long time. Goodness! I hope I don't sound like I am appraising a horse or a cow! Maybe that wouldn't be so bad: our personalities live in and are expressed by our bodies. Dr. Pullias

Debbie Bumstead

129.
Los Angeles
Jan. 1, 1973
Backyard Study
Dear Debbie:

Thanks for your beautiful letter written from Hemet. It is indeed wonderful when a person has those fine days such as you had during your vacation: those are the times that give life meaning and joy. There are many things in your letter I would like to respond to, but will select a few, not necessarily the most important.

Congratulations on your achievement in the first quarter: that was a very good job particularly as you are getting onto things. I am glad you like the psychology since that is likely to be the basic foundation for your career with teaching children - may or may not be teaching. I'll keep an eye out for special materials that might be helpful.

Your friendship with James sounds wonderful. You are very wise, I believe, in your attitude toward kissing and intercourse: not weird at all. These intense physical activities do often times spoil the fun of genuine friendship. They are inclined to get out of hand and dominate the whole relation undermining the slow building sensitiveness and understanding so basic to the kind of friendship you treasure so greatly. This is not to say that sex is bad in itself, but that unaccompanied by a deep mutual respect and long-time commitment, as in marriage, it is destructive. You have a lot of common sense which I believe will guide you in those very complex areas. I am not sure I have helped much in what I have tried to say, but let me know if you ever feel I can help. I hope your roommate doesn't get dragged into something harmful with the married man - often such men simply try to use a girl and then leave her hurt.

Your dreams are very interesting. Isn't it pleasant to have a positive, pleasant dream that foreshadows good days - and contributes, I believe, to self understanding which is so important in life. In many senses, you will "see your teacher" each Christmas: he taught you much.

I am eager to hear about Prieta's colt - foal. Surely hope all went well.

Your interest in children is a great thing - a great inspiration for your study. There is so much to learn from your formal study, but we should always try to keep that formal learning balanced with good common or horse sense.

Yes, I have had beautiful days like the ones you describe. I'll tell you about some of them sometime. They are almost always related to friendship (a special kind of love), which rests upon mutual respect and common interest; often they come from close contact with nature, sometime from doing something reasonably well, especially helping someone.

How wonderful it is to be thinking so many millions times beyond what you can write: that is the greatest freedom of all - the freedom of the mind!

Good wishes for your second term. Sincerely, Earl V. Pullias

130.
Jan. 11, 1973
Dear Dr. Pullias,

Today was a good day because I found a tutoring job! Its at a school about a mile or so from here in a 5th grade classroom - two boys, Jody and Roger. I will go Monday and Thursday afternoons and even though it's a long hilly walk I think I'll enjoy it. The teacher seems nice enough. She wants me to take each boy for a half hour and give them 15 min each of Math and Reading. Along with this I hope she will let me do my favorite thing - taking a dictated story, from the kid, down on paper - for about 10 min.

When I was with the children I felt very happy; I miss them so much! I could watch them all day. The teachers I've worked with don't seem to understand me "What is this?" they ask, "A person who just wants to be with kids?" They think of me as a person who doesn't realize how rotten kids are, as a person not yet shown the bothersomeness of children.

Dear Dr. Pullias

Why is it, I wonder, that every teacher I've worked with talk to children either as a teacher giving information or in a warning voice? What happened to conversation and humaness and laughing?

Do you think I am dumb to think this, that children are pretty nifty people? Do you think I am in for a shock as I work with more and more children?

Also today my roommate and I were asked to join the tennis team. This would be fine if I could win matches but it seems in tennis when it comes to playing 3 hours I'm sort of a loser. Maybe this year will be different; I could try anyway.

Prieta has not foaled yet unless she has done so sometime in the last couple of days. I'm anxious to have it out and seen!

I'm so tired from tennis I can't think of what to write.

My roommate does not see her married friend anymore.

Your friend, Debbie.

131.

Dear Dr. Pullias,

Tell your friend with the book of poems I'd sure like to try illustrating. I've been practiseing and am probably best in pen & ink and for color I can add watercolor. My drawings are imaginary rather than realistic. I wouldn't be able to draw realistic children but rather pictures children themselves might enjoy.

I'd really like to get into illustrating children's books. Sometime, too, I'd like to write a children's story or two. I'll get down to that when I get down to it! Maybe some poems, too, who knows?

I'm glad the war is over! I'm glad! It will be different.

When James and I went to Lake Hemet we made up a very detailed lovely fairy-tale about the five-inch people living in tiny castles on the edge of the lake and in log houses in the trees. I enjoyed that and with much thought afterwards I figured out that in a wonderful inside way I believe such fantastic things as fairy-tales and fables and myths. Now I know why I've never been able to find symbolism and deep meaning in stories; I literally believe them! In an inside way. Its always been a problem for me in literature classes to find meaning. Interesting phenomenon...

Nothing yet of the colt!

I quit the tutoring because I was assigned to a thoroughly wicked old first grade teacher who gave me a sweet little kid who couldn't read. I was to work with this girl 20 min with the teacher constantly googling over my shoulder. I didn't like that a bit! And 20 min seemed not worth an hour of walking. So...

I will look for the book, Spearpoint at this library. I doubt if its here, the library is quite behind times. Worst of all they don't have children's books! But I've heard they have a fair amount out at Elliot, so next year may be happier reading-wise for me.

I sort of kind of tentatively decided to stay in USIU till I graduate. And if I do transfer I think I'll stay in San Diego; go to UCSD perhaps. I like San Diego very much and might even like to buy a house some day and live here. Like forever? Well... I'd like to visit in Washington state again someday when I have a car and a friend to go with. That's about all the ambitions I have traveling in my life.

I liked your letter from the Far Winds very much.

Your friend, Debbie

132.
February 10, 1973 Sunday
Dear Dr. Pullias,

I feel like typing, OK? I haven't typed since last quarters English papers and this quarter I won't have any term papers. In my Develop. Psych. Class I have to give an oral report on curriculum in the Headstart program. I've found two articles in two magazines called Elementary English and Instructor. This library has these magazines in huge bound volumes and other magazines, too, in a special floor of the library. I've never explored this floor's content yet and it excites me to know that I will soon unearth many bookly treasures. I plan to go there this afternoon.

Thinking about what you wrote about my experiences with

Dear Dr. Pullias

children being not in the best conditions I will say this, when I remember things I always tend to remember pleasant events or feelings better than bad things, therefore I remember most the goodness of the children themselves and not the conditions under which I knew them. I pretty sure I will not ever be discouraged from my love.

Prieta's foal was born on the 27th of January and he is beautiful! You must see him while he's still little. He has a star like Prieta and two white socks on his hind legs. Otherwise he is a lovely unique gray frosted through with white hairs, darker on the back and head and gradually the gray is frosted more profusely down the legs and under, the tummy being a very pale gray. So furry!

My mother called me Saturday evening with the news and wanted me to come for Sunday to see him so I agreed. My roommate was gone home for the weekend herself so I was quite alone for the night with no one to talk about the excitement with. I went to sleep and had two nightmares, one with a gored kitten (in the basement) and one in which my mother was going to be killed. The latter dream scared me most but the former worried me exceedingly. I was afraid that the colt would die and I vowed that if he did within a year after his birth I would not again for a very very long time breed any of my animals. I even thought that I should not have any child myself for fear he would die.

The next morning waiting for my mom I became nervous, shaking. But when we got home and I saw him I was happy and sure that he would live and be a wonderful little fellow. Prieta was quite protective, biting and kicking at the other animals, becoming especially irate with the pigs. But she let me pet him all I wanted, in fact she acted proud when people were around like she was showing off her son, which she had reason to! Being only a day old, the colt seemed unaware of anything; he didn't even follow his mother, rather she trailed him and walked circles around him protecting. He was so quiet. And when he loped his gait looked so soft and floating that I wanted to burst. I couldn't get over the fact that here was the being that had spent a year inside my horse, growing. How is it possible that two individuals out of only themselves can bring to life a new individual? Life, a living being.

Last Friday was my roommate's birthday, she is 19. In the morning I sang Happy birthday to her and the rest of the morning every time I saw her I said, "Oh, Debbie. Happy Birthday." In the afternoon the

Debbie Bumstead

tennis team had a match at Palomar; we lost but that night Debbie told me what she had learned this nineteenth birthday. She said that during the game every time she went to hit she thought about Love and that there was no real competition in life, this was not two against two but four working together and it helped her to play better. I can't relly write what she said correctly. Later that night she asked me some questions about my philosophy and we discussed as I haven't for such a long time. And I told her things which I have never before voiced -- my life and my being. Though she had a hard time understanding because of the strength of her own beleifs, I think she knows me very well. I would write what I spoke of but strangely this is something I can speak of better than write. Why? I don't know.

My classes this quarter are going along fine, I think I may actually be enjoying them. They take up little of my time so I am thinking much and reading. I rather miss physical activities. I have tennis but I mean things like going places and seeing new things. My mother said I could have the car next year; she wants to get another one.

Hope everything goes well with you. It is stormy today here, wow!
Your friend, Debbie.

Debbie S. &
Debbie B.

133.
Feb. 17, 1973Sat. Morning
(I liked your typing)
Dear Debbie:

I wanted to write immediately to express my joy with you at the birth of Prieta's colt. I liked your picture in words of this new life and of Prieta's deep care. I hope I can see the colt before too long. Does it have a name yet? Names are fascinating and I suppose both reflect and influence what things are and become. In many cultures proper names have specific meaning.

It is good that your work this term does not create strain: thus you have a time to learn and grow perhaps in the deepest sense. I am glad you could talk so freely and deeply with your room mate. These relationships are, I believe, one of the most important things about college - and college is a great experience. Don't let these "easy" periods cause you to cease your development of good work habits: they help us to use freedom creatively.

By the time this arrives you will have had your 19th birthday - I guess that will be tomorrow. I hope it will be one of your good days. Beautiful, beautiful spring comes. Listen to it - I am really speaking to myself. It is clear and bright here today.

Your friend, Earl V. Pullias

Debbie Bumstead

134.
March 12, 1973 Monday
Dear Dr. Pullias,

Finally I am writing a letter! Trouble is I don't have much to write. Well, maybe I do. First of all my classes, right? We have only a week left to finish everything. In Developmental Psych. I think I've learned quite a bit, at least I've started to see the whole picture of growth and learning. I wish they had more classes here in development, but perhaps I can learn much on my own. My Statistics class is all mathematical mechanics which I enjoy solely for its wonder exactness. I like math when I'm learning it but after a few weeks all has slipped out of my mind again. In Drawing I've progressed somewhat further in my ability to see and potray forms and values. I think I've done my very best in this class so it makes me feel helpless when the teacher says, "You're doing good B work." But, oh well, I know I worked my hardest. And in the tennis team I've learned and enjoyed a lot. The lady coach is so very nice and we get to go out and eat after each match. We play all the different colleges in S.D. so I get to see what they're like.

Next quarter my classes will be as follows: Modern Art, which is a history course, Intro. To Philosophy, Children's Literature, and Tennis Team.

Now, life in the dormitory, OK? My roommate and I are the only two left living together still in this wing. The other girls have moved into single rooms. I don't know what that says about Debbie and me. I guess we both are very agreeable tolerant persons and can live easily with each other. I like everybody on our floor, but then I like most everyone in the world. But Ruth who lives singly down the hall three doors has something against me. She is friends with Debbie & Pam, my other very good pal. I think she feels competition with me or something, I don't know. It hurts me. One evening she was acting especially obnoxious and I started to cry. I went to bed and sobbed. Debbie asked me what was wrong and I told her, so she knows. I don't know what to do about this. Ruth and I are friendly, especially when we are alone but when Debbie or Pam are around she ignores me. It hurts because I don't mean to make her feel competitive. How can I act toward her so that she can like me? I'm such a child...

What next? How about James? OK. We have been writing back and forth and decided we'd live together in an apartment here in San Diego for the summer. Oh! Not really! I was just daydreaming! Sorry if I shook you up! Well, that's enough about dear James. I like him.

Now for thoughts, probably the most important, right? I don't remember if I wrote this to you or not: I am beginning to really believe I can get what I want. If I say to myself, "I want to have a small private classroom in four years." I know that there is absolutely no way that I won't get it if I really want it. If I trully want this I will work for it (though, work is definitely the wrong word, rather I am in the process of getting my wish since I said in four years). I believe that I can get what I want and no matter how hard I test this statement I still believe it. I walk along a curb and say to myself, "I want to stay balanced on the curb and therefore I will." and I do except when I realize that I don't really want to anymore, then I either jump or fall off. Once right after I started believing this I said, "I want to win my next tennis match therefore I will." (And I'd never won a match before even on the Tennis Team in Hemet) and I did win it. And I think that if I don't succeed then I really didn't want to accomplish the goal. Someday I might think I really want something and not get it.

Also this might work the other way, if I don't want something I can fight it off. I did this when the London Flu struck Chi Hall. Everyone on our floor had it except my roommate (because she is a Christian Scientist, whatever difference that makes) and me. I said, "Oh, man, I don't want that." and I denyed any thoughts that I might have it.

One thing this belief will not work on is people. If I said, "I want Ruth to like me, so she will." it wouldn't work. People can't be like that.

What do you think?

MOST affectionately, Debbie

P.S. from the 16th to the 26th I'll be home - P.O. Box 653, Hemet

135.
March 18, 1973
At home

Debbie Bumstead

Dear Debbie:

Your letter was here when I returned from seven days back East - about half time in Chicago and about half in Tenn. It was a hard trip, but interesting and often pleasant. I saw many students, who had studied with me, in Chicago; in Tenn. I spent the time with my mother who is 93, but very active and thoughtful - a strange thing, I guess.

It was good to get your letter. I had been wondering how things were going. Soon you will need to be planning for next year. What are you thinking now? I am afraid not much can be done about jealousy - it can be a very ugly thing, but usually passes. I hope you and your room mate can develop a good friendship - one that may last a long time. The writing with James would seem to be good. Your statement about living with him this summer didn't frighten me much. I have great confidence in your common sense. Sometime I'll write about that kind of an arrangement, as I see it. Beauty is fragile and easily destroyed.

I'm delighted with your tennis - a fine experience for you. I am sure it is beautiful there in the country. You will write me about Prieta and the colt - what is his name? I'll also write about the power of wishing - interesting.

I'm a little tired. Your friend, Earl V. Pullias

136.
Wednesday
Dear Dr. Pullias,

Did I write that I got a volunteer job at the elementary school? Well, I did, and this school is only one block away. I go everyday from 9:30 to 10:30. The class is a combined kindergarten-first grade with such quiet happily busy little kids that I like most just to sit and watch them all. But the teacher gives me children individually to read word flashcards. And when they talk they whisper and they fidget and when they smile they look at me open-mouthed at my laugh. I'm afraid to speak loudly for fear they'd be frightened. I want to play and swing them about and tickle them but this is not allowed. Perhaps as I know them better I can talk and be free. I like them, and especially I like to watch one little girl with pigtails and a tomboy face named Jessica.

My roommate worked up to be third in the tennis team line up so she and the coach and 1 or 2 girls are going to the Ohai tournament. I wish I could go just to watch. She's leaving today and coming back Saturday.

I like to rally in tennis, not play games, I just like hitting it back and forth. I feel the joy of my body working in a coordinated way and I hear the wonderful pop of the ball against raquet and its like there's nothing in the world more important than working myself this way. That's how I feel about horseback riding, too, when I am working Prieta to her fullest.

I believe my body is me, unlike my roommate who believes her body is an illusion, only her mind exists. And even though I may believe everything I sense is me, too, still my body is my very wonderful being as well as what I think.

You get into a rut of sorts when it comes to writing letters to specific people. I write about certain things to you and other things to another person and so on. I don't break out of the routine, though I tire of it.

And the only true writing I write is that when I write with no thought of the person who might read it. But I don't mind when someone does read these private writings unless it is the person I've written on, because no matter how many people know of my private feelings I still have the ultimate privacy - my mind inside.

Debbie.

137.
March 29, 1973
Dear Dr. Pullias,

It seems as if people around me ignore me in relation to my philosophy. And I must write that I do not look upon them and say they are at fault, rather it is me, my incapabilities at getting a responce from them that corresponds with my own view of myself. When I look at myself I understand that I am indeed sincere and loving in my thoughts and relations with people but somehow they do not see this. Something about me (and yes, perhaps it could be them not looking at me in the right way) must say to people that I'm out to get them, that

Debbie Bumstead

I'm hostile, and definitely quite dumb. Perhaps I am not reading them correctly but in fact there is some discrepancy between how I feel I am and how I am treated.

I guess I have a majority of relatively simple classes (2) for this quarter - one is Math 107 which is a general requirement and Children's Literature in which the teacher (Dr. Baker - quite sensitive and "with it") is holding a virtual open classroom. Then I have philosophy with Dr. Martin who speaks extremely slowly, repeating the statement in several different ways so that I can get notes down easily. I think it will be an easy quarter, but that is good, for at this time I am so tired of school I could scream.

Last quarter, if you're interested in grades, I received a B in Statistics, an A in Develop. Psychology, and a B+ in Art. Grades really get me down, though I'm sure I don't worry about them so much as others do. I don't worry about what grades are doing to me. I worry what they are doing to children and students. I think grades are very stupid. I don't believe anyone needs to be evaluated, no one should be bribed into learning something just for a grade, and no one should work in a panic at his classwork in fear of a bad grade. Why do we have this anyway? If its proven that grade point averages do not correlate with success in life why frighten, bribe, and stunt us with a evaluation that says you are as good as this and that's not as good as her, you're wishy washy because you got a C? It all makes me very angry and ill.

One day next week I think I'll go talk to the education major lady and ask some questions. I want to get in the program that lets you teach after four years instead of five and I'd like to see if there could be directed teaching in some liberal private or public school with open classrooms or something.

I went up into the hills over vacation. Beautiful and green, wow! I've never seen it so wonderful.

The colt is a bit wild though curious enough about us humans to nibble at my hand. His name is Warner's Rock - Rocky for short.

Your friendly Debbie.

138.
May 1, 1973 Tuesday
Dear Dr. Pullias,

Dear Dr. Pullias

I will herein list for you the important aspects of this year. They aren't listed in order of importance because they are all the most important differently. See? 1. Living away from home with no one to depend on except myself most definitely appeals to me. I am so fond of this independent feeling that I even enjoy it on deepest darkest nights when I am really alone, and I enjoy it when I wander alone by Saturday along city streets in such a vast city. This great feeling has pervaded the whole year as a pleasing under-theme.

2. The canyon, my canyon, to the left of the dorm, is very important. All year, at times, I go to squat under trees and watch birds and leaves, just to be.

3. I suppose the most significant (or not significant but the motif that took up most of my thoughts) theme was my rather passionate love for my roommate. If you can understand, not a sexual love, but a childlike worshiping one then you will see how I have felt and still feel. How anyone can be so intelligent and perfect as her, I just don't know, but I don't get silly over the fact because (we come to it again!) of my deadly deadly commen sense head who will never let me go wacky no matter how hard I try. Ha ah. I love Debbie now, but when now changes to the next now, I will dismiss the past; it will be a very good memory.

4. The library has been important to me this year though it is not so good a library. I found much of what I wanted.

Would you believe that is all? $3400 for the above. I would say it was worth it because we didn't have to pay.

And next year... and the summer... During the summer I want to ride Prieta, read children's books, go to the show of an evening, write late at night up in my new bedroom. I want to ride my bike and get brown and hot, I'd like to see my brothers and James, I'd like to play with my little cousins.

Next year I suppose I will get my general requirements out of the way. What a drag. Classes are so dumb for me. I'm learning, sure, but nothing of much use to me, and what is of use to me I would learn anyway. I am speaking of required classes and the fact that one is required to take at least 3 and so on. CRAZY!

Saturday I went around downtown with James. Interesting outing.

Sincerely, Debbie.

Debbie Bumstead

139.

Wed. May 16, 1973

Dear Dr. Pullias,

I was walking along the sidewalk by the cafeteria and saw Dr. Box up above. When I looked at him to say Hi he looked down, so before he glanced at me again I dropped my head to study the sidewalk. I smiled at both of our awkwardness and shuffled on.

Yes, today I am definitely not walking, I'm shuffling. The jeans I am wearing (and have worn for the last two weeks - how little clothes matter to me!) are limp and smell deliciously of the rosemary bush I always brush by on the way to class. My tennis shoes feel like soft moccasins, my hands in coat pockets, yes, today I'm shuffling.

****

All I really want is a small house, two or three small children, and a small job. All I really want is a simple loving life. As I grow older more and more I become childish I seem. I delight and laugh at the very simplest of things so that people gaze at me in stupification. Do you think I ought to try and grow up? I don't think I ought; I'm glad to be me!

I'd like to be a gardner. I 'd like to be a dog-trainer. I'd like to be an interior decorator. I really don't enjoy teaching, instead I like to talk with children and go places and take them out to eat and tell and listen to stories and wrestle and discuss. No, I'm afraid I don't place enough importance on math, reading, history, etc. for me to be a teacher and enjoy it. What to do?

We've been figuring out our classes for next year. All classes are scheduled so that we receive Tuesdays and Fridays completely free. Interesting. I wonder how it will work out. I'm taking mainly English, Psychology, and Science classes with one art class last quarter and one sociology class first quarter. Mrs. McKay, our tennis coach, wants me to take Field Hockey next fall. I suppose I will, but Field Hockey? Not the funnest sport in the world. I'll get to go out to eat though! And I really really like Mrs. McKay. A quiet fondness exists between us, the kind of feeling one needn't dwell on, just smile with.

So now that I've told you all about me why don't you tell me something about you? Are you shuffling today or walking, or wandering, sauntering, pacing or simply being motionless, standing in the middle of the air looking at the sky? And are you what you wanted to be when age 19? And have you figured out your classes for next year and do you know someone whom you are quietly fond of and the feeling is mutual?

Well, there's me. Maybe?

Affectionately, Debbie doo da.

P.S. Now a bit of sad news from a couple of weeks ago. Rocky, Prieta's colt, had to be killed because of a paralyzing spinal injury. Hmmm.

140.

May 29, 1973 - Tuesday

Dear Dr. Pullias,

Your trip sounds like it was fun (or do you use the word fun when you're older? I hope so). Wow, you just pick up and go all over the country! Have you ever been to Japan, Scotland, Germany, Spain or Africa? I like these countrys but I also like Russia, India, Arabia, Ireland, Brazil, and the Antartic. Have you ever been to any of these places? In fact I like almost all contries except France and Mexico; well, I like them, but they are not especially interesting to me. I wonder what makes our interests and disinterests in such far-fetched subjects as what countries one likes?

I don't think I've changed much since you last saw me, I <u>feel</u> taller but I haven't physically grown any and I <u>feel</u> lighter when in fact I've gained five pounds. I don't know if I look healthier but I am; I'm rarely troubled with my intestinal sickness anymore, in fact this quarter I haven't felt it at all, not once! What do you say to that?

Feeling and thought wise, well, these last two quarter's have been rather a trouble, a problem I can't seem to solve and can't ask someone else to solve for me. The matter will end, anyway, come June 9 when school is out. Someday you must read my journal. Anyway! Its been a wonderful lovely year!

Tonight was the Women's Intercolliegte Sports Banquet. I won the Sportsmanship Award in tennis. I think I told you before how much I like our tennis coach Mrs. McKay. Yes, I like her! For Mother's Day I painted her a card to be from my roommate and me.

Well, school's over June 9 and I guess that's all I have to write. Oh, except about the dream I had last night. In it I saw two children milling about in a driveway and something unseen was slaughtering their

---

bodies with an invisible knife. One girl held the other child's dismembered arm or foot. Blood (so realistically liquid and red) spurted around. Then I was the girl lying in my bed with my left leg sloshy with bloody cuts all along it and also under my foot. I wanted to clean off the blood because it was dry so I wiped it off on the edge of my sheet. And it hurt so much because the cuts were open, oh it pains me even now. And when my whole leg was clean it was white and bloated. Then I woke up and I felt so deathly still, I couldn't get up enough courage to move for five minutes (my roommate was gone for the weekend). My left leg was out of the covers and was cold and aching.

In my dream when I looked at my bloated leg I thought it might be completely dead. This makes me think of the girl here whom I like who had one of her legs amputated. She has a false leg.

What a note to end on! Your friendly Debbie.

141.
Hemet Soboba House
July 3, 1973 Tuesday
Dear Dr. Pullias

I went outside and it was oh, so hot, hot, hot. I could hardly beleive the lawn, plants, and trees were still green in such heat. It seems they ought to turn orange or dusty tan or bright yellow just to balance artistically with the warmth, and then turn green again at night.

Flys, hordes of them, hidden under the leaves of the undergrowth, buzzed around when I walked through and landed again while I sat on the dirt next to the evergreen shrubs. I sucked on some sickly-warm cherries and glimpsed movement a few feet away. It was a large beetle fumbling and thrashing amoung dirt clods. I think it was dying. It had a red-orange back, long black legs which were thick at the ends as if it were wearing boots, and fantastically long, flourescent, red and black feelers. Ooo, it gave me the creeps so that I jumped when I felt tickling on my thigh. This was a tiny beetle with yellow and black stripes and when I studied the ground closer I saw that thousands of these small beetles were dead and on their backs with tiny black legs neatly tucked around their tummies. I supposed that these were the insects that had been plaguing our elm tree when we had it sprayed with insecticide. Probably the large beetle was dying of the poison, too.

Dear Dr. Pullias

I came back in then because I felt so creepy - like I had grasshopper juice all over my hands - yick! And decided to write you. Ha ha. Nothing meant by that. When I was seven my friends and I caught huge green grasshoppers by the tens, twentys, thirtys and pulled their back legs off and had a grass hopper circuses. Tightrope walking, swinging trapeze, freak show, etc. What fun.

I received your letter and think you've made yourself quite clear. I don't know what to write back except that it seems true that the further one goes in learning the happier one becomes in life. And I think I know how you feel about potential; there is an exceedingly strong emotion I feel with everyone I become aqainted with because I see such possibility, so much there and so lovely. And I think, if only, if only that person will continue, keep going, keep going! I feel this with everyone I meet, maybe even just see, but it is especially strong with certain individuals. Stevie, a second cousin, who is about nine, wow, and Misty, and my former-roommate, Debbie, and my brothers. But especially Stevie.

Hey!

My mother is traveling toward Reno to stay for a week during which I have invited Debbie to come up and visit, oh boy, here. I hope she can, yes its true, I do.

Pow!

Bye, bye.

From Debbie

142.
July 30, 1073
Dear Dr. Pullias,

I can hear the crickets out in the night and I can hear cars going by and the record I'm playing. Children's songs are sung in mellow tones; I like to sing along softly. My mother sneezes downstairs and Joe reads the TV guide. Sound travels upwards. With the door closed the room seems very high, perhaps at the top of a tower or maybe floating in space.

Last night I dreamed of a college friend, Heather. In the dream I saw her in a classroom at the old high school and I was sitting under an olive tree outside. I waved to her. I felt very friendly toward her and then a group of others were teasing me in fun and she in fun, too, said, "Stop making fun of Little Debbie!" We all laughed. Then I woke.

Debbie Bumstead

I would like to write more about Heather because I have been thinking of her all the day. But what to write? I like her. And I can love people who do not especially love me without getting hurt as long as I don't live with them. Yes, I guess that about sums it up. I know that Heather, and others I know, like me, even like me very much, but me, I tend to become absolutely devouted to individuals, sacrificing all of my time and thoughts to them and if I live with them then I only think of them and it rather hurts to realize they don't especially think of me. If I don't live with them its wonderful to daydream and then I can go on with my life. I see. Yes, that does about sum it up.

Dr. Pullias, I really would like you to read my journal from last year. Mr. Hill, who read it as something to be published, said it was very "readable" so you won't become bored. When you come down in August stop by and get it.

Later in the afternoon I took a nap and had this dream. I was at the Olds' place leading Prieta out of the corral. Reggie was beside me; we were to ride together so somehow Prieta doubled herself and I had two black horses. Then Reggie walked alone around the old chicken pen to look into the corral. I climbed through a hole in some chicken wire into the paddock which now held all of a medium sized lake; I was on the banks looking down into clear water pebbled with large smooth stones on the floor. A couple of little boys were playing along the edge and I said, "Don't fall in!" There were hills surrounding the lake and strange wooden and wire constructions on the slopes. They were fancy corrals. I wondered if they would hold a horse and then I saw Mr. Anderson's face (the fellow from whom we had bought a horse) and it frightened me because he acted as I weren't a person at all, just some thing.

I like to write down dreams because they sound like fairy-tale adventures when you read them over.

I came downstairs because my mother went to bed and I could be alone in a room where the dark wood furniture and glass antiques and flowered chairs and sofa have personalities in the dimness. It's something I've known ever since I was six, that everything is ALIVE when the light is dim and dark outside; the buffet stares at me with drawer pull eyes, its expression frozen in a rather frightened gasping face, the tiny liquor set inside the shelf standing staunchily, the Vaseline glass candlesticks keep their hands curving along their skirts. Above a lady who knew Vincent Van Gogh holds her hands and looks calmly down at me. Oh! I feel as if everything is waiting for me to leave so that they may talk amoung themselves and move about. Yes, I know they do because I have caught them at it several times in my life. The first time happened when I was six and slept oppisite a bookcase. One night the bookcase thought I was asleep and all the book characters, goblims, leprechauns, fairies, came out and danced on the shelves. I vividly remember watching them a very long time.

It's great fun to catch them. Wake up late at night with the moonlight streaming in and look! The china animals are playing on their shelves. Or pretend to be working very hard under one lamp as if nothing at all could tear you away and then suddenly look, the horses in the painting are cavorting in the real green pastures, the trees are moving in the breeze. And soon they will all get used to you and let you just sit with a bed lamp on and watch quietly their secret life. Do you beleive me? It's quite true, my dear, and if you do beleive they will like you, all the seemingly inanimate things of life… of life.

I'm staying up quite late tonight; I thought I'd have a glass of milk and some ginger snaps and write you a very long letter because you are all alone. I wish also for a small devoted slave to do all the domestic work and play the piano and sing in a sweet childish voice funny songs.

I am watching a biography on TV of Eleanor Roosevelt and it is quite interesting. Very, in fact. I don't know anything about her and so far (the movie is up her debutant period) her life seems unfortunate. Then she married and had babies and then when the war started she began to act on her conscience and help better things. Hmm..now we are beginning to really get into a good story. Now she is fighting to have Franklin go on, even though he is crippled and she has won and they continue and etc. You probably know.

Sometimes I think of becoming great and famous, helping people, making good or writing excellent poetry and novels or starting something new in painting, you know, somehow reaching many people and helping them and becoming known nation-wide or world-wide. At times I feel as if it is a certainty that I will indeed "do something." But if I do I know that feeling was not a prediction but rather an ambition that I worked at to accomplish. And if I don't then I know the feeling was an ambition I didn't work at. I don't really mean "work" but anyway. Then again… sometimes I beleive in pre-determination and sometimes in determination but rarely in free will. No, maybe it is free will I beleive in. Oh, well, one thing's for sure, I'm open-minded.

Practically gullible.

If I was famous I wonder if they would depict my childhood and teen years correctly in the movies. Just think, you would be in the movie, too.

Dr. Pullias! I must be off to sleepy-time land!

Love to you, Debbie.

143.

August 9, 1973

Dear Dr. Pullias,

Actually I've accomplished much today though I had felt I was not. In the evening if I list up in my mind what good things happened then tomorrow seems a worthwhile day to live because more good is sure to come. During the day I feel I am not going any further than I am (but that is certainly not a bad feeling) yet the next day I feel further along in every way. That's hard to understand.

Anyway, let's tell about today, OK? In the morning I drove to the library and saw the fellow who works there in the parking lot taking the books out of the book drop. He is in my high school graduating class and we like each other secretly. We smile or take a sidewise glance (how funny!) or say "Hello" between the bookcases (I go to the library often but, believe me, it's just for the books!). Yes, what a fine figure of a guy, clean, intelligent, thoughtful, too bad his name is Bob, it just doesn't fit. Ah, well…

Silly, huh?

Then I went to Tim's house which is "The Workshop." Tim is making a wild wooden chair, Joe a walnut table top with carving, me, a set of children's blocks. I am sanding the blocks first, very slowly because the machine tires my wrist, then I'll stain and varnish them. I think I'll have different shapes and colors in a set of perhaps 25, I'm not sure yet. Today I sanded four square blocks. Joe and Tim are producing some lovely peices of furniture, my yes! They smoke a lot of pot and drink a black homemade liquor and that seems a little wierd to me but it's OK for them, I suppose. Personally I feel if a person is completely aware of where he is, what he is doing that moment and what for, etc. then that person lives his own life and will do what is best. I suppose the one thing you can't do is drift, you can take it easy,

Dear Dr. Pullias

you can be lazy, but you just can't drift. That's hard to understand, too.

And! After that I came home, laid around for awhile, than suddenly jumped up and made two mobiles - one with seven pale colored ribbon fish (oh, I love to see them wander in circles on their threads) and another with eight shiny shells clanking together faintly. I think I will hang them up in my room at college.

Well, my dear....

I will remember next time I am at the library (soon!) to look for the book you spoke of; it sounds fascinating. I'll go tomorrow, in fact, because I have to go to town anyway for a dentist appointment.

I had an awful dream last night because of a movie I saw before. The dream took place in a house on Buena Vista where as kids we played around. It was uninhabited. Something happened to us inside the house (we were kids again) concerning monkeys (the movie had monkeys in it) and we ran outside. I saw a hunched man creeping round the neighboring house with a knife. I was quite frightened; then the man came and there was a letter from you. It was typed. People were reading over my shoulder and the typed words invited me to stay at your house.. It was dark. I was relieved to know I would be in your safe place away from this darkness. I woke up rather frightened, went back to sleep and dreamt something about the name Jonathan L. Seagull.

Sometimes I don't understand things. I don't know, like evil things. Something is missing from my understanding. I am not even sure evil or bad things are true, I mean are real. That is, if we are thinking things then what we think is what happens to us. But if we all think so that we communicate then I expect we have a communication or intelligence we draw our thinking from. And if there is that intelligence then by the very nature of the word it would not have evil in it and so we could not draw from it anything bad and since it is all we have to draw from there is no real evil ever. So what is what we call bad? I guess it would be false thinking something into the world.

I don't know how to write it. Have you ever felt, though, that bad things seem always to pass but good keeps on going? Have you ever felt, like when you're sad or you hear about a murderer, that the real you or the real person is good the bad is just on top and passes away?

Well, I think I'll have a bowl of cereal and go to bed.

Your friend, Debbie.

144.

Sunday

Dearest Dr. Pullias,

Did I ever tell you about my room in this house? I like it because it's upstairs. I come up, walk in and think of girl's novels where there are two sisters with private rooms upstairs with white curtains and pale blue walls. There's some difference though, I don't have curtains at all yet and the room needs to be finished, painting-wise. An individual room in a large building, that's a nice thing to have.

I feel that way at college, too, even though one shares the room with one other. It is so pleasing to think of everyone having their own room and no one is the same.

Though I am enjoying the summer I am also looking forward to going away in September. I hope my new roommate and I will be compatible. This year there are a few things I will try not to do. I'll try not to be scared of dreams because they aren't real, I know. I'll try very hard not to cry. Last year I cried about four nights in the whole year and I don't mind crying; it doesn't make me feel babyish or anything, its just that there is that other person in the room having to listen. It embarrasses me even now to think of Debbie listening to me blubber. I appreciated her help but I could have taken care of it quicker myself because then I wouldn't pity myself so much. And then I began to enjoy her comfort and that was absolutely horrid. So I must try to stop crying, even though that will be very hard for me, a natural crybaby.

Oh, well.

I don't know what to write.

Have you seen the movie, "Cabaret"? I enjoyed it quite a bunch. The years of Hitler fascinate me plus I enjoy excellent song and dance routines.

For some weird reason I am exceptionally interested in genius and/or fanatisism: Hitler, Jesus, Lawrence of Arabia, Goethe, Beethoven, Rasputin, etc. What interests you in history? What makes our interests? Do you know of any people I might like to read about?

Your friend, Debbie.

145.
Los Angeles
Aug 13, 1973
Backyard Study
Dear Debbie:

It was a special joy to me to see you yesterday. Almost a year had gone by I guess since I saw you, so I wanted to see what time and experience had done - so far as one can tell from what is to be seen - which I suppose is not very much. In fact, we know each other more deeply through writing than in any other way. Perhaps it always will be so. That is all right. I suppose it is very hard to be sincere in other contacts.

I liked your home there: that is what I saw. I don't know how the inside would be, but the yard, the grass, the trees, the barn, the cow lowing across the way spoke to my heart. You looked good to me. Your legs were brown and firm, you arms likewise. I would guess you are in better health than you have been in a long time. Goodness! I hope I don't sound like I am appraising a horse or a cow! Maybe that wouldn't be so bad: our personalities live in and are expressed by our bodies.

I have thought a lot about the problem of evil or bad. I am still baffled by it. I guess I believe that evil in some ways is a powerful positive force - by "positive" I mean that it is not simply an absence of something, but that as a force it is actually at work in the world against that which is good, beautiful and true. It is forever trying to pull or push people in ways that harm or destroy them. On the other side, and stronger, there is light and truth. Our task is to be on the good side.

Your friend, Earl V. Pullias

146.
August 19, 1973
Dear Dr. Pullias,

It's quite hot up here in my room even though the hour is late. Is the weather hot in L.A. and do you have a room upstairs? Heat travels upward as well as sound. Indeed.

A friend and I went to the fair Friday night to watch the rodeo. I

Debbie Bumstead

like the bucking horses most because after the cowboy is off they run wildly around the arena dodging the herders. They look so frightened. One bucking mare bucked very high and coming down landed wrong and broke a back leg. She tried and struggled to get up but couldn't and made us in the audience concerned and sad. They brought in a tractor to hall her off.

School starts for me the 16th of September, exactly four weeks from today. So soon! Because after this week there's only three left and after that only two and after that only one! Oh, dear! I will be driving down in the Datsun my brother sold me.

When does school start for you?

Did I tell you my first quarter classes? Well, I'll tell you again. A sociology class that I'm taking to please the general requirements, Abnormal Psychology and Creative Writing. Also I've been invited to play in the College Field Hockey Team. Sounds deadly dull, huh (Field Hockey, that is), but we get to eat out after games and I do enjoy running. It always surprizes me to think of myself as athletic concidering my other interests - reading, writing, painting - but I suppose I am quite active. Well-integrated, right? Hurrah!

Have you read my journal yet? When you do any comments on style, form, interest as well as content, problems, my roommate's personality (she asked me to relay your comment to her - she's interested) etc. would be interesting. But again, if you don't want to comment, that's fine, too. Yippee! Tee hee!

My brother Tim is getting married to a little girl named Amy. She's very pretty and shy. I expect she's intelligent but so very quiet I don't know. Anyway I like her.

Marriage all around! My friend [in Reno], Marie is getting married in November. She wants me to be her Maid of Honor (what in the world is that?) but I'm not so sure it will be possible. We'll see.

Your friend, Debbie.

147.
August 23, 1973
Dear Dr. Pullias,

Ah, a nice evening alone; my mother is off to play bingo and I

Dear Dr. Pullias

don't expect my brothers 'til late.

So what shall I do? Shall I tell you about yesterday evening? (my brothers just came in - oh, well.) Well, yesterday I went to give Reggie and Randall their riding lesson - first stage on the longe line, "Randy! Don't jiggle the reins so much because it makes the bit hurt her mouth." "Reggie, loosen the reins." - second stage free in the field across the streets, "Remember, no running." Actually they're pretty good riders and I think I'll let them run in the field tomorrow, "OK, hold her on a straight course with the reins and if she turns a little toward home turn her the other way and give her a kick. Stop her if she gets out of hand."

After the lesson I was giving them rides with me so we could lope freely. We saw Misty on her horse, a firey snorting three year old gelding, riding him bareback. She has that horse in tip top condition; he gallops thundering fast, wheels on turns, stops with a slide.

We put Prieta in her corral and walked, Reggie, Randy, their family friend, Pat (who is 11, Reggie is 11, Randy is 10, and Misty is 12 and I am 19!), and I, across the fields to Misty's house. I think she was pleased that we would all think of coming to see her so we laughed and talked on the porch. It was getting dark, though, so we thought we better head back. Misty asked her mom if she could walk with us and she said yes and off we ran, tumbling and pushing; the boys bragged, the girls discussed the future (Pat wants to be a teacher for the handicapped, Misty wants to be a jockey or a teacher) and I breathed in the dusty smell of yellow weeds and kicked at dirt clods. What fun it was...

Interesting that all four of them are adopted. Anyway it was dark when we got to the Olds so I offered to drive Misty home. On the way we saw her mother out hunting for her. Interesting.

I must go outside before it gets dark; I like this time of evening...

Your friendly Debbie.

P.S. In our tutoring sessions Reggie and Randy have discovered the excitement of making up your own stories. They dictate to me fantastic adventures. Its so exciting to see them excited!

148.

Debbie Bumstead

Los Angeles
Backyard Study
Aug 24, 1973
Dear Debbie: Your letter came. Thanks for it. I have finished Vol. II of your journals. There are many things I wish to say about them that might be of interest to you, and possibly a little helpful. I am not quite ready to write them yet: there are deep, deep things, I want to say. I will try to say them sincerely; whether wisely or not, I probably cannot know.

We too are caught up in the wedding business. We are invited to three to-morrow. I am not in the mood to go to them. There is so much to do, and one fears not a little pretense. But there seems to be a great need for these formal weddings. We should study and try to learn from them, I suppose. I am sure it does no good to fight them inside. Besides there are better things to do. For example, walking among and communing with natural things.

I feel the precious Aug. days going by. They have been good days in many ways for me - a much needed chance to step back and look at things, mentally, physically, and spiritually. My study here in the backyard is really just a shack, but it is dear to me. A front and back door open welcomes the breeze, and the sound of the wind in the trees is good for the heart. And yet today my heart is sad. It is good that you can cry.

Earl V. Pullias
P.S. My school starts Sept 15, registration the previous week. Your classes good - Abnormal was my specialty for a long time. I'm delighted at your participation in sports.

149.
Los Angeles
Backyard Study
Aug. 25, 1973
Dear Debbie:

I finished Vol. III of your journals last night. Reading them was a good experience for me; I believe writing them was an extremely valuable thing for you to do. Your first year in college was a period of growth in many areas two of which interest me deeply: 1) in self-understanding which is almost of incomparable value, and 2) in observation and writing skill. Your Journal contributed greatly to both of these.

The first (self-understanding) is so important because many, perhaps most, of the things we do that hurt ourselves and others happens because we are acting out motives we do not understand. Equally significant, self-understanding helps greatly in our progress in realizing our potential. Writing helps perhaps more than anything else our attempt to understand ourselves, other people, and reality, in general. Also, it is a special talent for you which, as it is fully developed, will enable you to render the services you are so capable of doing.

Now to my reactions to the Journals, you will let me make this reaction in my own way? And you will just let your mind flow with mine and perhaps forget the years and other distances that lie between us. I shall not criticize your writing. Others can do that if they wish. There is a personal word I wish to say. Since you were a very small child I have been deeply interested in you, and I believe in the most beautiful sense of which you speak in your Journal, have loved you very much. But probably I have not communicated that feeling very well. I did not really know how, except perhaps some in these letters, to surmount that thick and high wall of shyness and perhaps other feelings and fears that separate people. I hope the deep, deep kindness I have felt has in some measure come across. Perhaps I have been too interested in what I believe is your potential and a great desire that it not go unrealized. I cannot help that. I would like you and respect you and love you if you were just a drifting worthless "bum" to yourself and to others - but the dreadful waste would be terribly sad to me.

Now to the Journals. (1) you write well and that ability develops steadily. (2) you have a fine tendency to see detail in all you observe. Continue to see and express that detail - just let yourself see and express what you see and feel. (3) Of course, you will use your judgment about keeping the Journal, but whatever you decide, <u>write</u>, for the very act of writing is a great learning experience. (4) One of your greatest strengths is

sincerity or honesty or authenticity in your writing and living. (5) Your study in love during the past school year was very important for you, and I suspect for your friend D.... Sincerely, Earl V. Pullias

150.
August 27, 1973
Dear Dr. Pullias,

James was going to hitchhike down here today to bring us a new puppy and do some errands in Hemet. He hasn't arrived here yet but I hope he does soon because he doesn't like to hitchhike at night. I expect the puppy is causing him problems getting a ride.

Did you know that my grandmother Marlow is buying a piece of property out in the hill here so that Joe and Tim can build a house? The land is near Mr. Bean's house. I think or feel that it's rather sad (somehow) another house will take up that land but it would be interesting to live there!

I wish Joe would come home. I feel kind of spooked for some reason and would like company.

I feel really wierd...

Maybe if I turned off the radio I'd feel better.

Oh, I don't know what is happening with me. I suppose it is a question as to whether to have a full life or a happy life. Or does a full life have to have sadness in it? Or what? You see, for instance, this summer whenever I felt a <u>little</u> sad I thought a happy thought and became content but I missed the sadness just a little, but again, I knew if the sadness went deeper then I would only become sadder and then it would be harder to think happy. But I have had such a fantastic summer. I expect it is better to be or have a lot of happy and a little sad than to have a lot of sad and a little happy. Yes.

Too bad, sometimes, thoughts lead to thoughts because if they didn't we could be very sad and then very easily up we pop very happy.

It's strange that I would suddenly take an interest in the problems of pain last year because I never had before. But it is wierd also to think of things...how when you have a problem and you ride it out to the very last, practically being smothered in the process (but never quite) and then afterwards, somehow you get a vacation from it and when you return it's all exceedingly pleasant; the problem simply disappeared, not from any fighting of it or crying or solving, only from it just vanishing.

Or maybe it just seems that way. Maybe it's like the time we were playing doubles tennis and I was at the net; my partner was receiving the serve. The other side served -FWAP!- the ball fizzed over right into my stomach and after the commotion and hurt was over I <u>automatically</u> avoided that spot where I had been standing. Then I had to make myself consciously stand there; but when the server threw up the ball I <u>automatically</u> moved away quickly so as not to get hurt again. But I didn't think about moving...

Oh, dear, do you think I think too much? But it's so fun to think! It's like math. Or foreign language or writing or almost anything. What a funny person you are, Debbie Do Da. But thinking isn't like watching or feeling; I think thinking comes after observing, do you?

Mostly I am glad because I feel so exceedingly aware and sensitive to the things of my life.

And I like you very much. So much.

Debbie.

151.

Monday

Dear Dr. Pullias,

I recieved my journal in the mail today and I have been skimming through it. Parts of it still brought tears to my eyes but the feeling was different; I was no longer bitter, only sad that I had been that way.

So I will put these notebooks away and despite everything I had written to the contrary, will probably continue to keep a journal. As you would say, "Ah, me.."

This past week a friend from Reno was down for a visit and for two days we went to San Diego to see the zoo and Sea World. She has never been ANYWHERE and was thrilled to be so independent. It rather saddens me to think of her upcoming marriage at only age 17. Perhaps she will be happy.

I don't really have much to write. I drive down to school this coming Sunday and I am getting myself ready now. I recieved my room assignment; and will be in the same building as Heather, a friend from last year. I don't know who my roommate will be. Well... This will be my address:

Debbie Bumstead

USIU, Gamma 25F
10455 Pomerado Road
Sand Diego, Calif. 92131

I am glad you said you would love me even if I never did ANYTHING because sometimes I feel people are only interested in me because of my "potential" or "talent."

Love to you, Debbie.

152.
Friday- Sept. 14, 1973
Dear Dr. Pullias,

I feel like writing tonight. I know, I'll write what I feel tonight and maybe tomorrow night and then Sunday night when I am in my room at college. Would that be interesting? Yeah, I guess.

All of my necessities are neatly packed into four boxes, two suitcases, and then there's my tennis raquet and typewriter and big pillow to go on my bed - all of this across the room from me on the floor, ready to go. And above on the desk is what I'm going to wear Sunday, new denim pants, a red flowered blouse, clean underwear, new shoes. The whole scene makes me feel very simple because I know most girls take twice as much stuff. But that doesn't matter.

I am excited and eager for a variety of things - what will the bedroom look like (will we have bunkbeds? Then I must have the bottom one), what will my roommate be like (at least let her be friendly), will my classes be fun and fascinating (it feels like they will; I am so ready for more formal learning), what is it like to live in a eucalyptus forest (I must explore!). All these questions? - I mean, All these questions! Hey! And it all starts day after tomorrow.

Today I figured out that if there are six suites to a building then I am in the last one because it's called "F." And since there are two rooms to a suite, that's twelve rooms and since I'm in room "L" I'm in the last room. My roommate and I are numbers 23 and 24 then because there's two people to a room, I'll be #23.

Sunday

Dear Dr. Pullias

The view from the window is pleasant and the walls are paneled and the desk is formica. It's much more attractive than last year's rooms but also smaller. I feel clausterphobized. And the beds are bunk but I decided to take the top because it seems privater and besides Zoe is short. I know Zoe from last year.

When people go down the stairs the room sways. The girl's stereo in the room on the other side of our wall is very loud - OH WELL.

Should I or should I not go to the ice-skating party?

What else should I write? I'm so tired and don't really wish to go and yet - do I want to be alone?

Friday - What a dumb letter. Last night I had an awful and ugly dream - I was on the bus coming home from the ice skating thing and we saw to the side of us on the road a huge furry bear and her cub. When we got off the bus they turned into reindeer. They were trying to tame the younger one; a guy held him and yelled at him. But the reindeer got away and turned into another fellow running and the first guy took a huge manure shovel, lifted it way up and walloped the second on the head. I felt like vomiting. The boy fell instantly to the ground still but recieved another bang, anyway.

Oh, well I won't write the rest of it.

I found out I don't care for ice-skating - too cold!

Your friend, Debbie.

P.S. We are in suite "H" so on my address put - USIU, GAMMA 25H

153.
September 23, 1973
Sunday
Dear Dr. Pullias,

Ever since I got here I have felt so different, so weird and isolated. I feel as if there is NO ONE here who would ever be interested in what I am interested in. It's very difficult for me to enjoy talking about boys, as if boys were the only thing to be dedicated to. AND THE GIRLS HERE CONSTANTLY TALK ABOUT BOYS. CONSTANTLY.

Do you think the boys only talk about girls?

I FEEL SO WIERD, DR. PULLIAS.

But of course, despite everything, I always have me and I have friends to write to. And I have fun teasing and being teased and of course there is schoolwork to enjoy and hiking.

The land around here is absolutely lovely and wild. Yesterday Heather, Diane, and I put on hiking shoes and set out. We went about two miles through eucalyptus, Manzanita, and undergrowth. Can you guess what Heather & Diane talked about? I smiled at the incongruity of communication problems with boyfriends and the green around us.

At night sometimes we hear the coyotes yipe and one night when I was walking around I saw a rabbit scamper away. And today I walked down a nearby gully and saw a squirrel. Of course, the plants, too are worth seeing - eucalyptus, reeds, long yellow grasses.

This is a very wild place. I like that. Oh, I love it! I pretend I am an Indian and I practice walking quickly without making noise - and it's hard with the crunchy eucalyptus bark underfoot - hopefully soon I will really move silently.

I'll have to see about getting you a picture - one worth giving because all last year's paintings I threw away except for one fine watercolor that Debbie wanted. Last quarter this year I have a watercolor class and I hope to learn more techniques. That media I believe is my favorite. I like to do pen and ink, too. WE'LL SEE!

Your friend, Debbie.

154.
Dear Dr. Pullias,

I feel very much like writing to you tonight to tell you of my thoughts. A shower has refreshed me and I feel comfortable up top here on my bed with the night outside the dirty window and Cat Stevens singing loudly in the next room.

Today has been—what?—a day in my life here and yours there, a day. Today, though, I think was especially special for both you and me. It was my day where I was and yours where you were and and and. Do you know, sometimes thoughts meet during the day even though one is far apart from the other; there are the times we two have written letters to each other on the same day; there is the time James and I, after a whole year of not writing or seeing or phoning, suddenly wrote letters to each other the same week (that was utterly fantastic!); there is the time, most recently, I went to see if I could locate Debbie at UCSD, couldn't, came back and received a letter the next day which she had written while I was looking for her, telling me her new address!

Life here is quite strange. I tire mostly of the noise; rarely do we have silent moments to think. I tire also because I never really relax. I think this is because the people around me are new and when we live together for a while I will begin to relax. This might be the reason for I find myself quite more comfortable when I go downstairs to Heather's suite.

A week ago I called the adoption agency in search for a job. The lady and I got to talking and I heard some highly distressing news —single girls can no longer adopt children! It sort of shot all my dreams. Then today Debbie and Ruth and I were talking over breakfast about it. I said I wished Debbie would make me a baby. She said she tried but I ought to make my own. Oh, isn't it strange how we can speak so simply about such a monumental thing. And isn't it fantastic, I, me with my little tummy, I could have a baby! Wow!

I'm so sleepy.

I got a volunteer job taking an 8 year old girl places on the weekends. Both her parents are in wheelchairs.

The food here is horrid. I'm not eating much except salad and jello and milk. Oh, it's awful!

With that cheerful note I bid you adieu…

Love to you,

Debbie

155.
Backyard Study
October 5, 1973
Los Angeles

Dear Debbie,

I have given much thought about the often strange relationship between friends. There seems no doubt to me that there are mental connections that we do not know how to explain very well. As you say, there are many evidences of mutual thought letter crossing in the mail and many others. We know so little about the mental and spiritual world: it is a great adventure to open oneself up to such learning. There is a novel by the

171

English writer Elizabeth Goudge called <u>The White Witch</u> that touches on this world that I enjoyed.

I appreciate your speaking so freely to me about your feelings and your concerns. Perhaps you can understand that because I think so much of you and am so deeply interested in you, I want very much to respond giving you, my friend, and fellow student , the benefit of such experience and thought as I have had. Yet an older person has such a strong tendency, sometimes unwise, to give "advice" or even to "preach" that I hesitate. But I will talk a little.

I wish so much your situation there was better. The noise and the constant preoccupation with boys and sex is really not very good for life: I suspect that in time you will find a friend with whom you have some affinity and some mutual interests. You need regular contact with nature, some time alone and quiet. It would be good I think if you could put a lot into your tennis or some other sport that is available – I wish you could ride a horse now and then. Through the years reading has been a great help for me – it has enabled me to escape the rather silly and wearing monotony of people – really reading is a great joy. And close to that is writing: putting one's genuine thoughts and feelings on paper.

(While I am writing this, on the radio which I have here in my study the announcer mentions that the program will now present Brahms' 1ˢᵗ Symphony, and I remembered as the music plays that when I was at Pepperdine many years ago your grandfather and I were working closely together and were very close friends – he had a very great heart, deeply kind, and much talent and sensitivity – and he used to come here to our house and he and I would listen quietly to this great music together. That would be about thirty years ago – long before my beloved friend was born: wonder if she existed in another state then? and yet as I listen to this music tonight the experience returns.)

You mention wanting to adopt a baby or to have a baby. I suppose that is the deepest longing of a girl's heart. I would guess when you are ready you will be able as a single girl to adopt a child. These things change. One word of warning from one who loves you: this hunger for a baby is very strong – in a sense, it is a great mystery – and oftentimes men who have no care or respect for a girl know how strong the need is and take advantage of the girl, and great harm is done to girl and child if there should be one. To speak more directly or bluntly a selfish man may lead a girl on to satisfy her hunger for a child using her as a sexual object and leaving her and the child without love or care. Although, I know it is not always so, a baby – a child – should be the result of mutual love and respect between two people. To put it in another way, to "make" with your marvelous body (as you express it) a baby, another human being, is a very sacred responsibility. Like beauty, love, truth and many other sacred precious things, it should not be dealt with lightly.

All of this I judge you know or sense intuitively, but I believe you do not mind my giving you my thoughts on this great subject. I have the deepest confidence in you, and especially in that fine common sense of yours.

My classes go quite well. Last night a young woman – perhaps 25 – became so deeply interested and moved by what we were discussing that she began to cry as she undertook to express her thoughts. Perhaps she needs help; perhaps she is just tender or has been hurt. We need each other so much in life, and yet often we can not reach one another very well.

This letter becomes too long! Good night, dear friend.

Sincerely,

Earl V. Pullias

156.
October 10, 1973
Weds.
Dear Dr. Pullias,

I came to the library tonight to study as it was exceedingly noisy in the dorm. Studying here is surprisingly successful; I feel like a serious intellectual student carefully reading her sociology. I've read for an hour, now I'll take a break. The book is interesting but I rebel against many of the ideas. Marriage means Encounter. I think I get angry, because they make statements from a moral basis only and I feel I have a right to learn the true facts. I wish we could learn about this stuff as we learn about other subjects like biology or psychology.

Debbie Bumstead

Grrrrr!

In response to your letter—I fail to see too much difference if you're single, between having a baby or adopting one. Perhaps you were speaking from a moral standpoint also. Maybe not.

Here is what I think: for a baby or a child it is infinitely good to have a papa and a mama both, I would choose that for any baby even mine— I wouldn't have a baby on purpose unless it could have a daddy.

That's how I know I will act but this is what I feel: If I had a baby accidentally I would raise it and it would be very happy and if there was a child I could adopt it would be very happy, too. Somehow I can't imagine myself devoting a lifetime to a husband. But I can to a kid. But not in a motherly way; I've never ever been able to be adultish around my little friends. They're my <u>friends</u>.

Who knows what I'm talking about?

My creative writing teacher is a neat fellow. He has me all excited about writing, words, and things. I like him.

I like my psychology teacher, too, because I think we are a little alike in many ways.

My sociology teacher, I suspect wants me to open up to him but I am rather rebellious against the course and so am quite angry in class.

Anyway I like everything here except the noise and that makes me cry. I really don't know why noise disturbs me, perhaps because I am so quiet myself. I step around the rooms as softly as possible, I carefully open the closet, I set my books down gently. I do it all quite naturally. My suite-mates, on the other hand, are quite naturally noisy. So I cry because the noise makes me feel helpless, especially when I'd like to study or sleep. Oh, well! What an incompatible person I am!

I suppose I ought to read more sociology and then journey back to the dorm. Maybe I will sit outside awhile.

Love to you,
Debbie.

157.
Los Angeles
Backyard Study

Dear Dr. Pullias

Oct. 28, 1973
Dear Debbie:

I am looking for a good Indian name for you. It made me feel very good and warm inside that you read my letter out in the lovely wild where you love to go and be. As I read your words I could see and feel the hawk, the surroundings, and the Indian maiden walking and thinking softly in that setting. Perhaps I mentioned before a delightful book of Indian stories – all about girls and women – called <u>The Inland Whale</u> by Theodora Kroeber. I will send you a copy in a few days. It might have a name in it that would fit, but beyond that I believe it might be very helpful in your writing class.

Your interest in and deep feeling for children, their nature and their learning and their growth expresses something very deep about your nature. If you follow that in earnest, acquire the knowledge and skills that are needed to make the most of that interest, I believe you will be able to make a significant contribution to education – it needs improving so badly, but it is not easy to make it better.

I hope the paying job came through. If that one didn't another one will. The value of pay is that it provides a means to independence and freedom – if we can avoid the slavery that comes from wanting too much. I am so pleased you have the same psychology teacher: she gives a picture of what is possible and good.

I must tell you a little about myself. My classes go pretty well, I think. We have not been able to visit our beloved rocks and hills at Hemet lately and that hurts: the place is very healing. I went again to Utah this last Thursday and Friday – spoke to college young people your age: snow college. I'll talk more about the <u>you</u> I see next time.

Sincerely, Earl V. Pullias

158.
Dear Dr. Pullias,

I received <u>The Inland Whale</u> today. Thank you! I'll probably read it in the next couple of days because there is a surprising and sudden scarcity of schoolwork. I need a small vacation from textbooks. A very good book I am reading is <u>Island of the Blue Dolphins</u> by Scott O'Dell.

I wonder why my hands tremble and my heart beats faster after I've taken a shower. Interesting.

I dislike the soap opera-ness of this place. Alison takes away Zoe's honey while Zoe goes out with Howard and forgets about Jim in England. Sue tries to get Scott. Nora has not changed her sheets since school started and comes home drunk or stoned. Meanwhile downstairs Sandy treats Bob like mud while Heather hurts and gives Shirl an "I perceive" because she had a boy in the living room.

But the one thing I don't like to do is write about it like this or talk about it. A girl, Janey sees all this and wishes to speak of it and comes to me. I'd rather she wouldn't because if no one talks about it I never notice anything.

How very strange that I should have such a very hard time telling if people are being mean to each other or insincere. I do not see very deeply. I don't know if I wish to.

I like James a bunch.

Do you know what? That's what. I'll probably get my first paycheck Monday - $90. My goodness!

I want so much to write something nice to you but I can't think of ANYTHING.

Here are two recent poems.

I

Panda swamp sprouts and a
Wee dew giraffe, my
Strawberry shy dream of
Sun earth and
Awakening to find myself turned to
Dusty tickle beetles
That have all wandered away.

II

Squash maroon child and
Dapple checker leaf—
when
My eyeglasses are lost the
Moon blade forest is water-painted on

Dear Dr. Pullias

Turquoise tremble sneeze silk
That someone up above is rippling.

Thank you,
Love,
Debbie.

159.
Dear Dr. Pullias,

Last Saturday little Cassie and I went hiking in a place called San Clemente Canyon. Sycamore trees and oaks were old and tall and we found a wild dense place along the creek bed. We followed this creek with yellow leaved trees doming over us and the sun touching on the soft red leaves of poison ivy banking beside us. It was a beautiful place but I will have to be more careful next time for at the time it did not register that the red leaves were poison; it looks so different from Hemet poison oak. Consequently two days afterward I woke up with one eye completely swollen shut and my cheeks puffed up also. Today it's a little better. Everybody around here has been awfully nice to me; yesterday I stayed in bed with an ice pack and Heather checked on me often and brought my mail (what a bright thing to receive three letters from friends when one is feeling bad).

I hope Cassie is not as allergic to it as I am.

What makes a person laugh? Is it all learned? When I laugh it feels like spontaneous music bubbling out. And I find so many things funny, or not all funny, just delightful. Not TV programs or jokes but the way humorous people act or what they say. It's hard to explain but I wish I could because it's an important part of me. I laugh an awful lot!

I think I will rest my eyes a bit and then go to the library. I'm looking into the procedures of publishing books and illustrating. Also I want to look at college catalogues. The tuition here is going up 4000 a year and if grants do not go up that high I suppose I ought to have somewhere to fall back on.

Thanks so much for the letter.

Your friend,
Debbie.

160.
Los Angeles
Backyard Study
Nov. 10, 1973
Sat. Night

Dear Debbie:

Did I tell you about the ivy in my study here? The ivy has been growing around this little building for many years. In recent years, it has creeped in through a window and a back door that does not close very tightly and has grown across the back of my desk: it is a dark green and gives a nice feeling to the study. Perhaps it communes with the leaves and the toadstools in your picture above and to the right of my desk—the one you gave me.

I hope you were soon over the effects of your encounter with the poison ivy. I guess they have drugs now that are good for it so that it doesn't hang on as it used to.

I wish you could have been here today. This week we had a new redwood fence just in on the south side of our yard. It is very good looking wood, and I like wood very much. Calvin and I stained the neighbor's side and we all worked on cleaning our yard: it was a pleasant day. I wonder if you have much skill in working with your hands as your father and Grandfather had in such marked degree?

Probably in a few days I will send you another book. This one a student of mine who is a dentist bought some copies of for me in Canada where the author has been a great scientist and doctor.

Your friend,
Earl V. Pullias
P.S. I enclose a leaf of the friendly ivy for good fortune— not poison!

161.
Los Angeles
Nov. 14, 1973

Dear Dr. Pullias

Early Morning

Dear Debbie:

Yesterday (Tuesday), Mrs. P and I went to our place in Hemet to check on things there, and to experience the hills and rocks and quiet. I had to be back for a meeting last night but it was a good day. We took a little lunch over to the juniper tree and ate there sitting on the soft bed of needles under the tree. Your letter was here when I returned.

There are many things in your letter to which I would like to respond, but can only write a little this morning. When you write to me express whatever is in your heart and that will be nice in the deepest sense. I liked <u>Island of the Blue Dolphins</u> very much. Must have read it last summer. That kind of story inspires me and lifts me up, and I need that very much. It seems that many books picture only the worst in people, and is a little like eating garbage. I don't mean we should not know about the dreadful evil in the world, but it should not be overplayed, and should be balanced by the True, the Beautiful, the Good, and the Loving (TBGL)! I need these things in reading too.

I suspect James is a very special kind of young man. I'm glad you like him so much. Perhaps if you wish you will tell me sometime where he is and what he is doing. Love is indeed a beautiful thing, but is delicate and must be handled very wisely, sincerely or it gets distorted and spoiled. Deep down your heart is pure and you can follow it.

It would be good if you could almost lose yourself in your work, in athletics, in reading, in nature, in writing, etc. and get entangled as little as possible in the "soap opera" of the dormitory. You can observe it and learn some from it.

I hope you like <u>The Inland Whale</u> stories. They will follow nicely the <u>Island of the Blue Dolphins</u>. Now and then I'll send you other things. They may or may not appeal to you. Getting your first pay check is a great experience. I want to write about that later.

Sincerely Earl V. Pullias.

162.
November 15, 1973

179

Debbie Bumstead

Thursday

Dearest Dr. Pullias,

There will be no studying tonight–its open house—oh my—the guys are comin' over— get cleaned up— clear the table—curl your hair—hurrah! Its so fun to see everyone so excited.

Everyone I know and, to a lesser degree, everyone I see, I feel a friendly affection for. Do all people feel this way–then it must be a wonderful world. But I suppose many people do not (would you say the majority?), but it's hard for me to see that they don't feel the affection because I feel it. It's hard for me to see many things or understand them (though I don't know <u>what</u> I'm missing I know there <u>is</u> something. There is a part of my mind gone that other people have to see what they see and I have a different part—or something like that.)

I have a friendly affection for myself, too, do you? It's funny because at night, just after I get into bed I smile suddenly into my pillow and say inside, "Debbie?" and the other me says, "Yes, my dear?" and then I say, "I LIKE you." "Well, I love you, too; now go to sleep."

Somewhere I read that little children talk to themselves and then society pushes that underground so that all of us talk to ourselves inside. That's certainly true of me—I tell myself what I could do, should do, and want to do. I tell myself and discuss thoughts (I like to be logical about it, too, so as not to miss anything). Sometimes I take two sides and have a conversation. Its funny.

Oh, I feel happy tonight. I have new warm knee socks on, they're blue with yellow and light green stripes. I like them bunches!

The music is lovely; it makes me feel the night is all around, just a little sad—in a calm acception way with stars far away and blinking.

I must tell you about yesterday—so much happened. First of all I was trying to find someone who might know if my grant could go higher, I checked the financial aid offices—they didn't know. So I went to see my advisor and waited for a half hour (oh, I dislike waiting!); she was busy so I saw another guy who didn't know and gave me no encouragement. I left and felt so tired and hopeless I cried.

Then I went to lunch and on the way back I stopped by to see my marriage/mental health teacher (who is also the Dean). Though not too deep, he is very nice and told me the cost was going up $270 a year and I thought that wasn't too bad. Then he said I could get into the University College here and that does not have the language requirement (and a couple others) for a B.A. He said my autobiography (we had to write for class) was the most beautiful he had ever received. We spoke of various things.

THEN...I had to go to my psychology class—that was OK. But my Crea/Writ. class was being held at "The Lodge" a place down by last year's campus. I rode with two guys in our class. The place overlooked the ocean; the sun was setting; the ocean was a turquoise tinged with fuchsia—mmm. I didn't know it was to be a drinking and smoking session—I politely refused. Loud music played, the sun lowered, gold came in the windows, I fell asleep on the couch Later it was dark and I went out onto the patio and talked with the fellow who had driven us. He had been quite considerate and had not drunk more than two glasses of wine. We talked all about ourselves as we watched the waves coming in and the sandpipers thinking of lazy fish. And when we drove away and back we talked more; he was quite thoughtful. We ate in the cafeteria and I did not like that because we became awkward and unnatural; the lights were too harsh.

When I came back to the dorm my suite-mates had to discuss the fact that Janey wanted to move up when Pam moved out. Zoe didn't want Janey here, Sue didn't care, I didn't know. So we had to go speak with the R.A. (Heather) and see how we were going to tell Janey we didn't want her even though we liked her. It was quite trying but I do not like to dwell on things, I do not like uncomfortable silences so I told Janey when she came up and let it be.

Later I went down again to Heather's (she's my buddy—I like her very much) and she asked me to spend the night. I said, "What fun!" And it was fun. I so like talking at night when we both lie in our beds and we both like each other and then I fall asleep and sleep so nicely because there is someone I love so near. DO YOU KNOW?

How does popcorn work?

I so enjoyed hearing about your picnic by the juniper tree— have I ever told you how much I love those hills? It makes me cry here with the music. Come thanksgiving I will be home and plan to go hiking alone—maybe because I know it so well and all it's places is why I like it more than even the forest I explored last summer in Idyllwild which was more beautiful. Maybe because I had so many fun times as a child there, I don't know. I like it in the early spring when everything is green and I like the late cold fall hills when it rains. In the summer the weeds smell luscious. I feel the land there and the plants and birds, and rocks are quite literally my friends. It seems I can hear them speak with me. Truly.

Your forever friend, Debbie

163.

November 28, 1973

Dear Dr. Pullias,

I have been having a rotten week because of what Mamma told me at Thanksgiving—that Daddy might come down for Christmas. Ah, I hope he does not. I do not even want to be around if he does. Maybe I'll run away. Maybe Debbie wouldn't mind if I stayed at her house.

Ah, come on, buck up, you know you can take it. You're quite strong.

Baloney, I don't even want to be around.

Maybe I can stay over at Tim's house. Except he's being complicated, too. Since his fiance said no and made another boyfriend he's taken up religion, becoming a Jehovah's Witness. There wouldn't be anything wrong with that except that it came so sudden and he's so solemn and different.

It's all enough to turn me away from—what? I can't even think of a word for all this complicated stuff. Mostly I would like to stay simple.

What should I do? I don't know.

Next quarter I will have Dr. Box for a class in Medaevil History. I hope it's interesting and imaginative because that is my favorite time in history. Also I'm taking Psychology of Learning and Biology and I'll again be on the tennis team. I only have Fridays free so I have to quit my job—easy come, easy go. I made about $150. Perhaps I can get a Friday job somewhere—I'd like to.

Surprisingly enough the last of a quarter is not usually very busy for me; I suppose because I anticipate being busy and so take greater care in organizing my studies.

I've made friends with Dr. Kirby (maybe I told you?) who is the dean and my sociology teacher because of a autobiography and a talk he had with me. He read my paper to the class one day when I wasn't there (my suite-mate told me all this) and he told the class I was such a "beautiful person" and everyone should get to know me. And he always takes care to speak with me.

Also my creative writing teacher—oh well!

I like you so much!

There's a fellow around here that looks so much like you I jump every time I see him.

Now I feel better. Maybe I'll now be happy. Heather said I looked as if I weren't content and that I should get over it because it is very hard to live with. I like her. It's just that I don't know what to do to keep from being involved in rough situations. Oh, well!

Love to you,
Debbie.

164.

December 3, 1973

Dear Dr. Pullias,

Tonight I called Debbie. She is exceptionally busy with studies; she worries so much. For Christmas I'm giving her a belt made of leather that the teacher my mom works for made for me. It has embossed flowers and the name DEBBIE. I would keep it but the buckle is too heavy and my stomach too small. It pulls my pants down!

So tomorrow I'll drop it off at her house as Sue and I are going into La Jolla to Christmas shop. Sue is one of my suite-mates. She's a freshman and I feel very much compassion for her. She seems so young. She badly wants a guy to date, but she's—I don't know. It's just that, though she's not at all like me, I remember how it was that first quarter. We all wandered around as if in shock. Sue makes me smile.

I get the feeling I should use both sides of the paper from now on because of the "energy crisis." And it's cold in here!

It will be pleasant having 3 weeks to laze around—I'm ready for it. Do you get 3 weeks?

The fern in the living room looks like a Medusa-head.

Dear Dr. Pullias, do you know what causes or keeps it going these "crushes" (for lack of a better word—what could I use?). I have had one each year since fifth grade. It's a way of life for me and I enjoy the feeling. But some aspects I would like to eliminate but I don't know how. Even if it's a way of life I still do not have a clear understanding of it.

> I hope you are all well.
> Your friend, Debbie.

165.
December 14, 1973 - Hemet
Dear Dr. Pullias,

Hi, hi, hi, hi, hi! Do you know what? That's what!

Our house is so very cold that I am shivering. My nose doesn't seem to want to get warm. Brrrrr. I wonder what makes one person (me) get cold easily and another (Mamma) stay warm. Quien sabe'?

My vacation to date has been thoroughly enjoyable. I've visited Mr. Hill. We drove in his new red sports car, oh my, to a coffee shop and we talked. He always seems just a bit sad, but I like him. He said he'd come visit me at college, that we might go to the harbor and walk along the waterfront. Once when I was still in high school we were talking together and he said, "Sometimes I wonder what you would have been like if you had been my daughter." He says everything with that tiniest touch of melancholy and I wondered that he could have thought such a thought, to have thought of having me as a daughter (of course it was one of my more common daydreams to have him as a "fatherly figure" [as well as you, and a few others—but then I am too old for that dream now...still I dream...]).

I have finally finished my room just today. Most of the china animals are out on two wooden shelves I hung on the walls; stuffed animals—an alligator, panther, tiger, snake, etc.—live on the window seat; Victoria, Curly, and Abigail, the dolls, sit in their little places; my watercolor painting of elephant, giraffe, zebra, leopard—my room is so full of friendly smiles! I have a room that likes itself and everything that lives in it likes itself, too. Cheerful.

The little boys came over today to clean up the yard, but they spent most of the time calling for me to come out of the house. Finally I agreed. And then they danced about, talking and talking and trying to pin my arms behind my back (but I fling them off like flys and they wonder at my strength—though I suspect it is more a matter of coordination). My mother tells me they are, for sure, in love with me especially Reggie. I smile because I love them; they are such eager happy little clowns.

Yesterday James and I went hiking up a clifferous (hurrah! a new word!) pine treed mountain in Anza. We had a picnic on a flat rock looking down into a manzanita crowded ravine; we saw a flock of crows circling far above us, checking us out. James wished to go further up to a ledge he had seen so I said I would start down and wait for him somewhere in the sun. I crawled along through the manzanita, seeing with delight, secret meadows for little people. And through the brush, I then hopped from stone to stone and looked around at the pale gray rock slabs and the pine trees; the better part of the mountain still towered above me. I realized how much more I enjoyed hiking alone, following and leading only myself, taking my own time, going exactly where I wanted. Still I liked James to be there on his own individual jaunt, a thread of thought connected us yet we experienced our own sights of loveliness, and anticipated our rendezvous, later, in the sun. James called, "Hi!" from his ledge far above and I waved, "Hello!"

Do you like to Christmas shop? I do.

Love to you, Debbie.

166.
Los Angeles
Dec. 23, 1973
Sunday Morning
I hope Christmas was good. Sometimes I like shopping for it.
Dear Debbie,

I wanted to write Friday night after I saw you but I was a little tired when I got home. The trip in one day makes about five hours of driving. But the day was good, especially I was pleased to see you again, and to walk among the rocks and hills at Luiseño Land—for the Indians that once lived there.

I am not sure I can say wisely what I would like to say. But I will not try too hard for you will understand and make up whatever my words lack. I am very thankful for our friendship: its authenticity, sincerity, genuineness. Often through the years I have wished I might have had a daughter with whom I might have had some affinity at the deepest level. But it was not to be. It was good to see your special private room and your "friends" there.

Perhaps our friendship must always be at the level of writing largely. Speech and physical nearness are always very different things. Perhaps it is harder to be sincerely oneself in those more direct relationships. What is is, and will be, I suppose.

Reading has always been a great joy to me. I was greatly inspired by the book about the Indian girl who lived so long alone on the Pacific Island, the <u>Island of the Blue Dolphins</u>. Have you read other books by that author that are also good? I greatly need things that are beautiful and inspire me—lift me up toward what I would like to be. To read the greatest authors is to be in touch with the best man has experienced. Since I saw you I have been reading some from a good translation of Homer's Odyssey: such beautiful language, music, and ideas. I wish I could have heard him, the blind minstrel, recite his great stories! Keep true to your deepest self: let nothing cheep or ugly draw you aside. Really I know you will not. Above all be your sincere self.

Your friend, Earl V. Pullias

167.
Christmas Eve, 1973
Dear Dr. Pullias,

I picked three violets from our yard. We are having spring where winter should be, aren't we?— The narcissus violets, and roses are blooming; fresh spearmint has grown round the water faucet. I suppose I like violets because of their perfume and they are February's flowers and because someone once told me I was like a violet—lovely in the woods but once plucked and taken home would only wilt and die.

Ah, well, my three violets in their tiny glass vase will last a couple of days here on my windowsill.

The day after Christmas we are going up to Reno for a few days. I invited James along; he will call me tonight to tell me of his decision. I know so well his predicament—you want so much to go, you know you'll enjoy it once it's over, you want so badly to see the city...but oh, the strange people, what will you say? What will you do when everyone's sitting around talking? What if you feel ill? How do you sleep in the same room as some girl's brother? You don't even

Dear Dr. Pullias

know him! And you have to say thank you after each meal and offer to wash dishes. Oh, no! But then Debbie will be there and she knows exactly how you feel and you don't have to be around them all the time, you can always go off to your room. And you've never been to Reno, it might be quite interesting. And they do have a piano, that's something, actually it all might be quite enjoyable—but then again....

Oh, Dr. Pullias! What strain it is to be shy!

I've been thinking a bit about shyness lately because of James (though he's not as shy as I am, it's really amazing the way he clams up around other members of my family and then, the minute they leave, what a jabborbox! Truly amazing...) and because the other day, Sunday... Well I was just going for a ride on my bike, yes, heading down this way, oh, since I'm going this way I might as well go visit Miss Kerr. OK, that'd be fun, she might invite you in for milk and cookies, you could talk about horses and you could tease one another, yes that'll be fun. So I began to pedal up the hill, past the eucalyptus trees. Still, hmm, you might interrupt her, she might be busy with something more important and then she'd be obliged to stop and talk. She might be just about to leave for somewhere. I coasted down the other side of the hill, "click, click," went my bike. My stomach began to feel strange. What if I rode up and she saw me from far away? She'd think I was dumb. What will we talk about? She'll think I'm so dumb! When I came to her street I turned the opposite way and pedaled home.

And yet I know so well Miss Kerr likes me and doesn't think I'm dumb at all and that she's just as shy herself as I am. Then why does that happen to me? I really have no idea why. It disturbs me because sometimes I really would like to do things that I want to. Oh, well. It's hard to believe that I'm almost <u>twenty</u> and still shy around new people—would you believe I'm even shy around babies?! Why? What is it to be shy?

I'm not shy if I actually live in the same house as someone, I get over it quite rapidly. It just takes a bit of extended association. That is why I don't especially think our friendship must always be from writing, though I expect I'll always write to you, still perhaps if you ever move down here we can sit around somewhere and just talk. Oh, I don't know what I mean.

I like books. I read Tolstoy's story—good.

Your friend,

Debbie.

Debbie Bumstead

P.S. My brother, Joe & I took several good pictures. When I get back I'll send you one of me (that is, if you want it—oh, I'm so dumb sometimes!).

More to my friend –

It's been a pleasant Christmas eve; Grandbee and Grandpa came over for a while. Momma opened the present grandpa had given her – a turquoise ring he had made. It is very exceedingly lovely and my mother was quite overcome and grandpa seemed pleased. The other day when I was over visiting them, Grandbee was in the other room, and grandpa was near me showing me something and we said something enthusiastic to each other about the jewelry, we laughed, and <u>he looked at me in the eyes</u> which I don't remember ever happening before. Interesting.

James called tonight and had decided not to go to Reno – which is just as well I suppose as grandmother is in rather a nervous state. It's just that I feel, if we're going up and just for a few days it would be nice for a person who wanted to come along. That's, I guess, the way I think, and if it were not such close notice I would ask other friends. But maybe I shouldn't since that very well might not be the way the rest of the family thinks. Yes, indeed and forsooth.

It will be a nice difference up in Reno where there is snow. And when we get back I must have Joseph fix my truck up, renew my drivers license, buy this and that for this and that and speed off to school again. I hope I have at least one day before I leave for San Diego to calm my innards. I always need a very quiet calm time before anything exciting or stressful happens. Then I can enjoy the excitement better. We will probably be back on the 31st and I leave again on the 3rd.

I must write more, but my hand is very tired. And tomorrow is Christmas. Perhaps I will read a bit before turning out the light. And then I will think a long while and then I'll fall asleep. And dream...
DEBBIE.

168.
Los Angeles
Dec. 31, 1973

Dear Dr. Pullias

The Backyard Study

"But you will go safely, and you will come home safely:
If you have followed the customs and the rules; and if your heart
is pure" (from "Umai", my favorite of the Indian stories)

Dear Debbie:

I appreciate all your letters, but I especially liked your last letter. I am not sure why, and I think that doesn't matter. My feelings about the end of the Christmas holidays are mixed: the freedom is very good; also, it will be good to get back to the classes and other activities. That is life: often, yes and no.

I have long been deeply interested in the problem of shyness. I wish I could say something wise and helpful about the subject. Many people suffer more or less all through their lives from this problem. Interestingly enough they are often talented and the most desirable of people. That is to say that often shyness goes along in a personality with very good traits. I can say one encouraging word: early in life I suffered greatly from shyness but over the years the problem has steadily become less severe. We must talk about this more in the future. The main thing to watch is not to be led into using harmful methods to overcome the shyness, for then the cure becomes worse than the disease. For example I have known many people who started drinking because they were told a little alcohol would keep them from being so shy. The same with drugs.

I hope your visit to Nevada was good. There is often a great distance between generations. I feel this is a great pity, for the old need essentially the same things in life as the young, and they both need each other very much. One of my dreams in life is to help overcome the many barriers that separate people. I am very glad you had a moment of special association with your Grandfather Bumstead: you might be of much value to each other unless it is too late: as is the case of all of us, he needs love - <u>he</u> especially, but we all do.

"What Men Live By" is a great story. In fact, I believe Tolstoy is one of the truly great writers. It is so good that you like books: they hold within them the rich experience of human beings as they have lived on this planet - the experience presented and interpreted by the most thoughtful and sensitive people who have lived.

There are two other sources of experience that I have found very helpful: one, the warm, close contact with nature; two, listening to one's own deep inner thoughts and feelings - the still small voice inside us.

As our friendship grows, there are more and more things I would like to say to you - things that might be of special interest and perhaps helpful as your life unfolds. I must not let my concern and love cause me to push you in anyway: you will find your own way, and I believe it will be a good and wise way. My desire is to walk some of it with you, and perhaps now and then point out some especially joyful ways, and maybe some dangers or some "wrong ways: do not enter." Every good wish for the year that starts.

Earl V. Pullias

1974

*I have believed since I knew you as a child that
you are a very special person, and that those good
qualities within you will unfold and grow as you
grow older, and that you will be able to be and to
do especially good things, especially for children
and perhaps also for animals. But I should not
like to talk about these things too much lest I
frighten them away. Yet now I feel our friendship
is deep enough that I can feel free to say whatever
I wish - I hope you feel the same way.* **Dr. Pullias**

*I feel a little like going home and never coming back.
But I will come back again and again. So far my "college
experience" has not been very enjoyable. Where is all the good
and growing you led me to believe was here? Where is the
learning and beauty of knowledge? It's not here; it's inside me
and college does not help me get it out. The only things good here
are the independence and the forest.* Debbie

Debbie Bumstead

169.
January 4, 1974
Dear Dr. Pullias,

I received two very good letters from you upon my return to school. Thank you. So we are back in school... The days are pleasant but nights I feel quite hopeless because of the noise our neighbors make; hopefully they will quiet down with a few pointed hints. Tonight they are out and all I hear is the rain on the roof-top – I love that sound. We have a new suite-mate from Persia. She is rooming with Sue. I like Sue, even though we can't really talk with each other, mostly she's boy-crazy, we realize, I guess, that we are essentially of good heart. She understands something about me (I don't know what) and I of her that Zoe, my roommate doesn't but she doesn't know. Zoe and Sue are real buddies, gabbing away. Mostly when I'm here I sit up here on my top bunk or in the chair by the window in the living room. Or if I'm not in, I'm sitting with my blanket around my shoulders, on the steps outside looking into the forest or on downstairs with my pal Heather. I always seem to make dry remarks that no one gets or I laugh at almost anything that is humorous or I speak rather pompously of honor when someone becomes hypocritical. Otherwise I don't talk much at all but listen and think and feel.

You asked about James. Well, he's an interesting fellow: in personality, I think, rather a lot like myself but not as practical, ambitious, and tolerant. He writes and draws and loves nature as I do, in fact we find so many of our thoughts and feelings running in the same channels, except as I mentioned, he's not too tolerant of ordinary folk and his ambitions are not set on fame. He's rather attractive and slender, etc. pleasant green eyes. He's extremely shy and, I think, sometimes he feels depressed as if he weren't worth anything but then I have felt that way, too. I like him quite a lot but not the way I loved, for instance, Debbie, and I don't really daydream very much about him or feel jealous, etc. I think if we should suddenly stop writing I wouldn't mind – it's very hard to explain. Not exactly any love like I've felt before, and yet more than just pals. Perhaps because we understand each other quite intimately.

Or something like that.

Zoe came in from her date so I guess it's time for bed.

Love to you,

Debbie.

170.
Los Angeles
Living Room by the Fire
Jan. 5, 1974

Dear Debbie:

What a joy to receive your picture in the mail yesterday! It is very good of you, I feel, catching something of the deepest and best part of you - a fine piece of art, I believe. You and the cat fit well together - his or her name I forget which is a shame: don't let him know! - and the two of you together say something important, also.   Really, I suspect we know extremely little, compared to what we could know, about animals. As is the case with children we don't reach them or listen to them very well. Maybe people can learn to do better in these and other areas.

But I was expressing something of my appreciation for the picture. I will keep it in my study out back among my other treasures and will value it always.   I am not out there today because it is chilly here - at least for Calif. And cold strikes through to my bones. The "shack" out back is quite breezy!

My work at USC got under way this week. We, as I may have mentioned, are on the Semester system and so we have two weeks of classes and examinations after the Christmas holidays. I am not sure whether the quarter system which you have there is better or not. As soon as you think it is wise, I hope you will see your psychology teacher to advise with her about your degree. That might be pretty important since you are likely to wish to go on for graduate work or almost certainly, to get your credential to work with children.

Even if it is cold, the clouds are lovely. I hope you will soon be back at your tennis.

Sincerely, Earl V. Pullias

171.
January 9, 1974
Dear Dr. Pullias,

I'm glad you like the picture – the kitty cat is a "she" and her name is Sari. Animals are interesting. I have never thought of them as less intelligent than me but just quieter and in different bodies, leading a different kind of life. I feel the same about children, that they're not stupid but just small, different from me but certainly not inferior.

In some ways I'm too different myself, to enjoy living here. I guess because I grew up in such a quiet environment; all the girls around here seem almost fanatical about sound – synthetic sound – like TV and stereo. I don't mind it occasionally but not all the time especially at night. Night seems to me to be a time to listen to outside sounds, the croaking frogs, the cars passing on a distant street. There are other ways but I expect the noise is the most distressing. There's the fact that no one here talks philosophically or thoughtfully or intellectually; sometimes I miss that. Sometimes I just plain miss companionship with someone I can relate to.

But I keep saying, "At least I have me," and I keep good company with myself most of the time. I am almost constantly talking to myself (not out loud!) And I take myself places that I enjoy – the woods, to see Cassie, the library. You know, most of the time I really enjoy being with me. And when I feel like it I enjoy being with others; my suite-mates are fun to listen to (99% of the time they are chattering about sex or guys [I must be awfully weird because I'm practically devoid of any "sex drive."]) And I like to be with Heather and enjoy my funny friend Sau-wah and Janey is nice, though she smells of antiseptic.

And there are letters (you and James are about the only regular writers) that I would not be happy without. I love to get letters and write letters.

Enough of that. I really like reading my Middle Ages text. It's quite fascinating. Dr. Box lectures like a preacher. The only thing really against that class is the fact that it's at 8 o'clock IN THE MORNING! Horrible. Also there's three tests. I don't like tests. But I wouldn't complain a bit about tests if the class wasn't at 8 o'clock IN THE MORNING!

I went to talk with Dr. Henry, as you suggested, and she was so nice. Oh, How I wish we could be good friends. She rather talks like I do when I'm not being shy and she has the quality of speaking to younger people as equals – an amazing lovely quality. (And guess what? I think I have that quality, too, with children.) She gave me a lot of ideas to help little Cassie and when I asked her about the B.A. She said there was only one B.A. that could be earned two ways – through the Cal Western college or University college. Either way it's still a USIU B.A. She was so nice.

That was a couple of days ago and then today I was walking back to the dorm and I saw the group of psych. teachers coming out of their building. And even though they had to step carefully through the left over rain-rivers, Dr. Henry looked up as I passed and said, "Hi, Deb." She called me by name!

Oh, my. That simply made my day!

I'm typing up some writings to send off.

Hurrah!

Dear Dr. Pullias

From,
Debbie.

172.
Los Angeles
Jan. 12, 1974
Living Room by the fire

Dear Debbie:
Both your letters came and I appreciate them very much. I have believed since I knew you as a child that you are a very special person, and that those good qualities within you will unfold and grow as you grow older, and that you will be able to be and to do especially good things, especially for children and perhaps also for animals. But I should not like to talk about these things too much lest I frighten them away. Yet now I feel our friendship is deep enough that I can feel free to say whatever I wish - I hope you feel the same way.

The fact that you are not so overwhelmed by a concern about sex and things that relate to sex is an important part of the deeper you. I think you can be thankful for this freedom. When and if you come to love someone in that way the need will develop. In the meantime it is wonderful - an expression of the deeper, richer you - that your needs are not so narrow and surface.

I am sorry you do not have a better place to live: quiet and thoughtfulness are important needs and should not be denied us. I especially liked you ideas about the wonderful sounds of the night: it is somewhat of a shame that these beautiful sounds should be drowned out by artificial and often raucous sounds. But that is often the case in modern life.

A person needs a friend or two with whom he can be sincere - in activity, fun, or silence. But such friendship is often hard to find, and so there is much loneliness in life. There is I believe much joy in observing, in thought, in writing, in learning, especially in reading.

We had sunshine and nice clouds today. Good after so much

197

Debbie Bumstead

rain.

Sincerely Earl V. Pullias

173.

January 16, 1974

Dear Dr. Pullias,

Wow – it has been some rough lonely week! Next week I hope I can cheer myself up. I expect a lot of this gloominess is due to the fact that my period is coming (interesting, isn't how that affects me – I always cry at least once before it starts, sometimes when there's nothing to cry about I cry at some song or picture, and one night I always feel like running a long ways. Sometimes I'm very sad or depressed before hand and other times I have a sudden creative sprint. It's all very interesting.) But mostly I've missed companionship. The girl who was my buddy with whom I enjoyed talking and being with has suddenly become busy with other girl-friends and a new boy-friend. I have been on the verge of tears all week. Next week has to be better.

For one thing I'm going home for the weekend where I can relax (go to bed early, cry really hard if I feel like it, wander around the house and play with the cat) and visit with Mamma and my brothers. I am going to see Mr. Hill and he is a very good friend.

Last weekend my little friend, Cassie, came to spend the night. Oh, she was so excited and had such a good time. We slept down in Heather's suite with H. and Shirl. Shirl is really some riot – very fun and funny. Sunday Cassie and I went on a picnic into the woods. I'm going to start tutoring her Fridays at her school as well as going places on Saturdays she's really quite a bright little girl (but her teacher doesn't think so – oh how that makes me mad! We'll show her!) With a sophisticated vocabulary and such a love of fixing and organizing.

January 17 –

It's going to be a lovely day today. After Science I'll eat lunch and then take off for home. I feel a little like going home and never coming back. But I will come back again and again. So far my "college experience" has not been very enjoyable. Where is all the good and growing you led me to believe was here? Where is the learning and beauty of knowledge? It's not here; it's inside me and college does not help me get it out. The only things good here are the independence and the forest.

198

Dear Dr. Pullias

Your friend, Debbie.

174.
January 28, 1970
Dear Dr. Pullias,

I wish I could read and just read. I like my history text; it's quite fascinating. But I despise taking notes on it and later having to answer someone else's questions about it. I do so dislike trying to think up answers to questions that someone else thinks would be wise for me to know. Maybe it would be good for me to know but the person could tell me, I would listen – honest, you wouldn't have to test me on if I listened. I don't mind thinking, but I don't wish to think someone else's way or my way on someone else's thought. Perhaps I do wish to but I don't wish to be tested on it.

I wish I could read and just read. And then write what I thought. It doesn't matter if what I think is wrong – I will learn because I do learn.

Bah. I'm disturbed over this history test I just took. I don't know what his questions were talking about but I would listen if he wanted to tell me. And I could tell him that I quite enjoyed the chapters and I could write my way on what I had gathered from the book. So what if my writing would be pure imaginary dreams – that's what I interpret into the Middle Ages. And if there is something else I should know, I'll listen to the teacher. Why am I tested on questions I don't understand – and it doesn't matter that everyone else understands, I me – and graded as if that counted most? What counts most is what I learned in my individual way of going about it.

Growl. I wish I could read and just read. I wish I could write and just write. I wish I could listen and just listen.

I feel so much like being at home. With my own quiet spring still room upstairs and with the life of quiet learning. I like to read and learn and I believe I do so even without school. And I like the calmness and green loveliness of the day in my home life; it's more natural than living here among a frenzy of complex relationships.

Ah.. home. I wake up early but lie in bed perhaps till 9 o'clock, thinking or reading or dozing and dreaming. The sun shines merrily through the window and I dress and go downstairs to fix my breakfast. The mail is very important when I'm at home, so that some days I sit outside in the yard to wait for the mailman.

And some days I go into town, sometimes I ride the horse. Some days I go to James's, some days he comes to my house, sometimes my friends come to stay a few days, Debbie or Marie, or my little cousins.

There is more time to do things at home. There is always time to read, and I probably read five times or more as much as I do at school and there's always time to write. But there's always time to do other things to – a day in San Diego with my brother, a shopping day to Riverside with Mamma. Mostly I live alone at home but I'm not even as lonely as I am at school.

In the evenings Mamma goes to bed early but I stay up with the music on, writing or reading till quite late and then I go up to bed. I lie in my quiet night plant room and fall into sleep and dreams easily; only the sounds of distant dogs and cars come into my room.

I do not like this place. I do not like it, Dr. Pullias. Interesting that some of the most intelligent thoughts come when one is half asleep have you ever read Green Eggs and Ham by Dr. Seuss? It's about a little guy trying to get this other guy to try green eggs and ham. The other guy insists that he does not like them, he does not like them, Sam-I-am. Sam-I-am goes through a long thing of asking, "Would you, could you with a fox? Would you, could you in a box?" "I would not, could not with a fox. I would not, could not in a box. I do not like green eggs and ham, I do not like them Sam-I-am."

Finally the guy says okay if you let me be I'll try your green eggs and ham. And he likes them! And he'll like them with a fox, in a box, etc. it's like you persuading me to try college and I say I do not like it. Then you say, well would you like it here or there, would you like it anywhere? I say, No! I do not like college. I do not like it, Dr. Pullias. Finally do you suppose I'll just suddenly give up and like it?

I wish I could do that right now; I wish I could just like it but I hate it, and I want to leave badly, but I've nowhere to go. I'd like this life to be over with.

Your friend,

Debbie.

P. S. And yet when I receive a letter from you I feel better, not so ignored and useless. Thank you for the friendship.

Dear Dr. Pullias

175.
February 2, 1974
Dear Dr. Pullias,

I'm down in my friend, Heather's room. She lets me stay here when she's out. Since she is the R. A. She gets a single room and fixes it up just her way. This room reminds me just a bit of my room at home – not in looks but the feeling. Because the bed has a bedside table and lamp and because there's a stereo to play lovely <u>soft</u> music and because the pillow I'm leaning against is comfy and because there are rugs on the floor and because the people next door are not very noisy. Suddenly, when I am down here alone, things do seem sturdier, more homey, not as crowded. Down here, alone, with the music, tears come to my eyes, not from irritation or frustration, but for the loveliness of life and being here.

These dormitories, I'm afraid, are failing to create an inducive environment for learning; they are even failing as a place to call "mine" or "home." We say, "Let's go back." instead of "Let's go home!" The lights are very harsh, the paneling, sterile, and the building sways when someone goes down the stairs, and everyone hears everyone else through the walls. Very poor idea, these dorms.

I think that, the dorms, is really the cause behind my depression – anyone can stand a bad class for one quarter, I can even forgo all my pleasure reading till the summer without getting too upset – but it's hard for me to live comfortably when I feel hemmed in with noise, people, paneling. The place where one lives – isn't that the place that one lives <u>from</u>? For me, where I sleep each night and where my friends and where I wake up each morning, is the base from which I strike out into the rest of the world. If the base is weak, I am weak.

But here in Heather's room, I am filled with contentment the music.... ah, makes my chest fill with warmth. And I love Heather for her understanding and her love for me. Dr. Pullias, there is so much importance in love, don't you think? Everything thrives best with the care of love, I feel love for just that simple fact – I love the way anything, person, place, or thing, ANYTHING looks, feels, is the best with care and love. That makes me love everything and everyone even more because I know love, oh! LOVE!

So you see I feel better than I did the last letter I wrote. Bad things change, disappear, reappear with the minute; Good things are

ever under, through and forever.
        You are a friend forever,
        Debbie.

        It's later and I finished my science lab write-up; I should be reading history but now I'd rather write to you. I promise I'll read at least two hours worth of history tomorrow, okay? I'm afraid I'm doing quite poorly in this history class; I'm glad it's the only one I have to take. Dr. Box probly wonders what in the world you see in me – "This girl? She can't even write a decent history paper; what's special about her?"
        Why is it so very hard to describe the feeling I get when I hear this music? Certain notes or melodies, I don't know. I don't know how or why music touches the nerves, but it's so beautiful.
        Heather is out drinking with a few friends. Too bad, but she's at least careful about it and won't drive till it's safe. What a strange kind of game it is here, drinking. Very strange. Oh well... to each his own.
        Last night I had an icky dream. At first it was nice because Jay was in it (he's a student here) and I like him. It seems there was a school activity at a huge stone castle. Afterwards Jay, Heather, and I were in one of the castle rooms; Jay sat by me on the couch to explain a map of the castle. Then I walked alone down a stone corridor where baby furniture stood abandoned, here an old wooden rocking horse, here an elaborate wooden high-chair. When I looked again a baby of about 2 or 3 clung to the chair. It was a baby that wasn't alive but he was. I don't know. He had blueberry stuff around his eyes and mouth but they were sort of like bruises, too. I took him into the bathroom to wash off the stain. He looked at me but didn't smile; he was deadish alive.
        Today I took Cassie and her friend Danny into La Jolla. We stopped by the bookstore and I bought a pretty book, Amanda, Dreaming, for Debbie (her birthday is the 8th of February; she'll be twenty. Can you imagine; soon I will be twenty, also. Twenty). Then we went to the beach; the two children ran off for the tidepools to catch fish, and I wandered with the ocean tumbling in, reaching almost to my shoes but not quite.
        Yes, I am on the tennis team again this year; I look forward eagerly to our practices. The coach is exceedingly nice; I like her; she likes me! Last time she and Jann were playing doubles with Franny and

me and during a pause, Mrs. McKay said, "I laugh a lot when I play with Debbie." And I laughed at my feet and smiled at her. Ah, how a simple sincere compliment lifts me!

Now I think I will cease the writing; I feel like I'm just driveling and maybe I'll read, maybe I'll think, maybe I'll go to bed.

Debbie.

176.
Los Angeles-to Debbie's mother in Hemet
Feb. 3, 1974
Dear Myrtle:

I guess this should be a sort of personal or confidential letter. I have been very busy this year, and have not written to you as I had intended to do. I have written regularly to Debbie.

I wanted you to know that Max [Debbie's father] wrote me from Hemet asking me if he could live out on our place for awhile. He said he needed and wanted some time to be alone. Of course, we were eager to do anything that might help him find his way. So we told him to move out there if he wished. Also, it might help to wean the vandals away. I wanted to write you before I made the arrangement. I wasn't able to, and I didn't see how it could hurt anything for him to be there, and it might do some good. Anyway I wanted you to know.

I am very pleased with Debbie's development. Her letters, in my judgment, reflect remarkable growth in many ways. I am always concerned, perhaps too much so, that something or somebody will pull her away from her education. I believe she will go right on, but there will be hard spots and she will need all the guidance and strengthening you and I can give her. The truth is if you could do it and you think she would like for you to, it might be good if you went down to see her now and then.

I hope too you will not let the rest of the family waste or unwisely use your Mother and Father's resources. Seems like there is always someone after money. I know they know how to look after their affairs, but you might be open to pressure or persuasion. I hope your work goes well. I surely like the place you have now. Let me know if I can help.

Earl V. Pullias

Debbie Bumstead

177.

February 6, 1974

Dear Dr. Pullias,

   With the strength of 10 men I got up this morning to come to history class. The only reason I came is because I ought to; it won't be so bad today because I'm writing you. This will keep me from constantly looking at my watch.

   The test I thought I so hopelessly failed turned up with a B. My, my! I received my report card yesterday – all As. So we think we are rather smart – heh?

   I think Dr. Box put too much cologne on this morning.

   This afternoon, finally, I hope to settle my plans for degree and credential. I've asked for help from professors; they either didn't know or weren't saying. Now I've an appointment with Mrs. Hayes who works in the education department. I certainly hope she helps me. I think she will.

   Tomorrow we have our first tennis match at Palomar. I asked Mrs. McKay if Debbie could come along and she said yes and I asked Debbie if she wanted to come and she said yes, hurrah! So tomorrow I'll go pick up Debbie and then she'll see my room and then we'll get into the van with all the rest of the team. All of the girls will be so excited because most have never been to a match before. Then we'll get there, warm up, play, and maybe win, maybe lose. Afterwards we get to practice on the courts; Debbie can play then. And then, off we drive with everyone chatter-chattering about what it was like, how to improve, etc.

   Dr. Box is getting quite excited about Charlemagne.

   To dinner we will go, in some pleasant restaurant and the school pays. Mmm, good food. Chatter and laugh, it's fun. When we get home, perhaps Debbie and I will go visit Ruth; I'll listen to them talk until Debbie wishes to go home. And I can spend the night at her house so I won't have to drive back in the dark. It's so quiet at that house.

   You would probably like Debbie; she's exceptionally nice and intelligent. I like her.

   My, it's five to 9 o'clock, only about twenty minutes left. The fellow next to me is coughing. Bothersome. He is also taking liberties

with my desk, bumping it. Stop please.
I think I'll just sit now.
Your friend,
Debbie.
Mrs. Hayes did help me, very much. I found that I can get my
B. A. With a major in psychology and with four extra required classes I
can get into a teaching program which lasts one year.

I have eleven required classes left to complete the major and to
get into the teaching program and twelve openings (three per quarter)
for classes till the end of my junior year so I shall try to finish all these
classes by my senior year. Then I can spend the senior year in the
teaching program. The only thing is, there is an art class sequence that
lasts three quarters that I'd really like to take. I'm going to see if I can't
take some of the teaching requirements (U. S. History, speech,
composition, music) at the junior college during the summer.

Boy, is it nice to have everything settled. The counselor was
very enthusiastic about the teaching program. They find teachers
positions for the student and you can pick what grade. I can even be
placed in an open classroom! How wonderful!

I'll have to take exams (a new law you probably know about) to
get the teaching credential. I also have to take some exams toward the
B. A. I don't really mind tests. D.

178.
Feb. 9, 1974
At home
Dear Myrtle:
As you know I believe it would not be wise for Debbie to
think we were writing each other about her. I know you would
understand that, but I was concerned that my letter to you may
have expressed more concern than was warranted. In a letter that
came yesterday she reported having got her courses all planned
to go right on for her degree and her teaching credential. (She
was very happy) There will be ups and downs, but I believe she
is on her way. I have great confidence in her and her future. Yet I
know there are many attractive detours in this life.

I hope things go reasonably well with you. We are about
as usual - really greatly blessed. I hope too your parents are all

right. They have worked hard and long, but that is life, and overall, I think, is better than working to avoid work. Life is complicated. Keep your faith and a good sense of humor and perspective.

     Sincerely, Earl V. Pullias

178.
Los Angeles
Feb. 12, 1974
Backyard Study
Dear Debbie:

     So I am back out in my alone place. When I mentioned I had been driven out by the cold and the need not to use the electric heater to try to save current, I mentioned the pictures and objects about the room that may come alive and be together when I am away. It was your idea or fantasy. An interesting one.

     Then I was in the living room and thought when I was out here again I would tell you who would take part in that party. Beginning to the left of my desk and going around the room: a photograph of a road in a forest two people walking together; on the desk two solemn owls - one red made of wax (a candle) and the other larger and more severe of grey cement; also on the desk a beautiful head and neck of a Native Hawaiian girl made of black coral which Mrs. P. brought me back from the state; and the small picture of a girl maybe fourteen or sixteen, a reproduction of a painting by a French artist, picked up in London one day - wearing a red scarf. Then the picture you gave me - would the leaves and toadstools take part or just observe. Next to that picture two pictures of my first grade teacher - one when she was sixteen and the other when she was 31 or 32 about the time she taught me.

     Then on the south wall to my right my friend Debbie B. and her cat; above them a brown plaque of an ancient Greek girl (from Greece); next to D.B. a beautiful white horse and her small colt both lying down in a meadow; above them sheep (all white I believe) grazing in a pasture; going on around a small Madonna called the Madonna of the chair (Mary holding Jesus and the

Dear Dr. Pullias

little John looking on - very nice colors); and the next little girl with black hair and a pink cape flying a kite - I think I sent you one of the cards once; next a picture of Francis of Assisi feeding birds and animals and in the picture a copy of his famous prayer - your friend Debbie S. would like it; then two pictures of Jesus when he was a young man - maybe your age. Finally, also on the west wall a picture of Gandhi given to me by an Indian (East) young man who was my student. The south wall is composed chiefly of windows and looks out on the back yard.

Now it occurs to me there would not be room enough in this little "shop" for them to be very free! Where would they go? Would they be afraid out in the yard under the bright soft moon that will shine tonight? I think not if you and your cat were with them.

Today I have been working on some talks I must make a little later this spring. Getting a little tired I stop to talk with you a moment. My classes are underway and I hope will be good.

If in your reading you run into something you think I would like let me know - or simply something you liked.

When you feel like it tell me how you found your friend D. I hope she is finding her way wisely. There are many paths that lead to good and beautiful places; many to bad and ugly places.

Sincerely, Earl V. Pullias

179.
February 14, 1974
Dear Dr. Pullias,

I am at home for the weekend; it's late and I sit curled up in a fleecy quilt on my bed. Sari, the Kitty is playing with my toes when I wiggle them – now she has decided to wash herself. I like her; she likes me! She's a good kind of friend.

Oh, your letter was so fun to get and read today! I so enjoyed picturing your study and its occupants; I am sure that some nights when the stars and moon are especially soft and lovely, there are quiet parties in your backyard.

The Hawaiian and Greek girls and your first-grade teacher and

Debbie Bumstead

the French girl, the baby Jesus, the mare's colt, the girl with the kite, little John, and I played tag on the lawn or hide and seek, running on silent feet; you will not hear us even if you are awake. Perhaps Mary sits talking to the white horse; the sheep lie peacefully watching us play; Jesus, Gandhi, and St. Francis talk about green pleasant things; the owls are not so severe as they look, not at this party, and they tease Sari, my cat. Maybe, if you are just falling asleep, you will hear the owls hoot, softly or the colt nicker or me, whispering into the night breeze, "Ah... The night."

Hurrah! That makes me smile.

Do you know what I'm doing tomorrow? No, not baby-sitting, horse-sitting! One of the horses out where my mother's friends' keep theirs is going to foal extremely soon. It's her first so she needs watching; I'll look after her until school's out, then Mamma will come. I do hope the baby is born before I go back to college Monday – they are such exquisite little creatures, foals. Prieta will have hers in June, oh joy!

I went downstairs to put on some records – Simon and Garfunkel are nice; I also like the record with Tchaikovsky's Dance of the Flowers, the Dance of the Hours, and the Mazurka. I don't remember who composed the last two but I like to whistle to the Mazurka.

Saturday my mother is going to Las Vegas with some girlfriend. My, my.

I think I will read up on St. Francis of Assisi; he sounds interesting. I've read three good children's books recently: Stuart Little by E. B. White (author of The Trumpet of the Swan. I read Stuart Little when in second grade – one of my favorite books), A Little Princess & The Secret Garden by Frances H. Burnett have you read any of these? Harriet the Spy by Louise Fitzhugh is a good fun book to read.

It was so much fun staying the night at Debbie's! Her birthday was the next day and her housemates gave her a surprise party that night I was there. She was so tickled and happy, oh, it was funny! I so love to be with her. She is a bit sorry that her classes require an exceeding amount of study, but she still gets mainly straight As. I would like to live in a quiet house like hers where one can sit alone in the warm sun.

I must be off to bed, I suddenly realized. Good-night.

Love to you,

Dear Dr. Pullias

Debbie.

180.
Los Angeles
Feb. 24, 1974
Dear Debbie:

It is a lovely Sunday morning - a good time to be out in your eucalyptus grove. Mrs. P. and I greatly appreciated your note expressing your feelings about the card and the gift. We love you very much - and did not have a regular daughter. The idea to get a special chair for your place out in nature seems good; we simply wanted you to get something you specially liked.

I like all your letters but especially the one about the party of the beings in my study. I shall listen for all of you on the lawn some night when the moon is warmly bright. But I must not try to see you for then all would vanish into thin air! Debbie, your imaginative letter gave me an idea. Why don't you begin writing stories or a continuing story for some of the children you know and love? I'm sure they would like them. Many writers I believe have begun their work by writing for children in the family. As I recall Charles Dickens, "A Child's Christmas Carol" was written that way - also his child's history of England. Of course, for various reasons you might not wish to do that kind of thing, at least yet. Just an idea.

I hope you will read some things about, and by Francis of Assisi - a very great spirit, I think. I am glad you were able to see something of Debbie, the friend you love so much. One needs such a friend. I am glad things go well with her. If she knows of me give her my regards and good wishes. Sometime I must learn more about the Christian Science faith. Are you aware that you Grandfather Bumstead was brought up in that faith as a youth? (I must write to him.)

What a wonderful day this would be to be at Hemet - but it is good here too: the goodness is largely within us.

Sincerely, Earl V. Pullias

181.

Debbie Bumstead

February 27, 1974
Wednesday in Dr. Box's class
Dear Dr. Pullias,

It's a foggy kind of day and I would like to be asleep in my warm bed but I have come to class. Why don't I listen? My head is too heavy, it is easier to write.

I'm going home again this weekend because, guess what! We (actually Mr. Heaton) have two new baby horses, a filly and a colt. And another is imminent! I'm bringing along the little 8-year-old girl, Cassie with me and will stay 'til Sunday. That ought to be fun.

I wish I felt better today, I seem to be aching all over for sleep. I'm debating weather to go or not to science. Yes, I think I'll go, no, maybe not. Science, sometimes, is so very interesting, I really like the class even though I'm not a science whiz. Next quarter I'm taking the second class in natural science; it's a requirement but I don't mind.

I'm also taking Psychology of Personal Development as an independent seminar class and advanced creative writing, which I felt I should take to help me in that vein. Next year I wish to take a special year class called, "Studies in Drawing." I feel it's very important that I don't let slip my small creative talents to receive such a scientific practical B. A. and credential. I would rather be an authoress and illustrator but it's a bit less practical than some nice steady job. But I think eventually I could be or have both. So, in my work toward one I'll not forget the other.

I just got my second history test back, another B -. "Debbie, this is a good expression of your subjective response to some aspects of the middle ages, but is a bit vague as an exposition of the reform movements. Or so it strikes me. But I will be glad to have you come in & discuss it." I would say to him, "well, if I get a B - on an objectively written paper that I hated writing and a B - on a subjective paper I thoroughly enjoyed, then I expect I'll continue the latter." But I doubt that I'll go see him.

I did come to science. After this class then I go check my mail and then to the cafeteria. In the afternoon I will take a nap and then wash my hair. I plan to go to a certain place in the forest where a particular type of eucalyptus grows to collect seeds for my Mama. Also I plan to do a bit of studying in my psychology books, go to dinner, then I don't know what.

Oh, I'll be so glad for our weeks vacation in two weeks. I just

210

Dear Dr. Pullias

want to relax or something, I want to sleep late.
>   Your friend,
>   Debbie.

182.

Dear Dr. Pullias,

I don't know what to do. Today I finally got a hold of my independent study teacher and took my work to her. I learned that I should have seen her ages ago to make out a "contract." She was very nice about it but stated that the work was certainly not sufficient. In other words I failed the class. Of course, being me, I began to cry, I had to leave and I wandered far into the forest to sit in the spring grasses and smell the white sage. I never feel lonely among the bushes, trees, and rocks but I feel free to let loose the sobs of my worry.

What do you think I ought to do? The only thing that concerns me is my scholarship. If I dropped the class right now I'll only be taking 11 units and I'm required to be taking 12 to receive the grant (however I can request permission to go under 12 units). If I take the failing grade my grade averages brought down quite a bit. I suppose I'll write them a letter explaining things – why was I so dumb? Rats. You think it will hurt me?

I kind of wish to change my major. Would that be unwise? I read the fine print of psychology majors to find that one must have 30 units of a related field in sociology or communications. I don't know – I don't know. I feel as if I could never take another ugly psychology class; I'm stuffed to overflowing with the pompousness of them. Perhaps I'd like to have an Art major – do you think I'd grow tired of that? When I spoke to Dr. Henry, the education counselor, and Dr. Brummer, they all thought I ought to have an art major, as it would suit me better and Dr. Henry said there was not much demand for psychology right now.

I wish wish wish I could take what I want want want.

I hate to listen to people kiss and kiss and fondle each other. How can a girl meet a guy just a week ago and now kiss kiss kiss? How? I suppose nothing's wrong with it for her, she has the wish to kiss as if she were talking – for me a kiss is exceedingly special even just on the cheek. I don't like sex on the porch.

211

Debbie Bumstead

183.

March 4, 1974

Dear Dr. Pullias,

I'm dressed nicely today; the pink and yellow bead necklace Debbie gave me for my birthday, my whale shirt and over that a rust colored pullover, My neat silver Croton watch, a pair of quite spiffy gray corduroy pants and navy blue socks embroidered with four red and green owls and lastly my suede hiking shoes with their striped shoe-laces. Hurrah!

The wind is cold today but the sun shines and I hear a bird singing; the radio is playing, too. This morning I registered for next quarter – I changed my classes to "Natural History and Cultivation of Plants", Modern Art History", "Advanced Creative Writing", and an introductory education course, and the tennis team. Also I called the scholarship commission and they said drop the course, we'll send you a form to fill out, and for the month of March you will receive 75 dollars instead of 100. I don't know if they will take off from my tuition grant or not, I should have asked of them. Later: no, they won't. They were very nice about it. Nothing affects the tuition part and once I am back to a regular amount of units I continue to get the monthly 100 dollars. Ah, now that's a relief.

Cassie and I had a good time in Hemet. Cassie loved riding Prieta and I loved the weather and the colors in the world, green fields, black windy-maned horse, brisk cheeks. Saturday we went hiking up to your cabin to visit my father. He was reading by the fire when we came – doesn't that sound cozy? I wish I could do that here. He and his friend Eileen have the place fixed nicely. Cassie played with the kitten and Daddy and I talked about school and writing. We had hot chocolate. Then we all went over to Joe's trailer; Joe doesn't look too well sometimes; I think he's worse than me at eating. He probably smokes too much marijuana.

It's funny the way I go. Now, when I am feeling good I think of myself as extremely healthy mentally (physically I know I'm pretty healthy) and I think of my life as pure and clean. I cry when I am sad but being sad doesn't carry into being happy, so I am happy when I am happy. Sometimes even when I am sad I see it is good to have it pass. How do I say it? My life is pure; I like pure, unshaded colors; I like bright patterns and I like details. I like things that are what they say they are; I don't like symbolism or icky wishy washy feelings I don't understand. I see things in colors and outlines and patterns and compositions that are pleasing to my eyes.

Some things are very pleasing, both to write about and do. There are certain things one is in the mood to do. Look in the catalogue, read books about growing plants, reading late at night or early in the morning or in the middle of the day, playing in the mud in the summertime. When you are in the mood to do something you go do it and you enjoy that and build on it in your mind. Really one learns that way. Sometimes when you are doing the thing you're in the mood to do you run across something new and when you are in the mood to do something new you go back to that and learn about it. That's the way I learn in the summer and on other vacations and to a much slower degree here at school.

I wish I could have a kitten here at school; I would like that. For next year I've been thinking of other places to live besides the dorms that would be just as practical. Across the road is a housing development that would be good to live in; one of the counselors here owns a house there that I've been to – I wonder if I could suggest rooming in her extra bedroom (she has a husband and one teen daughter) telling her that I could pay a reasonable amount. I think I would like that except I don't know if one could just go up to someone and ask if they'd like an extra person around. I thought I could ask my tennis coach because I'm pretty good friends with her she lives on Point Loma but drives here every day anyway. But she has quite a few children; I don't know if she has any room. Then there's going to be an opening at the house where Debbie lives but that's kind of far away. What do you think? Is your house two-story? Somehow I had gotten the idea that it was; it surprised me to hear you write of looking right out into the backyard. But I like the idea of glass doors and a bird feeder. What kind of trees and other plants do you have?

I have just thought that it would be nice indeed to live across the street at Dr. Kobes house. One evening we were invited to visit her for dinner. Afterwards when the other girls were playing around in the sewing room, I sat in the guest room. It was much much smaller than the daughter's room but it was snug and quiet.

Ah.. well. Perhaps I'll get enough nerve to ask her.

Your friend,

Debbie-debbie.

More: in the evenings an irritation settles on me. I think

evenings were made to have someone, a friend, to talk with or read with or just be silent with. An intimate kind of friend. I don't have that here; I suppose that was my wish last year, too – that I could have good company in the evenings. I like to be alone during the day but at night I like company. I wish you could somehow transport yourself over to visit me tonight; oh, I do, or better that I could transport myself to your house. Oh, how I have long wished I could do that – tesseract myself to faraway friends houses and sit in their rooms enjoying the comfort of comradeship. Or that they could tesseract to me. I have even thought of becoming a scientist to see if I could work it out. It would solve the gas problem.

I should study my history but I'll do that Wednesday okay? Tomorrow I have a science lab and a tennis match at USD. I like tennis even though I'm not especially fierce and competitive.

You know one thing about me that's kind of different than other girls my age? I tend to have a wide variety of friends with respect to their ages. Young and older and the same age. Most of the girls have friends their own age. What's that got to do with the price of tea? (Or something like that – Debbie says some witty remark like that but I can't remember quite how it goes.)

Debbie has left a lot of marks on me. I flip my hair back from my shoulders like she does and sometimes on especially inspirational sunny days I break out whistling one of the hymns she sings. I can't recall the tune when I want but sometimes it just comes. She certainly affected me philosophically. I sing much more than I used to and I just all round try and act cool like her. Last year she told me I was rubbing off on her! My slouch and my creative remarks and wishing more to draw and write. That's nice. Yep, I like her.

She knows of you; I often shared your letters with her. The last time I saw her she said to give you her regards. I will give her yours.

What were you like when you were my age?

Debbie.

184.

March 27, 1974 –

Dear Dr. Pullias –

I received your letter Monday when I came back – thanks. It

seemed as if I hadn't heard from you in a long time when actually it had only been a week. Whatever would I do if you quit writing altogether! What would you do if I quit writing? Probably live as well as ever!

Oh, have you ever read the "Pippi Longstocking" books? I love them dearly, Pippi is my most favorite heroine in the world, and I would like to think of myself as sort of like her in my friendships with children. And think of my older friends as being like Pippi to me. You need to read all of them (about 3 or 4 books) to get a complete picture of her personality. The authoress, Astrid Lindgren, has written other good children's books as well, one is Rasmus and the Vagabond. Gee, Pippi is so neat. I would like to have all her books for my library; maybe I will buy a set for a present to myself.

James is down in San Diego looking for a job, on Monday we went together to La Jolla and explored the beach, then we drove to downtown San Diego and wandered around. Downtown S. D. is quite ratty and grey, but I like to explore it... As long as I'm with someone. We had fun checking out each floor in tall old office buildings. We felt like adventurers. James's fun; I like that in a person.

Do you know what I'm glad for? That my friend, Pam, from last year is going back to school here again this quarter. Her two quarter absence has made no difference, we are still the best of pals. And I need THAT. She is similar to me sensitivity-wise. I wish she could be my roommate.

Does it take you a long time to write a letter? It does me. I wish I could just whip them off zip zip zip.

My classes may prove quite interesting.

Right now I feel kind of strange, it's been a strange day. Oh, I know what it was – in the orientation to Teach. Ed. And in my Crea/Writ classes the lights were terrifically blaring and I felt ugly and pimply, no one knew me or would want to. That's icky to feel.

Pam came over this evening and we conversed for a pleasant while. Now I am about to fall asleep. I wanted to write in my journal but that will wait till tomorrow; I'll take a quick shower and go to bed. My roommate Janey is out (how come I always get roommates who go out constantly?); I wish she was here so that I wouldn't have to wake up later. Oh, well, perhaps I won't – perhaps I'm so tired I'll sleep deeply.

Good-night.

Your friend, Debbie.

Debbie Bumstead

185.
Los Angeles
March 31, 1974
Bedroom
Dear Debbie:

It was good to get your letter written after you got back to school. I sent one to you at Hemet that probably didn't arrive before you left. Your mother will send it along. I have run into a little bad luck. I am threatened with a cold or a virus which has driven me to bed yesterday and today in the hope I can be better for tomorrow's activities. Lying here looking out the window onto the backyard reminds me that I never told you much about our house. I will sometime. Mrs. P wanted a two story or upstairs, but alas she never had it: did not think early enough to marry rich!

I must share some very good news with you. The book I wrote at Hemet and used to read chapters to your father when he was working on the gazebo has finally been accepted for publication. The title will probably be <u>These Things Are Fundamental</u>, but I am not sure. I believe it is the best writing I have done. It will be good to see it in book form and hold it in one's hands, and especially to smell the fresh printer's ink. Of course, I'll send you a copy as soon as they are available. I know you would like to be glad with me.

I look forward to the time when I will hold one of your books in my hand and in my heart. That will come, but we do not push it.

I am very glad your friend, Pam, is back in school and near so you can be with her. A single friend near who has some mutual feeling makes all the difference in the feeling of one's life. I wish you could room with such a friend in your junior and senior years. Perhaps that will come if it is best. Can you tell what is happening to James as he grows older. Some people change quite a bit, and some almost not at all.

I am eager to read the "Pippi Longstocking" books you mention. Mrs. P's sister who works in the public library can bring them home for me. I'll tell you what I think. The

216

afternoon has been beautiful - not good to have to be in. I like for
you to mention things good to read.
> Sincerely, Earl V. Pullias
> P.S. Make those courses the very best possible - just for
fun!

186.
April 6, 1974
Dear Dr. Pullias,

Its summer-y here; I am reminded of last year when it began to be summer. Not reminded especially mentally but almost physically. Interesting.

My roommate Janey brought the little girl she tutors over to spend the night last night. Janey magner 2835063 4333 cathy magner1/2p (she just decided she must try out the typewriter). I enjoy having children around. Some young girls, though, have an interesting sort of unnaturalness to the way they act, as if they had been brought up to especially act girlish. Or something. Do you know what I mean? I wonder if I was (or am?) that way. The little girl that I tutor here, Cassie, is not at all that way. I like her because she's natural and active and especially because of a certain sense of justice she has and a compassion for other things. Sometimes one finds that in children; it's good.

My mother has vacation next week so she is planning to come down and visit me for a couple of days. That'll be nice and then on Friday I'll take her home and stay the weekend. I feel like being at home. I wonder if the trees have grown out their leaves yet. I am looking forward to the summer. This year, it seems, has been tough or tedious, or something. Boring, I suppose, perhaps, I've had too much time on my hands. Next year I'd like to get a T. A. job at a elementary school and stick with it all year.

I hope your cold is all over and that you enjoy "Pippi" as much as I do.

This morning I took Janey and her little friend to the animal shelter. I like to look at each dog and cat because they are each different, individuals. I would like to take them all home to live with me. The kittens and puppies are so appealing because I see in them the need to be loved and reassured, the need for someone to look up to and learn from and model after. At home I like to watch our two new puppies, Mitzie and Kiska, try to imitate the older dog, Hobo. They are so fun.

I had a strange experience in my creative writing class the last time it met. We drove over to somebody's house and sat in the living room. Dr. Eulert asked me to read one of my writings. So here I was revealing my most inner secrets to a group of strangers. They liked my writing. It was a weird sensation, that's for sure and it will happen twice a week for the quarter. We will see what will come of it.

I am enclosing something I wrote awhile ago.

Your friend,

Debbie.

February 13, 1974 – Wednesday

I'd like to have a smallish house, maybe a cottage, in bright rich La Jolla within walking distance to the stores and beach and where I work. I work as a teacher at an open classroom school. I ride my bike to school every morning. I look rather young to be a full-time teacher, but I am, and my hair is blonde and long; I wear it in a single loose braid tied with pretty ribbons. Oh, I'm very neat and have soft-clothes to attractive printed dresses and thin-fitting nylons and shiny comfortable shoes. Maybe I don't ride my bike to school because I always wear dresses, instead I walk, briskly, and sometimes for fun I run, because I still love to run and laugh. I am always brown from beach-wandering summers, even in the cloudiest winter when I wear bright woolen skirts and pattern pull-over sweaters, still my hair sparkles and floats with cleanliness and my eyes are turquoise against my gentle tanned face.

The children in my class are five, six, and seven years old; they are small and quick. It's quite a large class so that there are two teacher's assistants. The children go about their work and play and we watch and help and suggest; I play pretend with them often because I still enjoy doing so. Outside I play tag or that I am the captured Indian princess or that I am the evil monster queen. And the assistants and I always think of new ideas for displays or projects. The class is mostly cooperative and happy and learning because we all enjoy our places, and I love the children and watching and listening to and laughing with them. With care and love they are exquisite little creatures.

Dear Dr. Pullias

(Dear Dr. Pullias, there is so much more that I tire of typing and I thought that perhaps you would read my journal anyway – – you are always welcome to though you don't have to. I don't think I write any different knowing that someone is going to read it, but I wouldn't really know because I always have someone who reads my journals. So you can, if you ever want to. Maybe at the end of each school year. Over spring vacation I put all my writings into notebooks; I have them since 2nd grade! I have some diary type listings from 5th grade and summer, interesting to read – – but I think I told you I have them already. debbie.)

187.
Los Angeles
Backyard Study
April 14, 1974
Dear Debbie:
Probably by tonight you are back at the University. I hope your mother came down and you had a nice visit with her there. It must have been wonderful at Hemet today and yesterday and the day before if you were there on Friday. We drove up on Thursday, and it was good, although the trip is a little long for one day. We had a pleasant simple lunch under the juniper tree over to the East - and thought of you. Saw a rabbit or two.

I finished my first of the Pippi Longstocking stories by Lindgren, <u>Pippi In the South Seas</u>. I like the stories very much, and am looking forward to reading others when Frances (my sister-in-law) can get others from the Library where she works. I am deeply interested in the great appeal of these stories. They say something quite profound about life, I suspect. I do not mean to destroy my direct enjoyment of them by thinking about them too much: as you know, thinking is a great part of my enjoyment.

I liked the list of writing you sent. Your greatness lies in your genuineness, your being yourself. Probably it is hard for any of us to be ourselves if we are very conscious of an audience. Your creative writing class procedure will be interesting to

219

observe. I guess a part of our learning to write is to learn to write for an audience while remaining sincerely ourselves. I am sure it can be done, but it may not be easy. I'll be very interested in reading your journals for this year this summer if you would like for me to.

My cold is about gone. The week has been good. Easter today has been beautiful.

Sincerely your friend, Earl V. Pullias

188.

April 16, 1974 – Tuesday

Dear Dr. Pullias,

I have had a lovely day! First off I had a pleasant dream. Sometimes dreams can leave me feeling good, cozy and loved, all day. This dream had you in it! You and Mrs. Pullias and I were walking along the dirt road down from your cabin. Perhaps you had your arm around my shoulders, I don't know. Then we were all walking on a straight dirt road with green fields on either side. It was in the evening. Oh, it was such a pleasant time of the day to be with good friends. We came to a house that was yours, an old house, something like ours on Buena Vista. I sat down on the couch. You sat down by me. Your arm was along the couch back of me and we were talking. Somehow I felt unsure of myself and you reassured me saying, "Not to worry, I'm sure your IQ is at least 200 if not 300." It sounds pretty funny now but in the dream it was comforting. I looked at you and wondered if I should tell you my secret. No, I would not, just yet.

The next part of the dream concerned itself with my secret. I was home and it was night. I slipped out of the house and into the driveway. Ah! Now! My experiments, my secret scientific explorations in flying! Without motors, etc. It was rather like swimming, only in the air.

That was a funny good dream. Thank you for being such a wonderful friend!

This morning I went over to tutor Cassie. I take her into the teacher's lounge, and she reads one book aloud to me. I have previously underlined certain words throughout the text. I keep a notebook in which I put a check for every page she reads and for every underlined word. It's a pretty good incentive just getting all those checks; she wants to break her record of "100 and 89." But toward the end of the book she gets SO tired. I really like her very much, she's quite bright and fun. I like her sense of humor. And I'm beginning to be quite good about this behavior; I relax and enjoy it – work with it, rather than fight it. I'm glad I'm being able to do that more often – I think it builds a better friendship. I'm not saying give in, exactly, to the child's wishes but work with them. Its different, somehow.

Yesterday James and I went down to Shelter Island to wander around the boat docks and eat seafood. We went to Old Town where, in a museum, James played an old out-of-tune piano. He plays very very well. Piano playing is extremely important to him. Such a pleasant fellow he is. It's funny that no one I know knows how enjoyable he is because if we're around someone new he never speaks a word but have that person leave and he rambles on and on – he speaks exceptionally well.

I don't know how I got onto yesterday when I was telling you about today! This afternoon we had a tennis match at UCSD. I played 4th singles and won! My, my, what a great surprise. And Debbie came to visit us there at the courts. And she came with us for a picnic on the beach. Gee.

When I won the match Mrs. McKay said, "Fantastic! What really amazes me is the way you play – so casually – just hitting the ball over and over and over."

"Yeah! Like me last year" Debbie added, "You know Debbie taught me to play."

Gee. I've never before made friends with an older woman but I have with Mrs. McKay. It's kind of different. I don't really know how yet. We'll see.

I have good friends, don't I?

My creative writing class is so very strange. I don't really know how about that either yet.

Next Wednesday the tennis team is going for a tournament up in Ojai. We will stay for a couple of days. That'll be fun, I think.

April 17, 1974 – Wednesday

I received your letter today, thank you, I read it as I ate watermelon for lunch out in the sun. The cafeteria had a picnic. Dr. Box was sitting and watching the proceeds, so I went over to see him. He said to tell you hello. So, hello!

Debbie Bumstead

I'm so glad you like Pippi. I don't remember if I told you about the funny little girl I've been writing about. Her name is Alice and she comes from my dreams. I just put my dreams in third person and there she is! Alice is very open and fun; I rather like her. My creative writing teacher does, too; he said last time we met, "Someday I hope to hold a book by you, called 'Alice!'" Who knows? Maybe it will happen.

Yes, it was fun when Mamma and Joe came down. Lots of fun. Keep well!
Your friend,
Debbie.

189.
April 30, 1974
Dear Dr. Pullias,

> "Here I lie sick in bed
> With wondrous dreams
> running through my head
> There's my friend, Joan by name
> Turning cartwheels in my brain
> And what's that on top of my knee?
> A yellow and black striped bumblebee!
> And dancing across the front of my eyes,
> Are thousands and thousands
> of secret spies!
> What fun it is to lie sick in bed
> With wondrous dreams running
> through my head!"

I wrote that poem way back in elementary school, and just recalled it today because I am lying here sick on the couch in the living room. I think I caught the flu from one of the girls who went to Ojai. But I believe it's on the mend because the cough always comes last and I'm beginning to cough! I enjoy a good cough every once in awhile; I even enjoy a sniffly nose and a sore throat occasionally. But I don't like to throw-up (and I'm not) and I don't know about fevers. This is the first time in a long long while I've had a fever and I'm not yet sure I like it. One thing interesting about fevers is the dreams they produce. Absolutely fanatic! The first night I had just finished reading <u>A Sand County Almanac</u> which is about nature and wilderness life, etc. I dreamt of cause and effect and chains and lines and this living on that and that on this other and oh, my! No plot, only fanatical ravings and as I dreamed I thought it was all extremely important, that it would be my life's work to carry out the orders in this dream.

I feel kind of fanatical right now – I'm writing very fast with no real thought for content.

~~~

I feel like answering questions so I'll answer yours, then I'll start a letter to Marie in Reno because I got a letter from her today asking me zillions of funny little questions. She's a smart little kid (but she's 18) and seems happy with her life and marriage.

As for your questions about James – he has been trying to find a college to go to because he really wants to go back to school. He feels he needs the discipline. I don't know why he can't get himself moving. Maybe he will, now that he's moved to San Diego and is getting a job. He thought he might like to go to Mt. San Jacinto Jr. College next year just to start. Mamma said he could rent one of our rooms. He is good pleasant company so she says she will enjoy having him around. But if he rents in the summer she said it would be improper for us to be alone together when she's up in Reno. That's kind of funny, but OK with me. I'm pretty agreeable, right? That's lucky that I am, I like my life to be simple and things seem to get complicated when one fights. If I don't agree then I won't fight, I'll just leave. That's lucky.

I hear the girls who play tennis downstairs, leaving. We will have a match today and I had to go and be sick. Phooey! Rats, rats, rats.

Some days I feel quite the ugliest girl in the world, other days I think I'm attractive. Today, even if I am sick, I think I look nice – my hair is clean and long and a pretty color, my face is brown, my eyes are blue – I like blue eyes. And I'm not fat and I'm not pitifully thin. What really pleases me is the way my arms are firm, perhaps showing a bit of wiriness. I like to think of myself as "in shape" and healthy. And I am healthy even if I have the flu. It's a healthy cold.

Several times a day I just say, "Debbie."

And the other me says, "Yes?"

And then I say to myself, "Debbie, I love you."

Sometimes I make it into a poem:

"I love you, love, love you
I love love love you
I love you...."

Do you think that's weird? Sometimes I say, "I <u>like</u> you. You are nice. I like you."

It doesn't feel weird. It's just like that.

"Debbie."

"Yes?"

"Debbie, I love you."

"I <u>like</u> you. You are nice. I like you."

Dr. Pullias,

I like you, too.

I love you, too.

Your friend,

Debbie.

190.

Los Angeles

May 10,1974

Backyard Study

Dear Debbie:

I have been dreadfully neglectful of my sick young friend. I hope she is not longer sick, although she seemed to be having fun even with the flu - and that is something not many of us can do. Let me know if you got well pretty fast. Also, when you write tell me when your school is out, and when you will be going home. I will not wish to write you there after you have gone home.

My school is out June 6. That day we have a breakfast for our doctoral graduates in the School of Education at 8:00 and then formal graduation later in the day. It will be a full day, but a good day. The students are pleased to have completed their formal school work. I hope they will go on learning always. My work between now and the end of school will be pretty hard. I have good classes, I believe, and I am trying to help my students to <u>be</u> and to <u>want</u> to be the kind of people who can be good teachers. The world needs them very much.

I have a problem: here in my small study I put up the card you sent based on <u>The Wind in the Willows</u> of the Mole and the Rat laying out their picnic. I put the picture on the South wall next to the one of you and your cat (that is a favorite of mine).

Do you think the Mole and the Rat will be friends with all the rest of the creatures when they come down from their pictures later tonight perhaps to have a party on the lawn? Or will they be afraid of the others? The horse will not step on them? The large solemn owl will not be tempted to eat one of them will he?

I am glad you love Debbie and can say so, and that you love me and can say that. I am a little tired.

Sincerely, Earl V. Pullias

P.S. I am very glad you like Sappho's beautiful word images. I am reading another Pippi book, and like it.

191.

May 13, 1974 –

Dear Dr. Pullias,

Hi! And I got well fast and our school is over on the 6th of June, too and what are you going to do this summer?

I went home this past weekend and thought about what I might do. In the summer, that is. For sure I am going to teach my mother's puppies to do things like sit, stay, come, and walk on a leash. They are both big big pups. Mitzie is very smart; she almost has her own opinion on things. Kista is sweet and a little dumb but she likes to be around people. It will be interesting to see how each learns.

Maybe I'll take some classes at the Junior College. There are a few general classes (speech, music) that I need to get into the teaching program here. But if I don't, I'll try to get a pleasant job, maybe at the library. I suppose I'll make the usual bit of money by tutoring.

I have an evening class to get to right about now; we will probably get our mid-terms back tonight. Uh-oh! I like learning about artists. Of course my favorite is van Gogh. I like Marc's animal paintings.

My science class's fun, too. Boy, and my creative writing class, too! This quarter's classes have been top-notch.

I received a letter from Debbie today, too. Yes, I can say that I love her but my poem (?) In the last letter was not referring to her (what a problem we have, having the same name!) but to me! I tell me that I love me! Only I talked to me as if I were two people – me and me-Debbie. And I was wondering if it was weird to love myself. I don't think so because it doesn't feel weird, it feels happy and funny. Yes! Sometimes I am quite pleased with myself.

Summer – come! Who invented summer? A wizard of wonderfulness, I'm sure!

It's a summer-night party. The grass is cool under barefeet. Dream people and creatures from the pictures wander in the summer-fragrant air. Crickets sound and there is the trembling of silken speech – you hear a whisper or a tinkling laugh, faintly, through the open window. The Rat and the Mole are timid at first, keeping close to the study door; the owl is so stern, do his eyes look hungry? The horse is so huge; oh dear! But someone has asked the Rat for a poem and the Mole... Well, he's a lovable fellow; the owl will try to look less hungry; the horse will be exceedingly careful. And the summer will be poem-pretty and dream-splendid.

Yours, Debbie.

Dr. Pullias – here is something I handed out to our Crea/Writ class – two of my Alice stories. You needn't send it back – I have plenty of copies. Each student writes comments and gives them back.

The Water Nymphs

Alice and her little brother, Mikey crept out of the house one stormy night and walked along the lane that ran through the farm fields. The wind blew Alice and Mikey's hair. The green alfalfa growing in the fields tossed in the wind, too.

"See, these green fields stretch forever," Alice told Mikey, "until they reach the mountains. But the sky goes on even beyond the mountains. There are outlines in the clouds but no stars tonight."

Mikey looked up at the night sky. Alice knew everything.

"When will we reach the land where the little people live?" Mikey asked.

They entered a line of billowing swaying trees beside an irrigation stream that was more than twice its usual size. Alice said, "Now we are here." and dived into the curling black water, and Mikey followed her. The current took them away, away back home.

As they stood on the streambank Mikey wondered how he had managed to get out of the current; he wasn't that strong.

"I saw a mer-man and a mermaid help you," said Alice, "They had pink scales on their tails and they placed you safely on the bank."

Mikey whirled around to see the water people but they had

already flipped their pink tails and disappeared into the tumbling black water.

The thunder began, and the lightning and then the rain. Mrs. Bugle ran from the kitchen and hustled Alice and Mikey into the house saying, "You'll have to take baths and get warm." Alice and Mikey ran, giggling and wet, upstairs to change. Alice would not take a bath, but Mikey did.

He thought he saw two water nymphs in the bubble caves of his bathwater.

Could he be sure? Afterwards, in his pajamas he snuck into Alice's room.

"Alice?" he whispered. Alice opened her deep blue eyes. Her damp hair stained the white pillowcase. The window was open; a fragrance of wild wet earth filled the dark room.

"Of course you saw them," Alice smiled, "Some kinds of water nymphs love to play in bubble baths." Alice knew everything, Alice! Mikey adored her. He skipped down the hall to his bedroom.

***

Alice in the Evening

Alice stretched out on the rug by the stereo. She listened to records through the headphones. The TV was on and Papa, in a rare mood, sat on the floor to play checkers with Mikey. Mrs. Bugle, on the couch, knitted an afghan.

Everyone except Alice laughed and commented on the TV program. Alice whistled to the theme from A Summer Place.

192.
May 20, 1974 –
Dear Dr. Pullias,

Thanks for the letter. I needed a letter today because I feel rotten. Maybe you have the flu for a long time but at least you don't have to contend with cramps! I really would not mind not going through this kind of pain every month. At least it's the kind of pain you instantly forget after it's over.

I'll look for the book you mentioned at the Public Branch I go to in Claremont. Thanks for recommending it – oh, I do like good books! Right now I am reading another series about a little mischievous girl; the one I'm reading today is called <u>Edie on the Warpath</u> by E.C. Spykman. It's rather good.

It's been good that I found that Claremont library and can get outside reading. It really brightens me up. I also get books for Cassie, whom I tutor on Tuesdays & Thursdays at her school. Last time we had an inspiration. She was teasing, I was laughing and shouting, "Read!" And she was wrestling with me. I said, "Here! Repeat the words after me." I pointed to each word in the book and said it loudly; she happily shouted after me and we read the whole book (Where the Wild Things Are by Maurice Sendak). Sometimes she looked away but because I was pointing to the words she felt inclined to look at them. It was fun. I called her, "Wild Thing!"

I think I would be scared to go ask the guy at the newspaper but that would be fun. Yeah, it would. My creative writing teacher thinks Alice should become a contemporary novel. OK, I'll agree to that.

Chow, chow, chow.

I don't know if I told you about getting my classes for next year. I have mostly Art classes, one communication and one general music. This summer at the San Jac. J. C. I'll take Health Science which I need to get into the teaching program. I was also going to take U. S. History there but I found this test you can take that if you pass 37% of it you get credit for the class. Maybe I can pass that.

I've practically finished my science class (3 weeks early!) And my creative writing class is a snap. So now I have time to write a short report on architecture for Art History.

Are you going to give a speech at the graduation?

Last night I had an exceptionally strange dream. I had taken two aspirins (I allow myself to take aspirins for cramps but not for anything else – I don't want to get addicted!) and my head was balmy. I dreamt my brother, Tim and I were at the bottom of an immense rock mountain. An earthquake started and I grabbed Tim's hand and said, "Come through here!" We went through a rock arch that led into a rock mansion with jillions of little carved granite figurines. Tim said, "Stupid! Don't you know you have to smash the Dragon on the arch to be safe in here?" He smashed the little dragon. But the earthquake caused the walls to crumble. We got out in time and found ourselves on a beach, a rocky beach, with rough waves. Tim turned into a doll with blood coming out its mouth. All the little figurines were fanciful animals, I liked them.

Your friend, Debbie.

193.

Los Angeles
Backyard Study
May 25, 1974
Dear Debbie:

It is a good feeling to have you sign your letter, "friend." I am thankful to have you as a friend, and I feel deeply that the many years of difference in age do not matter. In fact, perhaps because of that difference each can bring something special to the other. This will probably be the last letter I will write you before you go home for the summer.

And so you will leave completed two years of college, and I am very proud of you. I am glad you have done well in your studies. More important, is the fact that you learned the great joy of learning. Not only that but also you have made fine development in many ways that need not be mentioned. You are really in the early part of a great journey - often in writing called an odyssey - and it should become more meaningful and interesting as you go along.

Much of it will not be easy - indeed the journey will often be hard, and there will be suffering and disappointment. But you will learn to deal with those things. I believe you are learning the great place and value of persistent work in any significant achievement: tennis, art, writing, anything; except that when our heart is in any one activity it does not seem like work. The activity leads us on and the effort as well as the result becomes a joy.

I believe too you are growing in self-understanding. I was once uneasy - forgive me if this shows a lack of proper faith - that you might be led off into some unwise way that would hurt you. There are so many foolish and harmful ways in our time: sex, drugs, and many others. And since I loved you so very much, and wished such good things for you, I did not want you to take one of these detours. I have come more and more to respect your judgment and your ability to take wise ways. Still although I want you to be free and your genuine self, I want you to take good care. You have a good head and can use it, and I am thankful for that.

The summer should be very good - a change of environment and a change of pace. Your mother is right that it would not be wise for you and James to be alone in the house together. For many boys and men sex is an overwhelming and difficult-to-control need. It is not wise to put too great a strain on that need. And then once the physical part of a relationship goes too far - gets out of control - then other parts of what may be a beautiful relationship may be spoiled. I believe you will try to understand this rather complicated fact - and be wise about it.

Now I am afraid I have sounded "preachy." I didn't meant to. Just talking freely with a beloved young friend - even as she speaks freely with me.

I too am finishing up my school year - lots of papers to read many of which are interesting. I will not teach this summer. Hope I can write some and get all the details connected with publishing the book done. Best wishes for the last days there.

Sincerely, Earl V. Pullias

P.S. As I write this letter I am listening to Beethoven's 9th symphony. I suspect James likes it very much. It is a fine night for a party for the picture people.

194.
Los Angeles
Backyard Study
June 7, 1974
Dear Debbie:

We had our commencement exercises today at USC. It was a good day, but a little long and I am tired. The day began with a breakfast at 8:00 for our graduates who were receiving their doctor's degrees in Education. That lasted until about 10 o'clock. Then we all got ready (cap and gown and hood) for the general program at 11:00. When that was over we had a special program for all the graduates in Education from 1 to 2 o'clock. I thought of you and my anticipation of attending your graduation when you receive your B.A. degree. But in the meantime much interesting life and learning.

I miss your letters very much. Perhaps I had not quite realized how much our friendship means to me. I shall be interested to hear how your year rounded out at school and how it felt to be home - good I know. I am glad for summer to be here, but I suspect it will be good when fall comes. I am not teaching this summer, but am working with some of my students who are finishing the dissertation for their doctor's degrees.

I will be interested to hear what you are reading that is good. I forgot to tell you that here in my study I have a little picture of the drummer boy - do you know that story? He will be in the party.

Sincerely, Earl V. Pullias
Photos of P's papers

195.
June 7, 1974
Dear Dr. Pullias,

Today I went to see Mr. Hill at the high school and give him this quarter's writings to read. He took me to 31 Flavors and treated me to a banana split. I've never had one before; it was pretty good! Later I went over to Prieta's to dress her for a ride (I had seen Miss Kerr at the high school and she said we ought to go riding) and rode to where Miss Kerr keeps her horses.

We had a great fun ride and oh! guess what? Miss Kerr said that it looked like Prieta might very well be pregnant after all! And we had thought she wasn't. Anyway we'll soon find out! On June 24 she'll be a year since breeding so a foal can come anytime. Of course maybe she isn't pregnant – we can't get our hopes too high. We hope, though, still, and we hope it is a little black filly.

I don't remember if I told you Miss Kerr said she wanted to be my literary agent. I gave her some writings today; she said she would have fun sending them off, etc. maybe she will help me "break into print."

I suppose I've always wanted to be like Miss Kerr. She's a

honey!

So the summer begins....

Yesterday, before I left San Diego, I had to say good-bye to my little girlfriend, Cassie. She knew it was the last day which I would see her 'til next year so she wore a dress (!) for special. We sat in the teachers lounge and didn't do any "work." We talked and played around and I gave her some greeting cards that one colors. She was very pleased with them.

I had been invited to her house for lunch and after that I headed home.

Cassie taught me a lot, you know, about my capabilities for entering into her world of fun and pretend. I have found this year that I am becoming more like I was as a child! When I told that to Miss Kerr today she said, "Well, you're growing up! And that's what happens; you learn how to be young again."

My mamma is incubating some quail and pheasants that will hatch June 19.

The only thing sad about leaving school was having our creative writing class end. It was such a good class; I have never been so open in a group as that one, never been so much a "member." Dr. Eulert is an excellent teacher – helping us open our eyes and minds rather than stuffing them with this and that. He especially liked my Alice stories; the last day we were leaving and he turned to me and said, "I want a hug from Alice." That's me!

Two good books are <u>Ginger Pye</u> & <u>Pinky Pye</u> by Eleanor Estes. Have you read them?

Love, Debbie.

196.
Los Angeles
Backyard Study
June 16, 1974

"What is so rare as a day in June, then if ever come perfect days." Lowell.

Dear Debbie:

It was very good to see you and have a little time with you yesterday. I was glad you came up to the cabins: it is so free and open there. And I thought that was not a bad picnic under the

shade of the live oak, among the rocks, and listening to the wind. Yesterday I felt nearer to you physically than anytime before since I knew you. The old barriers from shyness and life's many problems were largely gone and I could feel the love that is so great in your heart. And I was thankful.

We wish there was something good that could be done with Luiseno Land that could make and keep it a place of healing and growth for those who can feel its natural spirit. What I don't know. Your father has some interesting ideas.

I wrote Dr. Box this morning. I am afraid he is facing a pretty rough time. I doubt if he will be able to get another teaching job at his age. I am afraid he was very unwise in entering the complicated struggle for control of the school. There are always so many sides to these things: as a rule in such a fight nobody wins.

I was very glad that your learning experience was so good that last quarter. That was beginning to be what college can and should be. I wish the general campus environment was better, but one of the things I have found is that in life there is always some good and some bad. You are on your way to getting your college degree and your credential and these will be a foundation from which much can be done. This June morning is unbelievably beautiful.

Sincerely, Earl V. Pullias

197.
June 16, 1974
Dear Dr. Pullias,

It is late and I am quite sleepy; I must go to bed soon. Tomorrow I'm driving to James's place for a visit. It's fun visiting him but perhaps a little tiring only because he's not comfortable with lazy conversation — a silence makes him feel awkward (so he tells me) — while with me lazy talk is the only comfortable way I can talk.

I thought our hot summer picnic afternoon was lovely. I was still dwelling a bit on the nightmarish occurrence of the day before when Mitzie got killed but I felt better with the heat and the desert perfumes of yellow weeds and oak leaves. I will think about what you and daddy want to do with the land. It would be fun to have a funny

,ororor

little burro around.

I am reading a good book by Elizabeth Goudge titled <u>The Bird in the Tree</u>. It's pretty good. If you have not read <u>Linnets and Valerians</u> by this same authoress you really must some time. I read it when I was quite young and I believe it affected my writing a little and it certainly caused me to look for magic in the world. It is a magic book.

Debbie called me last night to tell me that another girl had entered that house so that there won't be an opening for me after all. What will I do? Rats. But it was fun talking with Debbie.

I must be off to bed! I would write more tomorrow but I'd like it to get to you before you start your trip. I hope you have a pleasant time. What is the country like there?

If you tell me when you next come down I'll get my creative writings from Miss Kerr for you to read over the weekend or something. I'd especially like you to read them, but you can read my journal as well if you want. You can take that home. Maybe even the writings, I'll ask Miss Kerr.

Have a good trip!
Your friend,
Debbie.

198.
June 26, 1974
Returning home-
Memphis, Tenn. Left Nashville
About 4 o' clock
Dear Debbie:

It was very good to receive your letter at my mother's house. The letter arrived after I left, but Mrs. P. enclosed it in one of her letters which came last Sat. I was pleased she sent it.

I had a good visit. Really I gave almost all of the eight days to a visit with my mother. I probably told you she was 95 years old last Monday. That is the oldest person I have ever known and I was very interested in many things she told me. Perhaps I can write about some of them some time. I hope I helped her some: although she has many friends, in a deep sense she was eager to talk with someone whom she felt understands a little. I am pretty tired, but soon should be in my backyard study (if this plane flies well).

I am very pleased you are reading and liking the books by Elizabeth Goudge. She is a fine writer. I will read both the books you mention this summer and will tell you how I like them. I would like to mention two by her, books that I liked very much: (1) <u>The White Witch</u> (also about magic and also beautiful I think) (2) <u>The Child from the Sea</u> (I believe one of her best novels about a real historical figure - keen insight into the child of the story).

I would like very much to read your creative writing and your journal. Will work it out so I can get them. I too liked our picnic. I was very sorry about Mitzie. Maybe you will tell me what happened sometime. I hope also we can have a burro, but water and food may be a problem. We'll see.

Your friend, Earl V. Pullias

P.S. We are just taking off from Memphis, about 5:20 in the afternoon.

199.

June 29, 1974 –

Dear Dr. Pullias,

Last Monday I went to visit out at James's. He has a trailer and shack for a house below his parents house. First we sat in his living room and sort of talked and listened to records. Then I said, "Well, what do you want to do now?" So we threw pebbles into the trashcan. Then I said, "Well, what you want to do now?" So we built the castle of books in his bedroom and peopled it with old toys and finished it with knickknacks. We made up stories about the characters and laughed at them. It was very much fun and took up the rest of the afternoon so that I did not have to be bored and rude and say, "Well, what you want to do now?" again.

I still love to play pretend and I still can, I think as well as when I was very young; it's just that I don't so often. I do when I am with children and when I am alone. I love my toys – my dolls, stuffed and china animals, junk stuff I collect when I take a walk – just as I used to. That's interesting; why should a person lose the ability to pretend for fun just because he's grown up? My brothers and I still play a lot and now I have found that it is possible to play pretend with a person my own age, James. Are he and I special to have this ability or is it just that we are creative enough to think of playing pretend and that doing so does not require specialists, rather just thinking of it and then not thinking it's too silly.

Some time when another friend my own age comes over because there's nothing to do I'll suggest a fun time with my china animals just to see if they would be able to still pretend. That would be interesting. Do you think you would be able to play pretend? Let's see... yeah, I think you would, with me or with someone else younger than you, but would you think of it with your wife, for instance, or anyone your own age? Probably not. Probably if you did they'd cart you off to the funny farm where life is gay all day long. Hee hee ho ho.

Delighted is a good word and that is how I feel when I am dealing with what people call children's things. Children's books, films, cartoons, toys, games; they do not have to be just for children; I like them, too! But I am even luckier because I can enjoy grown-up's things, also! Grown-up books, films, work, etc. What a lucky kid, right? To be so smart and yet so simple!

Three days a week I am helping my mother and Mr. Heaton take their summer school students to the high school pool for swimming lessons. I get in, too and help teach. The children are so fun to watch and laugh with; some of the little ones are very new to water – such a large body of water, anyway.

I know these children are mentally retarded; they can't talk well and won't ever be able to read; yet my mind has the most strange inability to think that anything is stupid (except me). What makes me that way? What makes me feel that my puppy, though I know she won't ever talk or do math problems, is some form of a small god, much wiser than me? Why do I feel that the trees know that I am under them and that they are stronger and more intelligent than me so that they crowd close to protect me. I even feel the butterfly is more clever than me. What makes me feel this way? Is it an inferiority complex? A dreadful case of humility? Or perhaps a childhood belief that everything is a god except me?

I don't know if I ever told you the above feeling but I've been aware of it for many years; I suppose it's what keeps me shy – I don't know if I, the stupidest anywhere, am worth being considered. But then again somehow it helps in my relationships with children. And somehow, too, it is good to feel that the world of plants and animals can keep me pleasant godly company. Interesting...

So.. my thoughts for today! I am glad you had a good visit with your mother.

Your friend,
Debbie.

200.

July 5, 1974 –.

Dear Dr. Pullias,

Today I have been reading your book, <u>A Teacher Is Many Things</u>. It's quite interesting and very inspiring. After reading a little in it I feel so much like becoming a teacher that I want to be one right now!

And that's good because I just got a job that will be a kind of teaching. Miss Kerr directs a Campfire Girls camp in the San Bernardino Mtns. She thought I would enjoy being a counselor who guides and helps seven or eight little girls through their day. I wasn't sure if I wanted to go because it's for six weeks and you sleep outside and take care of the kids <u>all</u> day with one day off a week and you only get $5.00 a day. But I knew that my reasons for not wanting to go were really just fears. Like – fear of failing, fear of the children not liking me, fear that the bathrooms won't be private, fear that I'll get so tired I'll cry, etc. etc.! The only valid reason I had to stay home was that I wanted time, plenty of time, to be lazy before school starts. That's not terribly valid when one has a new opportunity to experience! And I would not let those fears get the best of me because I know they're kinda silly.

Besides that, your book made me feel a little more confident about doing that work. SO.... I called Miss Kerr and said, "Nnnnnyes!"

I'll give you the address in the next letter; I don't leave till 19 July.

Miss Kerr and I are going riding Sunday morning.

In the evenings I take Kista, the puppy, for her run. I like to walk back through the grapefruit trees to the cement irrigation ditch that runs through the middle of the whole block. The water rushes and gurgles pleasantly; Kista splashes in it, she likes water. I like to look at the tiny metal doors that lift up to let the water flow into the dirt runnels that go along beside the trees. I pretend I am the official tiny metal door checker. That's funny. I think Kista is my official irrigation ditch patrol dog. I wish that Mitzie didn't get run over so she could be the official tree inspector. Hobo, the old dog, is locked up because when he comes he only barks at me to throw him dirt clods. He is a dirt clod fanatic.

Today, hooray, I got the letter from the State saying that I was to receive 3,294 dollars for the next year at school. That's almost unbelievable; that someone or thing would think I am worth that much. To think that someone or thing that doesn't even know me would give me so much money. Wow!

I think I'll write another letter, get ready for bed, and read some more in your book. Yes!

PS I am painting your watercolor picture. I hope it comes out nicely.

Your friend,
Debbie.

201.
Los Angeles
July 10, 1974
Backyard Study
Dear Debbie:

Of all the letters I have received from you the one that came Monday was perhaps the best for me. It was all one hopes from a friend: genuine, sincere, honest, open. But in a way that is a bad habit of mine to be evaluating so much. I believe it is not quite judging in any critical or bad sense, but is a comparing of the ideals within one's mind - the dreams - with reality as it is and is developing. Thus to see you grow steadily into what you can be is a great joy to me. At its deepest I believe it is that you have great potential for life, for service, and for meaningful achievement, that I care for you very much and so am thankful and glad as you move toward what you can be. As I write this I know it may sound sort of abstract and not say what I want really to say. But now, after our years of growing friendship, I am confident you understand. Really I should have more sense than to try to say why I liked and appreciated your letter so much!

Dear Dr. Pullias

I am very glad you accepted the position with Miss Kerr. I liked very much the way you thought through the problem and came to what I believe is a valid conclusion. The experience will be excellent for you both in preparation for teaching and for your writing. The pay, including board and a sleeping place under the stars, is not bad, but the important thing is you will be learning, you will be doing a significant job (teaching), you will be carrying through on a task that will doubtless sometimes be hard and unpleasant yet over all deeply satisfying, you will be working with a skillful and thoughtful guide who is interested in you, etc.: all of this I believe will be very good for your growth - and often will be fun in the best sense.

I am so pleased that you like <u>A Teacher Is Many Things</u>. As you know much of my heart is in that book. That it inspires you and makes you want to be a teacher - <u>now</u> - encourages and inspires <u>me</u>. I hope you will like the new book that will be out a little before Christmas - if all goes well.

I am delighted that you have word about your fine State scholarship. It is a wonderful thing. I believe you are worth it!! At the same time such a scholarship is both a great opportunity and a great responsibility. It means in a sense that the people of the State of Calif. believe that such an investment in your education is a good way to spend money because of what you <u>are</u> and <u>can</u> be - and I believe they are right. Yet I don't want you to feel under special pressure because of the scholarship but just grateful as you are for life, and beauty and love and friends; to be used as best we can.

Debbie, at the risk of sounding preachy there is one other thing I want to say. Life will always be a mixture of joy and sorrow, of things that are pleasant and things that are hard and unpleasant. Many people are destroyed, turned aside, or discouraged when the going gets rough. Often we have to work though the hard problems to get over to the other side. I believe you felt this principle when you accepted the counselor's position, and I am proud of your insight. Enough of that.

Really I would rather talk of your lovely evenings with Kista and your experience there. Yesterday when we were at your mother's place Sari jumped up on the hood of our car, walked along to the driver's side and crawled in a window. Later I let her

Debbie Bumstead

out the door and she ran saucily to a grapefruit tree! Thinking what?

Sincerely Earl V. Pullias

P.S. I hope very much the watercolor turns out: I would like very much to have it.

202.
July 12, 1974
Dear Dr. Pullias,

I liked your letters, too. The July 4th one and the one I received today. Don't worry, I don't think you're too preachy; I think you're great, in fact!

After all that wonderfulness about teaching experience I don't like to tell you – but I'm not going to be a counselor after all! Miss Kerr called me and said she couldn't hire another one, but that there was an opening for a kitchen girl. From teaching to kitchen duty! Oh, well. I think I will still have fun even if I must wash dishes and mop floors for a living. I'll have free time to watch the children and be with them and to hike, etc.

Tomorrow I will wake up at 7:00, come downstairs to watch Bugs Bunny till 7:30, while eating breakfast. Then I'll dress and wash my face and say, "Ah!" At 8:00 Miss Kerr is coming by (I have to wait outside for her because she is bashful about coming to people's houses) to pick me up in her truck. I'll help her put her horse, Ida, in a trailer and then will go with her to visit the camp. She's leaving her horse there. I'll be able to see what the place is like.

Miss Kerr's a pretty neat lady. Sometimes it's hard to tell about her, what she is thinking or whatever. She says that she is shy so I guess that's the reason. Though it's hard for me to imagine it, she probably has almost as hard a time as me in breaking out and initiating a conversation. But when we get going we talk very companionably. I like her.

My music class is so much fun we are learning to make music with our bodies, our voices, musical instruments like xylophones, drums, etc., And our recorders. Oh, my! I've never made such music! And it just came, it just came out of me easy and pure. Before I took

240

guitar lessons it was such a chore, I didn't feel the music, at all. I thought, "I'm not musical" but this class tells me there is music in me, good creative music, too. The teacher is excellent – I'm afraid I've already fallen in love with him! Oh, dear! I wish I could have the class much longer (but not so far away). But this will at least tell me more of what I can do.

Sari is a saucy cat - I like it when she comes into my room in the morning to wake me up. She jumps onto my bed and purrs; I open my eyes to see the sun on the rug and my crazy quilt and Sari's pretty blue eyes. When I am lying on my back she likes to lay on my chest to look right into my face. And when I lie on my side she likes to sit on my hip. She's funny.

If I have room I'll take your painting to finish at the camp. I'll for sure take my drawing tablet.

Your friend,
Debbie.

203.
Backyard Study
July 15, 1974
Los Angeles
Dear Debbie:

How very good to come home from a pretty tiring day's work to find your letter here! I will not worry again that you might think I am preachy at you. I will feel free, as I usually have, to say what is in my mind and heart because you are my friend and you will understand what I wish to say even if I should not say it well. That is a good feeling.

Wonderful that you took the job as a kitchen aid! You may find that work to be as interesting, useful and meaningful as the counselor's job. Really I have found there are many ways to teach: in fact, in a sense we teach in all that we do and especially by what we are. You should have time to observe, to listen, to read some, and especially to write. I have found that if one does very well what needs to be done and what he has opportunity to do, that nearly always leads to the chance to do something else that you may like better. I believe it will be good to work with Miss Kerr and to learn from her. It will help you in getting ready

Debbie Bumstead

for your own teaching and other work.

It is dusk - perhaps my favorite time of day, although morning is good too. I like to hear about your friend Sari. She will surely be an interesting part of the moonlight party when my pictures' "people" come down for their play together. She might take charge!

Good luck as you prepare for a new adventure.

Sincerely, Earl V. P.

P.S. I hope this arrives before you leave for camp finally. The music class sounds wonderful.

204.

July 20, 1974 – Saturday

Dear Dr. Pullias,

All the girls (36 staff members this first week, then the little girls come) are at a Campfire Meeting except me. I ditched! Shame! But I had to write in my journal and I knew if I went I would be too tired to write afterwards. It's hard work in that kitchen! It won't be so bad once we get everything cleaned up, then we'll only have to wash dishes and mop. My legs are aching and I'm cold, oh me, oh my.

I hope Miss Kerr will not mind me not being at that meeting but I simply <u>had</u> to write of the two magical experiences that occurred today. The first came when I was sitting near the river against the tree reading (I am reading <u>The Torch</u> which you gave me). A ground squirrel scampered up a path toward me and I stayed very still. He came, jaunty and quick, right up to my shoe! Then he realized what I was and ran away! The second event came when I hiked up the hill a ways and sat on a rock. In front of me a stream trickled through a valley, the tree grown hills rose from it giving me the sensation of being in a boat. A tree earth rock boat! Floating on an unseen ocean drifting to an unseen destination – or perhaps it would drift forever and never land. All I could see was my boat and the sky.

This forest is like watermelon; I love it!

Miss Kerr just came in (we are staying in cabins this week) saying, "Debbie, how invisible do you think you are sitting there? You know you're not that invisible!" She took my foot and threatened to tickle it; I warned that I would kick. She tickled and I kicked! Then she

242

Dear Dr. Pullias

sat on another cot and said, "Oh, Debbie." I read the line above "I hope Miss Kerr... meeting" and she laughed and said, "It's very hard for me to mind. Because I think you are a more private kind of person than any of the others. But I want you to learn to be with a group like that, too. So... I put the burden all on Debbie's head." She got up and touched my hair and left saying, "You know you won't stay invisible all summer!" I heard her running down the path and she was gone.

I wanted to say, "Stay." but I couldn't say anything. After she left I felt like crying but I didn't, instead I wrote this and feel cheerful again!

You know sometimes I <u>am</u> very different from others. Not in an abnormal way. Sometimes I think the only reason I seem different is that I listen carefully to myself and so enjoy my own company. If Miss Kerr means, "private" that way she is right – I do listen and think with myself. But if she means private by not wanting to be with others that isn't so. I left that meeting because I was bored not because I was afraid or trying to keep things inside. I had something exciting to write so I left.

I'm not so much private as I am quiet. If someone asks and wishes to listen I'll speak. Quiet and shy and a bit private – in a way.

Do you think talking is as important as listening?

I will have to copy that incident over into my journal.

The other day I received a letter from my little friend Cassie in San Diego. She thinks summer school is bad because I don't come and play games with her. Hmmmmm.

Write soon, OK? I will love to get a letter from you and take it out to read under the forest trees by the stream. That will certainly be magic. This is a magic place!

Your friend,
Debbie.
Camp Wasewagan Angelus Oaks, California 92305

205.
Los Angeles
July 25, 1974
Backyard Study
Dear Debbie:

Debbie Bumstead

It was wonderful to receive your letter that came yesterday. I was concerned to know if you had gotten settled all right at the camp, and wondered how things were. I wish I was with you out in the forest by the stream. Few things in all of life are more lovely than a running stream in a lovely natural setting. I have thought if one could learn to listen carefully and deeply enough one could understand the language of the brook and thus we might hear many deep secrets - of truth, beauty, goodness, and love. (TBGL!)

I'm glad you are reading <u>The Torch</u>. The author is a very great doctor - one of the greatest living doctors and scientists now quite old. - but more important, I think, he has a heart: as you will note there is much about teaching at its best in the book.

Debbie, there is something I want to say to you because you are my friend and I love you. This summer will be a great test for you. I want you to meet it well. In all of life there are routine, unpleasant things we must do in order to be able to do the deep more important things. In my writing I have called the sort of drudgery things, of which there are many, the "profane" and the deeper more meaningful things the "sacred." If you brought <u>A Teacher Is Many Things</u> to the mountains with you I would like for you to look at Chapter 12 where I discuss this idea. This problem may be a major one for you, and I want you to understand it and conquer it. You can do it.

Sincerely, Earl V. Pullias

P.S. Again the family is on vacation and I am alone. Oh how badly I need a small slave to do the "profane" -the routine, and I have none! Yet life is beautiful.

206.
July 27, 1974
Dear Dr. Pullias,

It's strange how things happen. A few nights ago – when we were still staying together in the cabins – the girls were extremely noisy and excited, maybe about the campers coming the next day and I was exceedingly tired. So I started to cry, left the cabin, sat outside, etc. A girl came out to sit by me and she put her arms around me and talked. I did not know her especially but had observed her before around.

Anyway the next day I wrote the experience in my journal. And whenever we passed each other it was as if we were still unknown.

Then tonight we happened to be sitting in the lounge and I had my writing things here intending to write you. First I read over my journal. I wondered whether I could let this girl, Leslie, read my entry for that event since she was concerned in it. Finally I offered my papers to her and she read them. Then we talked, almost deeply. She said she had wanted to talk to me before but felt strange. How strange to begin a knowledge of a person with crying and comfort.

I made another friend today, too. I went hiking to the horse corrals down the road where the campers learn to ride. I watched a while and then came back with all the little girls. One girl walked especially slow and so I walked with her as I walk slow also, to enjoy the view. "Why do you walk slow?" I asked. She replied, "To be able to look around." A girl after my own heart! So we hiked together and talked. She is nine and talks very intelligently. I had noticed her before because when games are going on she hangs back and watches but doesn't play. Yet speaking she was bright and happy. I happen to ask her if she was going to college and she replied yes, she was going into medicine, she wanted to be a scientist. I told her about mixing baking soda and vinegar.

July 28, 1974

Tonight I am on "Hill Duty" which means I stay with the campers till a certain hour. I have to get them to go to sleep. The unit I am in is Bluebirds, the littlest girls. When I came they were ready for bed but giggling and talking excitedly. I laid down on two little girls cots and said, "Mmmm, I'm tired." So they decided to take care of me; they covered me, held my hands, and constantly told each other to shut up, "Debbie's tired and her ears are sore! Be quiet!" I pretended to groan but I couldn't help but laugh. Then I told them a story and they got quieter. I asked them politely to be quiet and they responded sincerely but I know it's hard when a kid is excited.

I went horseback riding today. It was fun but it rained.

Tomorrow is my day off and I'm driving home; I don't know why, it's just something to do.

Your friend,
Debbie.
unicorn unicorn
with your horn

Debbie Bumstead

ho. heh hey then.

207.
Los Angeles
July 28, 1974
Backyard Study
Dear Debbie:

It is early Sunday morning. It is cool and quiet here in my little study. My friends around the wall and on my desk look at me as if they knew something I did not know. Do you suppose they all came out of their pictures and other forms (including Debbie and Sari) and had one of those parties on the lawn last night?! The moon was very bright. But they do not say - just are very quiet and pensive.

I thought of you and knew it must be very beautiful there in the mountains under the soft moon last night. While you are there if you have a chance you might look again at Sappho's poetry - I doubt if you could bring the little book - but some of her loveliest and most vivid word pictures are of the moon.

My past week was a little rough. My regular work with my students was very hard, and then there were two of them who are having pretty serious trouble with their work toward their doctor's degrees, and I was trying to help them. They had failed some Exams and were very discouraged. Both happened to be women students. In a way, they did not do the "profane," the hard routine, that the degree requires - the problem you and I were talking about recently. A very complex one, and especially hard for some people.

I hope all goes well there. You can be yourself <u>inside</u>, and yet adjust to the demands there. That is what I have tried to learn to do.

What does "Wasewagan" mean?
Sincerely, Earl V. Pullias
P.S. Oh how I have needed a small loving slave this past

week to do the work about the house! Maybe I'll be more grateful.

208.

Los Angeles
July 31, 1974
Living Room
Dear Debbie:

It was good to have your letter from the beautiful mountains. Your letter brought the freshness of that good place, and the good spontaneity of children who are growing. You have a fine understanding of children, perhaps chiefly because you are interested in them and like them. This understanding and skill that comes from it will grow through the years. And you will write important things about and for children: that is my faith. Faith in a young friend I love.

To make friends is good, especially when it involves genuineness, or reasonable authenticity. I am glad for you. I believe your writing will have the power to reach many hearts. I have felt quite alone much of my life. One needs at least a few people with whom he can be sincere, totally himself. These relations are very precious and I suppose should not be expected very frequently. One can, I believe, (we have talked of this before) have a creatively close relation with living things (plants and animals), with non-living things and with the deep spiritual world which the Indians called, the Great Spirit. By the way tell me how you liked The Torch. We who are teachers are in a way the greatest physicians or healers of all.

My work is harder this summer than I wanted it to be. Many students are trying to finish the work for their doctor's degrees. I have not been able to write much. The lady who is in charge of the publication of my new book called from New York Monday to say the plans are going forward nicely. Should have copies before Christmas. Would a copy be all right for a present?

Sincerely, Earl V. Pullias

Debbie Bumstead

209.
August 5, 1974
Dear Dr. Pullias,

Yesterday I cried a lot. Some little thing hurts my feelings and tears come up. I can't stop thinking about what's hurt me so that when someone speaks to me I am on the verge of crying. Then I think of myself as incredibly stupid to not be able to swallow the hurt down. I leave to go cry down by the river. By that time often it is no longer hurt feelings that make me cry but just crying that makes me cry.

Yesterday after I had really begun to be weepy I honestly didn't know any reason why I was crying. The assistant director (Miss Kerr was on her day off) followed me to the river and tried very hard to find the reason for my sadness. I sighed and smiled at her, she gave me two aspirins and let me go lay down.

A steady steady rain started to fall and I cried with it and cried and cried until I fell asleep. And when I awoke the rain had stopped. The forest and I were rain-washed and bright again.

I am sitting alone in the staff Lodge. As I wrote I noticed a hummingbird caught inside banging against the window to get out. I got up thinking I could herd it out the door but it wouldn't be herded. I caught it in my hands easily; it fluttered and squeaked. I took it quickly outside and opened my hands on the ground and watched the bird fly, a green whirring, off into the trees. "It is magic," I thought, "to have touched such a magic high-flying thing that most likely was not and will not ever be touched by a human. Except for me. My hands are covered now with hummingbird magic."

It's interesting here. This morning I got a letter from Miss Kerr (she and I write each other though we see each other every day – isn't that nice?) And read it down past the Bluebird cabins. It was a sunny lovely morning and I laid back on a warm log to watch the sky.

And today I walked down by the river and sat awhile and threw rocks into the water. I heard a step behind me and looked around to see Miss Kerr. She said, "that's magic," referring to the way in which she had just found me. We threw pebbles then she left. After awhile I left, too, and wandered around until I happened upon her sitting throwing wood pieces in the river. I said, "It happened again!" We sat and talked about the hummingbird magic.

I surely admire her, more now because I understand some of her ways. Hearing some of the staff members talk of her – "sometimes

I feel like she doesn't like me." "Those eyes!" – I know what they see but I understand Miss Kerr's shyness around individuals and her peculiar watching characteristic.

Ah, ya ya.

There are so many things, so many people to love.

Your friend,

Debbie.

210.

Los Angeles

Aug. 7, 1974

Backyard Study

Dear Debbie:

Maybe sometime you will tell me more about Miss Kerr. Do you think she would like to have a copy of A Teacher Is Many Things? Or would it be wise to ask? I recall that Sylvia Ashton-Warner (the author of Teacher) says in one of her novels Bell Call, I think, that questions are pressure. I guess it is often so.

It was good to have your letter telling of your weeping and of the sky weeping with you and then of your being refreshed and renewed. I suspect the weeping is related in some - maybe many - deep way to your need and wish to love. As you say there are so many things and people to love - to be warmly and creatively related - I think that is what love is - at least in part. But the best of much relations are not easy to establish or to maintain. And I'll tell you a mystery: often those who are shy - who find many relations difficult - feel the deepest love and, in fact, have the richest personalities. And often those who seem to be so free to establish relations quickly and easily and without pain are thin, shallow, and easily changed. Strange isn't it? Wonder why it should be?

How is the work - the profane? Still hard? That is a lot of it that must be done!

We wanted your judgment this week. We had to choose between several designs for the jacket of the new book. We gave our first, second and third choices and then the publishing co. will make the final decision. Wanted your judgment on color and lettering. Hope the book will be out by early Dec. I think you

The stream sounds so good: absorb its peace and beauty.
Sincerely, Earl V. Pullias

211.
August 11, 1974
Dear Dr. Pullias,

Today I was sitting in the sun with my legs stretched out waiting for the girls to finish eating. When they did they all rushed out and scared a near-by chipmunk. The chipmunk ran onto my leg and up to my knee. I felt his little running feet and liked his stripes.

It is getting so I pretend I have special powers with wild animals – after all a ground squirrel came to me, a hummingbird breezed in my hands and a chipmunk ran along my leg. I pretend I am like St. Francis or Pan. Who else is like that in history or literature?

The work here is still hard but now we are faster. I don't know if the work is "profane." I enjoy it, in a way, especially when I'm finished! When I am in the process of working in the kitchen I don't think at all, I just do. But what I like is the way my body works; I feel it all working together and when I lift heavy trash I feel my muscles getting stronger. I like that. I like my body to work – but regularly, like something every day or three times a week or something. When I get into a good routine I like it. I do.

Miss Kerr is a pleasant lady and pretty and neat. I study her. Sometimes though, I feel as if she doesn't like me because she passes by and doesn't even look at me or something like that happens. But then later the same day she will tickle me or laugh and talk. It's just the way she is, I guess. I like the assistant director, too; she's the same age as Miss Kerr but different. She is really funny and makes me laugh, laugh, laugh. Ha, ha, ha. But she talks to me, more than Miss Kerr does but I don't value her words, though I especially like it, as much as M. K.s. Do you know what I mean? But I like her, too. I like Miss Kerr and her the best here. And then Leslie and Jackie and Linda and then everybody. Linda is one of my "Shack-mates". She's from Texas and tells funny stories.

What of the people who have a sort of covering of knowledge or information so that you don't think they have an inside. They seem all outside with their bits of definite facts. There's a girl, a staff

250

member, here who is like that, named "Hunter." She knows a lot and seems only to tell facts but she doesn't seem "no-it-allish." Once I almost bumped into her and I looked up to see her eyes very close. In that second I saw an inside in her eyes and we smiled inside smiles. I wonder if she knew it, too. Now I like to think of speaking with her, even just small talk (she isn't around much – we haven't even been introduced.). But I don't have to if it doesn't come. I will smile at her and that's enough if we smile our inside smiles. I don't know how it is with others but most of the time my smile is my inside smile (no, maybe not, there is my zip hi smile that comes quick and spontaneous, there is my mmm yeah smile for understanding, and my special just for me smile from some thought that pleases me).

I see a little mouse on the floor looking for crumbs.

It's interesting how I take pleasure in thinking I might be better in something I'm not sure of than someone else – OH I DON'T KNOW. Like the nature teacher, she acts as if she bouncing around all the time; I think I see more – but I only flatter myself, I suppose.

Your friend,
Debbie.

212.
John Ascuaga's Nugget, Sparks, Nevada
Aug. 14, 1974
Dear Debbie:

I suppose I had as well use this fancy writing paper although I can't say that I like it. It is too much like almost everything in this little suburb of Reno, Nevada: pretty artificial and phony perhaps. Perhaps you wonder what I am doing here. A school district (called the San Juan District) is having a conference here for their administrators (superintendents, principals, etc.) in preparation for the opening of school this fall and they asked me way last spring to make the main talk, and I agreed. I am glad I am here. It gives me an opportunity to say some things about education that I hope will be helpful. How education can be improved interests me very much - and you, I believe.

Your good letter came yesterday before I left for the plane to come here. I am sure you can develop a special relation with animals: there is magic there, and a beautiful kind of magic it is. To have touched and been touched by these wild usually frightened beings is a wonderful experience. Thanks for telling about Miss Kerr and the others there: people are so different and that is good.

I am very glad you are learning to like the hard work. That I believe can always be done and makes all the difference. In this life the work is always to be done, and the way we look at it is important.

Your friend, Earl V. Pullias

213.
Los Angeles
Aug. 19, 1974
The Shop
Dear Debbie:

I don't know if I told you this little study here in the back yard where all our picture friends live is called the "Shop." That is because we built it perhaps 25 years ago for our youngest son, John who as you may know was drowned when he was 18. When he was a small boy he was interested in all kinds of mechanical things including electrical things. So we built this shack in the back yard for his shop. Later we paneled it (originally it was very rough and unfinished) and made it like it is now. I suppose Shop is not a bad name for a place for study, reading, writing, music and just thinking.

I have never asked you if you like candles. I like them very much and like to buy different types, and even like more to burn them. Often when I am writing to you as I am tonight I like to light a candle both for its flame and its odor. Then later at night it is good to turn out the other lights in this little room and the candle casts interesting shadows around the room, and especially on the pictures and statues. Often times you and the cat in your arms seem to move. And at such times truth, beauty, goodness, and love (TBGL) seem more real and nearer and more possible to achieve in human life.

The summer goes by pretty fast. When is your camp over and when does your school start? My summer has been good.

Sincerely, Earl V. Pullias

214.
August 25, 1974
Dear Dr. Pullias,

My mother came up to this camp to visit me today. She enjoyed it and I liked her visit. She brought with her some mail from the college – my report card (all "A"s – my my) – when it starts, Sept. 17 – and the dorm room I'll have, Gamma 26A. All the college news seems a shock to me as I sit against the tree by the river writing this. Everything is so dreamy and happy here – oh, I dread living in the dormitory again.

I would like to have a little old house with a little old yard in a nice place with one or two nice housemates. Perhaps I will look for such a place in Claremont which is near USIU and is also where I will be working. My little friend, Cassie, has her home in Claremont, too.

I really and truly do not want to live in the dorm. The thought has tainted my day.

I will stay four more days here.

It is a Childs Garden of verses Winnie the Pooh place at this camp.

Night before last I had hill duty and was sitting in the unit shack when I heard a rustle outside. I took my flashlight out and shined it up the hill. I saw a deer look at me and then turn to leap away. It was very thrilling.

You know, before I ever finished The Torch I lost it. Tell me did Daphne marry Hippocrates and did they live happily ever after?

Wasewagan means "Camp of the Torch."

At night I love to watch the girls run through the trees. I like the campfires and the stars.

I like it here. I like the people.

Your friend,
Debbie.

215.
Los Angeles
Aug. 30, 1974

Debbie Bumstead

Backyard Study
Dear Debbie:

I liked your last letter from Camp Wasewagen very much. Isn't it interesting that the word means the "Camp of the torch." I like the symbol of the torch very much. I hope you can read the rest of Penfield's <u>The Torch</u>. Should I send you another copy? Yes, Daphne married Hippocrates and they were on their way to a good life together - "ever afterward," I hope. Dr. P. is a very great doctor and I believe, wise man. You will like the last chapters, and especially the way he develops the idea of the torch.

I am deeply thankful that the experience at the camp was so good. It is wonderful when an experience can be so satisfying and at the same time a meaningful service. That is what teaching and other educational work will be for you. It would seem to be good if you could do this camp work in summer as a variation from your college studies and later, your teaching.

It will be a little hard to get back to school from the beauty and freedom of the camp. But as we have often said your formal education is a necessary means to what you would like to do. And it is a great joy to me that you have learned to do the courses with high excellence. I am proud of your all As - not for the grades themselves, but because it is good to do whatever one does well: such achievement leads on to better things.

I am glad your mother was able to visit you and that you enjoyed the visit. Now for some good days at Hemet? I'll tell of my activity next time. Earl V. Pullias

P.S. Really you are not very well suited for a modern dormitory. Maybe you can find a suitable room outside and not too far away.

216.
Sept. 6, 1974
Dear Dr. Pullias,

Next time I go to the library I will look for the Goudge book you mentioned. If it's not there, when I go down to San Diego I can order it at the public library.

I've been reading and reading and reading lately. Especially children's books like <u>Rufus M.</u> by Eleanor Estes or <u>Emil and Piggy Beast</u> by Astrid Lindgren. Zilpha Keatly Snyder has some pretty good books like <u>The Season of Ponies</u> or <u>The Egypt Game</u>. I just finished one of hers called <u>The Witches of Worm</u> which I'm not yet sure I like. It reminds me of all the talk about <u>The Exorcist</u> which I haven't read, but have heard the story line to.

I like it when I am in a reading mood – then laying on the couch in the hot afternoons reading is the most pleasurable thing I can think of to do. Or staying up late in my bedroom because I'm just about finished with the book.

This afternoon has been fun. James, who had come into town for an orientation at Mt. San Jacinto College (which he is attending this semester) came over to our house afterward. We talked a while and then went to the little house he has rented in San Jacinto. He fixed tea and after tea we went out roller-skating. That was funny. Presently we returned to my house, listened to my mother's old 30s records and then James left.

Tomorrow we two are going up to visit Daddy at your cabin. Daddy had thought of James as a caretaker for you and this would seem ideal as J. needs to live around here because of going to school. So if you would have him for a caretaker, he's yours.

Today also I have been getting stuff for college ready; it's always good I guess, to get organized. Then my mind will be ready for the onslaught.

I'm pretty excited about learning more about drawing and painting this year, though I am a little doubtful as to whether I'm talented enough to be taking all these advanced classes. Each learns from his own level, though, I guess, if the teacher is good. And Dr. Fortbrook, the art teacher, though he talks too much, is a sensitive teacher.

It will be interesting, also, to be taking piano and voice lessons.

I learned many great songs at Camp Wasewagan   sometimes you'll have to hear the tape cassette I have of us (the staff) singing. It's really quite good.

Some days I really miss that camp. I really must go again next year. And the next year... And the next year...

First Reno, then Palm Springs – it sounds like you're really swinging! Where next? Tahiti? Or how about the hottest joint anywhere – Hemet! so much to do, so many people to meet, so many things going on.

I like Hemet.

A college friend that I might have mentioned Pam, wrote and informed me that we are to be roommates. That is good. She and I see in much the same way. She is an Art major, also, and has classes with me.

I decided that I would really make an effort to enjoy the dormitory for Fall quarter. But if I see that I just can't I will be on the lookout for some pleasanter place to live come Winter & Spring quarters.

Right now I feel like fixing myself some tomato soup with crackers and milk. So I will!

Your friend forever,

Debbie.

217.
Los Angeles
Sept. 11, 1974
Backyard Study
Dear Debbie:

How beautiful it is here today! Late red roses are blooming around the bird feeder. The backyard is quiet and beautiful.

I fear I may be running about too much! This afternoon I go to San Jose and out into the country from there to speak for the faculty of a small college called, Gavilau College tomorrow. It all has to do with my interest in improving teaching and helping teachers. I am not sure I help but I hope so.

Really this is a somewhat hurried note to say we would be very interested in talking with James about being caretaker up at the cabins. I have been very impressed with what you have told me about him. I'm glad he is going to college. As you know the conditions are a little primitive there, but if an individual liked that sort of thing it might be a very good thing for him and for us. Let me know what he thought after your visit there the other day. We would like for it to be a beautiful, good place as I think it used to be. Also, I would like to know what your mother thinks about the idea of James's living there. She has good judgment, I believe. I can understand your Daddy wishing to go north. Our relation is good.

I am delighted you have a good roommate. Tell me more about her.

Your friend, Earl V. Pullias

P.S. Remember me as you enjoy the riches of Hemet! A little honeysuckle enclosed to bring love - I looked and there was no honeysuckle - a rose petal instead!

218.
Los Angeles
Sept. 14, 1974
Backyard Study
Dear Debbie:

This letter is to welcome my beloved young friend back to her third year of college. I hope it will be your best year so far. A congenial roommate is a great help. This morning Mrs. P. got out a scrapbook she kept when she was in college your age about. She played on the basketball team - they had intercollegiate basketball for women in those days - and she enjoyed that and other things about college very much. We thought of you and hoped that your year would be a good one.

I hope you don't mind that I am very proud of your achievement in college. As I have often said this experience is a crucial means or door to your future. Also, I take great joy in your general development as a person. I was pleased that you settled yourself to the hard work to be done at camp this summer. An ability to work - sometimes unpleasant work - is extremely important in life.

I begin my teaching this coming week. I'll tell you about my classes a little later. I hope I can make them as meaningful as they should be. Perhaps I can.

It is lovely late afternoon in early fall : a favorite season and time for me.

Sincerely, Earl V. Pullias

P.S. I hope you find your wooded hideaway places undisturbed.

Debbie Bumstead

219.
September 16, 1974
Dear Dr. Pullias,

Yesterday I went with Joe and Daddy up to your cabin. They loaded stuff into my truck and took it down the hill. I stayed and wandered down the road on foot. I thought it seemed a very dry year and I liked listening to the insects click and the faraway airplanes buzz. The thing about a dry year, I thought, is that the crackly weeds and wild buckwheat smell especially sweet.

Do you feel that in natural places when you're alone that you are often hearing more than can be physically accounted for? When I walk alone in a place where there is nothing man-made, I think I hear silent things. I hear a kind of flowing breeze moving through my whole body. But I hear that anywhere that I am quiet – even walking through town or sitting here in Mamma's living room – there is something more to listen to in a natural setting. I don't know what it is, perhaps the plants, wind, animals, the sky, and the earth are speaking to me in their silent language, or maybe it is the good spirits that are keeping me company.

I think some time I should take pen and paper with me when I go into a natural wild place. When I come back to write I often forget the exact essence of things felt and heard.

Why is it easier to bring sights and tastes to mind than sounds and smells? And touch – it is practically impossible to bring a touch to mind. Maybe not. But what's that got to do with anything?

Yesterday afternoon James came to visit. Mamma was here so he and she talked while I listened. I don't know why I clam up when my friends are around my parents. I can talk easy as pie with Mamma alone but when a friend is over I can't say much of anything. Perhaps it's embarrassment. It's good then that J. and Mamma could talk; they have many interests in common – antiques, old music. And I enjoy listening. I liked looking at James's handsomeness. Some days, I thought, he looks very good – clean hair, trim beard, brownness, and green eyes.

Yes, it is good that he's going to school again. He has decided living in town would be more practical as he needs to get a job also. I don't think he liked the idea of driving up that road and down it every day from your cabin.

Yesterday evening Joe, Mamma, and I went over to Grandbee

Dear Dr. Pullias

and Grandpa's for dinner. Daddy and Eileen were also there. And Mamma had indulged in a bit of liquor before we went. And at dinner I thought I was going to cry. It was all too horrid – the repulsive smell of Mamma's breath, my stomach in knots, too much laughter – I found myself biting my fingernails. And the only person I loved then was Grandpa because inside we were together. Joe is on my side but sometimes he goes even further down and pushes me up to them. But he is mistaken, I'm not with them because their situation makes me cry and hate the world.

Because I can never forget, I guess, those things that happened when I was still in high school. Sometimes I read my writings from those years (maybe that's why I can't forget – but I think I wouldn't, even if I hadn't written it down); they're really enough to make a person cry. Again.

But after dinner last night mamma fell asleep on the couch and Joe, Daddy, Eileen, Grandpa and I went down to play pool. That was very much fun. Then I loved Grandpa and Joe; I liked Daddy and maybe Eileen. I don't know what I felt about myself.

That was yesterday. In another day I will be on my way to San Diego for another year of school. I am eager again for the independence, (though the independence at school does not match what I felt at Camp Wasewagan. There I was completely free to live up to my own ideals – which in my opinion are ideals fine and worthy to be lived up to – rather than those of professors, Scholarship Commissions, friends, and parents – which are fine ideals also – and no hard matter to live up to, all of them, at the same time even; it was just simpler and more satisfying to live up to only my own. [I hope you realize that I'm not indicating that I resent your or anyone else's thoughts for me – I consider that a way that people show they care. I find myself giving my ideals to children that I know and care for – it's just natural, I guess.]).

I will get a T. A. Job that will probably start next week. It would be great if I could get it at the elementary school across the street; then I could walk to work (I don't especially enjoy driving in San Diego.).

My first quarter classes are Advanced Figure Drawing, Color and Design, and Art History. Also I'll have piano lessons! That will be interesting.

Now I feel pretty happy about going.

259

Rose petals,
Debbie.
USIU Gamma 26A
10455 Pomerado Rd.
San Diego, California
92151

220.
September 21, 1974 –
Dear Dr. Pullias,

It's a quiet night; everyone is at the football game. I'm not. Pam, my roommate is playing solitaire. I had a good day today. Sometimes a day comes when you are struck with a new idea. Often it is a small idea but just as often it is important and grows and leads to other ideas. This is what I wrote in my journal:

"Today I went to Cassie's house. It was the first time I'd seen her for 3 months; she leaned against the doorway, shy, and smiled. I said, "Hi Cassie. How are you?"

"We drove to Frazee's to look for art supplies. On the way Cassie talked away as she always has. I laughed. We talked in German accents.

"She talks so freely, so easily with me that I want to sing out! It makes me feel that she considers me important, that she wants me around, that she likes me.

"And here is something I've not felt so strongly with anyone else – that through talking with me somehow she is learning. And in some kind of way knows she's learning. And is <u>happy</u> learning.

And that is a most wonderful compliment."

Those last paragraphs told the new idea I felt, an idea that I must think more on. 1.learning 2. knows she's learning 3. is <u>happy</u> with learning.

You know that <u>is</u> a compliment to me that Cassie knows I am her "teacher" but would describe me as "a good fun friend." I guess the two descriptions can fit together. What do you think? I think I love Cassie and her bright perky funniness. Even though I love Stevie, my little cousin and other children, I expect Cassie and I have the workingest relationship I've ever had with a child. It has something to do with seeing her regularly and having a kind of structure, loose

Dear Dr. Pullias

though it is. 11:00 on Tues. and Thurs. for school work, 10:00 on Saturdays to go places.

That is a refreshing thought – about Cassie – to think tonight. Last night I had bad dreams (I think I will tend to have them after I watch weird movies. I saw "Willard" about a guy and his man-killing rats). The first one was that I got bitten by a rattlesnake and my leg swelled up. The second Prieta was pulling a whole school bus and then she went lame. Her leg was horribly swollen and when I led her into her stall she collapsed. She had to be killed. It was my brother Joe's fault but he laughed. I hurt all inside.

Tomorrow, Sunday, I will relax. Monday I go to be assigned to a school as a Teacher's Aid. Also I must shop for more art supplies. When I go into La Jolla I will stop by Debbie's house to visit if she's there. Maybe I'll go to my favorite bookstore, too.

I'm sleepy. Good night. I hope you had a good day.

Your friend,

Debbie.

221.

September 29, 1974

Dear Dr. Pullias,

A friend of mine in Hemet made me a pottery cup colored sky-blue with fluffy white clouds circling around it. Today I put some yellow and red flowers in it. I am pleased with the insensibility of flowers above sky – I like that idea.

Beside the cup is the little cockatoo figurine Debbie gave me. It is white and has a mischievous expression. Also two flower-bead necklaces I made curl around the heart-shaped rock a friend gave me at Camp. The objects make a lovely arrangement to rest my eyes on. Today I have been working with pen and ink on contours. Eucalyptus trees, rocks, leaves, hands, and my head in the mirror. I like doing self-portraits for some reason. I like looking at them afterwards and seeing those little quirks of lines that give a touch of particular personality – sometimes graveness or pensiveness, sometimes humor and mischievousness.

I have been reading, too. I discovered another children's book by Eliza Goudge called <u>The Little White Horse</u>. It is very very good. She describes places that I have described to myself in daydreams. I looked for <u>The Joy of the Snow</u>. The public library has it but it was checked out. I'll look again.

My classes are going to be good, I think.

This week I am to hear if I am to get the T. A. Job. I hope so; I have such an amount of free time. And I really would like to earn some money.

I will tell you what I am thinking of for my year after I graduate. Of course it is a long time away but this is an idea that may change.

I wrote to Pacific Oaks College. They sent me a catalogue that interests me very much but I don't know if I like the idea of living in such a big city. They mentioned a child-centered school in Washington near Seattle that they work in co-operation with. This school, called "The Little School" takes teacher interns for a price (1560.).

I thought I might like to go there. I have had for many years a desire to go back to Wash. Perhaps a year there would satisfy me – I might see it's too cold or whatever or I might think it's just the place to live for awhile.

Right now, as it turns out, though in two years anything can change, Joe is living with a girl-friend right near the school in Wash. Perhaps this next summer we can visit him and get the lay of the land (before Camp starts, because I want to go back there, too.).

That's far away but something to think about...

I ought to do a couple more drawings for tomorrow. I like contour drawing.

Your friend,
Debbie.

222.
October 7, 1974
Monday
Dear Dr. Pullias,

I do feel like writing you tonight! Night before last when I was sleeping in my own bed at home I had a dream with you in it. It was in a place that was partly camp, partly a school, or motel, or futuristic commune. We all had rooms. My father was there. And you and Mrs. Pullias. Also a lot of other people. I noticed where your room was. I felt strange to know I would be living around you; I wondered what it would be like. At the dining table you left a letter on my plate titled Communication.

The day after this dream Cassie (who had come home with me) and I went hiking in Random Acres. I showed Cassie my cave. Have you ever been to my cave? It is a little oak-studded valley with sweet-smelling yellow weeds. Jeff and I made the cave into a fort. It has a place for a fire (but we never built one) and a natural chimney/escape tunnel (if you're little). Below it is a special cave for dogs. Just outside is a log leaned against the small rock cliff for climbing up that way. That cave is perfect. I'd like to live there now; if I curled up I could sleep protected.

Maybe over Christmas vacation I'll go hiking more often and pretend again. Not that the cave is a fort this time but a home, an elfin home.

I dream and dream of a home for me. I am deathly tired of living "in transit." I can stand it another couple of years but then I must do something about settling down.

I've some tiring news though. I'm 4 classes short of completing G. E. requirements and my Art major. I probably shall have to take those classes Fall of next year and so start the Teach. Prog. in Winter. Then I'll have to attend that next summer after I graduate for the 3rd level and my partial credential.

There are still more inquiries to be made.

Tomorrow I find out about a librarian job at a Jr. Hi. I certainly hope I get it.

Today was Zoo Founders Day when all adults get in free. So I took myself to the zoo. I love the zoo. It is like a fantasy world all come true. I took a few photos and bought two very small wooden antelopes for my collection.

I can't decide whether my favorite animal is the Giraffe or the Okapi. What's your favorite?

Wednesday

Hooray! I did finally get the T. A. job! Not at a Jr. Hi. but at an elementary school in La Jolla in a K-1st grade classroom. Hooray Hey! That's great! I didn't really meet the teacher but the principal is extremely pleasant. His name is Mr. Hill. I suppose every time I call him I'll think of my friend, Mr. Hill, in Hemet. I'll start work Friday.

Hey, I'm happy about that.

In my Art classes we are mainly doing assignment kind of

things – figures, fruits, etc. But on my own I've been doing some contour drawings of trees. I'll send you one. I like the eucalyptus trees around here.

My roommate Pam is quiet and shy (not as shy as me, I think). What she really wants to do is get married and have eight children (she comes from a large family). The only other thing she'll consider is starting an orphanage. But she is very talented in Art and is sensitive and thoughtful. I like her. We go around together, enjoying each other's company. She likes to read like me and be quiet sometimes. Really we are what you might call ideal roommates. Very compatible.

Our room looks better now because Pam bought a big rug and I put up my little shelf. The place looks more homey.

Today I'm happy.

Yours,

Debbie.

223.

October 17, 1974

Dear Dr. Pullias,

I don't know why I miss home so much so far this year. I do though. A couple of nights ago I lay in the darkness alone and listened to the teeming of girl life around, all around me, I wondered desperately, "whatever am I doing in this horrid place?" I miss calmness. I miss my brothers. Mostly I miss – Oh, I don't know. But I dislike it here more nights out of the week than I like it.

The days are full and good and yet even at times during the day I want to be at home with Sari (I really miss her!) and Kista and my grapefruit grove.

Oh, I want to be home.

Pam tells me that every few nights she wakes up to hear me grinding my teeth. Grinding my teeth! What does that mean? Maybe it's further evidence that I am discontented here at nights. What do you think? Pam is very interested. So am I.

I suppose I mostly miss the quiet I love to dream and think and read and listen in.

Yesterday I met Dr. Eulert. It was the first I'd seen of him this year, yet in a way he's been keeping me company in my thoughts. He is my good understanding friend here in San Diego and even if I rarely see him, still he's around. He asked me to bring some recent writings to him. Maybe I'll do that tomorrow.

My job is proving very interesting. I am learning some things I didn't know how to do before. Like explain things to both individuals and groups – I have always just listened. And like telling them to get back to work – I have always just let them do the things they want. I expect it is good to learn these things but I shouldn't forget what I already know. Listening is good and I will listen still. Today, for instance, I had to explain how to do some owls for Halloween to the kindergartners. They listened well and added comments also and I listened to them. We were really, though I was nervous a bit, conversing as a group. It was good. The teacher, Janey, who is with the 1st graders thought, I guess, we were too noisy. Oh, well. She's a likable person, though, and the children like her, I think.

I consider myself pretty resistant to colds but I seem to have caught one. Rats. I'm aching and have a fever.

Maybe I'll read a little before going to sleep.

As soon as I get somewhere to buy a long envelope I'll send the drawing. It's not especially good but I like the tree. I shouldn't apologize for my work though.

I'm glad you're my friend.

Yours,

Debbie.

224.
Lost Angeles
Oct. 18, 1974
The Shop
Dear Debbie:

This past week has been real hectic. In addition to my regular teaching my work includes a good deal of speaking and I am trying to help some colleges become better colleges and so I must visit them now and then - visited two this week. In addition, the weather here became very hot, so I began to wonder if I would make the week! But it went well and now it is Friday, a beautiful day and I can stop a moment to write a friend.

I had two bits of good news that I would like to share with you. The French edition of <u>A Teacher Is Many Things</u>

came this week. My French is not very good, but it felt good to hold the book in one's hand. This is the ninth language in which the book has been published - fun?! Then I received the copy of the inside flap of the jacket of the new book. I will send you a copy of the new book when it comes - I hope before Christmas - but I thought you would like to see the flap copy.

I suspect we have to learn to live with and make the best of our bashfulness or shyness. Except that more and more we see that it doesn't matter much, and so it becomes less painful. To me to get lost in some meaningful purpose and work to achieve it has been most helpful - and <u>time</u>, for time changes many things. Miss Goudge's account of her struggle with this problem is very interesting. I am always interested in what you are thinking deep down inside.

Sincerely, Earl V. Pullias

Dear Dr. Pullias

A COMMON SENSE
PHILOSOPHY FOR
MODERN MAN:

A Search for Fundamentals

EARL V. PULLIAS

The central theme of this book is that
what people believe to be true and important determines the quality of their
lives as individuals and as organized
groups. The extent to which belief coin-
cides with reality is a matter of degree.
No individual or society has perceived,
or is likely to perceive, full truth; yet no
individual or group could exist and function at any level without having learned
a large body of truth. The extent to which
man is in trouble is the extent to which
his belief is not based upon reality — the
degree to which he has failed to use the
truth he knows and to discover needed
new truth. This book is an attempt to
state some of the basic principles or fundamentals that man has grasped thus far
in his journey. In a deep sense, they are
timeless, classless, cultureless. Yet within
and beneath the emphasis upon fundamentals is the even more basic concern
for the dynamic quality of these fundamentals: of search, of growth, of moving
toward rather than static arrival. The principles have a living, emergent quality. In
essence, the book proposes alternatives to
the doubt, fear, futility, and cynicism that
threaten the quality of modern man's life.
  Dr. Pullias is Professor of Higher Education at the University of Southern California.

PHILOSOPHICAL LIBRARY INC.
15 East 40th St., New York, N.Y. 10016

267

Debbie Bumstead

June, 1974

A Teacher Is Many Things

A Teacher Is Many Things by Earl V. Pullias and James D. Young
(Indiana University Press Bloomington and London) is used for teacher
training for all levels of teachers and for in-service development
of teachers in the public schools and in colleges and universities.

The book strives to give a special view of teaching and the
teacher - a view that attempts to escape the harmful extremes of
either cynicism or sentimentalism - a view that places chief
emphasis upon the growth of the teacher as a person and as a self-
respecting professional worker.

A Teacher Is Many Things was selected by the U.S. Information
Agency for its Ladder Series - books especially written for students
in developing countries who are studying English as a second language.
In this special paperback edition the book is now available in Latin
America, Africa, Southeast Asia, and the Far East.

Also, A Teacher Is Many Things has been published in Spanish,
Burmese, Portuguese, Japanese, Sinhalese, Lao, Arabic, and Chinese
languages. Now French!

Debbie, I was glad you liked and was
inspired by ATIMT. Someday you
will be publishing things. E.V.P.

Dear Dr. Pullias

225.
October 22
1974
Dear Dr. Pullias,

You see, I <u>don't</u> know if I can spend many more nights here. Tonight I am beginning an account to see how many evenings I will cry. I am crying the first night. It's 12:00, I have to get up early. The girls in the next room have their music on loud. I was crying before because of the noise. Pam is out till late with a new boyfriend –

I am lonely and tired of the noise.

I am lonely and tired of the noise. I can't live in this damned hotel. I want to cry aloud and scream.

It is the second night and I have not cried. Pam is here and that helps. But if her friend comes over and she leaves – what then? I'll tell you what it may be with me – boredom. I think of home; there wasn't one evening or night that I wondered what I could do. I really had no time to be bored. Here I am desperate. I can't read, write, think for all these hours on end. I liked being with those good close people at camp. That kind of closeness doesn't happen here. There are not so many things in common (like working, living, sharing together) here as at camp. Still, I wish I didn't have to be so bored-lonely.

And the noise. The noise is not so bad when someone is here to share the quiet. Pam is like me in ways. We do share. But we're not close. She's not the kind of person I'll write letters to, etc. But we're very good roommates. Except that, like all my roommates I've had (I guess every girl is that way except me), she goes out talking with a young man until late at night. And I get lonely and bored and I cry. Nothing's wrong with crying but I don't like to be crying when Pam comes in. If you knew someone who cried every night, wouldn't you begin to wonder whether they needed help? I would. But me, I don't mind crying. Maybe I need help but not about crying, about what I'm crying about.

Never mind.

I certainly enjoy the full airy days. Fall has come; I almost thought it had forgotten me. It suddenly filled me up last Saturday.

Then suddenly, with that Autumn, rusty windy clean yet dusty feeling, Cassie and I went to watch some Country Club horses work out. A cool wind rushed through our ears and we dreamed of working Prieta. It was fall.

Sunday, too. I took my drawing things down into the yellow weed eucalyptus wild buckwheat forest. I stayed there with Fall filling me all inside for two hours and when I walked I felt happy and comfortable. I began to feel that good ole forest is mine, like Random Acres is. I go there often, the wood is a friend (but a day friend – I need a night friend) and I like drawing little natural scenes. My pen and ink drawings come out rather pleasing; I hope to keep them up. If you want, look at Maurice Sendak's drawings in the animal family by Randal Jarrell. They are my goal in ability. I love them! Next week and the next week our drawing class is going to the Natural History Museum and the Zoo. Free! Hooray.

I sorta changed direction in that paragraph, huh? Anyway autumn has come!

I expect I can't go home and stay a child forever but it can be a daydream and a vacation. I am going home this weekend.

I like the way your letters smell. I wish – wish oh wish –

Rose petals, Debbie. P. S. Tonight I seem to be writing rather like the first-graders I help teach!

226.
November 2, 1974
Dear Dr. Pullias,

Today is Saturday. I went to Claremont to the library and got the book you mentioned. I've read several of her books but not this one. Then I went shopping. I bought some railroad engineer pants. They're striped and they fit; I like pants that fit. I also got two large envelopes to send my pictures in. I'll send a couple pictures to you Monday. Miss Kerr asked for some drawings of mine, too. The large drawing you'll receive is of The Enchanted Grove at night. This particular grove of eucalyptus is a bit of a ways away so I rarely go there. I've never been there at night but drew this as a night picture so that when you light your candles in your study the drawing will show you a spooky enchanted place. The other drawing frustrated me some because I couldn't get it balanced, but I like the tree.

Dear Dr. Pullias

I have been looking for rooms to rent. Do you know how it would be to rent a single room in a family home? I feel like I might rather do that than rent an apartment of my own or even with some other girl. I wonder if I might like living in a family with children. There are some people asking for housekeeping or babysitting in exchange for room and board.

I really have to get away from here.

Lately I have been thinking a lot about Prieta. I am making plans to give her a riding program over Christmas vacation (a whole month for me!). She is very fat (yet furry and beautiful) and needs exercise. I think of putting the bridle on her, brushing her, putting the bareback pad on, mounting, and walking to the field where I can work her. I feel like riding, I feel like working on my body and exercising hers. She's a good old horse and I feel quite an affection for her.

What did you do when you worked with horses? Did you like riding them? I think that sometime you ought to get on Prieta again. I would look at you and think of Don Quixote! What do you think of that? But I like Don Quixote. Prieta is a little like Rozinante.

Somehow I think I have neglected to tell you of my new lovely friends I made at Camp Wasewagan. Their names are Michelle and Linda and Lucy. M. and L. live in Texas, but M. is moving to California this January. I think of them and we write often. Last weekend when I was home they called me. All the way from Texas! I loved hearing their funny accents again. Lucy is about Miss Kerr's age, we don't write letters but I think of her so often that I count her for a friend. She is different from Miss Kerr but I admire her in much the same way. I hope I can see her again next summer. I think of her very frequently in fact. She gave me three things that help me remember her: a heart-shaped rock with "Wasewagan helps your heart." painted on the back, a pretty printed pillowcase, and a funny straw hat.

My friends are:
Dr. Pullias
Mr. Hill
James
Dr. Eulert
Joe n Tim
Miss Kerr
Michelle & Linda
Lucy

Debbie Bumstead

Debbie

me

That's not counting my children friends. They are: Cassie, Steve, Scott, Kristi, Reggie, Randy, Misty. And that's not counting those I am beginning to feel close to at work. Oh, my, I do have many friends, don't I? I like and love them all.

That's good.

I think I will snuggle into my bed and begin reading, <u>The Changeling</u> – I feel pleasantly tired, tomorrow, Sunday, I will hike in my woods and take some photos with Mamma's camera she let me use. That will be fun.

Your friend forever,

Debbie.

227.

November 11, 1974 –

Monday

Dear Dr. Pullias,

I'm back from another visit home. I'm glad I went home because the elm and maple trees in the front yard are yellow-orange with Autumn. Here in San Diego, though I occasionally get the <u>feeling</u> of fall, one does not see many trees changing; they stay green all year. I like Hemet for its seasons. Sunday I took a walk down to Miss Kerr's house. She wasn't home but the autumn walk was lovely and I stayed a while in Miss Kerr's yard. The atmosphere was exceedingly Miss Kerrish; I felt a love for the place and felt at home. I think that it is a good thing to have friends that have been friends for years – you, Miss Kerr, James, and Mr. Hill – even though I am still shy, in some way I am at home.

There are wild rumors flying around campus. The campus is to be sold and we are to move again, where unknown. This year is to continue here but next year – ? The Education School is supposedly moving into the Law school buildings downtown. Crazy.

I talked with my advisor and he said I should go ahead and take twenty units (1 class more than usual) both next and Spring quarters. In that way I'd finish my B. A. by June. He said he was sure I'd be able to do well even with the extra class. I think so, too, as I won't be working anyway (I'd like to keep up with that wonderful job but my class hours don't work out).

I got my first paycheck today. It's great how I can learn, have fun, and earn money all at the same time! You know, I like to work.

Yes, I liked Ivy and Martha. Enough to wish the book hadn't ended. One question seemed unresolved – that of how one stays a child. Now I am reading <u>Julie of the Wolves</u>. It is good. Please recommend more books! Have you ever read <u>The Little Princess</u> by Francis Hodges Burnett? James recommended it to me and I enjoyed it. I read it last year so that at camp, working in the hot kitchen I pretended I was Sara Crewe. A little princess despite the menial chores.

I keep thinking about after I graduate and what I will do. It seems to be getting so close that it's almost not a dream anymore. It's unbelievable to think that come summer I can put B. A. After my name!

Mary Deborah Alice Bumstead, B. A.

My!

I don't think you knew that I am taking piano lessons this quarter. They're fun but it takes so much concentration! My fingers get sore! I like it though.

Your friend,
Debbie.

228.
November 16, 1974
Dear Dr. Pullias,

It always feels good to have finished up a whole bunch of homework that I told myself to finish. I had to do several designs of colored construction paper shapes. When I finished I noticed some nicely shaped scraps and glued them to your envelope.

Today Cassie and I went to the zoo. We looked at gorillas, wolves, kangaroos, and snakes. Cassie likes snakes. This time more than any other I felt the wildness of the animals and felt them in their natural settings. I almost felt frightened. I think because of a nightmare I had night before last about wildness and death. At the end of this dream I saw a dead child picked by crows. Throughout the dream I kept thinking, "But crows are supposed to be lucky." When I wake up from such a bad dream I can't move for several minutes though I realize it's OK now. Some chemical thing happens so that my body feels weighted; I am petrified!

Pam went home for the weekend.

Yesterday I checked once more with my counselors. And unfortunately we found that both of them had made mistakes; I won't be finished this year at all. I feel like giving up the hassle. I wrote to Pacific Oaks. I could enter there as a senior and not lose credit, I think. I might as well since I've exhausted the art courses here and everything else (except Creative Writing) doesn't look right. At Pacific Oaks perhaps I would learn more about children than here. I think it would be best.

I suspect there will be a certain amount of unease here next year as the rumors are true. Due to financial troubles we have to sell the campus and move – no one knows where. Crazy.

I will try to get I Heard the Owl Call My Name. Every time I check for Watership Down it is out – it is very popular I guess!

I am looking forward to Thanksgiving.

I liked your letter.

Your friend,

Debbie.

229.
Los Angeles
Nov. 22, 1974
The Shop - at night
Dear Debbie:

My last letter to you written last night or the night before was mostly about plans about your work. So in a sense it was about business, yet the practical affairs of a friend are in reality much more than business - they have the life given to them by mutual care and friendship. Much of life is composed of these things - these practical problems.

A week ago tonight I made a talk about college teaching at a college about 40 miles from here at Azusa, Calif. The occasion was a small conference of college teachers and Dr. Box was there. I was able to talk a little with him and he was quite complimentary of you as a student. My talk was about some of the ideas in <u>A Teacher is Many Things</u>, especially the last chapter which discussed the problem of the teacher as a person. They seemed to like the ideas, too but whether they can practice them is another matter. Yesterday I talked with some students at the same college and they seemed to think that as a rule college teachers are not too interested in the students. It varies I guess from teacher to teacher.

Some days I feel apprehensive and uneasy - as if something not good was happening and was about to happen. Today has been one of those unhappy days. Perhaps caused by an unpleasant dream I had last night which I could not remember this morning. I note in a recent letter that you had the unpleasant dream about a dead child again. Wish we knew what that dream is trying to say to you if anything.

The day has been beautiful; the shadows in this room have a charm: life really is a joy, I know.

Sincerely, Earl V. Pullias

P.S. Just wanted to talk a moment with my friend before the day was over. Do you like candles?

230.
November 24, 1974
Dear Dr. Pullias,

Two more evenings after this one and then I can go home. After Thanksgiving only four evenings before quarter break. Oh, how I hate it here. I wish I were dead. I won't go to school next quarter if I have to live like this. Every night I feel on the verge of some desperate action — getting in the car and driving all night or running down into the forest and sleeping there.

Maybe I will go home tomorrow. I think I will.

I'll try to be a little more cheerful. You know I remember

something you told me once — that often a person's unhappiness is caused by not knowing enough about things. At the very beginning of camp, for instance, I noticed Miss Kerr going around with the Assistant Director. I expressed to her a feeling of what I had always called jealousy and she said right back that she didn't think it was jealousy but probably just wishful thinking. And what magic that was to dispel my unhappiness! I haven't been "jealous" since; I like wishful thinking.

Somehow I think what I'm going through now could be that way. I'm quite confused and unsure of what's going on; what my feelings mean. I wonder if there are some magical words like wishful thinking that will let my mind break into understanding. Even if its solution doesn't happen suddenly I think I need a little help on this problem.

At the beginning of the year everything was peachy-keen. My roommate Pam and I were very good pals. We went around together and talked. I didn't love her but I liked her. Then suddenly she made friends with a fellow named Bob and I have hardly seen her since. I felt like she had just dropped me as no good. It was so sudden and complete. She is with him all day, sometimes all night but at least till 2:30 A.M. She was the only evening friend I had here. I need an evening friend, I think. I don't know, maybe I don't.

The things that bother me about it are that she once told me that she wouldn't live with a guy ever — she'd think of a girl who did as a slut sort of (I wouldn't, and don't think of her as such) and yet here she is — doing just that. She must have it justified in her mind but I see it as hypocrisy. There's nothing I hate more than hypocrisy — I may be so sometimes but I fight hellish hard not to be. Another thing is that she has said, "Oh I'll be home tonight to keep you company." and then she shows up at 2 in the morning! It <u>hurts</u> to be hit like that. Does she realize that? I thank <u>if</u> she were in my place and I in hers I would, no matter <u>how</u> much I loved the person I was going around with, keep my promises and live up to my ideals. I don't think I would sacrifice a friendship for another friendship no matter the degree of affection.

I guess I am expecting her to live up to what I would live up to. I guess that's what bothers me and hurts me. It's a kind of loneliness but not really. For instance when she works in the evenings (twice a week) I don't cry. I know that's valid and she keeping to a responsibility. I cry on nights when she's out with him because she's picked him instead of me, completely. I would understand her being out with him

<u>more</u> than staying me; she loves him.

So... she bothers me with her hypocrisy and hurts me with a brutal discarding of me. It hurts to be cast aside so abruptly.

Why do I feel all this? Maybe it's boredom — I conjure up unhappiness to occupy me and then get trapped in it. It takes a little more work to conjure up happiness but I'm too lazy.

But maybe I'm all wrong. Maybe you know something you could tell and help. Do you have magic words?

Your friend, Debbie.

231.
November 25, 1974
Dear Dr. Pullias,

Thank you for the letters; they help me remember that I have friends. I thought I'd stay here till Wednesday after all, as I should because of work and class commitments. But tonight (Monday) again I am not sure. It is open house and Pam and Bob are in on the couch groveling (my word for kissing and squirming). At first I was just sitting in the bedroom thinking but the sounds took me way back to the miserable time when I had to listen to my parents love-making. It's not so much the actual acts that bother me but the untruth, the hypocrisy of it, both then and now with Pam.

So I put the music on and started writing. That will keep me from crying. How sad it is that I am beginning to despise the sight of a once good pal.

Why do I worry so much about truth? We're all going to die anyway. Yet truth is vitally important to me; I don't want to be anything less than perfectly honest, with others and with myself. I want truth to be known and acted. I want to be <u>right</u> and <u>good</u>; I want to be <u>true</u>. It is of exceeding importance. Perhaps that's why it irritates me to see hypocrisy and weak action in others and myself.

Because of my occupation with truth I guess I am bound to be displeased with a lot of actions. Would it be truthful for me to accept and forgive? It might be good but I won't do it. I refuse to give into this wishy-washyness. How can I be happy, then, living with it? If I could accept it in others but keep to truth myself. That would be hard.

Perhaps in a college dorm people are especially hypocritical. I don't want to live this way any longer.

A young lady who is getting a divorce and has two children called me about having a room to rent across the street, in her house.

I wish they would leave. Open house's over and I have to go to the bathroom and get to bed. Well, I have every right to go into the bathroom; I can't help interrupting them.

I want to be away.

Your friend,

Debbie.

232.
Los Angeles
Nov. 28, 1974
The Shop - at night
Dear Debbie:

Your last two letters have touched my heart deeply. In a way, they made me sad, but in a deeper sense, they made me very proud of you and very thankful we are friends. Of course, I would like very much to help - to offer magic words and thoughts that might strengthen and guide you - but I am not sure I can, although I believe I can: I will give you my whole mind and heart. This will be a long letter - I hope not too long - but there is much I wish to say.

First a word about A Little Princess. My sister-in-law who works for the public library brought home to me the only copy she could find. It was a badly worn paperback that was dirty, but I didn't mind that. I read the book last week. I liked it very much, and in fact, I was greatly inspired by the book. I feel it is a great book. It felt very good to be reading a significant book recommended to me by you. To know Sara Crewe together will help us both.

I did not know the deeper part of you, except by intuition, until I received your last two letters, especially the last one, in which you tell me of your roommate, Pam, and her behavior over the past weeks. I believed in you, I admired you, and was confident that you are a very special person, but I did not know really how deeply you are devoted to truth and to principle. I don't know how to tell you how glad and thankful I am that this is true. You will understand. It is a foundation on which to build a great life.

I believe I understand, at least somewhat, why Pam's behavior and treatment of you hurts you so deeply. You had thought you were discovering a friend who might have similar ideals and interests. Further, you may have been beginning to love her in the way girls often love one another. To have this relationship destroyed almost ruthlessly - really apparently without concern - was like a betrayal - in a way a slap in the face. That is always a great hurt and pain. But I guess even deeper is the betrayal of truth or principle, when, it seems without concern or regret, she persistently behaves contrary to her word and stated ideal. Here the hurt goes to a deeper level, and becomes almost more than you can bear, and understandably so.

Still the problem has another aspect which touches something especially important in your nature and character. Publicly displayed, or carelessly displayed, sex behavior is deeply disturbing to any sensitive person, and especially to one of your nature. I am not sure I can do much to say why, but the feeling of revulsion involves the deepest levels of our minds. Sex behavior of that nature is, and should be, a deeply private thing, and when it is not it becomes cheap and vulgar and harms both the participants and the observer. I have considered the public display of sex behavior as harmful. It is not right that you should be subjected to such environment. The hypocrisy and the unfortunate childhood experiences add greatly to the pain. So what I am saying really is that your feeling about the situation is natural, and is a compliment to you.

You are right in feeling you must get out of the situation, and as soon as possible. Maybe you get the room with the divorced lady; maybe you could ask for a single room; if neither is possible before Christmas then after we have talked like this and you have had a little respite (this holiday at home), you could if you had to stick it out until the Christmas break, and work something out before you go back. I am very concerned that this ugly, and in a way foolish event doesn't damage your school work. You have made excellent progress. Nothing, certainly not a foolish, fickle, uncontrolled girl and boy, must be allowed to turn you aside from that growth or progress.

And now for my magic word: <u>the little princess</u> or <u>imagination</u>. You can and will rise above this hurt and disappointment. Really Pam and her behavior are pretty small. There is too much of beauty and love and friendship in the world to be turned aside by this kind of thing. You will find friends that will be true: you have many now that love you.

In the meantime, you need to develop and pursue interests that pull you: do more with your athletics, your music, your art, your writing. Give yourself fully to them - and to children who heal you. You are 20 years old and I believe deeply very strong, and will grow stronger. I am so glad you could write so freely and fully to me. I am glad you are my friend.

Sincerely, Earl V. Pullias

P.S. This letter is written to meet you when you return to school: I wish it could be in person. Let me know if there is anything I can do.

233.

December 2, 1974

Dear Dr. Pullias,

Thanks very much for your good letter. Besides making me feel I have a very good friend and giving me some insight into what I'm experiencing, your letter also gives me something enjoyable to do – write back! I like to write to friends. It brings them close.

The vacation was very recuperating and I think I can easily last out this week. The quarter ends Friday. That night I wrote to you last turned into a grisly scene. I began to cry from listening to them so I put on my shoes wrapped my blanket around me and left. It is the best thing, really, for me to do – to go sit on the steps that look into the forest and the night sky. Because when I see how immense and beautiful the world is around me I quite quickly let the small confining ugliness of a problem slip away. When I'm in this room with nothing to do the problem almost grows larger than the world. Anyway Pam and Bob, concerned with my abrupt departure, found me. Bob left and Pam sat beside me. The problem came close again and I cried. Pam tried to get me to tell her what she had done but it is one of my rules – you can't tell a person what is wrong with them, though you can tell them how they make you feel. I tried to tell her how I felt and when she asked what she had done to make me feel that way I said, "Look and see for yourself, I don't want to change you. I want you to change if you see that you want to." She thought a long time and then said, "I think I've been selfish." I told her to go away. I didn't want to hear anymore promises and ideals for fear they'd all be broken again.

Dear Pam. She cares, she's sensitive, but... I don't know.

For pretty sure I will live with the young divorcee in her house across the street. It's a fairly large place (with the pool); I'll have a private room and bath. I guess I'll eat supper with her and her children and then have cereal for breakfast and fix a sack lunch for at school. It sounds rather pleasant especially because of the children and the fact that I'll have access to the private tennis courts there! I miss my tennis.

My schedule for next quarter then will be to work at the elementary school two or three mornings a week and in the afternoons attend my art class – Beginning Painting and Special Studies in Drawing. I like my art teacher Mr. Fortbrook. He is extremely sincere, exceedingly so! I like him for that. I'll also have an independent study in Creative Writing with Dr. Eulert. I don't know if I've told you how much I admire Dr. Eulert. We are beginning to be <u>friends</u>. I think he is an excellent teacher; I really feel like I learn something even though he doesn't purposefully stuff information into us. I just learn by listening, watching, talking, and being with him. Since I know I learned from him and want to learn, well, it's good to take another class with him. What I say is "When you find a good teacher for yourself, stick with him!"

I spent yesterday with James. We went for a walk and picnic and in the evening at his place we talked and talked. I really really enjoy a philosophical thoughtful kind of discussion. At that time, when I am listening with absolute full attention or speaking with a most careful precision (and yet all in a relaxed way) I think I am especially alert and alive. It feels the way I feel when I'm out hiking. I wonder why.

I think it takes a certain amount of trust and assurance from the other to be able to discuss such important topics as dreams, death, God, etc., and with two such shy persons as J. and I it probably takes more. So it pleases me to see our ability to communicate so intimately – or honestly. It says that we are close friends.

I'm sure I could be just as close, talking-wise, to a girl; I could be just as intimate and honest. It does make a difference that James is a guy – I feel different just as I <u>feel</u> different with you or Mr. Hill or Dr.

Debbie Bumstead

Eulert, well, I just feel different with men, and different with women. And maybe with James I feel even differenter because he is my own age, but I feel different with each different age of men or women. I guess what I'm trying to say is that my feeling for James as a male and as my age is naturally different from the feeling for anyone else; it's not something to get excited about – it something to feel and feel good about.

. I don't know how to state the difference between J. and me and some girls and boys, that is the difference of our difference compared to their difference (got that?). Maybe you know how to state it? Maybe the difference is excitement. I'm not too excited that J. is a fellow and I know him and I am a girl, rather I am excited that we talk so well with each other and have good fun. Perhaps others are excited that they are man and women, just that. I don't know! But I do like James and being with him and talking.

Wow, you know, even though it takes in an enormous amount of talking to myself, explaining, writing, making rules, thinking, thinking, thinking, I am <u>very</u> glad I have myself to live up to. Yes!

<u>A Little Princess</u> is indeed an inspirational book. When I was quite young I read <u>A Secret Garden</u> by the same author and enjoyed its magic also.

Recently I've been reading <u>Journey to Ixtlan</u> and <u>The Teachings of Don Juan</u> by Carlos Castaneda. They are interesting.

Your friend, Debbie.

After a night mare
 and screaming,
the moonlight slipped through the window.
On the sill
a small ceramic pony
bowed his head,
and with the moon, whispered,
 "You are here."
Nov. 30, 1974

234.
Los Angeles
Dec. 7, 1974
The Shop

Dear Dr. Pullias

Dear Debbie:

Thanks for your good letter. I was especially glad to get that letter, because I guess I had been worried about you somewhat. That is one of the problems of having a dear friend: her problems, hurts and concerns become yours. But so do her joys and triumphs. Do you recall the chapter in <u>The Little Prince</u> where he met and "tamed" the fox. It is one of the most beautiful and thoughtful pieces of writing I know. Wish you could read it again during Christmas. I suspect you and James are experiencing that "taming" relation - and I am glad for you.

I would like to react at some length to many of the thoughtful and difficult problems you raise in your letter. Sometime maybe, but I am not quite in the mood tonight.

The arrangements you are working out for a place to stay next quarter seem quite promising. I hope you can make them work out. A good deal depends on what the lady is like. I believe it was quite important that you get out of the impossible dormitory situation. I believe it is wise for us to study ourselves as to what we can "take" and what tends to be more than we can bear without too much damage. I hope you can get back into your athletics (tennis for example), and it would be good if you had a friend, boy or girl, like James with whom to talk. The classes sound very good.

Do you think it is fair for some people to be out of school and walking the hills Dec. 7, and other poor people to slave on until the 18!? My picture and statue friends around me here say it is surely fair for Debbie!!

Sincerely, Earl V. Pullias

P.S. Hope you can go out to the Random Acres Area much while you are there.

235.
December 11, 1974
Dear Dr. Pullias,

My mother has gone to bed, I am in the living room with the radio on and Sari My Cat purring beside me. She wants to get into my lap but I have to say, "Not now, I am writing to Dr. Pullias." She is purring a hello to you.

Debbie Bumstead

My mother gave me an early Christmas gift – a crocheted pair of slippers. They look like elfin shoes for autumn, bright yellow and brown. Often I am an elf. I admire elves; I am glad I have enough imagination and humor to believe in such things. I'm glad we can pretend your picture people come alive and dance on the lawn. It's fun. And funny.

These are characters that I admire: Pippi Longstocking, Danny Kaye, Bugs Bunny, and my own Alice. I do like Alice. She is a little like Pippi but not as strong, in fact she's just a bit vulnerable; love counts for so much to her. Alice. She's bright, she's open, she's honest. She loves. She is loved. It pleases me enormously to know that I am Alice through and through. Only a thin crusting of manners and inhibitions keep me from acting completely Alice. I am a brat already; what a terrible wonderful brat I would be (Alice!) but for my manners keeping me in check!

Oh! You never knew I was a brat did you? When I write I'm not but when I begin to feel comfortable with someone I become a brat. Sometimes I'm sorry for it. I don't know why I'm a brat. Someone once told me it's a way of asking to be loved. Could be. And it could be a way of showing love, too.

Why do you suppose I've been so occupied with love these past three years? I think I'm learning a lot about life, especially about love and truth at college and it feels good to feel that I am changing and learning and progressing. Love and truth. Interesting to think about and feel.

I like vacations 'cause suddenly I have time to stop and think and dream and write all I want.

Oh! I like the song on the radio.... "time seems to stand still, in a child's world it always will.... what a day to go kite flying..." Some strains of music quite send me kite flying! A friend can play on the piano a piece called "Fur Elise" (by Beethoven, I think) which has a repeating pattern of notes that produces in me such a feeling of beauty that I could fairly burst! Have you heard it? I shall have to get a record with it on it. Or maybe I should learn to play it!

Love,
Debbie.

236.

Dear Dr. Pullias

Los Angeles
Dec 14, 1974
The Shop
Dear Debbie:

It is evening here in my little study. I have lighted a candle, and its flame gives the pictures and objects in the room a special quality. Today I have felt pensive, and perhaps a little blue. I received your letter yesterday, and had looked forward to this night when I planned to talk with you in this way. I especially like the picture of you and Sari on the wall to my right: I appreciate receiving a direct message from her.

Truth, beauty, goodness and love: TBGL. These I think are the great qualities in life and in persons. You spoke of at least three of them - truth, beauty, and love - in your last letter. Goodness doubtless is a manifestation of all these when it appears in its best form.

I am much inspired and encouraged by your deep interest in <u>truth</u>. The central emphasis I try to give in the course I give on college teaching (I will offer it again the coming spring semester) is that of the importance of genuineness, sincerity, authenticity - I don't know which word catches the spirit I am seeking for best. Your writing has the quality of authenticity - of being free. I believe your life does also. I, also, have wanted more than anything else to grow in this quality so that what I am and what I write and what I do would be more and more authentic - true. To know that you, my friend, feels so strongly about this quality makes me feel very close to you - gives me an understanding of you that I had not had before.

But truth alone (at least unless it is very broadly understood) is not enough. Alone it (truth) tends to be cold and in a sense detached. So beauty and love need to be added, and then perhaps we grow toward what might be called purity of heart which perhaps is the deep meaning of goodness. I was much interested in what you told me of how beautiful things touch and move you so. I will try to find the piece of music "Fur Elise" of which you spoke. I like many of Beethoven's creations, especially his 9th symphony - the 3rd movement is my favorite.

But of course of all the qualities we might seek to understand and to incorporate in our lives, love is the best. Love

285

is it seems tricky though, and without a good measure of truth and beauty love can and does lead us into strange blind alleys. Maybe then it is not really genuine love but some kind of distortion. Perhaps Pam's behavior is a kind of love unguided by truth and beauty. I wonder how one comes to value these deeper aspects of love and guide his life by them.

I believe I understand what you say about being a "brat." It is to be oneself in all one says and does - like a child - to be free from pretense or guile. When what one deeply is of truth, beauty, and love, then one can be free - be oneself - and what one does flowing directly from that self can be childlike, free, direct (in a sense, brattish) but really not in the bad sense of unwisely hurting oneself and others. Or am I right?

Alice is a projection of the deepest part of you. Let her grow becoming all she can become which is much, I believe. The in-be-tween time of which you speak is great indeed. I am very tired, and will be glad when my vacation comes. My love to Sari.

Sincerely, Earl V. Pullias

237.
Christmas Eve, 1974 –
Dear Dr. Pullias,

I got your letter today (I guess it was delayed in the mail). And today I went hiking in the hills.

Tomorrow is Christmas.

I've been having a good vacation. Twice I visited Miss Kerr; once at her house where we worked in her garden and another time at her horses' corral and we went riding (Prieta was sold and now lives in Fallbrook – but Miss Kerr said I could ride one of her horses, Buster, anytime I like). It's kind of like heaven being with her, she's so much fun to me. Not only is she a friend and a special person but also, because she is older and I admire her so much, she makes me feel optimistic about the future. Even though I may not become that much like her nor even want to, still she makes me feel good about the future.

Three times I visited with James and that is always fun. And twice I visited Mr. Hill.

Inbetween I've been hiking, biking, wandering around town,

reading, doing a little gardening, a little writing and such. Pleasant things.

Suddenly the weather has turned very nippy. Brrrrrrr.

Tomorrow we will open presents. The Christmas feeling has not been with me much this season. My brother Tim who does not celebrate Christmas is living with us and so I feel I shouldn't be too Christmasy. I wonder, sometimes, if I'm kind to the point of sacrificing my own happy feelings, or to the point of sacrificing my freedom. Only that's OK really. I guess I'm kind in some ways and a terrible brat, like you described, in other ways.

But then I don't know what right Tim has to hang around and influence us in this dragging kind of way.

Day after Christmas –

My father and I went to my cousin Linda's house for Christmas dinner. I played with my young second cousins the whole time and they invited me over for tomorrow, too. To spend the night.

We have violets in our yard.

Your friend, Debbie.

238.
Los Angeles
Dec. 30, 1974
The Shop - 9:45 p.m.
Dear Debbie:

I am sorry my letter was so slow in getting to you - probably because of the Christmas mail which often seems to make letters late. Your good letter written Christmas Eve and the day after Christmas came yesterday - Saturday. I was very pleased to have your letter, for I had been wondering how you were.

It is very good you could be with your friends there: Miss Kerr, Mr. Hill, and James. Wonderful - almost more than one has a right to expect. I like very much what you have to say about Miss Kerr, your relation with her, and the way she encourages you about the future. Such a friend is a precious thing, and I am thankful for your sake and for hers for I am sure you bring joy to her.

I hardly know what to say about Tim's situation. I like your loving and kind heart in such instances. I believe I know how you feel, for I have often had the same feelings about people, and even about animals. Tim is searching for answers to the big problems of life, especially about the meaning of life and proper actions toward it. In searching for answers people often take strange and sometimes, harmful ways. I suspect the same deep needs are behind the varied approaches. Some take the ways of the girls in your dormitory, some to drink or drugs, some to religion, and so on. I believe there are good and wise ways to live life and it makes all the difference if we can find them and follow them. Most people I fear spoil their lives because they take the wrong ways and persist in following them.

Because I love and respect you very much I long for you to follow the wise and good and beautiful ways, not only for your own sake but for what your life can mean to others. I hope my concern for you will not cause me to push into areas of your life where I should not enter. I would not wish to do that, but I would like to help when and if I can.

There is a danger in over feeling that every person has a right to go his own way - that we have no right to judge. There is some truth in that position, but the danger lies in our concluding that one way is as good as another. This is simply not true: there are ways that are wrong and lead to very painful results that hurt not only the persons involved but all who are related to them. I think you will forgive me if I say I am quite uneasy about your mother whom I respect very much. I don't know if you can help but alcohol is a very dangerous way to deal with one's problems. I feel I haven't helped her as much as I should, but I am not sure I could help. Perhaps you will tell me what you think. I hope she is all right.

But I am being too serious for this glorious Christmas season. My friends (your friends for I feel you begin to know them) around the wall and on the desk look at me and remind me that there is a beautiful moon tonight - very good for a party on the lawn. I am so glad your holiday has been good. Let's see what we can do with the new year. It will be better for me because you are my friend.

Sincerely, Earl V. Pullias

P.S. Give your new address when you write. I am sending this to San D. address.

1975

*We ate a picnic lunch on a sunny rock ledge. I lay
back on the flat rock, closed my eyes, and listened. To the
children's voices, a chirring bird, a passing insect, and I thought
deep down that I was almost hearing the very vibration of Life.*
Debbie

*Sometimes I think it is strange and wonderful, the
way my life is going. Life is surely a magical business!* Debbie

Debbie Bumstead

Dear Dr. Pullias

239.
January 1, 1975
Dear Dr. Pullias,

My mother gave me this stationery; I like the inside of the envelope. I'll use it tonight in memory of my sweet friend, Sari. She was run over and killed Sunday morning. I buried her under the old grapefruit trees. I miss her.

It was strange that the night before the night before the day she was hit I had this dream – I was walking along an old paved road (not ours) and many cats, alley cats, were following me. The cats walked on the street and I saw a car coming. It was a hot rod with jacked-up rear end. I was scared the cats would get run over. The car went very fast. It almost hit one cat. And then as it got nearer me it did run over one cat and killed it.

It was strange, too, that Sari would go out on the street; she was very frightened of it. I wish she hadn't.

I had my two young second cousins, Steve and Kristi over for an evening. In the morning we went out to Random Acres. First we headed for the jumble-tumble rock ravine just beyond Sleepy Hollow. They both remembered the tunnels formed by the rocks from a time before. We ate a picnic lunch on a sunny rock ledge. I lay back on the flat rock, closed my eyes, and listened. To the children's voices, a chirring bird, a passing insect, and I thought deep down that I was almost hearing the very vibration of Life. I opened my eyes and looked at Stephen as he sat, munching animal crackers, looking down into the ravine. The sun caught at his thick red hair; I wondered what he was thinking. He is 12 now, my favorite child-friend, he is really the child that, 10 or 11 years ago, brought my interest in children into a sharp focus. I still love him and am just as interested in his growing but I think I will always enjoy younger children for their charm. Steve is, as everyone must, I suppose, losing some of his child charm.

Then I looked over at Kristi, who is 10 and hasn't yet begun to lose her charm. But her charm isn't as charming as Steve's charm was

Debbie Bumstead

(and is, though lessening). But I like her; I think she listens well to her inside.

After we ate and rested I took them to my cave. We started pretending we were Indians riding Pinto horses (galloping on pretend ponies is something I've done almost all my life! And it can be so very real, so very very very real. I wonder how come?).

We galloped to your cabin and inspected it and the upper one. We decided to make the cabins our home. So we began cleaning the lower one up. There had been a large beer party and it was a stinky dirty job. We put cans and bottles in the trashcan, swept the floor, and arranged the furniture.

When we finished we thought it was time to go so we galloped away.

Last night I dreamt I lived in the Adobe and all Random Acres was under my care. I made friends with rocks and plants and encouraged animals to come stay. There weren't any more destructive stinky beer parties.

Sunday I will be going back to San Diego.

~~This is my new address~~ (Maybe I better give it to you after I get there – I'm not exactly sure how it should be written).

Your forever friend,

Debbie.

P. S. Last night I also dreamed Sari came into my room to sleep with me. I will probably dream of her often for a while – just as I did for my other favorite cat the world, Frosty, when he died. In that way, them coming to me in dreams, I guess death is not so complete as I thought. But it is sad.

My
Sari

The House Across from
college in San Diego
Dear Dr. Pullias,

Dear Dr. Pullias

I am settled into my new modern room and rich home. I slept here last night and had a night full of dreams. I dreamt of Miss Kerr. And I dreamt it was raining – there is a fountain always trickling out my window.

But the weather here is sunny like spring. Yesterday was like the sunny easy breeze days I remember over at Cal Western. I walked around the block here and felt the air, clean and moist, moving through my whole body. It brought a feeling back – what memory? Something... Then I saw a striped cat going into a garage and the memory and feeling came back in a rush. It was the cat and the air. I remembered those completely magical mornings at Cal Western when I would get up early to walk up the hill and down to the elementary school. Some mornings the magic cat, orange striped and friendly, waited for me at the top of the hill. I petted her and sat for a minute in the lovely sea air with the tall trees that lined the street swaying gently against the blue sky. I thought that if I stayed long enough the cat would take me to her magical world where it was always green and fresh. But always I got up to leave, to go down to the school and my child friends.

I like this weather. It is like spring. I have two art classes this afternoon.

Yours,
Debbie.

240.
January 13, 1975
Dear Dr. Pullias,

Oh, I've had such a horrible tiring day. What caused it all was last night. I had one extremely frightening dream and two other disturbing ones. All day my mind dwelled on that horrid terrible dream – oh, the thought of it makes me fear another one tonight. It wasn't even gory, just frightening. In the first dream I was at home only no one was there. I knew that they all had rushed away because either Aunt Raechal or Uncle Al had died. I was frightened of their death. I wasn't sure which had died so I called. Somebody told me that they both had died and I asked how. I suddenly visualized them, Aunt Rae and Uncle Al, in a head on collision in a car accident. But the person on the phone said it was their old thing, narcotics (?). When I hung up the phone I

293

Debbie Bumstead

thought. And the thoughts were all questions about how I should deal with the death of someone. I thought of Sari. And all the thoughts were like drifting in an unfathomable sea of space – I couldn't catch hold of any answers. What frightened me was that <u>Aunt Raechal and Uncle Al were dead</u> and <u>I didn't know how I should think of them now.</u>

It doesn't sound very scary but it was, it was horrible.

In the next dream I and a lot of people were hunting in the hills above my Grandparent's house and around your cabin for a dead child. I didn't want to find it. The rocks and brush stood out very realistically in my dream.

In the third dream the whole family was going to an opera or something. I had to accompany Daddy because he had gone simple in the head. That scared me.

I don't want to dream tonight. I'm so very tired. I had an awful night, then woke up at 6:30, went to a two hour 8:00 class, sat on the grass till 12:00, went to a 2 1/2 hour class, then at last at 5:00 I could come home! When I came into my room I had a strange strange sensation. I felt wavery and my head felt like it was going to go out like a burnt-out lightbulb!

I think I'll take a warm bath and go to bed early.

My father gave me <u>I Heard the Owl Call My Name</u> and I read it and enjoyed it. Come to think of that book – the questions of death might have been what prompted my dream along with Sari's death. I haven't any idea why I picked Aunt Rae and Uncle Al to die – oh! yes I do! I remember in the dream at the beginning I had thought of Grandpa and I feared his dying because he had been sick over Christmas, but it was too real a possibility to think of him so somehow I thought of Aunt Raechal.

I like all my classes but they are very long, especially those two art classes in the afternoon right in a row and four days a week. Creative writing meets twice and at 8:00, but I don't mind so much because I like Dr. Eulert a lot.

Your friend, Debbie.

241.
Jan. 20, 1975

Dear Dr. Pullias

Dear Dr. Pullias,

Yes, I wish the mail would move faster; it seems as if I'm not getting any letters at all! Also my address number is 10272 not 10292 – that confused the postman.

The weather is so much like summer here! I am sitting on a wooden sundeck in the backyard listening to a mockingbird. The backyard is fairly spacious with a patch of lawn, new little trees, sundeck, hammock, etc. The house is quite large. It has a big living room, a family room, a big kitchen, a den with TV, two bathrooms, and three bedrooms. One of the bathrooms is mine and my bedroom is larger than mine at home. It has an orange shag rug and a wallpaper mural of an imaginary place with trees and beasts. It has an east-facing window.

I am free to wander throughout the house; I can write in the living room, watch TV in the den, get something to eat if I want, etc. I fix my own meals except when Jenn is home and cooks dinner or something.

The house is one of many of the same kind in a project called Scripps Ranch; it's upper middle class stuff. It lies directly across the street (Pomerado Road) from USIU. If I want to walk in nature I can still go to my forest at school. I like walking in neighborhoods, too, and this is a friendly, though rather monotonous, one to wander the streets of. I like the mockingbirds.

There is a wire-haired terrier living here, named Flower, and a hamster, Whiskers.

I decided I couldn't keep up with working three hours a day and having six hours of class work. So I'll have to quit the job. Too bad… but my health seemed to be suffering and I couldn't find the time I need to sit and just think.

Jenn, the lady here, has some arguing crying hassles about her daughter's homework so she asked me to be the Official Homework Helper. That way she has only one thing to do – enforce the rule – and I can concentrate on helping. I haven't started yet because of a cold but I expect she will pay me in some way; she is very nice. And yesterday I felt a sudden quick affection for the girl, Lisa, who is a bit shy, so I will probably grow to like her very much. She is nine.

The thing I really like about this place is that I can be alone and quiet and still have company. That is, in the evenings, when my creative and thought juices flow the strongest, Lisa is in bed and Jenn often is also (she works) so that I feel quiet in the living room with the radio on – it's just comforting and comfortable to have people in their bedrooms asleep and me quiet and writing in the living room. Privacy yet company, somehow. And quiet.

I've been having very vivid dreams – not unpleasant, though.

This morning I wrote a paper for creative writing – it concerned my Grandpa Bumstead. You know, when I get on a writing I get so excited I sweat! My heart pounds excitedly and I smile and shift my position many times as I write faster and faster. It's a very exciting thing, to be inspired, even in such a simple writing.

In our writing class we ditto the papers to pass out for others to read. I'll try to remember to send you a copy.

I will think a bit on my dreams and death.

Love,

Debbie.

I did the ditto tonight and will enclose this copy tonight.

The college is still unsure of what it is going to do next year. I expect for insurance I ought to apply elseware. In my next letter I'll send you a recommendation form if that's OK.

The manner of our discussion

Grandfather and Aunt Rachel, my father's sister, were guests. My father was the host; my mother served refreshments, she sat near the kitchen. My place was the corner of the couch nearest the heater, where I sat with my knees drawn up, and my older brothers stretched out on the floor by the heater.

Even as young children we were members of the discussion.

Grandfather smoked a pipe, Aunt Rachael, cigarettes, and my father, cigars. My mother did not smoke; sitting near the window, when she looked at my brothers and me, she smiled. The lamp beside my father filled the room with a mellow amber light. I always watched the curling tumbling grey wisps of smoke; I believe my brothers watched the smoke, also, with heads resting on hands, or they looked for pictures in the water spots on the ceiling.

And the room and the night were quiet. No one spoke. The curling grey amber air and the silence grew upon us; our thoughts revolved and lifted; our bodies stilled and lowered.

My father shifted; he uncrossed his legs and crossed them the

Dear Dr. Pullias

other way. He spoke. I thought his voice and laughter were like the smoke, soft and drifting, his words drifting into the room, into the air, to filter through to our ears. My father's habit of speaking was to move his legs and give a quiet chuckle after each sentence. We listened and smiled.

Another silence rose after my father concluded. His comment revolved with our thoughts, circling around the room; our minds and bodies became somewhat more active, we worked on the thought. Grandfather nodded his head; lifting his hands from his lap and opening them to us, we knew he was going to speak.

We listened to the quiet Grandfather always let gather before he spoke. His voice, even quieter than my father's, traveled out into the amber room on his puffs of white smoke. Each sentence was proceeded a thoughtful silence as he pulled at the pipe. Grandfather fascinated me, as I watched him from my couch corner, my eyes drawn to his mouth. His lips were thin and straight, yet they seemed full to me, full of long lost silent green Indian things. His lips, his opening hands, his silence, and his leathered skin – as a child I thought he had once lived in a forest, a forest where brooks ran after the rains and the deer turned and winked and leapt into the night, where the smoke of campfires twisted and curled towards the stars.

The smoke of our amber-lit room drifted to the open window and out into the night. My mother, by the window, watched; she rarely spoke but smiled and listened. My brothers and I drank the cold glasses of milk she gave us on special days. She, Aunt Rachel, and my father drank fizzing glasses of golden beer; Grandfather only smoked his pipe.

Aunt Rachel took up her drink and inclined her head to one side. Her voice, gravelly with cigarettes, was still clear; after each sentence she laughed vibrantly. She quickened our thoughts and even lifted our bodies; now the discussion tumbled on in a lively animated manner. I trembled and played with my toes – oh! I had something to say! My brothers and I learned from our elders our ways of speaking; one of my brothers rarely spoke at all, like my mother, and when he did he used his hands as Grandfather did. My other brother spoke clearly as did Aunt Rachel, laughing quietly like my father.

And I, as young as I was, still had learned my manner of discussion.

I played with my toes and smiled; the grown-ups knew then

that I was to speak and they listened as a small quiet gathering. I spoke as Grandfather did, pausing often to watch the white smoke drift. I spoke as my father did, smiling and laughing softly after each sentence. I smiled as my mother did. And I trembled to think I was entering into the secret lost silent forest where life was green and mysterious and full of the joy of the brooks and the rain and the winking deer in the curling twisting sky-bound smoke.

242.
Jan. 29, 1975
my brother Tim's birthday –
Dear Dr. Pullias,

I'm not going to get my hopes up; I'll check over and over once more BUT my education counselor once again says I may start the Teacher Ed. program beginning fall '75 and I'll have a partial credential come summer of '76. What I need, according to her, is one more art, one more science, and Literature 102 (which I can take the test for credit) and she says I can take all that next quarter. In this way I will have a "Multi—subject Major" of Art / English (Creat./Writ.) /Psychology. Sounds reasonable but I'll check.

No, there's nothing that I know of that I'm worrying about, especially, unless it is the increasingly strange dreams I have been having these nights. They are not disturbing in a gory deathish way but in just a weird way. They are just weird and involved and icky. I wish I could go back to my good Alice dreams. I don't know why I am having such strange dreams – what could be occupying me deep inside?

I went home over the past weekend and felt the spring coming. We have violets throughout the front yard, even growing in the lawn, they smell sweet; I think a violet is my favorite flower. I felt something strange and safe and good lying on the front lawn. When I came back to San Diego I wrote it down and am sending you this copy. The writing is suddenly a bit frightening but the feeling that evoked it was good.

I really really like my Creative Writing teacher, Dr. Eulert. He's a fine fellow. He has an air of homeyness and comfortableness that I've not seen before in my highly educated college professors. He is very educated and speaks excellently, yet he is easy-natured and homey. He takes great care in assuring people, students, that it is OK to say anything – whatever we say is good and growing. I admire him as a teacher.

Read any good books lately?
Yours,
Debbie!

243.
February 9, 1975
Dear Dr. Pullias,

It is a rainy day today. The window next to where I am typing looks out on an acacia blossoming yellow.

For the past half week my weird dreams have gone and in their place have been having very pleasant dreams about wilderness places. Last night I dreamt I was riding a horse at a lope, across a large expanse of wet green meadow towards some hills. All throughout the field wild horses were grazing and deer, too. A friend was riding a horse with me and we were the last people on earth. I loved the dream of just loping along for such a long time.

I am very sorry you are rather tired and discouraged at present; I did not think your letters were especially flat. But I know that feeling and I am sorry if my own letters have not been up to par (you know what I mean) but I am fairly sure I know the reason. It has happened before. See, last quarter, for instance, writing letters was important and that's how I got my urge for writing out. But this quarter I have the creative writing class and really that is all I want to concentrate on when I write. And I write so much for it that my vim and vigor for writing is lacking in my letters. Now I will mainly be writing letters just to give information, and I know these kinds of letters are not especially interesting. Maybe that is why I was sending you the creative writings along with my letters. So you see my letters probably haven't been quite like me because of the writing of them not because of some worry I have. At least that is what I would expect the reason to be.

Yesterday Jenn and Lisa and I went to Hemet to visit. We saw the new baby horse and new bunnies. We visited my mother and my father, too; we went for a hike in the hills and picnicked. My mother has a new cat and I like that. I really enjoy having a cat around. This cat is frosty grey with a white bib and she's going to have kittens!

A week or so ago I talked with Mamma on the phone and she

said she had decided to not drink anymore and to not even have any drinks in the house. If guests wanted a drink they could bring their own. I'm glad.

I guess I don't really think life is a lot of pressure marked here and there by good points that must be earned; I suppose, rather I consider life a pleasant joyful experience marked, sometimes frequently, by worries that can be overcome. And in the long run I think an individual life for an individual person is the way the individual looks at it. I guess I don't see any basic rules that go with all lives. My life is how I make it. People certainly can help me or rather give me ideas about a good life but I am the one that must make my life work. And I don't think there are any outside pressures that can hinder me if I don't let them. I think there might be a magic formula called Lovetruth that if I learn as well as I can my life will be especially good and joyful. What do you think of that?

Lately I have been daydreaming about a little house with a garden and cats and a very well trained dog and a horse. And I would hardly need any money at all so that I could work somewhere with children and not worry about money and I'd go to work in the morning and have a satisfying good job and then I'd come home and ride or garden or visit or something. Ah.. Daydreams…

Do you like to daydream?

Love to you, Debbie.

244.
February 18, 1975
Dear Doctor Pullias,

Today I am 21. Interesting. Over the weekend I was in Hemet and went into the hills to hike. I didn't go up to your cabin but wandered around in the canyons. It was a sunny day and once I lay down by a rock and listened to the birds and breathed in that desert weed smell that I love. Lying there somehow made me feel wild, as if I lived as the rabbits do. I certainly can feel the different 'auras' that different places give off. In the mountains at Camp Wase., with the huge cedars and other trees the feeling when I'm alone is that the place is watching, in a high godly way, out for me — the place likes me and gathers me in, but I am small. In the eucalyptus forest here, in among the thin trees and bracken that feeling is that the place is helping me think, the place is more like me, not so godly. The hills of Hemet, with their rock wrens and passing buzzing flies, rock and sun, and weed smells, gather me in almost completely, when I am sitting or lying still, the friendly sun tanness makes me into a rabbit or another rock or a sunning lizard. I think, even though I so love the green wildness of the forests, that really I have more in common with a sunny desert hill.

Tonight Jenn and Lisa and two others are taking me out to eat. I hope it is not a dressy affair since I am not fond of dressing up (and so don't have dress-up clothes). I prefer my comfortable suede shoes, my corduroy pants, and a warm sweater, and so I believe that's what I'll wear and hope I'll not be uncomfortable if the others are real snazzy. Oh, dear, why must we worry about clothes!

Later — it was a fun evening, lots of laughter. Just thinking about the laughter— you know, it is very very hard or it takes great skill to write of a conversation that is ordinary and yet funny enough to make you laugh with delight. One of the problems is I don't remember what was said, just that I laughed. Interesting.

I got this neat packet of cards with birds on them, and since you like birds I thought I could use them to write to you.

Right now I'm pretty sleepy.

I'll try the books you mentioned.

Love,

Debbie

Mary Deborah Alice Bumstead — adult - 21.

245.

February 26, 1975

Dear Dr. Pullias,

I am reading a pretty interesting book about Pawnee Indians called The Lost Universe. The thing I like about it is that it tells of their daily life (very detailed, too). Also I like learning about outdoorish kinds of ways of living.

Next week comes time to pick classes for Spring quarter. At the end of that quarter I'll have finished B.A. requirements (except for number of units) but I have a feeling I won't have gotten all the Teach. Prog. requirements so that I couldn't enter it next year. I wonder, in that case, what I will be doing next year? Just taking classes that sound

Debbie Bumstead

interesting, I guess. There are a few Human Behavior classes that interest me as well as extended study in Creative Writing and Drawing. I hope there will be enough interesting classes to last a year!

I had an interesting thought come in a dream the other night. It came about because Mr. Fortbrook, my art teacher said this week he was going to give us each an assignment to work on, individual assignments. My thought was of a classroom with children and me, as a teacher, giving each child something fun and interesting to do, and then later as a group we would share our experiences. My creative writing professor, Dr. Eulert did this once, assigning each of us to go out and see a different place in San Diego (he gave us the places), write about it, and share it in class. I really liked that project. Because it seemed the teacher was giving each of us something special because it was interesting! That's an interesting thought...

Late this afternoon I took a walk up the block, and I saw what seemed to me an odd sight — a meadowlark standing on the peak of a house roof giving his territory call. I thought meadowlarks were shy and hid in field grasses and that if you saw one sitting on a fence post flashing his yellow breast you would have a lucky day. Here, I guess the meadowlarks are not quite so wild —so not quite as lucky.

I'm watching Cyrano de Bergerac on TV.

Oh these past two days have been irritating. What does an artist writer do when the Muse leaves her for a few days, when she wants him so much? Hopefully the Muse may return tomorrow or the next day. The trouble is the more you worry about it the longer it will stay away until one day the Muse must just burst out. But I don't want to wait.

I want to be away in a dreamland. In a vast greeny-moist and flat meadowland. The silky grasses are pale green and yellow; the sun is shining, not hot nor specially cold - in all in the world the silken grasses and pale sky, the warm sun, and hooray, the plaintive call of the curlew! I don't know what the curlew sounds like but it is probably suited to my dreamland tonight. If not, I will have the meadowlark, wild ones, singing back and forth into the distance.

And now I must be off to sleep to dream land..

Here is a song I learned at camp and sing often:

Dreamland opens here, sweep the dreampath clear
Listen, child, now listen well
To what the tortoise may have to tell

Dear Dr. Pullias

To what the tortoise may have to tell
  Dreamland opens here, sweep the dreampath clear
Listen child, dear little child
To the song of the crocodile
To the song of the crocodile
  Dreamland opens here, sweep the dreampath clear
Listen child, now close your eyes
In the canebreak the wild cat cries
In the canebreak the wild cat cries
    It is such a lovely song.
    Good-night.
    Debbie.

246.
3-10-75
Dear Dr. Pullias,

I knew your birthday was in March and this is the bird card I wanted you to have for it. I think you told me that you especially liked owls. The other weekend when I went hiking I saw an owl flying to his tree. Both being predator birds, you'd think owls and hawks would seem to fly the same. They do each have those long coasting flights but the owls have a soft quiet flight, the hawks a <u>sharp</u> quiet flight. I like them both.

Hey! Guess what! I'm going to have a poem published! My professor entered me in the <u>Who's Who in Poetry in Amer. Univ. & Colleges.</u> for 1974-75. They will publish my poem, "I feel Birds." In case I didn't send that to you yet here enclosed is a copy. Also I'm sending you a poem, "On a Man...", that I wrote just recently (when the Muse came back full flush!) and that Dr. Eulert feels is probably my best work so far. He says of my work this quarter that I have "turned a magic corner."

This quarter <u>has</u> been different from any other. Sometimes I wonder, having read Piaget's theory of learning in children, if I, even as an adult, cannot grasp certain concepts until I have reached a certain age no matter how much someone pushes me toward them and that when the time comes the concept comes no matter what. But then I wonder if it could be the effect of this new living situation which gives me so much time to feel freely and the books on Indians and Indian songs and the poetry books I've read recently that worked an effect on me.

I don't know the reason why but I have been different this quarter. I've never been so... what? Serious, concentrated, inspired... Involved. I've never been so seriously involved with what I am doing (in this case, primarily creative writing). I feel all at once that I am learning, teaching (myself) and working. I've never been so totally deeply involved with my work, my learning. The involvement has been so total that I have lost (temporarily, I hope) the wish to play with children (Of course I'm still interested in them) and that disturbed me a little. In fact I've been so involved that, other than responding in classes, I've been alone (in my thoughts) all quarter. I've not initiated any friendship contacts — other than through letters and even those, I guess, have suffered.

It is indeed very strange. I don't know what started it or what keeps it going. I sort of enjoy it — I like the creations that come of this involvement and I like this new feeling of seriousness. It is almost a joyful seriousness, if there can be such a thing!

But it does not block out other things that I feel are important — I just don't have time and room in my mind for all the important things if I am this involved.

This is very new to me, I don't know what it might develop into, where it might go, this involvement. What do you think of it?

You know what I think? I think you and your family ought to move into a two-story old house with tall trees around, in Hemet. I think you ought to learn to be lazy and quiet (in Hemet how could you not learn that?), write, maybe teach some classes at the J.C. or whatever. I think that because that is what I would like to do (exchange Elem. with J.C.)!

Have a good birthday!
Your friend,
Debbie
I love you.

247.
Hemet
3-26-75

Dear Dr. Pullias

Dear Dr. Pullias,

It is very windy here and cold. I have been doing nothing for several days and neither enjoying not disenjoying it. Already it is practically time to go back for a new quarter. My classes will be — Creative Writing 4, Literature & Culture, and Watercolor. I'm going to take about 3 tests in Lit, Science, and Amer. Hist. If I happen to pass them I'll probably be able to go into the Teach. Program next year.

I still can't decide what to do this summer. I want to go visit Washington because Joe invited us but I wouldn't mind working at Camp Wasewagan again either. What to do, what to do… Perhaps I can do both.

Everytime I drive home from San Diego just off the highway on Winchester Road I see a sign by a dirt road that says "Montessori Education Center ages Pre-school - 7" I keep wanting to go there or call. It sounds interesting. I imagine living in a house in Hemet and driving there to work in the mornings. It's something else I've wanted to do one summer — look into that.

Today I found some tapes that long ago my friend Anne and I made. It was fun to listen to our laughter and voices — it makes me want to get together with her again. Maybe I'll write her a letter. I made another tape myself today playing my recorder (I can't play songs but I do play some pretty random note music!), reading poems, telling stories, and even singing! I am always surprised to hear my voice on the tape machine; I sound like a little kid! It's fun. A tape machine is always fun.

Did I tell you I have a new cat friend? Her name is Spooks. She's gray with white touches. When I go outside she plays with me, following and running ahead and meowing.

Oh! I am learning to dance like an Indian!

Your friend, Debbie.

248.
San Diego
4-13-75
Dear Dr. Pullias,

I've decided to just let the summer come as it will. If a friend wants to go with me to Washington in June I will and be back for

Camp. If not I'll decide whether or not I want to go to Camp or up to Washington with Tim later in the summer. I don't expect any "unpleasant situation" in Washington. To tell you the truth I sort of resent your suggesting it. Of course you are my friend and I'm not angry with you or anything but as a matter of interest I've been thinking about whether any person has the right to discourage another's plans even when the plan may not be beneficial. I don't know. I think there can be discussions, even opinions stated and suggestions given if they are asked for? But not discouragement — that is wrong, I think. It sort of says, "My way of what you should do is better than your way, period!" It may be, but its not the way to go about showing or teaching it! I don't know... what do you think?

I've been thinking about what I'll do after next school year. Daydreams... I suppose college, besides giving me time to grow more, has been valuable in showing me the process of learning — get the basics, go into an interest, follow the interest as deeply as you want. Its just been a strengthening of that process really, since I had that even when I was a little kid. I'm pretty sure I'll keep at it — learning about my interests — as long as I live. I hope. Besides that I guess I'm learning, at college, about relationships of people, how to be independent, etc. I think I've found that finding out things from classes which is supposed to be the reason I came to college is really not as important as the other things. Some classes stand out and are important but not the majority. It's like all my years at school — the teachers are the important thing in a class.

Your friend,
Debbie.

249.
5-2-75
Dear Dr. Pullias,

I have had a day of sitting out in the sun taking notes from books for a report entitled, "Culture as Mirrored by Fantasy Books for Children." Interesting! It is for my Lit. & Culture class. This is the first academic class I've taken that doesn't resort to tests. The teacher gives us books to read which we discuss in class; we each are to do two

Dear Dr. Pullias

special interest (our own interest) reports, keep a scrapbook of culture (which may be anything), and write a couple of short essays on this or that. The class is very well organized, vital, and interesting. And you can actually sense the atmosphere of "we aren't going to have any tests!" It's an atmosphere of relaxation, and, I think, heightened interest in learning.

This week we are reading <u>Slouching Towards Bethlehem</u> by Joan Didion. I like it, not just for her stories, but for the fine accurate sense she gives of Southern California. She exactly captures the mood (at least as I feel it) of California living.

Which leads, in a way, to my new decision for the summer (a decision for every letter, right?!). This is really going to be my last summer as a college student and I wouldn't want it to be worrisome. I applied at Camp for kitchen girl again but was assigned as Tent Counselor. I suppose I am over-qualified for the lowly job. But I see counseling, even if experience and learning, as a thing of great worry and much complicated thought, though I'd appreciate it in the end. But that is not what summer is for. Summer is only for that which comes easily and naturally even if it is static compared to what could be happening. Do you see that? Summer <u>has</u> to be summer or I won't accept it at all. So I <u>think</u> (things could change again!) I'll not go to Camp. I think I'll stay in Hemet. A Hemet summer is nothing to complain about — I love Hemet in that hot dry heat! I can work, volunteer at a summer school, read, write etc. and be happy. When Mamma goes up to Reno perhaps I will go with her or to Wash. with either Tim or Mamma to spend a couple weeks. Still, I'm not sure, I'll have to continue thinking about it.

My mother came to stay the weekend here last Saturday. We went to La Jolla and looked in the shops, ate lunch, and had a pleasant time. The only times we wouldn't would be when I was extremely irritated at her drinking. She seems to have stopped all that though and to me seems quite the better for it.

Oh, could you tell your wife that if her friend can wait till summer I'd be happy to play around with illustrations. Right now I am already illustrating two consignments (what a popular artist I'm becoming!) — one of horses for my mother and another of "Alice" for my creative writing teacher, plus working in my watercolor class.

I seem to be very well occupied this quarter but not enjoying it. Say, only two bird cards after this one — I'll save the one I like most for last.

Your friend, Debbie

250.

5-19-75

Dear Dr. Pullias,

I went to the Teach. Program place the other day and found they had my name on their list to start Fall. I don't think I belong there, but maybe they won't double check. A lot of the good staff there, including my advisor, are quitting this week; I don't know why.

Do you have any brothers and sisters? Sometimes I go through a stage of dreaming with my brothers in the dreams. Last night I dreamt Tim and I were outside with his parakeet in her cage. Somehow the bird got out. The minute it flew out the door it become a beautiful brilliant blue and I felt a wonderful sense of freedom. But I said, "She will be dead in a few hours because she's not used to flying." It always seems strange to dream about my brothers as if they were people like every other. They aren't. I feel incredibly close to them both, not because they are good people, though they are, I think, but because we have experienced the same upbringing, we have the same parents, we even attended the same schools. There is no one else that I can be so very close to, in that way. It is not an exciting closeness but certainly the most comfortable I've experienced so far.

The other weekend Tim cornered me and gave me a lesson in religion and politics. I found it interesting. It reminded me of the times I'd listen to Debbie talk about her religion. Religion is an interesting thing.

That same weekend I talked alone and a long time with Grandpa. Really it was the first time we had talked about ourselves to each other. It was like the we were just meeting. We had to ask funny meeting questions like, "Do you like to read?" He told about when you two were pals. It was a strange encounter — It seemed I was just now meeting my own Grandpa, whom I have always admired from afar. I think we could be good friends if we got started again like that conversation.

My mother started drinking again. I told her it hurt my feelings and I got mad and didn't speak to her.

Dear Dr. Pullias

I don't know how she can stop. I just wish she wouldn't when I'm around. I don't know why it makes me so "uptight."

Oh well.

Your friend,

Debbie.

P.S. Oh! We have the most lovely brand new baby horse in the world. He is light gray with white splashes on his rear — a beautiful Appaloosa! Appaloosa! Appaloosa!

You know.

I like Tim Weisburg's beautiful flute music.

251.

Hemet

6-22-75

Dear Dr. Pullias,

This is the last of the bird cards and my favorite. I guess because of the color, silver-blue. And once, in Washington a long time ago, I saw a heron. It wasn't blue but I remember the long neck and long legs. I think the heron is a strange magical bird to see in the wild.

This is a magical letter not only because of the heron and because while I am writing I am wearing a turquoise ring talisman (silver & blue) but also because while I was reading your letter outside under the Chinese elm a magical event occurred. On the paper of your letter was a design of leaf shadows and one of the shadows fluttered about like a butterfly. I looked and there was no butterfly. I continued reading and saw the butterfly shadow again — looked up, nothing. The third time I studied the leaves, perhaps it was a green butterfly, I thought. But I didn't see anything. Finally I finished your letter, stood up, and walked into full sun. A Black Beauty butterfly fluttered from me and away; it was as though he had been sitting on my head. But I thought the butterfly had been inside my head casting a shadow from the light of my eyes onto your letter and when I stood up it flew out of my forehead. That was magic! (And it might make a good poem besides!)

I wish to thank you very much for your book. It is exciting to hold a book like that that someone you know wrote — Interesting. I will begin reading it soon.

Speaking of books, I will begin typing my Alice book this

week.

Sometimes I think it is strange and wonderful, the way my life is going. Life is surely a magical business!

Last night and early this morning I reread some of the stories in The Inland Whale. I certainly enjoy them. It makes me want to write my own magical legends or read more. Do you know of any that are written as clearly, simply, as these?

Did I tell you I have a horse to ride this summer? His name is Buster and he is a tall cheerful chestnut-colored fellow. Unlike lazy Prieta he likes to get out of the corral and go for a little jaunt. He's a good horse. He belongs to Miss Kerr. She has another horse (a flighty one I wouldn't want to ride.) So sometimes we can go riding together. But I can ride Buster alone, too.

I've been thinking maybe it was you who wrote that magical fluttering shadow into your letter to tease me and you made it so that when I stood up the shadow would turn into a butterfly and fly away like magic!

Yes!

It was good to see you.

Butterflies, Debbie.

252.
July 14, 1975
Dear Dr Pullias,

What a week I am having! Last Tuesday I had my interview at the college for the Teach.Program I will be entered in September. I think it will be an interesting year.

Then Saturday James and I went on an Exploring Expedition through San Diego County. We explored the coastal towns and then the hills to the east. We went to Palomar Observatory. And we visited Dr. Eulert and camped there, staying up late talking around a fire. The visiting was rather strange, though, because everyone except me, had drunk and smoked and were sort of wrapped up, I guess, in their own private trips. That's okay with me, but not as fun as real visiting. I've decided the thing about drugs is this: marijuana makes things, objects, events, sounds, project their qualities in a surreal manner into a person and for that person, it is a passive experience, but true awareness is an active experience in which a person projects qualities into things, and the more truly aware the person teaches himself to be the more beautiful things can be. Marijuana may have some good use but I believe true awareness is a happier thing and can go farther, perhaps, than any drug.

Anyway it was, in all, a good weekend. Now, tomorrow, my father and I are heading up to Washington. That will be interesting, too. We're staying till the first week of August. I had better go to bed now, we are getting an early start. I'll write again, soon.

Your friend always,

Debbie.

253.

July 26, 1975

Saturday in Washington

Dear Dr. Pullias,

I'm sitting on a ragged green lawn overlooking a flat of mud — the tide is out — with dots of white birds hunting and hills forested. It is warm breezy day. I had a dream about you last night. I was driving the pick-up through a hilly residential place. The houses sat on banks above the road. I looked up at them: they were all old and wooden. I parked the car and got out. I thought, "This house can't be his because his is a two story." So I walked down the block to your house. I was let into your living room. My brother Joe was already there and you were talking to him. You didn't greet me though I sat down and smiled. I realized you were beginning to like Joe and I was glad because before you hadn't known what an interesting person he was. I got up and went outside into your backyard. It wasn't very large. I saw roses and a yellow dollhouse that I thought the cats might sleep in. Behind a chain fence was your study. I saw it out of the side of my eye but didn't look straight at it or in it because I thought you would want to show me that. I went inside again and we sat down to have supper. Mrs. Pullias talked about birds, she could make whistling noises like them. I stood up from the table and you stood up and looked at me and said, "I'm so glad you're here. I was so pleased that I could not speak to you before." I was interested that I could affect you that way. I said, "That's OK. I was too shy to talk anyway." Then the dream finished in a murky kind of way with me walking back to the car to bring it down to your place and the street being blocked by children.

Debbie Bumstead

I'm having a pleasant vacation here. It is all green. Sometimes the bay is so still I wish I had a little rowboat to go around in, paddles dipping in blue water. It is strange to be here after 14 years of thinking that this state is the best place ever. With all those years of dreaminess the state seems magical and it seems magical to be here. Sometimes in half-sleep after a nap or in the morning I feel a great leaping inside, "I am here!"

Still the place and people are all too new to me. I can't seem to write much about it all. I just want to bring it all in.

Your friend, Debbie.

254.
Hemet
August 11, 1975
Dear Dr. Pullias,

I read three good children's books by a Swedish author, Maria Gripe. They are <u>Josephine,</u> <u>Hugo & Josephine,</u> and <u>Hugo.</u> I liked the first one best, but the second and third were interesting because Hugo is like my friend James, and J. and I have a relationship similar to Josephine & Hugo's. They are good books even aside that interesting feature.

These days I am typing up some writings. I typed Alice, now I'll do the short stories and essays that I think are as finished as they can be. Then I will have typed up all the things that are ready for sending out. It will be good to have all that neatly typed and in notebooks — I figure I'll type one copy on good paper for sending out, give a copy of everything to Miss Kerr for her to keep, and then have one copy for myself to give to those around who want to read them.

Oh, these summer days. I wander around the yard, water plants, play with the cat. I sleep late and daydream. I just wander through the days. I heard coyotes one night in the groves yip-howling in their high wild voices. How long does the summer timelessness go on? It is August - -

A sudden thought — I've been writing so much, that when I put pen to writing and stumble onto a thought that evokes a mood I can almost automatically follow the mood out with words. My feeling doesn't come to me sometime and later I write it down, instead the feeling comes out in words. The feeling knows how to come out in words, I have been writing that much! Do you think I could go so far as to live on paper? My life all coming on paper.

I have been sleepy lately, adjusting to the altitude or tired after vacationing, or just summer-sleeping disease.

Read any good books recently?

Yours, Debbie.

P.S. This is rather a sleepy letter — oh well.

255.

San Diego

Dear Dr. Pullias,

A couple of weeks ago I started writing a story and I couldn't even stop to write in my journal. That's my excuse and I don't really believe in excuses but... I suppose out of politeness I give them. Which is not to say I didn't want to write you. I suppose if I were to be truthful I'd say I could have written but do to circumstances I felt disinclined to write letters. And I go through all that not to excuse myself but to be honest. Being honest doesn't need to take that much time, if I could dispense with all the excuses and reasons beforehand. But the reason I'm not truthful at first is because I don't want to be mean.

What do you think of that mess? Sometimes, to some extent, I enjoy thinking that kind of thing out, but I've a feeling I do it too much. The feeling I get after reasoning everything out and putting it to order, is a feeling of tiredness. After writing that paragraph I feel tired of life. Life is so big and it hurts to put it in little words. Especially the rules and abstracts of life — like honesty and working out problems. It may help, but it hurts. At least with the world we see or we feel well-chosen words can evoke a certain mood or impression of some thing or some event. So I begin to think I should write only of that which I see with my eyes or feel. And lately I have even been writing the feeling of an event or person in terms of seeing.

Then I see myself standing up; I am a person who sees out of her eyes and hears out of her ears. I am someone who feels and puts feelings into sights. And I can write the sights into words until my writing is all something you can see. No paragraphs that go in circles. What I see can not go in circles; I'll never see one thing again. Everything in life is new. I can't go around in circles like my first

313

paragraph.

So now that I've gotten past opening my letter I'll you the news —

First, a magazine called "Rocky Mountain Review" is planning to publish two of my poems in its next issue. Exciting!

Second, I'm back to school. I haven't received my student-teaching assignment yet but I know the general format of the year. I'll be working in a class every morning. Three afternoons a week we student-teachers will meet to discuss and learn from our professors. So far it looks like a very good exciting year ahead.

And I'm sleepy. Good-night.

Your friend, Debbie.

256.

Dear Dr. Pullias,

My grandmother Marlow said she was giving me money for my graduation to send my friend James and me to England. It would be interesting to visit the land of <u>The Wind in the Willows</u>, <u>Peter Pan</u>, and <u>Winnie the Pooh</u>. Those books give the country of England a pleasant flavor-thought. Other countries I like the thought of are Spain (for its paintings by Goya and El Greco and for Don Quixote), Australia, the animal parts of Africa, and Russia (for its boiled-up history and <u>Dr. Zhivago</u>).

I would like to go to England, too, to study a little in their primary schools. If I wanted a place to go that I could study my interests at other than England, I'd be interested in learning about American Indians.

My student-teaching is not exactly what I had hoped for. The teacher, Mrs. Murdoch and I are so different from each other that we don't understand each other too well. She gives me the impression that she thinks I am lazy and careless. I try to speak to her honestly but she often misunderstands my meaning. Still I will try to keep myself open and friendly. I decided that since her way of teaching doesn't work with my ideas, I'll just play like I'm at a job. I'll learn to <u>work</u> with children not teach them.

But I think I will really like my college professor, Dr. Baker. We meet with him three days a week. We have to keep a journal of our classroom experiences so he knows of my writing and my feelings already.

Thursday was an interesting day because the teacher left me in charge of the whole class (36) for a ½ hour. I read a story but afterwards when I had them line up for lunch they were very rowdy and noisy. I didn't know what to do.

I guess I'm to have that experience every Thursday. This Thursday I'll tell the children that if they don't take the responsibility for their own behavior they'll have to wait until they can. In other words, though, I guess I'll have them go back to their seats if they're especially rowdy and do it all over again. I don't want to force them to be good; I'd like for them to take it upon themselves to be polite.

So Thursday I'll have that half-hour. Then three other days I'll teach a P.E. lesson. I think it will be good for me to learn to work with children in these active situations. Right now it is somewhat frightening.

Did you go through a teacher-training like that?

Yours, Debbie.

257.
Oct. 26, 1975
Dear Dr. Pullias,

I feel pretty bad about not writing to you as much as I have. The thing is, I am tired of working at being friends. I've given up totally on Debbie Sjoberg. I no longer even care about getting letters from Miss Kerr. I seem to not care about having friends anymore. Maybe I am just tired of the strain it takes to stay friends by letter and infrequent visit. I want friends around me, seeing me every day or week. I seem to be giving up on my letter friends.

I have had a strange week. The Teaching Program is not working out for me. I may have to drop out of it after this quarter and just finish my B.A. with regular classes. I think I could be a good teacher if I could resolve the conflict between my personal nature and having to lead and control children. Well, to be a teacher I'd have to resolve on the side of control. But it is practically lethal to go against personal nature. No matter how well and democratic my control is over children I feel ugly and unnatural.

I want to join in with children's games and conversations; I do not want to hold myself separate so that they will remain respectful of my position. I do not want to lead them formally in "Sharing" or "P.E." or "Reading." I don't want to be the one to say, "Let's all be quiet," or

315

"Settle Down."

So that's it. I feel a little unsure of what I will do with myself but I guess teaching formally will not be it. Remember how every time you asked me, when I was little, if I would become a teacher, I always said, passionately, "No!"? I don't remember my reason, but perhaps it was something like the one I've given here.

Yours, Debbie.

P.S. I'm sorry I sound so gloomy in this letter!

258.
Hemet
December 15, 1975
Dear Dr. Pullias,

Winter is here in Hemet, I think. The trees around the yard are bare; the days are clear and cold. At night the wind machines in the groves whir and purr until morning. The machines are loud, almost as if they were right under my window, but it is a steady comforting purr. Last night I thought my mother in her bed and I in mine were little kittens snuggling against a huge mama-cat who purred to us all night.

I have been having a pretty good vacation; this house and land is a good place to think and read and dream. Some days James and I wander around town together. And I've talked with my father a couple of times.

Things are a little strained between my mother and me. Her drinking disturbs me but she doesn't think it is that bad. I guess she can't see the difference in her actions and speech that I do. I told her how I feel but to no avail...

Next quarter my classes will be two literature and one poetry. I'll have a lot of reading and some writing. The next quarter I'll have to take a science class and two electives. Then in June I'll graduate.

I've sort of decided against going to England. It is so far away. Maybe a trip to Canada, it would be just as fun to explore. The only place I could really get excited about is Washington! But some other states intrigue me like New Mexico.

Well, dear friend, I hope you have a pleasant holiday season.

Merry Christmas, Debbie.

Dear Dr. Pullias

1976

I must always be sure I'm doing what I want. I don't want to drift away from myself. Debbie

I guess you haven't heard from me in a long time. I have even been back in Hemet for a month or so, yet if you thought of me I was still in Washington. I came back. I was wrecking my dream state with the practical problems of everyday. Here I have the same problems but the scenery can take it. Debbie

Debbie Bumstead

Dear Dr. Pullias

259.
January 26, 1976
Dear Dr. Pullias,

This afternoon I'm watching cartoons. I rather enjoy the old ones.

I have a little disagreement with the way my literature classes are run. I've never enjoyed interpreting writing. I would just take them as they appear to be. Wouldn't you say Art is the appearance of itself? Or does art always have to represent some principle; does it always have to mean something else that its surface appearance? Anyway my head just doesn't work that way. It refuses to. Even though I might try to learn to interpret my head doesn't work. It seems to work in a different way. Still the readings are enjoyable.

But I'm not concentrating as seriously as I have in previous classes before this quarter. I play around with thoughts and I don't worry about quizzes. It's all probably because I'm a senior...

I was talking with my mother about the graduation ceremony. She said she knew how much I'd gone through, etc., work put in and that sort of thing and she wouldn't need to watch a public ceremony to prove it. I don't really mind one way or the other whether I go through the ceremony, but if no one was particular about seeing it I wouldn't. What are your feelings on this? I sort of feel like there should be some sort of ceremony — but it could be me alone going on a magic picnic with magic food in some magic alone place to celebrate my accomplishment. Or it could be a special dinner or something. That would be, I think, as much as any cap & gown thing, maybe more. But I don't mind any way.

I hope you are all well, your picnic in the hills sounded good.
Love,
Debbie.

260.

Debbie Bumstead

March 1976
Dear Dr. Pullias,

Hey, you! I'm not <u>21</u>, I'm <u>22</u>! I'm older than you thought.

I just received news that the magazine which published my two poems has accepted two more poems for its next issue. That is exciting! Now I will be published three times and I can call myself a Published Poet. Maybe it is something like the saying, "When you have fallen off a horse three times you are a horseman." I've fallen off a horse five times — three times off Prieta.

This is what I'm thinking about for the summer and next year. I want to go visit my grandparents in Reno. Actually I guess I want to visit Reno itself. Perhaps I'll stay there a couple of weeks. I should say we, because James is coming along on these summer excursions. He has said he would like to and I want him to come. After Reno I guess we'll go to Washington to visit Joe. Joe is living in a 17 acre forest near a small town. He's working in a foundry there.

I want to see if I want to live in Washington. First I will see this summer; I'll look around and feel myself there. Then if my inside says, yes, then I will try a year there. And that year I will see, I'll feel if I want to be there.

There are many kinds of jobs I can look for — I think of nursery schools or Teach. Aid or anything, working in a cafeteria, I don't care. What is important to me, my main lifestyle goal, is to always be creating. Writing, painting, thinking. I'm glad that that is my goal because it doesn't depend on anyone else, on getting a particular job, on having enough money. But I must always be sure I'm doing what I want. I don't want to drift away from myself.

This quarter in my 19th cent. Literature I've read "Self-Reliance" by Emerson and some things by Thoreau. That's sort of the way I think of leading my life. Deliberately and honestly. But I also want to lead it with a sense of lightness. I do not believe that I have to stand for heavy or ugly situations. Not one will teach me anything about another. I don't learn from pain; I just suffer. So I will allow myself to leave if the going is ugly. The only pain I know that I stay around anyway is the pain a person you like or love gives you. That is the most painful pain but I never can run away. Not until the pain has finally caused me to dislike the person and that makes me even sadder.

I think it would be interesting to get all those letters back and read them...

Dear Dr. Pullias

I am so dispassionate about that graduation ceremony that I may either decide to attend just for fun or not to because it's too much bother when I want to be thinking about the summer.

Last week I got in that summing up mood that comes as something ends and I wrote many of my thoughts about college in my journal. My teacher has that right now but when I get it back I'll copy some of it down for you. I probably won't get in the mood again till the end of the next quarter.

It's been a good day today. Thank you.

Your friend, Debbie.

261.
May 16, 1976
Dear Dr. Pullias,

Hi there. Did I tell you that I had dropped my science class? I did so quite early in the quarter and the reason was that it was too easy and boring and when I asked to work by myself the teachers got me all riled by commenting on my need for interaction, etc. So like the person I am I dropped the one last general requirement which I need for a degree. I then took the science CLEP test, the score of which I will probably receive this week. If I pass that I will get the B.A. If I do not, so be it. Because of this mix-up at the beginning of the quarter I got upset with staying around. So I spoke briefly with my teacher, Dr. Eulert, with whom I have my other two classes, and came to Hemet. I am attempting then to do these classes independently though I did not get specific permission from him to do so. My writing class is already independent so I know I will pass that. As for the other literature class, I don't know. But I did take two other CLEP tests, one of which I am sure I passed, so I think I will have enough units for the B.A. It all really hangs on the science test score. And that is my life story.

My brother Tim is getting married this month. The girl already has a baby so I will be an aunt.

Ah, life — Debbie

262.

Debbie Bumstead

Dear Dr. Pullias,

Today I got a note from the college saying I was graduating with high honors. Now I get to put some Latin words behind my name as well as my degree initials! I don't know if it's Cum Laude or Magna Cum Laude. Either way is kind of fun. I was surprised, pleasantly.

My mother and I are leaving Tuesday (June 15) for Vallejo to watch her horse race. Then Thursday I'm taking the train to Reno. I'll be there about two weeks, then my father and I are going to Washington. I'm ready to go!

Suddenly I feel like writing and writing things that I am feeling these days, dreams that are whirling in my head. But I am too overwhelmed right at this moment to settle into writing. I will have to wait and write in my journal. My journal has a calming sorting-out simplifying effect on me. I get overly excited in letters so that if I'm already full it's hard to write. Even though, I so want you to know. Oh, dear.

Yes, I see Miss Kerr fairly often and we write semi-regularly (like you and I these days, I guess). She is a good friend.

Now I have finished my Schoolway part of life and I have done well. First comes Summer and then what? The Beautyway, I hope.

I hope the summer will fill you with health.

Love,

Debbie.

263.

Debbie Bumstead.
5021 Jackman St.
Port Townsend, WA 98368

Dear Dr. Pullias,

There are five fir trees by the house. When the wind blows it is full of the ocean because the Straits of Juan de Fuca are only two blocks away. It is hard to get used to the seawater being north instead of west. The sun seems to set in the south.

I am renting this house and my father is living here, too. In exchange for part of the rent the landlord asked him to work on the place. It needs work. Today I painted the living room.

This house is three miles from downtown Port Townsend. On the way to town is an old graveyard with stone crosses and statues. In

Port Townsend there are three bookstores and a library. The town is very small, filled with Old Victorian houses and tourists. It is surrounded by forests and water. The roads are corridors through forests and they always seem to lead to water, mirror-still bays, beaches with huge pieces of driftwood, or harbors where the ferries that take cars over to Seattle blow their loud horns. It's beautiful! I think I will stay here a year.

Yesterday I went to see if the schools wanted a Teacher's Aid or something of that sort and they said they doubted it. Then I asked at the library and they said not right now.

The sun has gone down but it won't get dark for another two hours. It doesn't get completely dark till 10 o'clock. Out my window I can see seagulls and swallows making their way home. I suddenly feel lonely.

Your friend, Debbie.

264.
August 5, 1976
Dear Dr. Pullias,

A couple of nights ago I had a dream-thought that really got me excited and thinking. I dreamed that I would watch and listen to and play with children in school for part of the day and then I'd come home and write what I had seen and heard and thought very clearly and carefully. I wouldn't write about the school or particularly about a way of teaching — I'd write about the children in the school. And I dreamed that the first year I wrote about a kindergarten class, that I would visit every day from beginning to end of the year, and the next year I'd study a first grade, the next a second grade, and so on.

That is what I want to do! It would be a good job for me because 1. I like children 2. I'm good at seeing 3. I'm good at listening and 4. I'm good at writing things down.

The only problem is there isn't such a job. I made it up and I don't think schools pay you for a job you made up. I could do it this year, though, if I wanted, because I have enough money in the bank to live on. But I was just wondering about government grants for study. I've heard of them but I don't know anything else about them. Do you? What I like about Washington is you can't miss being involved with the nature of the place. In San Diego all the days are so warm and nice you almost forget to notice it's the earth you're standing on. Here you can't help but notice, the forests, the bays, and the animals. If somehow you get through not noticing them, you've got to notice the weather! And that's what I like about those hot Hemet summers. I am a little homesick for the summer. If I should decide to live here I think I'd spend my summers in Hemet.

Sometimes I feel like going home, but I want to stay, I need to stay. If I went home I'd live with my mother and here I'm living with my father. I want to live alone! Don't you think I ought to live alone for a year? I do.

Oh, well, perhaps I will presently.

I read a very good book called <u>Pilgrim at Tinker Creek</u> by Annie Dillard. It is excellent reading, in fact.

What are you up to this summer?

Your friend,

Debbie.

265.

Oct. 22, 1976

Dear Dr. Pullias,

I guess you haven't heard from me in a long time. I have even been back in Hemet for a month or so, yet if you thought of me I was still in Washington. I came back. I was wrecking my dream state with the practical problems of everyday. Here I have the same problems but the scenery can take it.

In the past month I have found that 1. it is hard to find an apartment or house, and 2. it is hard to find a job. I applied for four school related jobs and almost got one as an aid for a pre-school, but then they chose another. I applied for a greenhouse worker and wasn't chosen and etc. This week I put an ad in the paper saying I would tutor kids. I got two calls about it: both "tutees" 7th grade girls. One I will tutor three days a week (one hour a day) and the other two days a week. I will get five dollars an hour. Maybe if I kept the ad going awhile I might get a few more kids. It would be good, I think, if I could be self-employed like that. Tutoring is the kind of thing I'm not exceptionally interested in but I do well. And that's OK. That's really the way I like to make money: by doing something well without too much emotional involvement.

I also put an ad in the paper about getting a place to live. I got an interesting call from a woman who might want her house sat with for a year while she and the family go traveling. I would only pay utilities. I may consider that. I'm going to meet her next week.

I feel very good about getting those tutoring jobs. I was discouraged for a while.

I got the puppy I wanted, an Australian Cattle Dog. They are supposed to be the kind of dog that likes to be trained and the kind that makes a good watchdog. His name is Rex. He's a strawberry roan color.

Are you teaching new classes this year? I hope you feel better this year than last! (Funny how I count years from Sept. to June, instead of Jan. to Dec. [Summer lives by itself.].)

Your friend,
Debbie.

266.
November 11, 1976
Dear Dr. Pullias,

I think you read our minds! My mother and I were considering coming to visit you. My mother also suggested that you and Mrs. Pullias could come stay at our house for a day and spend the night if you wish. She wants to give you a special quilt made by her children at school. It is a gift in a appreciation of the care you show for us.

I have not yet moved into any place of my own. The house-sitting may not be for another six months or so. I do not know if I will want it then or not. The house is one of the new stucco gravel-lawn houses that look the same as all the other homes on the street. I don't like it much. The tenants in the back apartment of 324 N. Buena Vista are speaking of moving... James and I have been dreaming of building me a little house on my mother's property in the hills. It would be a guest house to the main house that Tim wants to build. It's just a dream right now...

As I write I am listening to a good record I checked out at the library. It is called "Golden Slumbers" and is a collection of traditional

Debbie Bumstead

lullabies sung by a variety of individuals. Sometimes I'd like very much to make music. I thought yesterday I might take singing lessons at the college next semester if they offer them. I think my voice is all right; it's just that I'm too scared to sing out, and sometimes if I do it comes out all wrong. Oh, dear. (But I can whistle!)

Yes, I read <u>Theophilus North</u> and found it good. I advertised a second time for tutoring but received no calls. So I still have only two girls in 7th grade. Virginia has problems in reading. We do her spelling homework and then we write stories. She is beginning to get excited and that pleases me. I love to hear the stories children make up! The spelling workbook is not touching her at all but the stories are getting her interested in reading and writing, I think. The last time her father said the teacher had noticed an improvement in Virginia. I liked that. Darlene has problems in math. We just do homework. Once I taught her a card game that helps with multiplying, but her dad came in and got mad. I felt crummy, but that's the way it goes sometimes.

My grandma called me and said a friend of hers was having sight problems and might like me to read her mail to her (just like T. North!). She lives in a rest home and said she knew several people who might like me to read to them. I don't know if I will be paid, but anyway it might be interesting to go there once or twice a week. The past year I have been looking at older people with great interest and respect — even if I don't know them. There is an old woman who goes to the library and she looks exactly as I picture myself old. It gives me a strange feeling to look at her, a <u>very</u> strange feeling. I will have to think about it…

One last bit of good news. A good literary agency has accepted me as a customer. The office is in Sun City, not far from here. I will drive over next week and find out how it all works. They charge a reading fee for the first work and then after it is sold, the rest are free. I have been writing a new story. It is really memories of my ninth grade year set to a slight plot. I suddenly wonder what my letters to you were like that year. Perhaps when you or we visit I may acquire your gift of all those letters. Oh dear again!

That is all for now —
Sincerely yours,
Debbie.

Dear Dr. Pullias

1977

Sometimes during the day, sometimes when I'm alone, sometimes when there are many people around, I'm frightened. Like everything is a dream. Like I don't just think, philosophically, that reality is a dream, but I see it is a dream. Everything wavering. Everything without meaning. I mean as if it were a dream and in a dream the dream can end any second so that everything has no future — or I don't know... Everything exists only just now. That's scary. I'm scared.
Debbie

I am confident you will be all right. There is genuine greatness in you, and you'll have your opportunity to express it.
Dr. Pullias

Debbie Bumstead

Dear Dr. Pullias

267.
January 11, 1977
Dear Dr. Pullias,

I think I need some counseling or some sort of help. Yesterday I was afraid of going crazy. I wondered if a person could go crazy from being afraid of going crazy. I was very frightened.

Today I have been depressed. I tried to find an explanation for my fear.

I have so much free time that I think too much. Thoughts go in circles till you know no thought is truly real and you feel like you're crazy. That can scare you.

Today I thought that perhaps too much freedom can be a problem. I am free to do anything. There are so many possibilities that I can't decide and when I try to go ahead with one, it just doesn't open up for me and I think this other will be just as good, oh, till I'm just lost.

What can I do? Where am I? Yow! School's out and I don't know what to do. There's too much to do. But none of it happens.

Today I have had the horrid feeling that nothing is worth anything. My mother and I kidded around with words and I felt like it was all useless, so useless.

I'm tired of planning out things to do and them not working out. I'm afraid to plan anything more because it won't work out anyway. So I don't have anything to do. So I think and get caught in the webs of thought and get scared. Getting scared really frightens me. I fear fear.

I feel like I want something to do which I can do for a long time. I feel like having a steady thing so that I won't have to keep dealing with all this freedom.

What can I do? I am very lonely and lost and scared and sick.

Bother, bother, bother.

What do you think? What's wrong? Why do I get afraid?

I think I will send this letter to you, but I don't want to trouble you. Something has to happen sometime.

Debbie Bumstead

Your friend, Debbie

January 13, 1977

Dear Dr. Pullias, I wrote that first page two days ago. I feel better today, though there is still a slight fear hanging inside me.

I got two very small jobs. One is 1 ½ hours a day as a noon supervisor at an elementary school. That will be regular and good and I hope I can learn to do it. Also on Saturdays I can work as a cashier at Alleen's Cards — my father's friend's little card shop. Also I am to be tutoring a little girl again.

But it scares me to plan things. There is a Women's Writers conference in February and I want to go, but I'm scared. I'm scared to plan it and register and everything.

What do you suppose is wrong?

Debbie.

January 16, 1977 - Sunday

Sometimes during the day, sometimes when I'm alone, sometimes when there are many people around, I'm frightened. Like everything is a dream. Like I don't just think, philosophically, that reality is a dream, but I <u>see</u> it <u>is</u> a dream. Everything wavering. Everything without meaning. I mean as if it were a dream and in a dream the dream can end any second so that everything has no future — or I don't know… Everything exists only just now. That's scary. I'm scared.

268.
Los Angeles
Jan. 19, 1977
Backyard Shack
Late afternoon.
Dear Debbie:

Your letters came yesterday - were here when I got home from a pretty hard task. I wanted to write you immediately, but couldn't.

Let me answer your questions somewhat in order, and more formally than I would like. Then a little later, this week I hope, I will write to offer some practical suggestions that might be helpful.

1. Really, as a rule one who thinks she might be going crazy or is badly afraid of that is not likely to have serious trouble. Try to believe that if you can. I do not mean to imply that your misery, your unhappiness, is not serious or important - it is, of course, but with a little precaution it should not be bad.

2. The idleness is real bad - too much time as you say to think. I wish you could write out your feelings, but maybe you can't. I would like for you to write me in as much detail what is worrying you as you can. The important thing is to hold back nothing. Whatever disturbs you whether it seems important or not tell me about in your letter.

3. Get much physical exercise - tennis, swimming, walking - and take care that you sleep as regularly and as much as you need.. Watch also your eating - regularly and wisely. If you feel you can, go to see Miss Kerr or other former friends.

4. I am confident you will be all right. There is genuine greatness in you, and you'll have your opportunity to express it.

Your deeply concerned friend, Earl V. Pullias

P.S. I don't think I need to say this: but feeling as you do and in the circumstances, there may be a temptation: absolutely no drugs - alcohol or whatever.

269.
Los Angeles
Jan. 22, 1977
Sat. afternoon
Dear Debbie

I hope by now you are feeling much better. I believe you will be telling me when you feel like writing again what seems to be bothering you most and most deeply. I would guess it is principally what you can do with your future. You have been going to school all your life, and now with that ended things probably look a little uncertain and empty. Work, if it is not too unpleasant, is extremely important for anyone. Just the work itself as activity is very good even if it is not always pleasant. And then it is very important if it can be a means of self support and this is most important, independence and self respect. I am confident you will find something that is not too uncongenial. Just a few suggestions:

1. I saw Dr. Hight who you recall is at the Community College there on campus at USC the other day. I spoke to her of you, and she said she would be very pleased for you to come out and see her. She has many contacts and might be able to help.

2. You might consider taking a class or two out there if there were something interesting or that might be helpful.

3. Let the people know at the school where you have the hour and a half work that you would like to help in other ways especially helping children that might need special help.

4. Try not to be afraid to ask people you have known to help you find work. Often times they want to help. Don't forget the personal practical things I mentioned and try to keep your sense of humor.

Your friend, Earl V. Pullias

270.
1-23-77
Dear Dr. Pullias,

I will send you some journal entries. It was hard for me to make myself write, but afterwards I saw that it was good to do so. I will try to every day.

I am better. I do not feel I'm going crazy now, but I do feel somewhat depressed, as if nothing was much worthwhile. That feeling may have something physical behind it, too — the neuritis which the doctor said I seemed to have. It dulls my body. Still I am afraid sometimes.

I think some of the things mentioned in my journal will need explaining. In September or October James gave me a marijuana cigarette. I have smoked a little before and had no experiences to fear. But this one time I had a time which I will never want to duplicate again. Probably the most frightening thing that has ever happened to me — including this past week, including the food poisoning, which was quite scary, also. We ate at a good expensive restaurant and the next day both James and I were sick.

Dear Dr. Pullias

Also, when I mention giving up James, it means mainly that I stop thinking we will get closer, because now I know we won't. We were in a rut, not a pleasant rut, rather a bothersome one, in which we seemed to be using each other for looks and for someone to be around. That's all. We'd used up each other's interests and we didn't have any emotion to keep up together. I didn't regret my decision to let him go from me — but it does change my normal procedure quite a bit and that might be depressing me some.

I am a little afraid to be alone. My mother has been very helpful. Perhaps because James isn't around I feel friendless. The only other friend I see regularly is Miss Kerr. We won't give up our friendship, because there is a loving feeling in it. I could have that feeling for James, but he wouldn't let me. He can't have any loving feeling (and he would be the first to say so — he is rather proud of his inability to love, but I guess that means friends come and go). And even though you are in L.A. you are a friend, because we have a loving feeling. And even though Dianna and Debbie are in San Diego, they are loving friends.

I sort of have a new friend. She is one of the head librarians at the public library.

I will give Miss Kerr the paper you sent.

I enjoy my work at the elementary school. Surprisingly, the constant reminding — "Hands off" "Out on the playground, please" "You're not to hit!" etc. doesn't disturb me. Maybe because I don't have time to stop and listen to myself and take myself seriously. Most of the time the kids don't either so what's the loss? I wish the job was longer than an hour and a half.

That's all. Thank you for your letter and I hope your hard tasks are accomplished smoothly.

Your friend,
Debbie.

— It is a few days after. I have received your second letter. I feel pretty crummy. Sometimes physically and mentally, sometimes just physically — but not just mentally. It makes me wonder.

It's like a dullness spreading all over my body from the back of my head. Do you know anything about neuritis? I have some questions. Like — can it make it hard to move your arms and legs? And can it make your eyes see differently? Can it press on your mind and make your dreams different? Does it make your head full of lead and pain

333

that comes in waves?

It's like my bad feelings come in waves. When I get up I feel so heavy and crummy, my head hurts in back. It is hard to eat and I have diarrhea. Then I move around and get going and feel better. But after I have been busy and am still active in the later afternoon my whole body suddenly becomes weak and it is hard to move and the back of my head gets heavy. Then in the evening I have my mental worries and my tiredness and my head burns. I think I am seeing like I did when I had the marijuana and it frightens me.

I think you are right about my feelings about the future. I wonder if it is worse because of the physical — or is the physical all mental, too?

Reading that over, it sounds like I don't eat enough. It is like that, except that it all comes from the base of my head, spreading out. I am trying very hard to eat as much as I can.

What do you think about the physical and the mental here in my case? Am I thinking myself into physical excuses or is my physical illness affecting my mental health?

Reading your paper inspired me. I feel like rereading A Teacher is Many Things. Your writing is very inspirational.

The principal increased my job for one more half hour. Now it is two hours.

Debbie.

Journal - January 19, 1977 - Wednesday

First I had that marijuana trip. It scared me in this way: it told me, suddenly, that reality is a dream. It's not real in the same way for everyone. Instead, every individual dreams up his own world. That realization shocked me. It threw me into a state of terror for a few minutes. Then I became catatonic. I was afraid I was going to be crazy for the rest of my life. But it only lasted one hour.

Then a couple of months later I got the food poisoning. I had diarrhea and vomited for two days. The third day I woke up feeling very strange. I half-way fainted and that frightened me. I was so scared I insisted that I go to the emergency ward. There they took tests and I felt safer. I got better. When I went back to have the tests read I told the doctor I still felt funny right at the back and bottom of my head, where my spine meets the brain. He didn't say anything about it.

A couple of weeks after that came a week of being alone in the evenings with complicated thoughts and worries about giving up James. I was alone for a weekend. The last night I lay on the couch and was suddenly horribly frightened. I felt like I was going crazy. It didn't have to do with James, it had to do with thoughts going in circles and circles, never solving anything and never coming to any conclusion.

Mama got home that evening and I liked her to be there. But I had a bad night. The next day I thought it was all due to my having too much time and too much freedom. It was getting to me — I couldn't take all the freedom after 17 straight years of scheduled time in schools. I thought, There is nothing I <u>have</u> to do, so I have too much time for thinking, and thinking too much leads nowhere.

The next day I went into action. I got a noon supervisor job and for four days I was active. But in certain moments I was frightened, moments when I was surrounded by people or moments alone at home; I'd look around and see, actually <u>see</u>, that the world was a dream.

Physically I was affected in this way: a numbing burn spreading from the base of my head, a burn in my stomach, clamminess, and diarrhea. There were all the symptoms I had with the food poisoning.

A week after that first day of fear I had another attack. I thought I felt better and was beginning to get used to my new view of things. But Mama was out and it was evening. I was afraid of the world being a dream. I was afraid of being crazy.

That was last night. This morning I wanted to be dead rather than go crazy. I thought about killing myself. But it came in waves so that there were moments when I felt well enough to continue. I went to visit the TMR class. While I watched the kids I didn't think of my fear. But when I sat with Mama and Mrs. Olds I felt it again. While I was working I didn't feel it.

In the afternoon the numbing really grew in my head. It deadened my movements. I didn't feel afraid of craziness, instead I just felt physically weird. Mama took me to the doctor but he can't see me till tomorrow. I want him to tell me if it is physical — perhaps a continuance of the food poison, that affects my nerve center and makes me think I'm going crazy. Or if it is mental. I wish it was physical, but I think it is mental.

Either way I believe I need help.

January 20, 1977 — Thursday

The doctor said it sounded as if I have neuritis, which is

something that affects the nerves of the cortex or spine. It comes as a burning and can produce a slowness in the muscles and a sweatiness. It can be caused by — among other things — certain kinds of poisoning and by vitamin deficiency, both of which could be my case.

I recognized that this is what I have, exactly. I was glad there was a physical reason to fit my case.

Does it explain away my mental problem, too? Does the pressure from the nerves make me see with prickles of light so that I think I am seeing a dream? The pressure causes me to be frightened, afraid that I am going crazy? Does that explain it?

Fear, worry, memory — fear of craziness, insanity, worry about what's happening, memory of my marijuana vision. Perhaps they all combined because I didn't know what was going on.

Still I am afraid. I'm afraid to be alone. I'm afraid to plan things like I am inclined to do. I'm afraid to be as I used to be. I am even a little afraid of writing in my journal as I used to do.

271.
Los Angeles
Jan. 29, 1977
Backyard Study
Sunday Afternoon
Dear Debbie:

I received your letter and enclosed pages from your journal. Both of them meant a great deal to me. I especially appreciated your thoughts about love. They are beautiful thoughts, and, I believe, true: genuine love gives meaning to life, and it may or may not involve sex or physical instances of any kind. It encourages me that you liked the article sent and that you feel you would like to read A Teacher Is Many Things again. Also, I hope you will read or re-read chapters 5 "Love and Reality" and if you feel like it, Chapter 17 in A Common Sense Philosophy - these thoughts between two friends might help just now. Don't make yourself read them, but just try to see if they speak to you. I am glad, too, you know how very much I think of you - I believe it is not too strong to say, I love you. And I am glad this helps.

Dear Dr. Pullias

In the deepest sense your mother is a very fine woman and of course loves you very much. Give her my love. I am eager that you not make certain mistakes she has made and that is not to judge her in the bad sense. I am very sorry that James has been a disappointment. I'm glad you are able to face the facts about his nature, and the fact that he is not good for you. I suspect a break, as wise and necessary as it was, hurt you more deeply then you might think, and may have been an additional factor in the way you feel.

I am glad you have a good doctor. My judgment is that your problem is largely physical. Yes, a physical condition can produce all levels of mental feelings or symptoms, and of course, worry and strain (technically stress) can cause or aggravate the way one feels physically. I know you pretty well, and I believe you are quite sound psychologically. You are very sensitive and delicately put together and therefore will need to live with certain care both physically and mentally.

That is the reason I have warned you (perhaps you have resented it sometimes) against all kinds of drugs, including alcohol. They are probably quite dangerous for you. The playing with the marijuana was quite unwise, as you know now. It effects different people in different ways, but for some, many probably - we don't know for sure - it is quite dangerous. One experience is not likely to damage you and the feelings you describe will likely soon pass away. I, of course, don't know, but what you thought was food poisoning might have been some kind of drug someone put in the food. Sometimes a person thinks this is a joke. May not be true at all, so don't take the idea too seriously, but I want very much for you to learn from the cigarette experience. Your body, mind, and soul are very precious and in a sense delicate. Respect them and treat them with care. I am glad your principal gave you another half hour of work. There will be more. I am a little better I think.

Your friend Earl V. Pullias

P.S. I will return your journal pages a little later. I am enclosing another copy of the paper for you especially.

272.

Debbie Bumstead

Dear Dr. Pullias,

What do I do about James? I told him in a letter that I was giving up the game we were playing and getting out of the rut we were in. But he doesn't seem to have caught my meaning. He is in New Jersey visiting his grandparents and he writes letters continuously. I have not returned with even one letter. Every letter I get from him I don't want to read. Because I want to give him up. I have to. I am. But it is painful, especially when he ignores my intention or doesn't realize its seriousness.

It would be easy if I could just give him up like that, and then his letters wouldn't matter. I'd just passively toss them aside. If he called when he gets back I'd just say this and that and then, "Good-bye now."

But I have had three dreams in which he has been trailing me, hanging on, trying to argue me out of my intention. In these dreams I will not be budged; I just don't care for his company any more. I shrug my shoulders and walk away. Part of me is that way. I really know that I <u>am</u> discontinuing our relationship. But another part of me has him hanging on, not wanting to drop away; and because he really is being that way it is hard on that part of me.

Now I see, though, that in those dreams the first part of me really can't be swayed by the second part. So I don't have to worry too much by what might happen; the main part will not be affected.

It feels like a great wheel that's been whirling one way for so long that it has to grind and churn and hurt as it changes to go the other way. No matter how it churns and hurts, though, the change will occur and soon the wheel will be spinning along smoothly the other way. That's how it feels. I want the churning to be over with.

Why do you suppose it helps so much to write it down to someone? Maybe because I am writing it in a way so that you will understand and consequently I begin to understand.

Thank you. Debbie

273.
Los Angeles
Feb. 13, 1977
Sunday night
Backyard Study
Dear Debbie:

Dear Dr. Pullias

I can't recall if I wrote to you before on this paper that a student from Egypt gave me. I think it is sort of interesting, and a folder in which the tablet came is very beautiful tool work which I'll show you some time.

As I mentioned to you a time or two, I have not been feeling very well the last few months, and I don't seem to be my best self. So I am concerned that in writing I might say something to you that would not be as wise as it should be. My hope is that our relationship is good enough that you would not mis-understand if because of haste or not feeling too well, I said something I would not otherwise have said. I have greatly appreciated the frankness of our writing. I feel you have said whatever you wanted to say, and have felt the same freedom.

I hope so much you have been feeling better. I feel confident that you are basically in quite sound condition mentally, although as I have said, sensitive and delicately balanced, so you will need to take care with your body and mind perhaps all of your life. My judgment is that when you get to feeling well again and you get to work, you'll be all right. I will be thinking of you. Earl V. Pullias

P.S. I have been feeling better.

274.

Dear Dr. Pullias,

I'm sending a bit of writing I did a couple of months ago. It is a memoir of my ninth grade. I just reread it and was struck by the very roughness of form it has. And I think I like that. It is not smoothly crafted at all. Instead it seems honest and simple, written not to present a story, but to put down a clear and precious memory. And that's why I did write it: to put down the memory. So it is true in every detail. The daydreams are dreams I dreamed then. Every event happened and every feeling was felt. That doesn't make much difference to other readers — but I think this was written for me and those it concerned and friends who are interested and that's all. Tell me what you think. (I wonder, suddenly, if I ever wrote you then about Mr. Basile, my art teacher.)

Well, I think I am getting better. I feel a little depressed in the mornings and the evenings, but the days go well. The neuritis is not constant. Instead it comes in occasional fits along with shaking and diarrhea. I'm taking vitamins and eating well in hopes that that will help. I said to myself I wanted to be noticeably better by my birthday and all better by the end of February.

Two things are helping me cheer up: reading good books and writing. I read My Antonia which you recommended a couple of years ago. I tried to read it then but it wasn't right. But I read it now and it was perfect. Funny how that works with some books. I started writing down my experiences at the elementary school. I'm keeping away from writing thoughts for awhile but I like to write my observations of children and other people.

A good children's writer is Meindert De Jong. He writes differently. I liked Journey to Peppermint Street.

Your friend, Debbie

275.
Los Angeles
Feb. 21, 1977
Backyard Study
Evening
Dear Debbie:

The night is chilly. A lovely crescent moon hangs low in the West not far from a very bright Venus. I know that you can see the same beauty if you walk out into the night and look to the west. Perhaps you do.

Your two letters in the folder of writing came yesterday. It was a special joy to me to receive them. I am so glad and thankful you are better. I believe you will soon be quite well again, and you will have learned much from the episode of illness. It is wonderful to be well.

Your letters are beautifully written. It may not be easy to break with James, but I have no doubt you can do it: you can get the wheel spinning in the other direction. (a vivid and insightful figure)

I have deep confidence in your judgment, and in your ability to follow a path you believe is best. Perhaps you will tell me what about the relation was so harmful if you wish to, and think it would help.

Dear Dr. Pullias

I have read Part One of your account - that is not the right word - of your 9th grade. I like it very much. I feel as you do it is the best writing I have seen of yours - it is genuine, authentic, sincere and in my judgment is a fine expression of your talent. You can write. Such writing is very good for you: it is healing and will refine your skill.

I wanted to write on your birthday, but couldn't. Keep your vision for life steadily before you.

Your friend Earl V. Pullias

P.S. You had not mentioned Mr. Basile: a fascinating aspect of your development. I am glad you liked <u>My Antonia</u>: you may like others of this author's books. <u>Death Comes for the Archbishop</u> is very good.

276.
Feb. 23, 1977
Los Angeles
Backyard Shack
Mid-day
Dear Debbie:

After my last letter to you when I had read only "One" of your memoir of your ninth grade I could not resist the desire to complete the writing that night. I was and am deeply impressed with what you have done in this writing: it is a fine piece of art about many things, but especially about the most important subject in the world: love and how we deal with it in human life. It flowed out of something very deep in you.

I am greatly tempted to try to say what it meant to me - its deep implications for numerous aspects of life - and especially for your developing art - but I shall resist that urge to elaborate and to analyze, lest it inhibit the flow of your thought and writing. Later perhaps I can wisely talk about what you have done or begun in that writing.

There is something I want to say that I fear I cannot make clear, but I must try: your recent letters and your "memoir" (we need a title for this piece of work) shifted deeply my feeling about you. Now I see you for the first time, perhaps, as an adult (who is very talented and special - I have always felt that), but as

Debbie Bumstead

an adult, with whom I am now speaking man to man, on the level, in a very special sense. For this I am deeply thoughtful. If what I say does not make much sense, give it time and perhaps it will.

I hope you are handling the James thing: I am eager that you not get trapped in anything that would hurt you and your future.

Your friend who loves and respects you. Earl V. Pullias

277.
Dear Dr. Pullias,

I had another attack last night. I guess I'll call it a nervous fit. Now I'm not afraid of going crazy, now I'm afraid I'll commit suicide. I feel depressed and nervous but not crazy. I am afraid that this troubled time will go on forever and that makes me want to be dead. Still that was the first "fit" I've had in a couple of weeks and I suppose it is significant that I mostly am depressed on weekends, rather than the days I work. I would like to work more.

After that bad time last night I had a little dream. I dreamed my father had a boat. This father looked like my real father but he was a doctor-helping-kind-of-person; his main concern was a child about ten. The boat was small, but big enough for a cabin; it wasn't a sailboat; it was the kind with the motor inside. There was a person in trouble in a far-away dangerous place up north. This person was thinking of committing suicide. The people on shore asked my father if he was really going to go that dangerous route up to help. For my father there was no question; he was going and he was going cheerfully. But for me, the child, it was a fearful decision — whether to go along or not. It was even frightening and dangerous to step from the shore onto the boat. But even though I was very afraid, I stepped down onto the deck. Then everything seemed right and I woke up.

I guess the people inside me want to help me, too. They are optimistic and cheerful and brave, so there must be hope, right?

James called this evening. He is home from the East. I don't really know how to deal with him. This is how I would like it to be. I would like him not to call on the phone or write. I would like us not to visit and do things together. But I would like us to not be unfriendly or hurt when we pass by on the street or have a thought run through our

342

minds. And I don't know how to go about getting my meaning to him. Should I write? Perhaps I should, and hope he doesn't write back wanting to discuss and talk me out of my feelings. Or should I just go about my business and give him the message by living it? I think I'll do both.

O, life. Anyway it is a challenge. I will have to have courage, do you think? Courage to keep caring, not fall into apathy.

But I tell you, I am tired of this nervousness, this depression, and this fear. I'm tired of having to think about it, that's when I feel it the most. Perhaps I should have other things to think about, huh?

I'm glad you liked the ninth grade story. I'm not good at getting out titles so I don't know what to call it yet.

I wish I didn't have to write such troubling letters to you. I feel a little guilty. I'm sorry. But thank you.

Your friend, Debbie

278.
Los Angeles
March, 11, 1977
Mid-day warm
Bright sunshine
Dear Debbie:

Your letter came two days ago. A friend is to be available when needed. I am very glad you feel free to write to me as fully as you wish and when you feel the need to share your misery or your joy. The free expression to someone who cares, and I hope, understands, helps.

The fact that it was two weeks between the spells or symptoms is, I believe, a good sign. I believe if you can use reasonably good judgment they will go away completely. Now let me give a few suggestions:

1. Continue to check regularly with your doctor - let him keep an eye on your physical condition. A physical problem can cause much psychological misery. Stay clear of any psychological treatment. If you need that kind of help, and I don't think you do, let's be very careful: many of them don't know what they are doing, I fear.

2. Follow through if you can, and I believe you can, in

settling the James relationship. Tell him very frankly what you feel you must do and plan to do - and <u>then do it</u>. Perhaps it would be good to tell him you will either destroy his letters without reading them or return them to him - the former might be better, but use your judgment - and tell him firmly you do not want him to call. Of course, I cannot be sure, but it seems very likely that your relation with him is your major problem. If you can do it, it might help to write me just what the relation was like and what went so wrong. It would help to write it out to someone who would understand and understand if you do not wish to write about this. You will, you must, find a solution to this problem. Keep in mind your nature and your sensitivities as expressed in your very insightful 9th grade report.

3. I don't know if it is possible or you would consider it wise, but you might think of going to see Miss Kerr and talk with her about your difficulties. She evidently liked you very much, and of course, you liked her: I am confident she would be interested and it might help to just visit her now and then.

4. Continue to build your general physical condition as consistently and wisely as you can: eating, exercise you like, writing, etc. It is a good sign that the work helps: you will eventually get full-time work that you like: work is a great healer.

5. The suicide feelings are very unpleasant but I believe not very unnatural or unusual. I suffered greatly from this feeling in my early years. The joy and beauty of much of life has great appeal for you - and I believe the promise is good: you have much to <u>do</u> and <u>be</u>. There will be much pain and tragedy, but a part of your hope is to make life better.

6. Try as best you can to keep your perspective and sense of humor: remembering the great saying: "this too shall pass."

Tomorrow is my birthday - March 12 - and I'll be 70: some kind of milestone, I guess! There is much I would like to say, but this letter grows long enough. Suffice it to say that I appreciate your friendship very, very much, that I have great respect for you and confidence in you, and that I hope the broad span of years between us will not separate us too much.

With kindest good wishes,
Sincerely, Earl V. Pullias
P.S. Let me think a little more about the dream.

Dear Dr. Pullias

Remember me to your mother and to your father if you see him. I care much for them both.

279.

Dear Dr.Pullias,

Your letter makes me feel better.

Somewhere I read that there were as many stars in the sky as there have been and are people on the earth. I think of that sometimes, and think that one of the stars is mine

Did you ever get a hold of the book <u>A Pilgrim At Tinker Creek</u> by Annie Dillard? It is very good and the way the author thinks — which is indescribable — reminds me of the way Miss Kerr is. Like, I seem to try to simplify things into easy sentences, but Miss Kerr lets everything that has any connection at all into her sentence. I do visit Miss Kerr often, but I haven't spoken to her about my troubles. I keep hoping the troubles will go away.

It made me think when you suggested that James might be the major problem. I hadn't really thought he was, but you know, the night in January when I suddenly fizzled in my head was after three days of considering him, thinking and worrying. Then the next day I thought it was too much freedom and so on. James didn't seem that serious a problem — to make me fear insanity and all that.

And it isn't that serious a problem — it just has a lot of years behind it and a big change to it.

First James and I were friends because we both wrote interesting letters and had interesting dreams to exchange. Then we were friends because we were companions in exploration and adventure. Those were both good times. We were close friends. We never really loved each other. But I thought we might grow to that. That was my mistake. About a year ago I realized that we were beginning to pretend that we were something we weren't. I don't know if I can quite express it; but it seemed we were acting like we were boy and girl friends, like we were intimate, close and loving; we acted or seemed to be that to the outside world, we went around together everywhere, called on the phone, talking constantly. But the interest in me was going away, and there wasn't any good love to keep it alive. We weren't really intimate. I found I was pretending and when I became conscious of it, I had to quit. It might not have been pretending for

345

Debbie Bumstead

James; he just might be that way: not being intimate may be his way of being intimate or not loving may be his way of loving. But I couldn't act like something I wasn't.

It's too hard to explain. But because we, or at least I (because I was the only one with problems with our relations), always spoke my mind to him, then it was fairly easy to tell him what I was thinking and for him to take it. Now I feel better because I wrote him and after he got the letter I called him and he understood as much as he could. So that now we can act true — which means friendly when passing on the street, but no calls and visits and constantness. That wasn't true.

I'm so weird. Will I be lonely all my life because I refuse to be intimate with people I don't love and because the people I do love are always distant in some way? Will I become cruel with all those I try to love and find I can't? No, it's not so bad as that, is it?

Your friend,
Debbie.

280.
Los Angeles
April 16, 1977
Backyard Hideout
At Night
Dear Debbie:

I have not written since you wrote me - I had asked you to tell me a little about the situation if you could and wished to - and you told me something of the problems with James. I am not sure I understand fully, but a good deal, I believe. Perhaps deeply it was sort of like a dream dying and that is always very painful. Edna St. Vincent Millay wrote a beautiful poem on the subject. It is no 32 of her collected Sonnets which is in paperback. I believe you might like it. I suspect you could adjust to and love deeply only a very special man who would fit your soul in a very special way. Any other type will bring you much pain and little joy. It will need to be a love not unlike that you described so sensitively and beautifully in the last part - the "dream" part - of your 9th grade account - we must find a good title for that work.

I am glad you continue to see Miss Kerr: she I believe is

good for you. And I guess you are wise in not talking to her about your illness and special problem: it might change something about the relationship.

I was sorry we missed seeing you when we were in Hemet for a little vacation. I wanted to look into your eyes and see you smile and know if everything is all right with my friend - I mean deeply; of course, there are always things wrong in this life. I appreciated your mother's invitation, but I didn't think it would be good to go to lunch under the circumstances. Another time.

I hope so much you are well or nearly so again.

Sincerely, your friend, Earl V. Pullias

281.
Los Angeles
April 30, 1977
Later Afternoon -
Backyard Study
Dear Debbie:

Can it be today we are finishing the fourth month of what only a moment ago was the new year? And that lovely April is almost gone? I can hardly believe it. The roses in the yard here have been beautiful again this year - a gift of God for which one can be deeply grateful. I have not been able to get out of the crowded cities as much as I would like. I need so much the openness of the country. Perhaps a little later when the demands of this special spring are over.

Which reminds me, that within two or three weeks or so Mrs. P. and I hope to come back to Hemet for another brief visit. Since your graduation from college I have had your letters all ready in a box to return to you. You will recall I promised to return them to you if you wanted them. There is no hurry if you do not want them yet, or if you do not want them at all they could be destroyed. I believe they should not be left unpossessed for the hands and eyes of strangers. You can let me know.

I hope so much you are well again. There are few things so good as being well in this life. One's body and mind and spirit are such good and precious things: they deserve as good care as we can give them but yet not too much concern or conscious

attention.

 I trust you were able to work out the James thing all right: my confidence in you is very deep. I hope to your writing is coming along nicely. I believe I have recently felt a little better.
 Your friend, Earl V. Pullias

282.
May 10, 1977
324 N. Buena Vista
Hemet, CA 92343
Dear Dr. Pullias,

 I very much like my apartment. I have fixed up the living room so that it is cozy like a home. All of my books are against one wall in shelves and I've framed several pictures and they're up. Now I have two more rooms to finish. I would like to be a good home-maker. I am good at decorating rooms and I find I'm pretty good at working outside, pulling weeds and so forth, but I still have to get going with cleaning inside regularly. I like to make meals for me and my animals (one dog and one cat), though.

 I am feeling better and better. I am glad I am staying here at my new place. It is what I've long been wanting to do, but was afraid to — live on my own. I am reading a book which concerns itself with living on one's own, making one's home, etc. — the experiences of May Sarton as she tells it. The book is <u>Plant Dreaming Deep</u>. Have you read it?

 What do you think about giving me the letters? I might be embarrassed to read some of what I've written you. Still you never can tell when such things can come in handy. For example, I am now writing a piece that was brought on by reading some old letters from two girl friends who live in Reno. So I don't know. Anyway when you come down you can come see my apartment if you want. Remember it is in the back of the house.

 My work is getting to be a chore. I'm getting tired of being a meanie. Anyway school is almost over. The only time I feel depressed now is when I consider the future, oh dear. Oh, well.

 I hope all is well with you.
 Your friend,
Debbie.

283.
Los Angeles
May 14, 1977
Living Room
Dear Debbie:

Your letter came yesterday. Thanks for it. I guess I had been uneasy about you and wondered if you had gotten into your apartment, and how it was working out. I know I should not be uneasy, but we do not always do what we should do in this world. I never want you to feel any pressure to write me: that was one of our agreements long ago. But I believe you understand my deep interest and concern.

I am glad you have your own apartment and are using your skills and interests to make it your own a place of special beauty and comfort and peace and work and life. It is a very fine project for you - a first step toward the little house of which we have spoken in the past. That will come in its time, I believe, but perhaps a good deal later in our very practical world. You will be a good homemaker, in the most genuine sense.

I am not sure how you will feel about your letters, but I believe you may find them very useful in many ways later. So it will be good for you to have them. You can always destroy them if you wish. They show a remarkable development in your life and thought. I am not sure when we will be able to come, but it will be good to see you, your place. And to leave the letters, if then you wish them. I am so pleased you are feeling better - that is wonderful, and I am thankful.

I will read <u>Plant Dreaming Deep</u> as soon as I can get it. I like her books very much, and have read a good many of them, but not that one. Thanks for recommending it. You might like to grow some things - to have a garden. Your Grandfather is very good with a garden: there is something very creative about working with growing things.

I understand how you feel about your work. I have often felt that way about school work, both as a student and as a teacher, but found what all could be done with and for people has been very satisfying and meaningful. I suspect any work has its

Debbie Bumstead

boring and discouraging periods: you will find a way to surmount them and even make them a means of learning and growth.

I wish I could help with the problem of the future: providing a livelihood for oneself is a very big problem. But it can be done and I believe you will find a way. I'll tell you a little more about myself next time. I have been feeling better.

Sincerely your friend, Earl V. Pullias

P.S. It is fun to know this is my first letter sent to your own apartment. It is chilly out back - I write on a board on my knee before the fire.

284.
Monday May 30,1977
Dear Dr. Pullias,

We had a good visit, didn't we? I enjoyed that.

Today my sister-in-law and the baby and I went out to the horse ranch to look at the colts. Mr. Heaton, the owner — who is also the teacher my mother works for — was there and when we started talking he said if I could find a place to keep a mare he would give Rotezza to me. He has to let a lot of the horses go, but he doesn't want to sell Rotezza. So you see I may have a horse in a few months (right now she has a young colt to take care of). Rotezza is a fat chestnut Arabian mare who, in her youth, won some championships in riding shows. She is a gentle horse, but I think she has a little fire in her, too.

I think my mother's landlord might let us keep a horse there. If not, Miss Kerr once said I could keep a horse at her house. She has three corrals and only one horse.

Sounds like fun, huh? I'm excited and also flattered. I do like Mr. Heaton. Even though my taking the horse would relieve some of his financial difficulties, still it is pleasing to be asked to take her. Or something like that.

Last Saturday I had another "attack." The night before I had bad dreams and once I fell asleep I felt my heart and breath were stopping. I woke with a jerk. It seemed very real. Then in the daytime I was visiting my mother and Jackie when suddenly I felt a spark burst in my head and it was like the marijuana experience — all that had gone on before fell way into the past. I was frightened, but as I thought I decided it must have something to do with James. Because he has been around again. He's selling a car that is parked at my mother's so he is over there occasionally. Maybe the split affected me more than I feel on the surface and my body reacts to my inner feelings. Maybe the drug experience connects with those inside secrets and punishes me when he's around in my thoughts.

I don't know, but the explanation made me not frightened and I got over the attack very quickly.

Today I finished a project I have been doing for my "agent." It is a read-aloud story that I painted pictures for and finished up on good paper. I hope she thinks it is good enough looking to send out. If not, maybe I'll bind it together and put it in my own library. The story is one I've had in my head a long time — about mountains being sleeping dragons.

School is almost out! I love the children.

Your friend, Debbie.

285.

Dear Dr. Pullias,

Now I am not getting Rotezza, the mare, but I am getting for my own her yearling colt. I like him more, even if I can't ride him yet. He is intelligent and gentle; he doesn't fight against Mr. Heaton like the other colts. Perhaps I can train him. Sometimes I have a hard time with names. I have thought of calling him Jet, because he is black (with a star and two white anklets). When he runs he sticks his tail in the air. He's an Arabian beauty.

My mother's landlord is letting us have a corral at her place for the horse.

Last night was graduation at the dog training class. We had a regular obedience trial like they have at dog shows. Rex and I got the third place trophy and our picture taken with the other winners for the paper. It was very much fun.

I do like my animals, you see. They are rather like having children around, I guess, without so much worry and bother. Rex and Sara are very much a part of my household. It's funny.

The man in the front apartment may move and I may decide to go up front. The yard is better and Tim, Jackie, and Beau, who plan to move back to this house would be better in the larger back apartment. Actually I think the front place is cozier. I think I will move — if the man goes.

That's the news. How is it with you?
Your friend, Debbie.

286.
Los Angeles
July 1, 1977
Backyard Study
Evening
Dear Debbie:

You are a very lucky girl to have a beautiful black colt named Jet! Or did you decide to give him that name? I think it is better to get a colt rather than an older horse, because in that way you will get to know him more deeply and thoroughly. When I was a little younger than you are I had several colts in various years that I took a keen interest in and loved very much. A horse, I think, is a very intelligent and charming animal, can be a great friend. I had one colt that I liked very much that I kept until he was perhaps three years old, and then I left the farm to teach.

In those early years I had a dear friend who was a veteran of the Civil War, (1861-65). He was by then (when I knew him) quite old but had some fine horses and was good with them. He and I, the boy in his teens and the old white haired man, used to prepare our horses for showing at the fairs and go together to take them. We would sometime win prizes with them because of their good qualities. That was fun.

Let me know if you decided to go into the front apartment and how you have things fixed up. Congratulations on the success at the dog training school.

After I finished my year of teaching, I have been trying to rest a little. I have been a little tired and for the last year or two have not felt very well. I think I am beginning to be better now. On June 15 I made the only commencement speech I made this year. It was at Citrus College - a community college some forty miles east of here. It was a pleasant evening, a large group of young people and their parents. They have the commencement outside in their stadium. It was about sundown: a lovely evening. The young people seemed to like my talk. Perhaps I'll tell you about it sometime. I hope to get a little writing done this

summer, but as yet have done none. I hope later. Let me know how things go with you. Any plans or projects for next year? Your beloved friend, Earl V. Pullias

287.

Dear Dr. Pullias,

Do you know this about colts? Whether after they've been gelded and then healed up and then moved to a new place and then been under close care for a week, can they then be left safely under general care for two weeks? The reason I wonder is because my mother wants me to go to Reno with her on the 25th or so. I will have the colt this weekend. My father would feed and look after him for the two weeks. I guess it would be alright if the horse seemed well and content in his new home. I haven't decided yet, though, if I'm going to Reno. There's a lot going on here, but it might be nice to have an interval of differentness.

Sometimes I feel a little panic about I should be working to pay myself's, my animals, and my horse's way. I began a factory job that paid well, but it was so deadly boring I didn't last but two days. That scared me because what if I find all jobs boring? Hopefully none could be as boring as that (stripping plastic off tips of wires) but I'd hate to become a quitter just because something doesn't suit me. That job was eight hours a day and I don't think I need to spend so much of a good day making money. Five hours would be enough.

I looked up the mailman job in the library. They work eight hours and have 1-4 weeks vacation. When I really began to consider the job it lost its desire. It's the kind of job I imagine me into, all independent and robust and continually active — the kind of job I'd have if I had a husband and children and a farm and never wrote. That's what I want and to be happy. But I can't be that. I feel very dull when I'm not writing and watching. I have a tendency to stop and quietly stare. I watch. I don't act as much as I react. I thought the second choice — school librarian — might be possible and suitable. A librarian reacts while a teacher has to act. A librarian watches and helps and introduces. She also gets first looks at all the brand new books!

Now — how do you get to be a school librarian?

I have had the colt for several days now. I still lunge him twice a day but I can stop that in a few days. He's all healed, I think. So I may go to Reno next week, Wednesday or Thursday.

I'm going to go to the school office and remind them that I can be a Teacher's Aide next year. Rumor has it that they're going to hire a bunch more for next year — because of added programs and different school hours.

It is hot here.

I liked your letter and I hope you are well.

Your friend,

Debbie.

P.S. During a nap a week ago I dreamt that I titled the ninth grade account — The Dream Time. I rather like that.

Yes, I've moved to the front apartment and I'm just getting it fixed up. I like it and I like the yard.

288.
Los Angeles
August 18, 1977
Early morning
Dear Debbie:

I was sorry I was not able to write you before your plans to go to Nevada. I hope your plan went well and that if you went you had an interesting stay. You are a good observer and everywhere there are things to see and feel. I'll be interested to hear about your experience. I am sure the colt - did you decide to call him Jet as you were thinking you might - got along all right. Doubtless he missed you very much, and it may take a little time to reestablish your close relationship with him. That will come as you associate with him. The relationship between a horse and a human being can be very beautiful and satisfying. There are some great historical accounts of such relations - Alexander, the great, is one. Don't get discouraged.

The problem of work to secure sufficient resources to support oneself is one of life's most difficult problems. There are many for whom a factory-like routine, relatively monotonous job is hard or impossible to take. On the other hand, meaningful work that has some interest and possibility of creativity can be found. Of course in any work there will be dull spots and boring times which a person must deal with. I believe you would do well as a teacher aide or in library work.

I believe you can find work that will have time and energy and spirit for your writing, and yet will supply your basic needs which are not great. I hope you will let your friends, including your mother, help you to get in. For example, I know a man here at USC who used to be Supt. at Hemet who knows the present Supt. who will and would be glad to put in a word with him about you as a teacher aide on my recommendation, but I didn't want to do that unless you wanted me to. Also, I am sure Miss Kerr could, and would be glad to help if you told her frankly what you want and need. I believe there is good possibilities for half time or so work at the library or one of the school libraries. Let me know if I can help.

I have not felt well this summer which as you know is a drag. I had hoped to write some, but have not been able to yet. Apparently nothing too serious but just don't feel well which tends to cast a shadow over everything. It will be good to hear from my beloved friend.

Sincerely, Earl V. Pullias

289.

Dear Dr. Pullias,

I have had some interesting thoughts on relationships between animals and humans. I often entertain myself with these peculiar beliefs I have which I can hardly believe I really believe. See if you can acknowledge any truth in them.

There are at least two, maybe three, different parts to every animal. In a domestic animal one part is the dependent less intelligent animal which you must care for and teach with love, firmness, and the belief that your orders must be obeyed. The other part is an animal of great wisdom and unique spirit, an animal that teaches you with only love. The third part is an animal in his freedom, being what he was born to, having nothing to do with you.

Prieta, for example, was a horse who spooked at silly things and often had to be calmed or scolded (she used to bob and shake her head in the silliest way when she was scared), but even so I could not throw off a persistent belief that she was much wiser than I ever will

Debbie Bumstead

be.

Another example of my crazy beliefs is when rabbits, deer, dogs, cats, etc. out of ignorance — an ignorance that can't be taught out — get hit and killed on the streets, I can't shake the feeling that they do it <u>on purpose</u> to show us our folly, in hopes that we will take heed and change.

Perhaps, because I'm always looking for teachers and things to learn, I developed this idea. But it seems more than that because I <u>believe</u> it — I don't just think of it and say, "that's true" — I can't <u>stop</u> believing it. It's like my very funny belief that my china animals and dolls and pictures comes alive and lead normal lives when I'm not with them. I don't believe it, but I can't help believing it. And so I don't try to not. Really, it is more interesting to believe such things.

The colt ended up being called "Diego" instead of "Jet." His naming was a hard thing to do. His official name became "Prince Harobed" because when I was little my imaginary Arab horse was named Harobed — which is Deborah spelt backwards. But I couldn't go around calling the colt that imposing name, so one day I watched a movie "Zorro" with Tyrone Power, and Zorro's real name was Don Diego. That name hit me full force because I used to be quite taken with the dashing Zorro. I mentioned the name to several people and they started calling the colt Diego, and there it is.

Since this seems to be an all-about animals letter I'll send you a couple of pictures to look at. The color isn't too good in the corners, but you can see how beautiful he is anyway, right?

Your friend,

Debbie

P.S. Certainly you can put in a word for me — Teacher's Aide-wise — if you want.

My application as a Library Clerk for the County was accepted, now there has to occur an opening.

Meanwhile I am writing a new story.

Dear Dr. Pullias

290.

Dear Dr. Pullias,

I waited before writing to you because I thought by today I'd be a Library Clerk. But they didn't choose me. And the Teacher's Aide position didn't even produce an appointment for an interview. Maybe they're tired of me at the District Office. I must really come across as an incapable person to have been rejected by so many interviewers!

Today I thought I might try the Tutoring thing again. Do you think I ought to? I made up some rules to get rid of the problems I had last time:

1. child comes to my house (avoids distractions)
2. Conference held a week before beginning (learn difficulties + get textbooks)
3. Make schedule of coming sessions
4. No homework or workbooks done
5. Three twenty minute periods, two five minute breaks
6. Two periods of textbook instruction, one period of learning games.

I'd try to be more prepared if I took this up again. I'd want ideas and materials all ready for reading, writing, or math games. And I'd study the children's specific textbooks before I started teaching it. I'd make out brief but clear lesson plans and I'd try to follow them strictly and not let my easy-going ideas of learning make me lazy and bored. Do you think I ought to try it again?

Next day: This morning I got up and decided I couldn't do the tutoring thing again — no, never. I took a walk and felt like being a mail carrier again. So later I called the post office to see how it's done. First there has to be a vacancy, then you take a test, and so on. There are no vacancies here. So this evening I'm thinking about being a tutor! I really need a job. Not just for money, but also because I <u>need</u> to work. When I'm working I don't worry about my life. As much.

I am reading a biography about the poet, Pushkin. I remembered you saying he was interesting. I like this book because it creates a picture of Russia at the time as well as showing Pushkin's life. Some biographies are flat, because they only show a person's life, not the time and place as well.

I just finished reading <u>The Count of Monte Cristo</u> by Dumas. You know how some books seem to fit your life and the character fits your character? Believe it or not, the <u>Count</u> affected me in this way. I, like Edmund Dantes, entered full of love and eager innocence. Like him I was betrayed (by the schools) and like him I nearly went crazy, nearly committed suicide in my prison of fear and betrayal. Now I suppose I will find a teacher (perhaps inside myself) who will teach me all he knows. After ten years I'll escape, discover a great fortune, and travel and continue my education for ten more years. Maybe I will find myself like the Count; educated, attractive, rich and refined. But he did it all with one mission in mind: to reward and punish his friends and betrayers. Does that mean I will seek to bring about the downfall of schools?

I have more to tell you but I'll save the news for another letter!
Your friend,
Debbie.

290.
October 5, 1977
Dear Dr.Pullias,

I wrote a poem about Don Diego, the horse, tonight. This is the way it goes.

My Colt
His eyes are forests —
He leaps the fallen trees;

Dear Dr. Pullias

He tosses his head in the leafy branches;
He is more fierce than the wild animals.
    His jet coat is a jewel of Spain —
His hooves beat castanets;
His ears know the history of castles;
His tail is the flag of picador.
    His nostrils breathe Arabian deserts —
He prances through the oasis;
He gallops through the fiery sands;
His mane is more flowing than the nomad's robe.
    His neigh is the ocean's roar —
He jumps the crested waves;
He nickers into the night mist —
Then he beats a roving thunder back to me.

It needs a little straightening up, then it will go to my creative writing class. That is one bit of news I was going to tell you — that I've started in a writing class in the adult education program. I finished the book I was writing. Now I have written four (in four years) and published none. In fifty years will I have written fifty books? Wow!

The other news was this. My mother is planning on retiring this year so she can go up and take care of her parents and the motel. This means that I will have to move also, if I want to keep the horse. I have two choices. One is that I, too, go to Reno. There is a cottage on the motel property that I could have and I could build a corral next to it. The other choice is to live here in Hemet on my mother's property on Gibbel Road. My father is building a small house there (financed by my grandmother) and then he is going north afterwards. I could live there with all my animals.

At the moment I'm working on choice # two; I'm helping straighten up the property and planning on planting some trees. Though I might have a better chance at a job and contacts in Reno, there are two disadvantages in going there. One is that Grandmother puts so much fear into me I'm practically paralyzed with ideas of murders, rapists, and kidnappers and the other is, though the property there is large, it is surrounded by highways and streets with no where to ride horseback. Here in Hemet I'd have places to ride, but I'll be all alone up there (though three neighbors are within running distance). I suppose my final choice depends on which challenge I want to accept — that of contending with Grandmother's fears or with my own fears.

Debbie Bumstead

Since they're the same I guess I ought to just pick the place I like best. Maybe I ought to live away from my mother a year or so. And so on. What do you think?

My father thought you might like to sponsor a tree out on the hill. That'd be fun.

Your friend,

Debbie.

291.
Los Angeles
Backyard Study
11/4/77 mid day
Dear Debbie:

Do you suppose I am slipping my rocker, or is the tense wrong, and I have already slipped? I don't know how or why I should have put the wrong zip code on your letter: I didn't realize that a letter goes to the large area like a state by zip. To Indiana! Your letter was very good to receive. It gave me information I wanted, and even more important, gave me a part of you in the form of an important thought. I liked the drawings, too.

The idea of a donkey sounds interesting, if you think we can afford another mouth to feed! It might not be wise to count on a "modern" donkey living chiefly on brush or nearly nothing. See what you can find out.

Your description and analysis of the deep inner struggle about the job or work problem was I thought very good and insightful. I suspect you have the conflict very well worked out in terms of the Indian and the white settler. (Were you able to read the book Tisha by Robert Specht: Throws much light on your idea). The mixture of Indian and White which many of us seem to be is very hard to manage and is often very painful, particularly in the white society with all its demands and values. I guess I still hope we can some way have the best of both worlds. Maybe that is what a reasonably good society would be. But even our world being what it is, I believe you can, when you set your mind to it, get a job that will provide the necessities without destroying an important part of you. I hope so.

I believe the visits were good - with your friends or former friends. Even the overheard conversation contributed to your

360

steady growth in self-understanding. Reasonable self-understanding helps one to avoid making foolish or harmful reactions to the internal struggle you understand so well. As I have said perhaps too often, the wrong ways can be destructive of the best of you and your dreams - your writing, the good life, etc.

Sincerely, Earl V. Pullias

P.S. (Later) I am not satisfied with my letter written earlier today. It does not clearly convey the thought I want to convey - even to a friend who by now comes to know me pretty well.

It would not be undesirable at all if you had a patron or sponsor who believed in you and who had the resources to provide you with the things, the circumstances, and most important of all, the un-pressed time you need in order to follow your writing. Such has often been done in the history of the world. People of wealth have often believed in some person's talent and provided that person with the means to develop and use that talent: writing, music, art, etc. Of course, there is always the danger that the patron will want to control or in a sense own or dominate, the receiver, but it need not be so. They may give the person helped complete freedom and allow him or her to retain complete self respect. The other danger is that the person who receives the help may not use it wisely, or getting the means of life too easily may be spoiled by it - that is, may come to simply take or receive and not feel the responsibility to give or in this case to create because of the opportunity the gift or support provides.

Frankly, I don't think you are capable of being "spoiled" in this sense. The deep need to cultivate and fully express your writing art is too great to permit such spoiling. I think your grandfather, Bumstead, might have done significant creative things had he had such freedom.

I don't know if you could receive it either directly or through your mother, but I have often wished your grandparents on the Marlow side could provide such support for you. Yet I realize you may need the zest that would come from making your own way. You will find an answer - tutoring, riding horses, ??

E.V.P.

Debbie Bumstead

292.
Dec 1977
Dear Dr. Pullias,

I especially liked your last letter. I like it when you say something about what you're doing and thinking. I often think the subject of me is monopolizing our correspondence (though, I admit, it is an interesting subject!).

Last Sunday I had a battle with my horse. Occasionally he takes it into his head to fight me when I'm working him. So far I've won all our battles (three since I've had him). Afterwards I wonder if he's really the sort of horse I want. Even though he's good-natured and affectionate, he is very spirited. I may be a fair rider, but I'm not at all a confident one. I'm afraid that when the time comes to get up on him, I won't be able to handle him. I'm afraid he'll run away with me or buck me off. But then I think how much I like him and he likes me (I like the way he likes me — Prieta couldn't stand me, even though I loved her). Maybe in the end he will have taught me to be a confident equestrian and I'll have taught him to be a good pleasure horse. I hope so.

I've been accepted as an enrollee in a federal work program that starts in January and lasts a year. I'll be called a "forestry aide" and I'll work outdoors with a group of 16-23 year olds, both men and women. I'll work eight hours a day and get the minimum wage. Probably at the end of the day I'll crash onto the couch at home and never be able to get up again. But I might as well try it. I want to work hard. I like the idea of working in the wilderness park (in Idyllwild — they bus us to the work area — I'll just have to drive out a little past my mother's house to the meeting station). I hope it works out.

What do you do on Christmas day? This year I'm making presents and each one is something I haven't done before. I sewed a robe for my mother and did some elaborate embroidery for the pockets. I'm making a wallet for my father, tooling, painting, and lacing up the leather is new to me. I carved a wooden plaque for a girl-friend and I'm going to cook some health candy bars for my brother Joe (who is down visiting). My father is making a walnut wood dulcimer instrument for my mother and my mother's making presents, too, but she's very secretive, I can't find out what she's up to! I think I want to make you something special, but it will be after Christmas.

Early this month Tim and his wife Jackie had their baby. It is a girl and I like her. I like Beau, too. The girl is named Winter Fawn. That's an unusual name, isn't it? My father says, with a name like that, she'll grow up to be a poet. Who knows? It will be fun to watch her and Beau grow.

      Love, Debbie.

Debbie Bumstead

Dear Dr. Pullias

1978

You have learned much these ten years since 14.
So it will be through the years that lie ahead.
Keep your dreams and march steadily toward
them. **Dr. Pullias**

Once, during a very exerting climb over a steep crop of rocks,
with my tree bag bumping my leg and the hoedad scraping on
the granite, my mind stopped itself and realized what a very
good time I was having! Debbie

Debbie Bumstead

293.
1-8-78
Dear Dr. Pullias,

I like my job so far. The first day we (a crew of seven with two foremen) learned how to use some cutting and digging tools. The second day we hiked a long way into the mountains to clear an old trail. The third day we sat in a classroom and learned fire safety rules. Then Friday we went to Lake Hemet to pick up trash. I was glad for the weekend to come, but now I'm looking forward to tomorrow, Monday. It is fun, mostly: driving around in the van, gabbing, taking long lunch breaks, going to the market for food, etc. I don't know if this easy-going feeling will continue, but it'd be nice if it did. The two foremen are not too much older than I am; five of the other six crew-people are 18 or under; three of us are girls. There is another crew with three other girls and more boys. We work with them sometimes. I feel a little old. Next month I'll be 24 — six or seven years older than most of them! That's OK.

I feel my age sometimes when I'm watching teen-agers. Just recently I felt a change in me. I no longer feel adolescent. I feel much calmer about many things. Looking out of myself, I no longer connect so many things to my security or insecurity. Like if a person looks at me, I'm not as likely to worry about what they are thinking of me. Instead I think about them. My mind's point of view has changed somewhat, I guess.

Oh, now I am sleepy. I have to get up at 6:30. So here is just a short letter for you.

Your friend, Debbie.

294.
Los Angeles
Jan. 29, 1978
Sunday Morning

Debbie Bumstead

Dining Room Table

Dear Debbie:

I have been concerned that much of this first month of your work project has been pretty bad weather: much rain earlier, and a good deal of chilly weather not very usual for Calif. I hope these conditions didn't make the work too unpleasant or got you sick. Probably before long you will write and bring me up-to-date about the work, your apartment, reading, and especially your writing - if that is not too much to ask even of a good friend. And your thinking - that is the best!

I believe I am beginning to overcome missing my teaching so much. I had grown rather tired of the long classes and the detailed work that is always a part of teaching if one does it well. I always liked to have my students to write papers about things that interested them, and liked to read the papers and give my reactions. I never felt it helped much to be very negatively critical. Rather I liked to point out what I thought was especially good in a paper in the hope that I could encourage the students to write more and as sincerely and freely as possible. I expect that it is by writing that a person learns to write. Of course, observation, thought, reading, all help.

I am still serving on the County Board of Education, helping some small colleges, and trying to help our little church to do as good work as possible. Recently I haven't been able to read much because I couldn't wear my glasses which is a long story. I see where the lady who wrote <u>I Heard the Owl Call my Name</u> has a new book out. Should be good. How is our friend Don Diego?

Your friend, Earl V. Pullias

295.

Los Angeles

Feb. 6, 1978

Shack in

Backyard

Dear Debbie:

Your letter helped to make this a good day for me. I

guess I was a little worried about you, fearing as I mentioned, that the bad weather in Jan. might have made you sick. So it was very good to hear you are fine and enjoying your work. Your drawing interest and skill might prove very useful. It might be something will open up for you in the Park Service or the Forestry Service or something of this nature which would provide pleasant work at which you could make a living and still have time to write. We'll see. Let people who know about such things know your interest.

I shall be delighted to serve as your guinea pig in the letter writing experiment. Try your hand at the way of writing you mentioned and see how it goes. When I was growing up on the farm and working there, I found it was very hard to do mental or creative work during the work days. I was usually too tired at night. But many people have been able to plan their lives so they could write during off hours, and I believe ideas can come while one is working.

I am glad you are getting the Alice stories ready to submit to the publisher. I am confident the 9th grade account will publish: it is very good. We must have a good title. Have you thought of one yet? There is great interest in adolescent experience and the slant on sex in your account is very special.

Your friend, Earl V. Pullias

P.S. I am very proud of the attitude you are taking toward your work experience. You are learning. I feel better.

296.
Los Angeles
The Backyard
Study - Feb 18, 1978
Sat. night

My beloved young friend, Debbie:

It is almost a perfect night. Perhaps a little colder than I like since by nature I like warm weather, but outside this little room it is beautifully clear; the moon half-way up the eastern sky casts its soft light over the back yard. The stars are dimmed a little by the moon, but can be seen. But surely you too can see this loveliness from your view in Hemet. I hope it has been a good day for you and that this evening is especially good.

I have thought of you often today and wondered what thoughts and feelings your were having on this your 24th birthday. Perhaps you will write to me about some of them. Probably you feel that 24 is pretty old. Compared to 5 or 10 or 15, it is surely older and has brought deep changes in you. I have been interested in observing the remarkable growth toward maturity as reflected in your letters: from a high school girl to a college young woman to a woman. And yet the central you, as I suppose is true of all of us, tends to remain much the same - different and yet basically the same. You have learned much these ten years since 14. So it will be through the years that lie ahead. Keep your dreams and march steadily toward them.

But perhaps you do not like for me to talk so much about you. It maybe better to just let the growth and life take place and not analyze or discuss so much. In a sense, I guess that is true, but it is the nature of some of us to observe and discuss - perhaps too much so. Yet I hope this observation and thought may add somewhat to our understanding of ourselves and others; and sometimes may clarify our goals and purposes and help to make some progress in achieving them.

I hope you have worked out a scheme through which you can continue to write as a part of your work. I am sure there will be much opportunity to observe and feel nature and people. The problem will be to make room for recording your thoughts first in your journal and later to use those notes in your more finished writings. I believe this was the way Thoreau worked; also, Emerson, and I suppose many other less famous writers.

Perhaps sometime you could tell me a little more about how things go with your mother. It was not quite clear when she planned to go to live with her parents. Or does that plan still hold? Of course, today I have thought some of your father, and your grandfather Bumstead. I hope things go reasonably well with them.

Someway, this letter does not quite show or sound as I want it to. You will understand if I tell you for some cause I have not felt very well today. So that is reflected in my writing to you even on your birthday. Yesterday was good - maybe tomorrow

will be again.

Surely if the objects and pictures, etc. would ever come down from their places and take on life they will do so on this moon lighted night which is also your birthday. Perhaps they will do so tonight at midnight and dance in their special way on the lawn. Since I last told you of the furnishings of the walls, I believe I have added the picture of a beautiful black stallion on the East wall here in front of me. He will have to stand by and observe perhaps.

Debbie, my love and very best wishes come to you on this special day.

Your friend, Earl V. Pullias

P.S. Mrs. Pullias would wish to send her very best to you especially today.

297.

Dear Dr. Pullias,

In the mail today I received two books which I ordered from a small press in N. California. One is a novel and the other is a Publish-it-yourself Handbook (without vanity publishers). I like getting things in the mail. I subscribed to three magazines, also. I can do that kind of thing now that I have my very own checking account.

It was especially good to get things in the mail today. I'm staying home from work trying to recover from the flu. I still have a little fever, but not near as much as I had over the weekend. Do you know why whenever I get sick it's usually over a weekend? This time though I'll probably miss several days of work. I feel incredibly weak. I'll try to go back Thursday and Friday, since those are my sign-painting days anyway and I can stay dry inside. I wish it would quit raining.

Sometimes I wish I could live as an animal. Animals seem to lead peaceful lives. My life is so complicated and busy. Sometimes I have dreams that I'm a horse. Once I dreamt I was a killer whale. When I woke from that dream I felt sure I knew the killer whales personally and they knew me, even over the stretch of land that separated us.

I'm afraid of death. I think about it every day. Any dream that isn't a fun or a gentle dream always deals with my or another's death. Recently I've begun to tire of my preoccupation. I don't mind death being there, if only I wasn't afraid.

Tomorrow, for sure, I'm going back to work. I've been gone four days. Whenever I have free time around me I begin to feel like writing. But I know I shouldn't, because I won't have time when I start to work again to finish anything well.

This writing thing preys on my mind quite a bit. So many people, myself included, have convinced me over the years that I am "destined" to write. Though I am working hard and feel good about it, I also feel like I should be writing. I feel like I can do both, but when I try, I can't.

I didn't go to work because I woke up speckled like measles. I went to the doctor and he said I'm allergic to penicillin (which he had given me for the fever). That's interesting.

There's a Master's program in creative writing at San Diego state. Do you know of others? Do you think I might go back to school some day?

Tuesday: I got your birthday letter today. Actually birthdays aren't the best days. I think I expect too much out of them. Sunday was nicer. I hiked back from Gibbel Road and followed a stream that is running down from Hemet Butte. It is so green along that little valley (I've always called it the Valley of the Shadow of Death) that I could pretend I was in a different country.

Then today at work we hiked 3 miles into the mountains. Everyone else is used to the climbing but I have to hang back and rest. I wonder if I'll make it through the year. It's hard.

Your friend, Debbie.

298.
Los Angeles
February 27th 1978
Dining room table
Monday evening
Dear Debbie:

Well you see the rain and chilly weather have driven me into the house again. Your letter came yesterday and I was very pleased to hear. I was very sorry you had had the flu, many people have had it here, so let us hope it is just going around attacking people, and soon it will let you alone.

But I can't help but be concerned about you. My hope is that your body will toughen to the out of doors and to the work, and eventually you will feel better than you ever have. If the long hiking and heavy work can be varied with some of the sign painting and other lighter work, that will be good. Unless it becomes unbearably hard, I hope very much you can stick out the year. Did you get to read <u>Tisha</u>, the book about the young girl in Alaska? That might give you some ideas, and also encourage you. (I think I wrote you about the book last year.)

I don't know what to say about your writing and how to relate it to your work. I believe you will find a way to do this, but it may not be easy. John Muir, the great naturalist, worked a half year and then checked off half the year to write. But I'm afraid such work would be hard to find in our time. (And I believe he married some money!)

Perhaps later you will tell me if you had any special thoughts on your birthday. I remembered where I was and what I was doing at 24. I was at Duke University working on my degree and teaching and tutoring some. Yes, I imagine you will go back to school, perhaps for your masters degree, or for special learning. In a deep sense, you are now going to a great school of experience. I hope it won't be too hard. Try to be well. Your long walk sounded very good. I wish I could have made the journey with you.

Your deeply interested friend, Earl V. Pullias

299.
3-3-78
Dear Dr. Pullias,

I feel good tonight. Sometimes I feel a great peaceful general sort of love in me, for all the people and things I meet and all the things that happen. It's like there's a love inside the acceptance and the entering-into in the world.

You're a good friend to have.

Don't worry too much about my quitting. I suppose I will complain and want to quit quite often, but I've already told myself I can't leave the job. I said that I could leave only if I was given or found a better job or if the foreman told me I was too weak.

There are seven girls on the three crews; three of them are rather thin and weak like I am. That makes me feel better. Really, I guess the only reason I ever feel bad is because of four Indians (3 on our crew) who spend a good part of their time making fun, telling secrets, and laughing at everyone. I wonder why they do that? I wonder if it has to do with the Indian laughing at the white man or the man laughing at the woman or just if you're with your own kind you get to laugh at the other kind. But why? I don't know. Maybe they are immature. Maybe they like to see hurt. It hurts almost like junior high school. I'm surprised that even though I'm older and I understand (vaguely) their motives still I get hurt feelings. It makes me laugh. I can't help but like the very silly little me. I'm not grown-up. I'm glad.

That's what I think at 24.

Yes, I liked <u>Tisha</u>.

Yours,

Debbie.

300.
Los Angeles
March 18th, 1978
the shop evening
Dear Debbie:

Perhaps I have come to care for you more than I should. But then how could one care more than he should?! I have been eager that this growing care be such that would not infringe upon your freedom or your ability to be honest and authentic with me. I am thinking of how very much I liked and valued your letter that came today. It told me much I want to hear about you. But I would always want you to tell me the truth as best you can perceive it, even though that would be less pleasant and perhaps even painful. It is a great joy to know that your greatest and deepest trait is the need to be genuine, yourself, authentic.

But it was good to read your first paragraph in which you describe that wonderful feeling of peace and deep satisfaction that arises naturally out of the state of and consciousness of an all-pervading love: a love that some way escapes the bounds and complications of the narrowly physical. Your 9th grade account especially in the last major section develops this theme. You come close to the meaning of life, the essence of truth, the nature of God or reality. I liked also to hear what you said about your work that you had made up your mind about certain things you would do and would not do - as to giving up your work - that then you would no longer be at the mercy of chance circumstance or internal whim. I have known, of course, you have great strength - I speak of spiritual strength - but I like to hear you relate that strength to decision and life. You see, what you said encouraged me because I care.

Sincerely your friend, Earl V. Pullias

P.S. About the attitude of the Indians and a little about myself next time.

301.
Thursday March 30, 1978
Dear Dr. Pullias,

I have felt happy all this week. Sometimes on the long drives in the van to or from the work project I'd find myself smiling as I gazed out the window. We are all usually quiet during the drives. It seems like we fall into a timeless void; through and through the mountains we weave — I never want to get to where we're going, whether it's to the work or back to the center to go home.

This week we have been planting trees in a part of the forest that burnt down a few years ago. It is hard because you have to carry a bag full of little trees and a hoe-dad (I love the names of our various tools — Polaski, MacCloud, Hoedad, Poonjar) to swing and make a hole. You have to climb rocks, push through brush and snags along steep mountain sides and be very careful to follow the person below you to keep the lines equally far apart. It sounds interesting, doesn't it? Actually I rather enjoyed it though most of the crew people said it was the worst job we've had. I liked the rhythm of the planting and the fun of whacking through the bushes. Once, during a very exerting climb over a steep crop of rocks, with my tree bag bumping my leg and the hoedad scraping on the granite, my mind stopped itself and realized what a very good time I was having!

I think I like hiking through untrailed countryside more than I like following trails.

But today while the others planted trees in the rain I stayed

375

back and painted signs.

Tomorrow we each get evaluated for our first three-month period. Uh oh.

Your friend,

Debbie.

302.
Los Angeles
April 12, 1978
Dining Room Table
Wed. night
Dear Debbie:

Your last letter to me was dated March 30 and opened with the wonderful sentence "I have felt happy all this week." I wish we could have many such weeks, but I suppose it would not do for all weeks to be happy, for it is probably by contrast that we know and feel: it is by feeling the pain of unhappiness that we sense the wonderful goodness of happiness? Whether or not it is necessary or good, surely life is full of contrasts.

I have been negligent about writing. I appreciate your letters. I especially enjoyed your description of your work planting trees: a good activity with a good purpose. Do you know Robert Frost's poem "The Way not Taken." You might like his poems. But I started to tell you about my not writing and a little of why. For many years I have gone to Chicago, usually in March, to an educational meeting. I planned to go this year but had a sort of cold or allergy and feared I would not be able to go. I delayed a day to try to feel a little better and took the plane on Monday March 20 instead of Sunday as I intended. Spent two days in Chicago and then Wed. went to Tenn. and visited three days with my very old mother. She will be 99 if she lives to June 24. Her mind is reasonably clear, and I was eager to know what a person with that enormous amount of experience with life feels and thinks. Someway I was not able to reach her as deeply, or as widely as I had hoped. Surely it is not easy to reach another personality. In a sense we are all deeply alone, but now and then by the wonderful process of love we are able to move across that loneliness and reach another person, or some aspect of nature. I returned Sat. of that week very tired.

I thought of you often on the trip and wanted to write, but usually did not feel like writing. So it has been since I returned. Before long I believe the spirit will return and the words will wish to flow. Perhaps we will see you Sunday.

Sincerely, your friend, Earl V. Pullias

303.
April 25, 1978
Dear Dr. Pullias,

I'm planning on quitting my job even though I haven't another to take its place. Guess I'm just a quitter. I break my own rules, too.

I learned how to work hard.

I learned that I can do much more than I thought I could do.

I learned how to walk a long ways.

I learned how to stay active outdoors rain or shine for eight hours daily.

But now I'm tired of working 8 hrs 5 days a week.

I'm tired of the teasing.

I'm tired of the dull days when I feel like I'm wasting my time.

I wish I didn't feel like quitting. I wish I could make myself continue. But I know it's already decided inside me.

Lost of others quit before I did, but I still feel bad about leaving the ones who haven't. It's hard to leave people you are around a lot and interested in. But once you're gone they don't care and you don't care. It's done and you are left only with a feeling of failure.

Alas and alack.

Do you know anything about USC's ISOMATA's new MFA program in professional writing? I read a short article in the paper about it. It sounds interesting, but I bet it's very expensive. Maybe I could get a scholarship. What do you think?

Thank you for the candle.

Yours,

Debbie.

304.
Los Angeles

Debbie Bumstead

April 29, 1978
Late Saturday
Back yard Shack
My dear friend, Debbie:

Your letter of the 25th came yesterday. It was very good to hear, for I was concerned about you, sensing that you did not feel well when I saw you, and that you were in the process of making a difficult decision - one against a sort of agreement you had made with yourself. That is always painful. But sometimes such decisions must be made, especially if one has a certain nature not yet conquered or transformed - conquered by self, I mean, or transformed by self understanding.

I do not feel too badly about the decision, although I had hoped you might get some breaks and stick it out. Really the breaks went against you: perhaps most important the weather since you went on the job was horrible. That together with the fact the physical work was perhaps beyond your basic strength made the situation difficult.

Your analysis of the situation is very good. Personally, I do not feel the experience was a failure, although I can understand that feeling. You, as you say, learned much: perhaps the most important being that you "learned how to work hard." Anything you wish to achieve will require such hard work, and the ability to stay with it until results come - and really the work becomes easy or seems easy as one learns to do it well and develops an interest and joy in the doing. That will come, I believe. You are battling a basic trait not easy to overcome, but surely possible.

I don't know about the USC Isomata program. I'll look into it and let you know. Hope so much you can find work. In the meantime, have faith.

Your friend, Earl V. Pullias

P.S. I hope the candle brings you some joy: it brings a message of care and love: let it speak to you.

305.
5-18-78
Dear Dr. Pullias,

Dear Dr. Pullias

Here is a picture of Don Diego. You can see how he has filled out and grown up. He acts a little better when the weather is warm. My friend, Carrie, who trains horses part-time, said she would train him to ride in a couple of months. Then she and I can go riding together. She has a big red appaloosa. I think you have met both her and her horse once when you were up at the cabin and I had Prieta still. No, I guess she had a gray filly then, not the red horse.

It will be fun to go riding again.

I'm sitting outside in the front yard of 324 with my feet up on the lawn table. The bottlebrush is blooming. It is about 6 o'clock and the air feels good. The train going by a block away is whistling and ringing. The moon is up in the light blue sky.

Now I can hear the train clacking along the tracks.

I'm reading an interesting book about Emily Dickinson by Polly Longsworth. I also checked out a book of E.D.'s poems. Her life and poems sort of fascinate me.

I was speaking with my mother tonight and she said I might be able to arrange a "writer's allowance" from her and her parents. She is moving up there at the end of the summer, for good. She's retiring.

It might be a good experiment for a year to just write and draw and not worry about money. What do you think?

Your friend,

Debbie

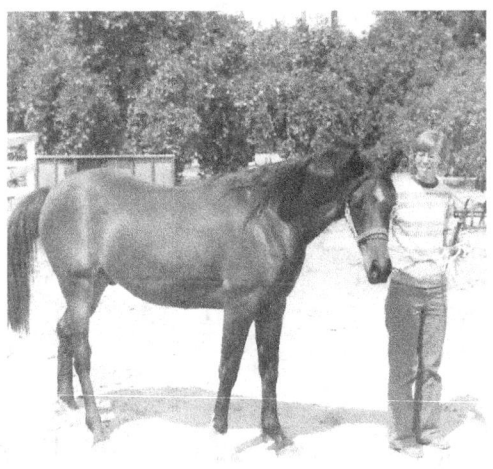

Debbie Bumstead

306.
6/10/78
Dear Dr. Pullias,

One day I was walking in the land of Me and I met three young women who told me their stories, which I have typed here for you to read.

I guess I am a bit of each one. If I happened onto a fitting sort of job I might become Bianca. The way it's going, though, I see myself as somewhat like Mabbie ("Maybe") striving toward Debbie.

Remember at my grandparents anniversary you said something about the good was in striving to be something not actually being it? You have said that before. I never really believed it. But recently I read a biography about Henry Thoreau and it seems he also said something like that.

Then I wrote these papers and saw that lately I have been working really very hard and steady on accomplishing the one about Debbie. And I saw (though it is an outward thing rather than inward) that I was striving, I was working, I had a rhythm, and it was good. The work felt good, the striving, not just getting it done, the accomplishment. (And yet — maybe that is the accomplishment.)

The cabin on my Mother's property is made of the timbers of your two cabins which were up above. Isn't that neat?

Your friend,
Debbie.

BIANCA STARBUCK

Bianca Starbuck is my name. I am an attractive well-dressed woman. I am a veterinarian or a child psychologist or a school librarian.

I have a dark green Datson 510. I painted yellow stripes and swirls around its edges.

My Arabian horse is well-trained and I ride him at the stables and in horse shows. He is a dark bay. I keep him shining and healthy. He responds to my every cue. We are a perfect match. People like to see me ride.

I live in a neat small white wooden house. The lawn is always mowed on Saturdays. The edges around trees and fences and flower beds are trimmed. I have a rose bed. I have a few blossoming fruit trees in the back yard.

Dear Dr. Pullias

I have one cat. She is a spotted calico.

Inside the house it is full of light and dreamy comfort. The floors are golden oak. The rugs are handmade. Every room is clean and uncluttered. There is a living room, a bedroom and bath, a study, a kitchen and a dining nook. The windows are large and have many panes. There is a fireplace in the study.

On Saturday nights and Sunday afternoons I spend time with a steady male friend. My girlfriends and I visit on weekday evenings.

Quite often during the year I go traveling to attend writer's conferences or visit the ocean or a favorite village or on business trips.

People think of me as active, attractive, intelligent. I am quiet, but clear-spoken. I am friendly and I like children. Everyone loves me.

Everyone loves me.

DEBBIE BUMSTEAD

Debbie Bumstead is my name. I am a plain modestly-dressed woman.

Early each morning I ride my horse. I groom him carefully. We keep each other company through the hills. We keep each other in shape.

I grow vegetables, fruits, flowers, and animals on a small ranch in the hills.

I live in a tiny cabin that has one big room for living, kitchen and bath, with a loft above for the bedroom. I clean house, and fix meals. I have fruit and nuts for breakfast, sandwiches and milk for lunch, and stew for dinner.

I write stories and poems and print them up into books with illustrations. People like to read my writings and look at my pictures.

I make ceramic animals. People like them also.

Friends come to visit me some evenings.

Other evenings I listen to music and write.

On weekends I play tennis. I belong to the tennis club and play hard and well. I am a steady friendly player. People like to play with me.

Some Saturday mornings I go to the open market and sell fruits, vegetables, and ceramic animals.

Occasionally I take small trips to visit the zoo or the museums in San Diego. Each summer I got to Nevada or Washington state for a vacation.

People think of me as an interesting, unusual, and pleasant person. They like me. They love me.

Everyone loves me.

MABBIE BUMBLESTUFF

My name is Mabbie Bumblestuff. I am a homely ill-dressed person.

I don't know what I want to do. I take a job first here and then there, never staying more than six months.

I am sick often, and complain of headaches and cramps.

I have an apartment, but it is usually dirty and the lawn grass is dying. I do not fix meals regularly and so do not eat well.

I have a horse, but I'm not sure how to train or ride him. He stands in his corral day after day swatting flies with his tail.

I do not have any friends. I sit at home and stare at the walls.

People think of me as a lonely dull person.

Nobody loves me.

307.

Dear Dr. Pullias,

I am in Reno visiting my grandparents and my brother, Joe. My mother and I are staying here a week, then we will head back to Hemet.

In Hemet I'm going to try very hard to get a part-time job that fills up just mornings or just afternoons. That way I'll have time for my other projects, but I'll also be earning some money to feed the horse. I keep thinking about tutoring; the idea seems to circle around my head, popping up every few months to inspire me. I don't know if that means that is something I should do, something that will never happen, or something that will happen naturally. What do you think?

On July 1st my friend Carrie and I walked Don Diego down to Carrie's house for training. He is living there now and learning new things. He learns very quickly and he seems to be, as they say, a "natural athlete" — he does everything well. But he is not a quiet gentle horse; he is hot and eager, and something of a brat. I will have to build up my courage to ride him. I hope I will do as well riding him as he is doing at learning to be ridden. I hope I will do better, actually, so that he won't get the best of me! But I like him, and he likes people, and that will help a lot on how hard we try to grow and be good together.

For part of the horse training fee I am training Carrie's dog, Toby, a collie. Every Wednesday we go down to the Fairgrounds to the obedience class. I am making friends with the teacher. He says I have a talent with dogs. That pleases me; because it is such a new talent. It's not one of my old talents, like writing or drawing or being with children. It's new. I like that.

Still, I like my old talents, too. They are my good friends.

Do you remember the ninth grade account I wrote? Well, even while I was writing it I was thinking I'd make it Part One in a four part book. Part Two would be my freshman year in college, Part Three would be about Camp Wasewagen, and Part Four would be about James and me. Though I haven't written parts 2 or 3 I just finished writing up a 40 page thing about James. Writing-wise it seems to be like a summary or a rough draft. It needs filling out. But I was surprised (as I always am with every writing), when I read it over after I finished, to find that it says something different, than what I thought it would say. I thought James would be the villain, but he's not. We were both having problems, but it was me that had the deadly obsession. In fact, that is what I call the writing — "The Obsession." If you read it, I don't know if you'd like the me in it. I will ask you if you want to read it, but first I'll tell you that it's very much about sex and you don't like that, do you? But I'll also tell you it's not about real sex, it's only about wishing and dreaming and being obsessed with it. There. Now you can say whether you want to read the story or not.

I hope to hear from you soon after our long silence.

I am reading The American by Henry James.

Your friend,

Debbie.

308.
Los Angeles
August 4 1978
Garden study -
the evening
Dear Debbie:

It was a very special joy for me to receive your two letters today, partly because I have been alone in this huge city for two weeks, but more because you are a very special friend - in a sense a daughter or granddaughter. It was good to hear.

I like the idea of making the four parts of your account into a book. I was very favorably impressed with the 9th grade story. Still we must look for a good title for the whole story and for each of the parts. You will have to find a way to disguise names without damaging the vividness of the writing. That may be a little difficult to do, but you can do it. I should like very much to see the part you have finished and the rest as it takes shape.

I probably have given you the wrong impression of my attitude toward sex. It is an extremely important and powerful part of life. I guess I have wanted to help you to understand how tricky, difficult to handle wisely, sex is and this has given you the impression that I was some way against it. Sex is a major factor in human life, and of course, in my own life and in my years of counseling I have worked closely with this problem. I would like for you to do me a favor get out your copy of my book <u>A Common Sense Philosophy</u>, and read the chapter on "Love and Reality," and especially note the section "Love and Sex" beginning on page 68. I would like very much your reaction to my ideas there.

I believe it is good you are writing out the James experience. That was evidently a rough experience for you, and writing about it should help to clear it up, and put it in proper perspective. I knew at times the experience was very hard for you, but I did not wish to press as to why. Sex in all its forms is a very intricate, complex and often delicate thing, and so often needs special handling. Perhaps we can talk more of this complex subject.

Keep knocking at all the doors of employment that are reasonably appealing to you, and one of them is bound to open. It would be wonderful if you could work on a paper, even on some routine type job, until you can break into the writing. I believe you have learned to work, and can hold a job over the inevitable dull and discouraging spots. I don't think it matters too much what the work is, but to be self-supporting is in our world is very good for a person. Without reasonable self-support there is a danger that a person will drift into all kinds of bad ways that lead nowhere or worse. Tutoring or reading like the

Dear Dr. Pullias

playwright and novelist did in Theo. North - Thornton Wilder. You probably do have special talent with animals. That would not be bad work. Keep searching.

You are probably right that I would be better if I could get back to my writing. I guess the two go some what in a circle: if I could write I would feel better and I would feel better if I could write. You understand this I am sure - the need is very great. I hope I'll be able to break the circle. This week for the first time in quite a while I was able to write a book review I promised to have ready in Sept. That was good.

I hope the family situation works out all right. These things surely can get complex. I believe the decision about the advanced degree in writing is wise. In the meantime you might study a little more what their program is like. I am glad you are reading Henry James - evidently a fine writer. By the way did I mention a book called <u>On Moral Fiction</u> by John Gardner (the novelist). Maybe the library would order it for you. It might interest you. A little technical about writing in parts, but very interesting.

As yet no small, willing, gentle, little slave, but I'm learning to do fairly well. The family returns tomorrow. You will <u>win</u> Diego or he will <u>win</u> you or both.

Sincerely your friend, Earl V. Pullias

309.
August 9, 1978
Dear Dr. Pullias,

I am looking at a large painting I just finished. It is of a horse and rider galloping through a wild stormy night. The horse is fairly well painted, he is colored like Diego. The rider is myself, dressed as Zorro. Her cloak covers up the fact that I couldn't draw her quite right. In the background there are three tossing trees — from one a man is hanging. In the sky a zigzag of lightening spells out "Zorra." It is a fun painting. I like it. When my friend, Carrie, who also paints saw it, she asked if I painted backgrounds first or last. Supposedly you are to paint background before foreground, but I told her my "technique" was to paint it last. Yes, she said, but then it looks like background is eating up the foreground. Exactly! I like that. I really do — it makes the painting

385

Debbie Bumstead

wild and alive.

The newspaper didn't have a job for me. The Dial-A-Ride place will call me Friday. Do you think I will look sharp, driving around in a shiny blue and white van, talking on the CB, greeting passengers graciously, and keeping cool when someone hijacks the van to Tijuana?

I also have an application in at the schools. They have 17 openings for Teachers Aide. Surely I could be just one of those 17! They won't interview till September.

Sometimes I go to Carrie's house to watch her ride Diego. She circles him around the arena at a walk, clucking at him and nudging with her heels. If he slows and wants to stop she pops the quirt against his shoulder and talks to him. She turns him across the arena and goes the other way. At first, last night, he was excited. He danced forward and tossed his head and put his tail flat against his rump. Carrie talked to him and circled him until he was calm.

She said he turned very easily, and gave to her heel aide. I told her that when I had him I had taught him to pivot around to my touch on his side. That's probably where he learned to give to her heel. I felt good to know something I taught him helps him now. I started him from a book I have — Understanding & Training Horses by James Ricci. You might like to read it. It's interesting even if you aren't training a horse.

I'm rereading The Idiot by Dostoyevsky. For some reason I really like this book.

I will read the chapters you mentioned in your book and send my ideas along next time.

Yours,

Debbie.

310.

Dear Dr. Pullias,

Last week one evening my grandparents came over to my mother's house to visit. My father and brother Joe, who is down from Reno for awhile, were there, too. We all talked in the living room as it grew dark outside. I remember such evenings from my childhood — quiet discussions in the warm dark. Now it is one of the things that makes me feel the most comfortable — listening to voices and stories in the night.

Dear Dr. Pullias

Your name came up in the conversation. Both Grandbee and Grandpa said they thought your talk at their anniversary was beautiful. We all agreed that yours was a commanding figure in any room, and that Mrs. Pullias was as bright and lovely as a songbird, and that Calvin was certainly a big handsome man.

Then Grandpa began to tell us how you two used to get together and listen to music, how close you were then.

When I got your letter today I thought it was interesting that you had both mentioned the memory within the space of a few days. Grandpa has told of the memory once before and you have written of it before. I think it must be a memory treasure that you both hold within yourselves, to be opened sometimes for pleasure.

Today I went out to Red Hawk Hill to hammer staples into Diego's corral. Possibly I will be moving out there to the cabin next week. I'll be glad. I've never been as content with this front apartment at 324 as I was with the back. I think it is the orange carpeting. Some shades of orange just oppress me.

But the cabin on the hill is a small cheerful place where I can grow trees and flowers and a plot of lawn. Isn't it strange that most of my life I have wanted a little farm with a place for dogs and cats and a horse and now, like magic, it comes to me? I have noticed that many things come to me that way. I fight and fight and cry, while the thing I've dreamt of comes around the back quietly and settles and there I am!

~~~

9-8-78

So I am here. My new address is: 40616 Gibbel Rd. My phone, when I get it, will be the same: 658-0279

Today I'm going to try to build a little fence for the dog. Tomorrow I go to work for three days. I am a Dial-A-Ride driver. It is a fairly pleasant job that you don't have to think about when you get home. Also you can pick what sort of hours you want which makes it even better.

~~~

Here is the story for you to read. Any comments, on either structural or thematic content (oh, brother) would be appreciated.

Your friend,

Debbie.

311.
Los Angeles
Backyard Study
Sept. 14, 1978
Night
Dear Debbie:

Your letter and <u>The Obsession</u> came two or three days ago. They both meant a great deal to me. There is much to talk about in both of them, but first, let's talk about the story. Of course, it is hard to separate my strong feeling for you and my evaluation of the writing, but I believe I can do so. I feel the <u>The Obsession</u> is excellent and that it will publish in a good magazine. It is keenly interesting, and more important for me, and for you in the long run, the story has something extremely important to say to parents and young people of this time. The condition and consequent suffering you depict so well is remarkably widespread and needs to be known about, and let us hope, better understood. But you will not write these important things because <u>they need to be written </u>but because you wish to and must. The results of which I will be conscious will be incidental to you as a writer. That doesn't matter, and is probably as it should be.

Having said this I am very sorry I cannot help you to find a publisher. We must find you a good agent or representative who would know how and where to place a story of this kind. There are quacks and cheats in this field so it is important that you have a reliable person of integrity. Maybe Miss Kerr would have an idea, and in the meantime I'll try to check a little. (By the way, I expect you'll have to change all names (except you can keep your own) as you did in the case of James). You sense intuitively better than my analysis will ever do the profound complexity of sex and the importance and beauty of love - and how it needs to be related to all forms of beauty as in houses and furniture and gardens and nature. (Did I mention the book <u>On Moral Fiction </u>by the novelist, John Gardner to you? It is about writing, a little technical, but I believe significant).

Now I must say a few other things and this letter may be too long. It is wonderful you have moved out to Red Hawk Hill. When you are in the mood you must give me more detail about your little place there. Better still before too long we hope to visit you there and go again up into our hills. It is good to have your address, and the phone when it is put in.

I liked your discussion of the quiet talk over at your mother's house when your grandparents were there. I too remember the warmth and beauty of such talk. I am glad your grandparents liked what I said at the celebration: it was deep from my heart. And the words about Mrs. Pullias were thoughtful and good.

Yes it was interesting that my beloved friend, Mr. Bumstead and I should mention this memory of our association at so nearly the same time. The friendship was very dear and precious, and there are many memories that can be brought forth now and then, and can perhaps enrich the lives and friendships of others. I wish he could talk more with you about life and love and truth and beauty and goodness. If he felt like it he could help you to get things to grow at your little cabin on the hill. But you'll know if that is possible or wise.

As my friend, I must tell you of a special experience I have just had which was more painful than I had thought it would be. Over the years I had mentioned my mother to you, particularly when I used to go down into Tenn. when I went back to the Chicago Conference. She was very old - 99 last June 24 - and the last year or so had not been at all well. Last Wed., Sept. 6, the phone call came saying she was dead - had passed over to the other side of existence. I had been expecting the call for many months, but when it came it was a strong, strange feeling. I had not been well, but I felt I wanted to go for my sake and the family's, so I went to Nashville on the plane a week ago tomorrow (Friday), attended the funeral 35 miles into the country on Sat, and came back on Sunday, arriving here very tired in the late afternoon. I am not sure why I tell you this, except as my friend, I wanted to speak with you about the experience. My mother was much interested in education and urged and helped her sons (she had no daughters and longed for them in her old age) to learn and learn, and as best we could to help others. By the way, love was hard for her too, and she never worked it out very well, I fear, but that is another and a very long story. How sad it is that love is so satisfying and healing and yet so difficult

389

for most mortals.

     Your friend, Earl V. Pullias

     P.S. I liked the folder you sent the story in. (Back to my last sentence in this letter: you will help us understand love better with your writing).

312.

October 5, 1978

Dear Dr. Pullias,

     I am sorry that your mother died. Death is a strange thing. All that is left on this side is the memories of relatives, friends and acquaintances, but I wonder what is left on the other side. I once read a little novel, <u>A Fine & Private Place</u> by Peter S. Beagle, that suggested that the spirit of a dead body remembered itself, at first, in its usual earthly terms. Then as the spirit gradually forgot details of movement and speech it finally ascended into its truly spiritual world. What that world is like one can't imagine. Movement, words, thoughts, images — are they needed by the spirit? Or does the spirit become intangible like the spirit of goodness, the spirit of love? Does the spirit depend on the living for its existence? No, that would only be memory. The spirit is more than the memory of itself and others left living. But that memory helps the spirit be different from other spirits. Maybe.

     Sunday Carrie and I moved Don Diego to Red Hawk Hill. Tuesday I rode him for the first time here. I was scared, but he was good. We just walked around the parking area. When he learns to go up and down hills we'll go up the road to your old place. I wish I had someone to ride with.

     So now Don Diego, the horse, Rex, the dog, Sylvester and Sara, the cats, and I live here. We would like you to come visit.

     I like it here. I like taking care of the animals and the trees. There are two cottonwood trees, a silver leaf maple, and a Christmas pine tree. There are also two small raspberry plants.

     Most of the time I have four days in a row without work during which I have been working on the place and later can write. I'm driving the bus weekends and Mondays. It is a mechanical job which I enjoy in a mechanical sort of way.

     Next week my mother is having an operation. She's having some problems with her organs, I guess. She will be weak for a long time. I'm not very good around sick people, but I'll try to keep her company a little each day.

Thank you for your encouragement about The Obsession. That helps me.

Your friend,

Debbie.

313.

Oct 1978

Dear Dr. Pullias,

I have had a very pleasant day off today. In the morning after I fed the horse I came back in, sat on the bed, and looked through some books and magazines. Later I went to town and wandered around a shopping center, eating ice cream, looking in stores, watching people. I came back to the hill, went out behind the cabin and sat on a rock in the wind and sun. Finally I began what I'd been getting ready for all day — to type the first draft of "Part Three" — my Camp Wasewagan experiences. After I typed a while I made some delicious hot cocoa. Now I am writing you a letter by flashlight.

I hope you are feeling better.

Don Diego is not happy here. He's lonely. He paces at one end of his corral or he stands looking off toward Wuthering Heights where there is a pony living. Sometimes at night he snorts and thumps around as if he were afraid of the wind in the weeds. I have advertised wanting a pony or donkey to keep him company. Perhaps that will make him happy. Also then I will be able to invite people to ride with me (if the pony is big enough).Today I received your letter. Yes, I have ridden up to your old place. It was very strange. Have you seen the area since the rains? Rabbit Meadow and all around the lower cabin it has become a damp swamp-like place, with long green curling weeds — that reach up to the horse's shoulder — growing thickly everywhere. I think the land that was yours missed you and left and another land came to take its place. Everything is completely different.

I think I will do some more typing this morning. When I get copies I'll send you one.

Your friend,

Debbie.

Debbie Bumstead

314.
Los Angeles
Nov. 11 1978
Backyard Study
Saturday afternoon
Raining and chilly
Dear Debbie:

   This first rain of the season is cold and my little electric stove has to work hard to make this study, as small as it is, cozy. But it is beginning to be comfortable. That makes me wonder how you heat Red Hawk Hill. We found it can be pretty cold there through the winter. You spoke of writing your letter by flashlight. I wondered if you do not have electricity. We didn't have current up at our cabins, but we were able to do well with kerosene lamps, even for reading. But current is near you there. I appreciated your sketch of your place - it gives me a better sense of how and where you live - that is good to know about a friend.

   I found it hard to picture Luisena Land (as we called our place among other things) as you described it. It is hard to believe that the smooth Rabbit Meadow where so many rabbits used to meet and dance by moonlight has grown up so as to touch the flanks of Don Diego. Some complications here have kept us from coming up there as we had hoped to do before now. I guess it will be a little sad to see the place where we spent some of the best and happiest days of our lives. But with a little rain and time everything tends to go back to nature. I am glad Don Diego is now good for riding. I hope you and he are steadily becoming better friends: a horse and a person can become very close friends helpful to each other. I may have told you one of my most vivid memories is of my Grandfather, a Greek immigrant who was a Cossack Calvaryman in the Crimean War fought in that part of Russia, telling us of his horse. He was wonderfully trained to help his rider. I wish I had taken down more details about his color, name, special habits, etc.

I am pleased you are working on the third part of your autobiographical story. I'll be very interested in seeing it when it is ready. I have not heard from the lady in New York I wrote about your writing who is an agent, but perhaps I will. In the meantime, I know you will write all you can - and read things that speak to you. Sometime tell me a little more about the Dial-A-Ride job. I am interested to know how it works. Also, a word about how your mother is. Think of us as you ride up into the blessed hills.

Sincerely your friend, Earl V. Pullias

315.
Los Angeles
Dec. 22, 1978
Back Bedroom - it
Is too cold in the little
Study. Friday morning.
Dear Debbie:

Can it be I haven't written since we saw you at your interesting Red Hawk Hill?! The days and weeks go by, and often times routines eat up the time. I suppose a certain amount of organization and discipline are necessary to deal effectively with life, but many of us like to be free, and often the freedom means drift and in a sense waste - and by the way I do not mean the lack of some kind of "busy" activity: reading, thought, being alone, walking, listening, etc. etc. are very important. I am speaking of myself: as I mentioned to you, I have been writing a little again for publication, but I find it difficult to stay at even that activity

Debbie Bumstead

which is so satisfying as I know it is with you, because the routines of life get in the way. Perhaps I could not have done <u>A Teacher Is Many Things</u> or <u>A Common Sense Philosophy</u> had we not had the cabins there and were the able to give steady concentrated time to them. I hope you can find a way of working that will enable to do your writing.

Our visit there did me a lot of good. I was glad to see your place and your animals. It was quite an inspiration to me to see that many of the materials in the cabins we enjoyed so much went into your little house. It is a delightful place. I have worried a little about your being warm these cold days. There is much trash lumber around there that I guess could be used to keep you warm. It would seem to be good if a congenial girlfriend wished to live in the trailer and you could ride together, but I know all human relations are complex.

It did us good to visit up at our old place. Things, as you had mentioned, were so grown up and changed that they seemed no longer like the place where we had spent such good days. Beautiful Rabbit Meadow strangely grown up, the cabins on which your father did such a find job gone, no inviting paths - so it was largely gone except memories. The area over towards the large slide rock, and the two oak trees, and the juniper tree have not changed so much. We ate lunch over there. We missed your mother - you might tell me a little about her when you write. We had a nice visit with your grandparents. So it was a good visit: and I didn't mention how good it was to rub Don Diego's nose and speak with him. Your Christmas card from your own hands was beautiful.

Your friend, Earl V. Pullias

316.
Dec. 27, 1978
Dear Dr. Pullias,

I am sitting by the fire tonight with the lamp on a chair beside me. I've spent the lonely day fiddling around on the hill. I began a shelter for the dog in his yard, but couldn't quite figure out how to build it. I'll save its completion for another day, I guess. I've spent most of the day reading <u>All Creatures Great & Small</u> by James Herriot. It is a

Dear Dr. Pullias

good book.

My mother had been planning on leaving for Reno early in January, but the doctor wants to see her again later in the month. So she is delayed again. She has a comfortable room. I often go over there (especially when it is very cold) to watch TV in the evenings. She doesn't miss her work. She says she was very ready to stop that. Now she busies herself with a few friends and me. I wonder where I will go, who I will rely on, when she's gone to Reno. It is frightening to think I may have to rely on myself.

I'm glad you like the cabin. Everyone who visits wants to take one home for all their own. Every couple of weeks or once a month three or four of my old high school friends meet out here for discussions and chit-chat. We are all still single. We seem to have a lot of things in common — the same sort of worries and fears, concerns and pleasures. They are all living with their parents at this time (though each one has lived on her own in the past) so my place is the place to meet. That's good. I enjoy the parties.

The letter I am enclosing was written a long time ago, before you visited. Tell me what you think of my bratty ways.

Love,
Debbie.

Dear Dr. Pullias,

Tonight I am thinking about some old friends I used to have - James, Miss Kerr, and Mr. Hill. Why have I lost them? I miss them. I still love each one.

First I told James to go away; then I left Mr. Hill in the middle of an angry conversation; and then I wrote an unpleasant last letter to Miss Kerr. Like a horrible selfish brat I told them all they weren't being good to me. I got mad and stamped my foot and then ran away.

There's no return.

I feel lonely this evening. I'm crying.

Why did I send them away? All at once, during that sad bad sick year, I did it. I was angry and impatient with the clouds sticking to me. I punched and kicked to reach light. My love felt sticky and heavy and painful. I kicked it away.

I hate them all for leaving me. Why didn't they stop me? Why didn't they hold my arms and legs and hug me til the clouds went away? Why didn't they call me back when I ran away? Then I could have

Debbie Bumstead

come back later.

Now I can't go back, even though I've come out of the clouds, even though I've learned not to be so selfish. My lessons of the year have no use: there is no one on which to test them.

I'm alone. I'm lonely.

Dear Dr. Pullias, I wish you could live here. I wish you and your family could live in the Bean's old place. I wish I could feel like a member of your family and come down to watch TV with you or play cards or sit and talk.

I'm not good at being a grown-up responsible for myself. I need help. I am little and lonely; I'm kicky and cruel; I'm shy; I run away. I need those who are firm with their love. I need those who will tell me to come back after I've run away forever. I need friends who will love me even though I am childish and mean. I need friends who will tell me to return after I'm certain I can never return.

Oh, I am still selfish, aren't I?

Debbie.

Dear Dr. Pullias

Epilogue

January/February - 1979

I felt your deep painful loneliness, .. for much of my life I have felt the same pain. **Dr. Pullias**

It seems like an age to end the age before. Debbie

Debbie Bumstead

317.
Los Angeles
Backyard Study
Jan. 6, 1979
Evening
Dear Debbie:

I am here again among all my friends including a picture of you and the beloved cat in your arms, and many other things I have told you about. It still intrigues me to think of our phantasy that at certain times on special nights these pictures and objects all come to life as we think of life and dance in the moonlight on the lawn. Much of this winter as you doubtless know, it has been too cold for me to be comfortable out here especially at night. I have a little electric stove, but I am cold natured - need to be warm.

I was very glad to receive your two letters. They were among the best you have written me in the long years of our friendship and correspondence. I was especially pleased that you sent the letter you had written earlier: it spoke so frankly and sincerely from your heart and from some of the wounds that heart had received. Before I respond to a few of the things you mention in your letter, I wish to say again, and probably I will say it many times again in such years as may be ahead, how very much I appreciate our friendship. I guess I regret that it has been almost entirely based on our correspondence. Could we have been better friends if we could have been together more? Walked together, talked, listened to music, worked together, sat in front of an open fire? I don't know. I hope so. I liked your idea of how nice it would be if we lived in the Bean house and you could come down from Red Hawk Hill and sit with us, and listen to music as your grandfather and I used to do. I felt your deep painful loneliness, expressed in your letter, for much of my life I have felt the same pain.

Debbie Bumstead

Surely I understand your feeling about your mother and her not being available. It is natural that you need her, and I suspect that she equally needs you. I would guess she would come back. I wish you had electric current, although I know it might add too much expense, so you could have a phonograph for music and a radio. Just tonight I was listening to our fine music station (KFAC). I wonder if you get it out there all right? The Chicago Symphony was playing that beautiful Brahms Symphony No. 1 that Mr. Bumstead and I used to listen to together when we worked together. That would be almost 40 years ago now. Beautiful, haunting melodies.

I think it is good that your school friends can come out to your place for fellowship. Evidently, you need deeper friendship or companionship, and perhaps even love, but oh how subtle and "tricky" love is - as you as a person and a writer know so intuitively and so deeply. But nearly everything in life has its risks, its price. From what I understood from your writing, and what you told me, the cutting off of your relationship with James was wise: there did not seem to be too much good for you there. Perhaps he could not love you, although you apparently loved him, at least, in a way. It may be he could love no one - I'm not sure. I was sorry to hear of your break with Miss Kerr. She was of special worth to you. You learned much from her; she respected you and at least in someways, understood you; you could have learned much more. If you feel you can do it, I would like for you to tell me a little more of how and why you broke with her - and especially, why you cannot go back when you are hurt like that or perhaps hurt someone else, and say you are sorry and rebuild the relationship on an even better basis. (And the same with Mr. Hill) Why not go back first to Miss Kerr and let her know you love her still: it would be much easier than you think. And promise me that if you should ever become angry with me you will tell me, but not run away. We need each other too much. There are dozens of more things to say, but two pages are enough tonight. Thanks for the picture of Diego's grandfather.

Your friend, Earl V. Pullias

P.S. I want you to overcome the "Bumstead" curse, the Indian curse, and learn to work hard and persistently at things that matter - to you.

Dear Dr. Pullias

318.
February 23, 1979
Dear Dr. Pullias,

What is it like to be 25? About six months ago something changed, suddenly but quietly, with me. Not internally, but externally. The external which I had been worrying and dreaming about for ages suddenly settled. I got a job which contented me; I moved into a home which fit very neatly my daydreams; I began to acquire a tiny, but reliable, circle of friends and acquaintances.

It seems like an age to end the age before. After crying, fighting, dreaming, and wanting all through high school, college, and after graduation, suddenly matters are settled, answers come, and decisions are made.

A couple of months ago I went on a "blind date" with a couple of girlfriends and some guys. It was dull. There was no bright conversation or active fun. When I went home I had a sudden decision and realization hit me. First that I was no longer going to worry about getting a man and second that I was and would probably remain all my life a spinster. I had always pictured myself an unmarried woman, but the truth of it had never hit me. Now I realize the fact.

That's the kind of time it is — when you see things that are true about yourself and you accept them. I do not fight against myself as much as I have in the past. I am not as passionate, but I am more contented. I don't think as much about philosophies and politics; I am more concerned with fixing the house or building a fence for the dog. Yes, that is it very much — I used to be terribly concerned about my ideas, my beliefs, what I was like in the eyes of other people. Now I am interested in the outside of me. Inside I am quieter.

Still I do not think my passion has died. I think it is just resting and will come back later to plague me again.

Right now at 25 I think I am living quietly, contentedly, and, in a calm almost scheduled way, productively.

In general I am living that way, I should say.

I also wish warmer weather would come. I am cold. I have either to be in my sleeping bag or busy moving around. I can't sit to write or read unless I start a fire, which can be a problem because of the wood. There is plenty of scrap lumber here, but most of it is too big or long to get in the stove. I need to ask my father to cut the wood up for me, I guess. By the time that happens it will be summer!

Thank you for thinking of and writing to me on my birthday. I had a good day. My grandmother and brother Joe in Reno talked to me over the phone in the morning. I worked, driving people to church and home again, till one. Then my father, his friend, Beth, brother Tim and family and my mother came out for lunch at Red Hawk Hill. Afterwards I had a surprise visitor — Debbie Sjoberg. She was down from San Diego with friends camping out in Sage. It was fun showing her the cabin, the animals, the view. She couldn't stay long. After she and her friends left Carrie came by and she, Anne, and I talked awhile. Then I went into town to watch television with my mother.

I thought of you the other day when I rode up the hill. Just as we came into view of the wishing well roof and the two parting roads I saw a cottontail bob across the road. I thought of you and remembered Rabbit Meadow. I had a feeling the Meadow was still there, but hidden in our memories of the past under the tall curling weeds.

Your friend, Debbie.

319.
Los Angeles
Feb. 27, 1979
Backyard Study
Tuesday Morning
Dear Debbie:

Today is one of the times when I wish I could drop by your cabin and talk with you instead of writing - or perhaps we would walk up the hill together, and there would be much to talk about of life and all its beauty and complications. Your last letter meant a great deal to me. You have become a daughter of whom I am very fond, about whom I care very much. Your report of how you feel and what you were thinking at 25 encouraged me very much. You have made and continue to make fine growth in self-understanding. That I am thankful for. You I believe have been patient with me when I was perhaps too concerned about you, even worried about you. But deeply all through the years I have had deep and unwavering confidence in your integrity - in your basic common sense and in your special gifts and talents. I like the things you tell me about yourself at 25. They fit somewhat what I had hoped for you. Still you must learn, I think, the art and joy of work which is the key to many things in life.

I believe your decision about the man problem is a good one for you. I suspect much of the sex, man-woman relation, so common in life is really not for you. It is possible a man may come along that would love you and deal with you as you must be dealt with and who you could love and enjoy much more than just physically, but such men are scarce and so the odds are not high. To be a spinster with self respect can be a very good life - and for some natures the best life. I am very pleased the cheap side of sex or drugs or other artificial means toward the release of tension you have wisely resisted. I would like for you to try your hand at this point at reading a book by C.S. Lewis, The Four Loves. It may be a little difficult in spots, but very keen thinking, and Lewis is a very good writer. Has written many other things. His analysis of the four kinds of love might be very helpful at this point in your growth. In our world, the love involved in friendship has been greatly neglected, and the narrow largely physically based type of love has been stressed out of balance and proportion. As I have said to you when we have discussed this problem on previous occasions, I am not saying at all that sex is ugly or bad, but taken out of a larger whole of genuine love and beauty, which you expressed so well in your writing you sent me, it often is very destructive of the best in us. You understand this deeply and I believe will eventually write significantly about love in its deepest and most creative manifestations.

I am glad you like your work: it is something you can do well that is a good service, and leaves you relatively free. Your task is to use that freedom as wisely as you can, making some demands on yourself particularly in the area of your writing. Eventually it will pull you, but nearly all writers have to push themselves over a certain point. For example, I still wish you would agree to send in some of your stories regularly to the local paper: they would appeal and would give you the much needed practice or experience in writing, and receiving the response of readers.

Debbie Bumstead

How glad I will be when the wet, damp, cold weather is over. I am cold-natured - to be cold is a misery for me, and so thinking of you as cold hurts me. But spring will soon be here. It has been 18 years now since we were there writing <u>A Teacher Is Many Things</u>. Can it be? And you were 11. And it was spring.

Sincerely your friend, Earl V. Pullias

Additional Material

A Note from Debbie on The Epistolary Mystery of Dear Dr. Pullias

List of Books Mentioned

Suggestions for Discussion

Online Sites to Visit

Afterword by Flora M. Brown, Ph.D.

About Debbie Bumstead

Debbie Bumstead

Dear Dr. Pullias

The Epistolary Mystery of *Dear Dr. Pullias*

Readers may have noticed I had a mystery in me that Dr. Pullias and I recognized and investigated, but we never found the solution together, never discovered the initial crime or caught the villain, (my Uncle Hersey), to bring him to justice. How I wish I could tell Dr. Pullias how the cold case was opened, studied, and solved when I was in my late 40s and early 50s -- but my beloved friend left me before then, having died in 1994 at 87 when I was 40. If he could know, he'd see that all the hints and clues that he and I spoke about in our letters back and forth for years would have become clear. My problems of nightmares, shyness, fear of sex, strange sufferings from relationships, all so incomprehensible to me and troubling to him would have become explained. My path would have become clearer. I might even have succeeded in those areas of life I had such problems with, had Dr. Pullias and I known the solution to my mystery early enough. For those readers who are interested in this mystery or in psychology and early sex abuse accounts, please visit www.DebbieBumsteadianLit.com for the manuscripts of *It Happened* and The *Epistolary Mystery of **Dear Dr. Pullias*** with The Clues in the Letters.

List of Books Mentioned in the Letters

Joanna and Ulysses; Plant Dreaming Deep - May Sarton
A Killing Frost; Moss Grows on the North Side - Sylvia Wilkinson
Lord of the Flies - William Golding
Dibs In Search of Self - Virginia Axline
Brothers of the Sea - D.R. Sherman
My Friend Flicka - Mary O'Hara
The Lion - Joseph Kessel
Kinship with All Life - J. Allen Boone
A Search for Understanding; A Teacher Is Many Things; A Common Sense Philosophy for Modern Man - Earl V. Pullias
The Wind in the Willows - Kenneth Grahame
The Little Prince - Antoine De Saint-Exupery
Manxmouse - Paul Gallico
The Strange One - Fred Bodsworth
The Family of Man - Edward Steichen and Carl Sandburg
The Hobbit - J.R.R. Tolkein
The Last Unicorn; A Fine and Private Place - Peter S. Beagle
The Annotated Alice - Lewis Carrol, Martin Gardner
All Quiet on the Western Front - Erich Maria Remarque
A Crack in the Sidewalk - Ruth Wolff
A Walk to the Hills of the Dreamtime - James Vance Marshall
Tistou of the Green Thumbs - Maurice Druon
Winnie the Pooh - A.A. Milne
Brer Rabbit - Joel Chandler Harris
I Never Promised You a Rose Garden - Hannah Green
The Trumpet of the Swan; Stuart Little - E.B. White
Rabbit Hill - Robert Lawson
Person to Person: The Problem of Being Human - Carl R. Rogers and Barry Stevens
I'm OK - You're OK - Thomas A. Harris

Dear Dr. Pullias

My Antonia; Death Comes for the Archbishop; The Lost Lady - Willa Cather

The Diary of A.N. The Story of the House on West 104th Street - Julius Horwitz

The Teaching of Young Children - Jean Piaget

The Primal Scream - Arthur Janov

Fig Tree John - Edwin Corle

Notes to Myself - Hugh Pratner

Spearpoint; Teacher; Bell Call - Sylvia Aston-Warner

The Inland Whale - Theodora Kroeber

"What Men Live By" - Leo Tolstoy

Island of the Blue Dolphins - Scott O'Dell.

Green Eggs and Ham - Dr. Seuss

Amanda, Dreaming - Barbara Wersba

A Little Princess; The Secret Garden - Frances Hodges Burnett

Harriet the Spy - Louise Fitzhugh

Pippi Longstocking; Rasmus and the Vagabond; Emil and Piggy Beast - Astrid Lindgren

A Sand County Almanac - Aldo Leopold

Edie on the Warpath - E.C. Spykman

Where the Wild Things Are - Maurice Sendak

Rufus M.; Ginger Pye; Pinky Pye - Eleanor Estes

The Bird in the Tree; Linnets and Valerians; The Child from the Sea; The White Witch; The Little White Horse; The Joy of the Snow - Elizabeth Goudge

The Torch - Wilder Penfield

The Season of Ponies; The Egypt Game; The Witches of Worm; The Changeling - Zilpha Keatly Snyder

The Animal Family by Randal Jarrel; illustrated by Maurice Sendak

Don Quixote - Miguel De Cervantes

Julie of the Wolves - Jean Craighead George

I Heard the Owl Call My Name - Margaret Craven

Watership Down - Richard Adams

Journey to Ixtlan; The Teachings of Don Juan - Carlos Castaneda.

Who's Who in Poetry in Amer. Univ. & Colleges for 1974-75

The Lost Universe - Gene Weltfish

The Dream Time - Debbie Bumstead

Slouching Towards Bethlehem - Joan Didion

Josephine; Hugo & Josephine; Hugo - Maria Gripe

Peter Pan - J.M. Barrie

Dr. Zhivago - Boris Pasternak

Debbie Bumstead

Pilgrim at Tinker Creek - Annie Dillard
Theophilus North - Thornton Wilder
Journey to Peppermint Street - Meindert De Jong
The Count of Monte Cristo - Alexandre Dumas
Tisha - Robert Specht
On Moral Fiction - John Gardner
Understanding & Training Horses - James Ricci
The American – Henry James
The Idiot - Fyodor Dostoyevsky
All Creatures Great & Small - James Herriot
The Four Loves - C.S. Lewis

Dear Dr. Pullias

Suggestions for Discussion

*Could **Dear Dr. Pullias** be read as a "Coming of Age" story about a teen girl becoming a woman?

*Dr. Pullias wrote that Debbie would most likely write true things about love as she develops her writing talent - could this be proved if only by reading the letters, which reveal such a deep loving friendship between herself and Dr. Pullias?

* Taken as a book about a time and a place, **Dear Dr. Pullias** gives a picture of late 60s and 70s home, high school, and college life, which readers, both young and old, can compare to their own growing up years, such as how they found their places in high school society, and the importance of friends, life in dormitories, and how they dealt with feelings of independence, emotional problems, and so on.

*The importance of a mentor, or one person in a child's life to whom she or he can turn at times of both achievement and problems, has been shown to keep disadvantaged or troubled children from falling into bad pathways in adulthood. How is **Dear Dr. Pullias** a story of this kind, and what achievements has Debbie accomplished by age 25 (that may or may not be tangible) due to her mentor?

*The theme of "the Bumstead Curse" stands out in **Dear Dr. Pullias** as a challenge for Debbie. A creative person's need is to work at his or her own spirit's creations, yet so often the creations, of art or writing or invention, don't succeed financially. Is there any solution to this problem of "the starving artist"?

* If you have read Debbie Bumstead's **The Dream Time**, see if you agree with Dr. Pullias's assessment of it in Letter #277. Does it reflect his favorite ideals: TBGL – Truth, Beauty, Goodness, Love?

411

Debbie Bumstead

Online Sites to Visit

21stcenturyscholar.org/dr-earl-v-pullias- This University of Southern California site has several short pieces memorializing Dr. Pullias. My favorite description is from Tom Garrison, professor emeritus of marine science at Orange Coast College: "an old man in a dark gray suit trailing chalk dust came into the room and placed a large clump of papers on the front desk. I don't believe he said anything, but nodded at those of us who were early....When he began to speak, I knew I had made a serious mistake. A very slow, soft-spoken, careful professor with a Colonel Sanders accent just wasn't going to work out for me, a young hotshot former naval officer with big plans. ...In that first hour, I came to realize that either (a) this guy was a parody, or (b) that I had run into something truly astonishing....[Then] the magic began to flow. By the end of that first day, I was hooked. As one of Dr. Pullias' last students, I moved down a road traveled by hundreds before me: first, disbelief, then astonishment, then inspiration, then decades of deep introspection and very hard, rewarding work.

Uscrossier.org/Pullias Lectureship Series – Every year at the Pullias Center at USC the Pullias Lecture, dedicated to the memory of Earl V. Pullias, is arranged to bring a nationally recognized scholar to speak. For the 2014 Lectureship I sent some quotes from the letters, which were printed in the event pamphlet.

Dear Dr. Pullias

DEAR DEBBIE

The letters of Dr. Earl V. Pullias to his young pen pal and family friend,
Debbie Burstead, 1968 – 1979.

"There are few things so wonderful as learning and
developing more and more the great things that lie
undeveloped in you. In most people they are never developed and this is one of the saddest facts of life. There
will be hard, unpleasant, discouraging days. We must
learn how to deal with these and not be turned aside by
them."

"I was very glad...we were able to talk a little while there
before 'The Four Winds.' Wouldn't it be interesting if we
could meet and talk there again two days before your 20th
birthday? And even your 30th? We would see what we
have been able to do with life, and what it has done with
us. The rocks, the sky, the hills, the clouds, the birds will
be quite the same. They have not changed much since the
Indians sat where we were sitting and perhaps talked of
what they thought was fundamental."

"The ideas related to Earth Day are wonderful. Perhaps
eventually we can build a world in which all days of the year
will have the spirit of Earth Day and people will hurt the
earth and its creatures, including other people, less and will
teach and heal and help them to grow into what they can and
should be more."

"I was interested in your feeling about the teacher. My school
experience was bad – teachers were often, for many reasons
I suppose, much they shouldn't be as teachers or as persons.
And I too came to almost hate teachers and even learning. And
then somewhere along the way I came to feel that one of the
great needs of the world is good teachers. So I have tried to be
one and later through writing and in other ways help others to
be. So life goes."

"...As my friend, I must tell you of a special experience I have
just had which was more painful than I had thought it would be.
Over the years I had mentioned my mother to you, particularly
when I used to go down into Tenn. when I went back to the
Chicago Conference. She was very old - 90 last June - and the last
year or so had not been at all well. Last Wed, Sept. 6, the phone
call came saying she was dead. I had been expecting the call for
many months, but when it came it was a strong, strange feeling.
I had not been well, but I felt I wanted to go for my sake and the
family's, so I went to Nashville on the plane a week ago, attended
the funeral 35 miles into the country on Sat, and came back on
Sun, arriving here very tired in the late afternoon. I am not sure
why I tell you this, except as my friend, I wanted to speak with
you about the experience. My mother was much interested in
education and urged and helped her sons to learn and learn, and as
best we could to help others. By the way, love was hard for her too,
and she never worked it out very well, I fear, but that is another
and a very long story. How sad it is that love is so satisfying and
healing and yet so difficult for most mortals."

September 14, 1978

413

Library.Pepperdine.edu for the Earl Vivon Pullias papers and photos. Dr. Pullias left his large collection of letters and other papers to Pepperdine University, where he worked as a Psychology professor and Dean of Students in its first founding years.

If you google the book **God Said It, Don't Sweat It** by Neil Clark Warren (the founder of eHarmony) you may "look inside" at a short essay, titled **Influence People Through Your Humility**, which is lovely appreciation of Dr. Pullias, who had been a professor of Warren's.

ColorYourLifeHappy.com is one of Flora M. Brown's online sites. Flora lived across the street from Dr. Pullias when she was a young woman, and was encouraged by him to go back to college to earn her Ph.D. She has kindly contributed the Afterword to **Dear Dr. Pullias.** Her life seems to me a positive active learning/teaching life, just such a life that Dr. Pullias wanted for all his students, family and friends.

DebbieBumsteadianLit.com As mentioned above in the Note from Debbie, check out **The Epistolary Mystery of Dear Dr. Pullias.** It explains Debbie's problems with nightmares, sex, shyness and fears by analyzing **The Clues in the Letters** in addition to more recent evidence in **It Happened**, an account of Debbie's early childhood abuse by pedophile, Uncle Hersey.

EarlVPulliasPhD.blogspot.com For quotes from the Pullias letters to Debbie, go to this blog and find **Dr Earl V. Pullias via Debbie Bumstead.**

Dear Dr. Pullias

Dr. Earl V. Pullias:
My Neighbor, My Mentor, My Friend

by

Flora Morris Brown, Ph.D.

When my husband and I moved into our first home in 1968 in South Central Los Angeles, we were expecting our first baby and eager to start our new life together. We couldn't have picked a better neighborhood. We were about six blocks from the original Pepperdine University campus, five miles from the University of Southern California, my alma mater, and freeway close to many of the attractions that tourists come from around the world to visit.

I had just completed my first two years of teaching English at Markham Middle School (originally Markham Junior High) located in Watts, nine miles from our home and the location of the infamous Watts Riots of 1965. When I began teaching in 1966, government funding and volunteers were pouring into Watts to help soothe the racial tension and unrest that incited the riots in the first place.

My new neighborhood was unique. Located near the original Pepperdine University campus in a predominantly white neighborhood, many of the homes in the 1960s had been owned by college professors and other university staff. After the unrest and tense conditions resulting from the 1965 riots, it was common for the white homeowners to flee to the new suburbs at the first sign of a black or Mexican homeowner. But our neighborhood didn't fall victim to the typical white flight. Our white neighbors continued to live in their homes until age or death brought about their departure.

Dr. Pullias and his family were the last white family on our block, and he and his wife were two of the first neighbors to welcome us to the neighborhood. He lived across the street from us with his wife, sister-in-law, and adult son. He had been dean of faculty at Pepperdine

Debbie Bumstead

University and a visiting professor at USC when he was asked to help form USC's Higher Education Department. When I met him he was a full-time professor of higher education and much revered by his colleagues and students. Although our neighbors knew he was a teacher, they didn't know much more than that.

In our early conversations in my driveway, Dr. Pullias was pleased to learn I was a teacher, but he was visibly moved to discover that I was a USC graduate. After my first daughter was born in 1969, I returned to USC in the summer of 1969 to finish my Master's in Education, much to Dr. Pullias' delight.

We often seemed to be stepping out of our front doors at the same time, so we always waved to each other before getting in our cars. Some of those times, however, he waved with a distinctive twist of his hand that meant he wanted to talk to me. Then leaning slightly forward he would make a beeline for my driveway before I could get in my car. With his easy-going Tennessean accent he asked about the family and began to encourage me to consider entering USC's doctoral program. Again, he was elated to learn this was already my goal.

After my first child was born I returned to full-time teaching until two years later, when I took another maternity leave in anticipation of my second daughter. As my family grew, so did our friendship with Dr. Pullias and his family. He invited us to the lovely literary gatherings he occasionally hosted at his home, where there were discussions of books or ideas, poetry reading, and usually a piano solo by the latest young mentee he had taken under his wing. His wife and sister-in-law served melt-in-your mouth treats and tea. I always felt like I had been transported to one of the cozy and intellectually stimulating literary salons of 19th century Paris.

Throughout the years he and his wife shared items they had received from friends and colleagues. I especially remember a box full of beautiful fall leaves he had received from East Coast friends. Not sure what he could do with them, he gave them to us, hoping that my kids and I would be able to create a centerpiece or craft project. Another time, after I complimented his wife Pauline on some delicious cookies she had prepared, she gave me a copy of her cookie recipe for what were called Jelly Slices, a thumbprint-type cookie perfect with tea.

During the four years of my doctoral studies at USC, Dr. Pullias kept a watchful eye on my progress. He had a close view of my work when I enrolled in his Introduction to Higher Education course during the very first year of my studies. I was delighted to be able to finally get to know him as teacher. I sometimes felt self-conscious when I caught myself hanging on his every word in lecture. Fortunately, I had received a generous grant that made it possible for me to buy every supplementary book he recommended. Being in his class was reminiscent of British classrooms portrayed in movies like *Goodbye Mr. Chips*, except that Dr. Pullias was beloved for his gentle manner and engaging college lectures, but never even came close to being a strict disciplinarian.

Although I greatly appreciated the advice and wisdom he shared throughout my studies, I began to worry that as his neighbor I was gaining an unfair advantage over other students. In an effort to minimize too much frequent contact with him, I began to peep out the window before leaving my house to see if he was in sight. If not, I'd herd the kids into the car, jump in the driver's seat and back out of my driveway.

Whenever he spotted me leaving, however, he'd wave with that distinctive twist of his hand that meant he wanted to talk to me. Then, with that forward lean, he'd rush to my driveway before I could get in my car. He'd always ask how things were going with my studies, and where I was along the way. No matter what stage I was in, he had invaluable advice, like recommending classes for me to take or advising how to select my doctoral committee.

When I was nearing the completion of my studies and had set the date for my dissertation orals, he asked me to invite him and his wife to attend. Normally, the orals were attended by the dissertation committee, family, and friends. Of course I was honored to have him attend such a significant event. After all, this is where I would formally explain and defend my dissertation and learn if I was officially a Ph.D. How wonderful it would be to have my key mentor present.

Dr. Pullias had retired in 1977 and was awarded Professor Emeritus status. As I was completing my doctorate, in 1978, The Pullias Lectureship was established and presented annually at USC, bringing a nationally recognized scholar to campus to participate in an ongoing academic dialogue on significant topics in higher and postsecondary education.

When Dr. Pullias and his wife arrived at my orals that June 1978, he was headed for the family and friends seating behind the table reserved for my committee. When the chairman of my committee spotted him entering the room, however, she invited him to join the committee at the table. I knew Dr. Pullias was revered at USC, but it was at that moment when I looked around the table at my committee that I realized they were not only his colleagues but his former students as well. On this momentous day, I was a bit nervous, but having Dr. Pullias there put me at ease.

After I presented the key points of my research and findings, the committee began to ask questions or seek clarification. I addressed all of their concerns until finally my chairperson turned to Dr. Pullias and said, "Would you like to ask Flora any questions?"

I can hear his response to this day. "I think we've asked Flora enough questions."

At that moment, the committee chairperson quickly wrapped up the event by explaining that it was customary for everyone to leave the room while the committee deliberated on whether I had satisfied the requirements for my doctorate. Before my family and friends could rise to leave, however, one committee member quickly spoke up and said, "I don't think that'll be necessary." He stood up, stretched out his hand across the table toward me, and said, "Let me be the first to call you Dr. Brown. Congratulations!"

My journey to the doctorate and my growth as a writer and educator were enhanced by having had Dr. Pullias as a neighbor, friend and mentor. He lived his life as a bridge between generations, just as he had advised teachers to do in his book, *A Teacher is Many Things*, which he coauthored with James Y. Young.

He cautioned college teachers to avoid complacency, in particular resting on their own accomplishments. He believed that teachers play many roles as they facilitate the free flow of ideas, insight, and creativity between themselves and their students.

Pullias was the author of more than 100 research and theoretical articles focusing mainly on philosophical issues in higher education, the author or co-author of numerous books, and a member of the Los Angeles County Board of Education from 1954 to 1977, where he was board president three times.

None of his work was as meaningful to him as teaching, learning, and fostering the careers of the thousands of students who were fortunate to have him as their professor.

That's why I was overjoyed to learn that with a generous bequest from the Pullias Family Estate, the USC Rossier School of Education

Dear Dr. Pullias

renamed the Center for Higher Education Policy Analysis, the Earl and Pauline Pullias Center for Higher Education. It's no surprise to me that this gift now allows USC, one of the world's leading research centers on higher education, to continue its tradition of focusing on research, policy, and practice to improve the field. Most significant to me among the goals of the newly named Center is its focus on financial aid and access for students of color, successful college outreach programs, and the retention of doctoral students of color.

After twenty years, I moved from our home across from that of Dr. Pullias, to accept a teaching position at Fullerton College in Orange County, California. I was saddened to learn of his passing five years later in 1994.

I feel very fortunate to have known him and his family. The impact they had on my life and that of my family remains deep, rich, and enduring.

About Debbie Bumstead

Debbie continued to grow. She did go back to school, earning her Master's in English. She married a gentle man who tamed her as The Little Prince tamed his shy fox. Though she struggled with finding work, she experienced several different jobs from city minibus driver to community college teacher's assistant, from furniture store worker with her husband to library clerk. She wrote and she writes, many books and memoirs, and she always found and still finds time to volunteer with children, helping them to read and to be artists.